# Beyond US Hegemony in
# International Development

China's initiative to establish the Asian Infrastructure Investment Bank (AIIB), attracting membership from G7 countries against the vocal opposition of the United States, has been recognised as a significant moment in an ongoing hegemonic transition.

This book examines how power transitions have played out in the World Bank over the last five decades, offering the first authentic account of the international diplomacy behind donor financing of the World Bank's International Development Association (IDA). Jiajun Xu decodes how the United States amplified its influence at the World Bank despite its flagging financial contributions to IDA. She further demonstrates that the widening influence-to-contribution disparity provoked other donors into taking 'exit/voice' measures, contesting the hegemon's legitimacy.

A rising China initially decided to become an IDA donor, seeking influence from within. But the entrenched hegemonic position of the United States in World Bank governance drove China to initiate the AIIB and New Development Bank, putting competitive pressures on the US-centred multilateral institutions to adapt.

DR JIAJUN XU is the co-founder (together with Professor Justin Yifu Lin) and Executive Deputy Director of the Centre for New Structural Economics at Peking University. Xu worked as a Junior Research Specialist at the United Nations' High Level Panel Secretariat on the Post-2015 Development Agenda responsible for the research on development financing and South–South Cooperation. She also worked as an international consultant on debt sustainability in the World Bank and productive capacity building for least-developed countries at the UNDESA Committee for Development Policy Secretariat. Xu holds a DPhil (PhD) from the University of Oxford.

# Beyond US Hegemony in International Development

## The Contest for Influence at the World Bank

JIAJUN XU
*Peking University, Beijing*

# CAMBRIDGE
## UNIVERSITY PRESS

University Printing House, Cambridge CB2 8BS, United Kingdom

Cambridge University Press is part of the University of Cambridge.

It furthers the University's mission by disseminating knowledge in the pursuit of education, learning, and research at the highest international levels of excellence.

www.cambridge.org
Information on this title: www.cambridge.org/9781107172845
10.1017/9781316779385

© Jiajun Xu 2017

First published 2017

*A catalogue record for this publication is available from the British Library.*

ISBN 978-1-107-17284-5 Hardback

# Contents

# Figures and Tables

# Foreword

The rise of China is changing global economic governance. China's accession to the World Trade Organization in 2001 heralded a rapid growth in trade and investment flows with each region of the world. Its participation in the Group of Twenty Finance Ministers after the East Asian financial crisis in 1997 signalled an increased engagement in governance. This was followed by a closer engagement in the International Monetary Fund and an increased attention to international cooperation in development finance. Most recently, China led the way in creating the Asian Infrastructure Investment Bank in Beijing and the New Development Bank in Shanghai. However, alongside these developments, China's role in established institutions such as the World Bank is changing. This book offers an explanation of these changes, by dissecting how previous rising powers have sought influence in the World Bank and with what implications for the organization.

Jiajun Xu's research unpacks the negotiations which establish how much major donors give to the World Bank's concessional funding arm – the International Development Association (IDA). This is a crucial window into change in the organization. Although the World Bank's formal voting structure is virtually immutable, regular IDA 'replenishment rounds' offer a unique forum for countries to translate changes in economic power into shifts in influence in the World Bank. Every three years, countries engage in a long process of negotiations, vying for power and influence.

The World Bank's own public explanation is that IDA burden shares change to reflect the changing relative weight of the contributing countries in the world economy. But Xu's historical research offers a new analytical framework for understanding who ends up contributing what amount and what share of the total. First, she highlights the hegemonic interest of the United States, fluctuating in line with the intensity of the Cold War and with an ongoing persistence in exercising influence in the governance of IDA even as its burden share fell sharply, especially after the Cold War. Second, she decodes the competition for status and influence among secondary powers in the developed world. Finally, she weighs in the exercise of exit and voice options as counterweights to US influence by other contributors to IDA.

The book contributes the first ever detailed history of the IDA replenishment process. As a doctoral student under my supervision at Oxford University, Jiajun analysed the dynamics of sixteen replenishment rounds from 1960 to 2013. In this book she details the political processes at work. We read about how the UK and Germany each tried to resist the first attempts by the United States to reduce its contributions whilst retaining its influence. We learn about Japan's bid for voting power as it rose to become the second largest economy in the world. Uncovered are the standoffs over US arrears and the ensuing birth of a special facility for Africa, as well as struggles with Bank management over independence, accountability, and incentives. The account is pieced together from the archives at the World Bank, in the United States and in the UK, as well as through countless interviews.

The role of China is examined in the latter part of the book, based on a set of interviews Xu conducted in Beijing during 2011–2013. She writes up the debate among Chinese policy makers that led to the decision to put its major multilateral funding through new institutions rather than lifting its contribution to IDA and other established multilateral financing facilities. That said, in January 2016 the US Congress finally stopped holding out support of a package of reforms in the IMF and World Bank which will increase China's voting power in each organization. This may encourage greater participation in the World Bank. But Xu's work highlights that China has exercised an exit and voice option vis-a-vis the World Bank that has already made its mark.

*Ngaire Woods*
*Oxford, April 2016.*

# Acknowledgments

My supervisor at Oxford, Professor Ngaire Woods, then Director of the Global Economic Governance Programme and subsequently Dean of the Blavatnik School of Government, played a central role in guiding me through the DPhil project that is the basis of this book. As a leading international scholar on global economic governance, and the Bretton Woods Institutions in particular, Ngaire inspired the focus on the donor financing of the World Bank's soft-loan window to anchor my ambitious inquiry into how a US-led hegemonic international development financing system adapts to power transitions. To search for a solid empirical ground, I focus on resolving the central puzzle of why shifts in burden shares in the International Development Association (IDA) were *not* always driven by rise and fall in economic fortunes. This required developing an analytical framework for disentangling the complex relationship between material capability, financial contributions, and policy influence of donor countries at the World Bank. I am immensely grateful for her active interest in my work and the speed of her feedback to my detailed drafts of empirical chapters and my evolving hypotheses.

During the course of this research, my work has been greatly improved thanks to the constructive feedback from Professors Walter Mattli, Kalypso Nicolaïdis, Duncan Snidal, and from Dr. Karolina Milewicz in the milestones of my DPhil studies. I am also grateful for vibrant discussions with Professors Rosemary Foot, Edward Keene, and Yuen Foong Khong. I am particularly thankful for the deep knowledge and wide perspectives brought to bear on my thesis by my examiners, Professors Andrew Hurrell and Robert Wade, during and following my viva. Professor Wade kindly provided detailed editing suggestions to clarify the material and render it more easily readable.

I owe deep gratitude for two long-term mentorships, from Richard Carey (the former Director of the OECD's Development Co-operation

Directorate) and Percy Mistry (the former Director & Senior Adviser, Finance Complex from 1981–87 in the World Bank). Their wisdom as both practitioners and thinkers guided me in grasping the essential dynamics of the international diplomacy behind the donor financing of IDA. They helped to put me in touch with key players, opening up doors for further interviews. They read several drafts of each chapter with keen interest. For their help, advice, and friendship, I owe deep gratitude. I recognise particularly my mentorship with Richard, which has evolved into a productive intellectual partnership enabling us to co-author several frontier articles on development finance.

I also want to give special thanks to Richard Manning and Alex Shakow, who held senior positions in the UK development agency and the World Bank, respectively. Without their support in contacting key decision-makers, my fieldwork would not have been possible.

More than one hundred former and current actors in the IDA governance and financing system (they were fused in the replenishment processes) gave their time to recall and explain events and behind-the-scenes debates and dramas in the IDA history. They made this history come alive for me, and I hope for readers of this book too. And through these fascinating encounters I have been able to position the IDA story in the wider Cold War context and the ongoing geopolitical developments of our current times. Too many to identify, I do offer here my deep thanks to them all.

Archivists from the UK National Archives, the US National Archives, and others helped me to access to official documents. I am particularly grateful to the World Bank archivists: they worked strenuously to declassify more than 180 folders. Given the limited materials available on IDA replenishments, my research would not have been feasible without their professional support. I gained enormous encouragement when an archivist in the Bank smiled at me in front of a pile of newly declassified documents and said, 'You are a pioneer breaking new ground.'

My fellow classmates at Oxford made this journey a stimulating and enriching one. I appreciate the feedback from many, including Eliza Gheorghe, Julian Gruin, Nina Hall, Ivo Iaydjiev, Seth Johnston, Helen Campbell Pickford, Suwita Hani Randhawa, Ruben Reike, Michael Sampson, Jack Seddon, Nora Stappert, Vinícius Rodrigues Vieira, Jeffrey Wright, and Makio Yamada.

Turning my dissertation into an academic book has been a rewarding journey. Feedback from two anonymous external reviewers has greatly helped me to get the core insights across and speak to a large audience. I am particularly grateful for professional support from the editorial team at Cambridge University Press, including Chris Harrison, Phil Good, Joshua Penney, and James Gregory.

This book is dedicated to my family – my parents, Xu Chengwei and Dong Xiaoyu, and my husband, Song Fangtao. It is their enduring love that enables me to find the essential energy to pursue my academic aspirations.

# Abbreviations

| | |
|---|---|
| AfDB | African Development Bank |
| AfDF | African Development Fund |
| AIIB | Asian Infrastructure Investment Bank |
| AsDB | Asian Development Bank |
| AsDF | Asian Development Fund |
| CASs | Country Assistance Strategies |
| CIA | Central Intelligence Agency |
| CIEC | Conference on International Economic Co-operation |
| CPIA | Country Policy and Institutional Assessment |
| CRS | Congressional Research Service |
| CRW | Crisis Response Window |
| DAC | Development Assistance Committee |
| DAG | Development Assistance Group |
| DFID | Department for International Development |
| EDF | European Development Fund |
| EEC | European Economic Community |
| EMS | European Monetary System |
| FCO | Foreign and Commonwealth Office |
| FSOs | Fund for Special Operations |
| FY | fiscal year |
| G-5 | Group of Five |
| G-7 | Group of Seven |
| G-24 | The Group of Twenty-Four |
| GAO | General Accounting Office |
| GCI | General Capital Increase |
| GEF | Global Environment Facility |
| GNI | Gross National Income |
| GNP | Gross National Product |
| GPG | global public good |
| GQR | General Quota Review |
| HICs | high-income countries |

| HIPC | Highly Indebted Poor Countries Initiative |
| IBRD | International Bank for Reconstruction and Development |
| IDA | International Development Association |
| IDB | Inter-American Development Bank |
| IEG | Independent Evaluation Group |
| IFAD | International Fund for Agricultural Development |
| IFC | International Finance Cooperation |
| IFIs | international financial institutions |
| IMF | International Monetary Fund |
| IO | international organisation |
| IR | international relations |
| ITF | Interim Trust Fund |
| LDCs | less-developed countries |
| LICs | low-income countries |
| MCC | Millennium Challenge Corporation |
| MDB | Multilateral Development Bank |
| MDGs | Millennium Development Goals |
| MDRI | Multilateral Debt Relief Initiative |
| MICs | middle-income countries |
| MIGA | Multilateral Investment Guarantee Agency |
| MOF | Ministry of Finance |
| MOFA | Ministry of Foreign Affairs |
| MOFCOM | Ministry of Commerce |
| MOV | Maintenance of Value |
| NAC | National Advisory Council on International Monetary and Financial Policies |
| NATO | North Atlantic Treaty Organization |
| NCBP | Non-Concessional Borrowing Policy |
| NGOs | Non-Governmental Organisations |
| NIEO | New International Economic Order |
| ODA | official development assistance |
| ODI | Overseas Development Institute |
| ODM | Ministry of Overseas Development |
| OECD | Organisation for Economic Co-operation and Development |
| OED | Operation Evaluation Department |
| OPEC | Organization of Petroleum Exporting Countries |
| PBA | performance-based allocation |

| PBOC | The People's Bank of China |
| PEPFAR | President's Emergency Plan for AIDS Relief |
| PRC | People's Republic of China |
| RDB | Regional Development Bank |
| RMS | Results Management System |
| SAL | Structural Adjustment Lending |
| SCI | Selective Capital Increase |
| SCO | Shanghai Cooperation Organisation |
| SDR | Special Drawing Rights |
| SFA | Special Facility for Africa |
| SSA | Sub-Saharan Africa |
| SUNFED | Special United Nations Fund for Economic Development |
| UAE | United Arab Emirates |
| UN | United Nations |
| UNECAFE | United Nations' Economic Commission for Asia and the Far East |
| UNEP | United Nations Environment Programme |
| UNHCR | United Nations High Commissioner for Refugees |
| UK | United Kingdom |
| US | United States |
| USAID | US Agency for International Development |
| WTO | World Trade Organization |

# Introduction

In a tectonic shift, by 2030, Asia will have surpassed North America and Europe combined in terms of global power ... largely reversing the historic rise of the West since 1750 and restoring Asia's weight in the global economy and world politics.[1]

*– The US National Intelligence Council*

We live in an era of unprecedented power transitions from the West to the East. This brings to the fore a perennial theme in world politics: whether and how shifts in material power lead to a new balance between costs and benefits of maintaining the international system.[2] This book aims to contribute to the scholarship about hegemonic transition and world order by anchoring this grand inquiry in a solid empirical ground to examine how the World Bank – a cornerstone of the US-led contemporary world order – has adapted to changing power balances in the past five decades.

This chapter proceeds as follows: first, it discusses why exploring the implications of hegemonic transition for the contemporary world order entails looking inside international organisations (IOs); second, it explains why the World Bank-IDA is a crucial case for exploring how IOs adapt to contemporary power transitions in a US-centred international system; third, it moves on to analyse why exploring the question of how member states distribute the costs of financing IOs (i.e., burden-sharing) offers a unique analytical angle for examining whether and how power shifts might redistribute the costs and benefits of maintaining the international system; and, finally, it explains why the in-depth investigation in this book of the international diplomacy behind donor financing of the World Bank's aid window helps to reveal that the process of hegemonic transition is far from a smooth and technocratic adjustment. The chapter concludes with the roadmap of the book.

---

[1] National Intelligence Council (2013: 15).  [2] Gilpin (1981); Kennedy (1988).

## I.1 Hegemonic Transition inside Multilateral Institutions

The contemporary hegemonic transition from the United States to China has sparked heated debates about the prospect of the American world order.[3] Will some kind of Chinese 'authoritarian model' dominate the twenty-first century, at the risk of reversing political democratisation and economic liberalisation?[4] Will the US-led 'liberal international order' be resilient enough to survive tectonic power shifts from the West to the East?[5] Or, will the twenty-first century be 'no one's world'? Is a dark era of ideological contention and geopolitical rivalry looming large?[6]

The above grand debates offer vital insights. But our knowledge about the contemporary hegemonic transition is fundamentally incomplete if multilateral institutions are left out of the analysis. There are two compelling reasons why we cannot afford to ignore the role played by multilateral institutions in these processes of hegemonic transition.

First, multilateral institutions play an indispensable role in the contemporary US-led hegemonic system.[7] At the close of World War II, at the zenith of its hegemonic power, America led the construction of an international order designed to save the world from falling into the kind of chaos exemplified in 'the twenty years' crisis' during the interregnum of power transitions (1919–39).[8] As manifested in the creation of the World Bank, the International Monetary Fund (IMF), and the attempt to create an international trade organisation (later evolving into the World Trade Organisation [WTO]), the United States committed itself to creating a liberal international economic order. The United States was also dedicated to building a more democratic and stable international political order, with the major institutional expression being the United Nations (UN). Hence, multilateral institutions are the very fabric of the contemporary international system.

---

[3] Power transitions here refer to shifts in material capabilities among states. It is analytically useful to distinguish 'power transition' (from one dominant state to another) from 'power diffusion' (from states to non-state actors) (Nye 2011: 113).

[4] Halper (2010).     [5] Ikenberry (2011: 336–42).     [6] Kupchan (2013: 5).

[7] Ikenberry (2001).     [8] Carr (1946).

Second, multilateral institutions are exactly the spaces in which competition between states plays out. The pursuit of international cooperation does not rule out the possibility that states wield power to seek national interests.[9] Indeed, IOs are vital vehicles for ruling the world.[10] Rising powers actively use these institutions to promote their international status.[11] Amid power struggles between states, IOs are by no means passive puppets fully controlled by member states. In fact, 'Management' in IOs (or, international bureaucracy) can play an independent role in shaping power politics.[12] Thus, multilateral institutions are arenas for intensifying power struggles as material power shifts among states.

This book aims to fill the gap in the grand debates about hegemonic transition by engaging with the inquiry of how the World Bank – a cornerstone of the US-led contemporary world order – has adapted to changing power balances. Filling this gap is of crucial importance to understanding the United States' relative hegemonic decline and China's corresponding rise. Although the literature examining the implications of the hegemonic transition from the United States to China for international security is numerous,[13] little is known about why rising China, a former World Bank recipient, decided to become a new donor of the Bank's aid window in 2007 before launching a new set of multilateral institutions, including the Asian Infrastructure Investment Bank (AIIB), outside the US-centred Bretton Woods Institutions and other established multilateral agencies.

## I.2  The World Bank-IDA: A Cornerstone of the US World Order

As a foundation of the Bretton Woods system, the World Bank is the most prominent multilateral development institution in the post–World War II period. The Bank's aid window is the first international aid organisation established under US leadership.

Founded in 1960, IDA was born out of North–South and East–West power struggles. In the wake of unprecedented decolonisation

---

[9]  Martin (1992: 765–92).      [10]  Gruber (2000).
[11]  Rosecrance and Taw (1990: 184–209); Lanteigne (2005: 1).
[12]  Barnett and Finnemore (2004).
[13]  The literature is vast: see Ross and Zhu (2008), Buzan (2010: 5–36), Friedberg (2005: 7–45), and Schweller (1999).

movements, newly independent developing countries had been vigorously campaigning for a sizeable international development fund under 'one country, one vote' UN control throughout the 1950s. This proposal was initially dismissed by rich industrialised countries, especially the United States. Yet, as the Soviet Union expanded its influence in the non-aligned developing countries, the United States took the leadership role in establishing IDA under the aegis of the West-dominated World Bank in an effort to counterbalance the Soviet influence in the Third World and to exert a strong influence on how and where to use the funds in recipient countries.

At first glance, IDA appears to be insignificant, as the role of IDA as a finance-provider is diminishing: IDA only provided about 6 per cent of official development assistance (ODA) to developing countries in 2013 – down from nearly 10 per cent in 2001.[14] As the new millennium dawned, growth engines in LICs ignited, reducing their aid dependence. IDA's financial leverage was thus declining.[15]

Despite its recent dwindling share of external finance to developing countries, IDA was once the linchpin in the international aid architecture. In the 1960s, IDA was 'the single most significant' multilateral channel of concessional loans to low-income countries (LICs).[16] IDA's pre-eminent position was strengthened in the 1970s.[17] As debt crises exacerbated aid dependency of LICs in the 1980s, IDA played a key role in leveraging market-oriented policy reforms in LICs.[18] After the end of the Cold War, although IDA was facing increasing competition with proliferating multilateral aid channels in an international aid market that was shrinking as the collapse of the Soviet Union obviated the need for the West to offer aid to counter the Soviet threat, it still provided about a third of total multilateral aid to LICs.[19]

Furthermore, IDA as a key strategic instrument has enabled the United States to project its influence worldwide.

---

[14] Net ODA disbursements of IDA as a percentage of total ODA provided by Development Assistance Committee (DAC) donors, from OECD DAC Aid Statistics.

[15] ActionAid (2011).

[16] The UN development agencies mainly provide grants rather than loans.

[17] While bilateral aid was the principal channel for disbursing aid, IDA's share of total ODA rose from 8 per cent in 1970 to 14 per cent in 1981. See IDA-7 Replenishment Agreement, para. 1.2.

[18] Mosley, Harrigan, and Toye (1991).     [19] OECD Aid Statistics.

First, the World Bank-IDA is a critical lens for deciphering East–West and North–South geopolitical power struggles. During the Cold War, IDA was a pivotal US geopolitical instrument for accommodating the Third World's demand for development assistance in order to gain an upper hand in the East–West aid-giving contests in non-aligned peripheral states.[20] In the mid-1970s, as the united Global South called for a New International Economic Order, the United States led Western donors to boost their financial support for IDA in order to pre-empt an overhaul of a West-dominated international system.[21] Then, as the bipolar rivalry faded away, IDA has been a key instrument for integrating developing countries into 'a liberal-capitalist world order' consistent with US interests and values.[22] Hence, the wider East–West and North–South geopolitics plays a pivotal role in grasping power struggles within IDA.

Second, the World Bank-IDA is a norm-setter in the field of international development. As an idea shaper, the United States usually pilots new 'best practices' in IDA, which then spread to aid windows of Regional Development Banks (RDBs) and other aid agencies. For instance, the performance-based aid allocation rules have been replicated in RDBs after the United States first pushed it through in IDA. As China is rising as a development financer, will China's aid, with 'no strings attached', challenge the mainstream proper rules of conduct promoted by the United States? Exploring the battle of ideas in IDA helps us to better grasp whether China's rise poses an ideological challenge to American leadership in the arena of international development.

In summary, the World Bank-IDA is a crucial case for examining how a US-led hegemonic international system adapts to power transitions.

## I.3 International Politics of Burden-Sharing

Exploring how power transitions play out at the World Bank leads us to examine an understudied research question of how donors distribute the cost of financing the Bank's aid window. IDA raises donations from donor governments and then offers concessional loans and grants to

---

[20] Kapur, Lewis, and Webb (1997: 1127–28).
[21] See Chapter 4 for more information.    [22] Walt (2005: 30).

the world's poorest developing countries. Unlike the IBRD – its parent institution – which functions as a self-sustaining business by raising funds from capital markets, IDA has to be regularly 'replenished' by donors since IDA's concessional financing is far below market interest rates. From 1960 to 2010, IDA completed sixteen rounds of replenishment negotiations, normally at three-year intervals (in shorthand, known as 'IDA-1', 'IDA-2', etc.).[23]

At first glance, burden-sharing appears to be simply a financial issue, but it is actually deeply political. Burden-sharing arrangements matter because of the close relationship between providing resources and influencing outcomes. Member states proactively deploy their financial leverage to vie for their desired influence both within and beyond IOs, in line with the common wisdom that 'he who calls the tune should pay the piper' (i.e., financial contributions and influence should be commensurate in IOs). Therefore, exploring the politics of IDA burden-sharing offers a unique analytical angle for unpacking how rising powers and declining powers engage in the redistribution of financial cost and state influence in the World Bank as power shifts.

Despite a large body of literature on World Bank governance, no systematic effort has been undertaken to examine the history of IDA replenishments.[24] One major reason for the gap is a lack of data. Only the information about recent IDA replenishments since 2000 is publicly available online. The IDA replenishment process itself also receives scant attention. For instance, the two official histories of the World Bank offer only a broad-brush description of IDA replenishments.[25] To contribute to the grand inquiry into how the US-led hegemonic international system has adapted to power transitions, the author took the initiative in requesting declassification of over 180 folders of the World Bank archives and conducting some 100 intensive interviews to make a first authentic account of IDA replenishment history, not possible before this point.

---

[23] The most recent IDA-17 was completed in December 2013. For a review, see Manning (2014).

[24] While Clegg (2014) examines the politics of concessional lending in the World Bank, it fails to systematically investigate the politics of IDA burden-sharing throughout the replenishment history.

[25] The first official history offers a short account up to IDA-3 (Mason and Asher 1973: 406–13); the second gives a brief review of 'the replenishments in sequence' up to IDA-10 (Kapur, Lewis, and Webb 1997: 1141–44). This may be understandable, given the comprehensive nature of their endeavour.

While there have been numerous burden-sharing studies, this strand of literature primarily focuses on military alliances, especially the North Atlantic Treaty Organisation (NATO).[26] While the burden-sharing literature has later extended to other issue areas such as refugee protection,[27] so far only a few 'exploratory' studies statistically test burden-sharing of multilateral or bilateral aid.[28] And little has been done to study donor contributions to a specific international aid organisation.[29]

Given the apparent lacuna in the literature on IDA burden-sharing, unpacking the international politics of IDA burden-sharing makes an original empirical contribution, shedding light on the wider debates about hegemonic transition and world order.

## I.4 Hegemonic Transition in Action

The grand debates about hegemonic transition and world order have concentrated on the central inquiries of (a) whether a declining hegemon would continue to maintain the burden of maintaining the existing order, clinging to its hegemonic influence, and (b) whether a rising challenger would bear more burden seeking incremental influence within the old order, or erect an alternative order at the expense of the waning hegemon. In essence, at the heart of the debate is whether and how shifts in material power can lead to a new balance between burden-sharing and influence-sharing in the existing (or newly extended) international system. To anchor this grand inquiry in a solid empirical ground, this book makes an original analysis of what drove changes in IDA burden-sharing patterns embedded in changing power balances within the US-led hegemonic international system over the past five decades.

The baseline explanation suggests that the cost of financing IOs will be redistributed in line with changing relative economic fortunes, resulting in concomitant shifts in member state influence in IOs. This prediction accords with the perceived wisdom that 'countries should give more aid as they grow richer' and that 'he who pays the piper calls

---

[26] The literature is vast. For a summary, see Sandler (1993: 446–83).

[27] For a special issue, see Thielemann (2003: 225–35).

[28] Addison, McGillivray, and Odedokun (2004: 173–91); Mascarenhas and Sandler (2006: 337–57).

[29] For an exception, see Roper and Barria (2010).

the tune'.[30] This indicates a smooth and technocratic process of hegemonic transition, as power shifts, burden-sharing, and influence-sharing would automatically adjust to new power balances.

But when we look inside the actual dynamics behind donor financing of the World Bank's aid window, we see a much more complicated picture. An in-depth investigation of IDA replenishment history reveals that adjustment in burden-sharing and influence-sharing amidst power transitions is far from a smooth and automatic process.

Three salient deviations from the baseline prediction may be identified:

1. Capacity-to-Contribution Gap: The hegemon honoured its traditional burden shares despite its relative economic decline, when faced with looming external geopolitical threats;
2. Contribution-to-Influence Disparity: The hegemonic influence at the World Bank persisted and even amplified, despite its flagging financial contributions to IDA;
3. Contribution-to-Influence Discrepancy: The hegemonic legitimacy began to be contested by other donors to the tipping point where, since the new millennium, the US hegemonic influence progressively eroded, despite only a mild further US share cut.

An in-depth investigation into the IDA replenishment history reveals two new insights: First, changes in US burden shares were not simply driven by the rise and fall of the hegemon's relative economic capability, but shaped distinctly by the intensity of geopolitical threats perceived by the hegemon. Looming geopolitical threats could arrest a potential US share cut even in times of its relative economic decline. The hegemon strived to honour its traditional share so as to expand total IDA resources to counter the influence of the Soviet Union and a united Third World. Hence, burden-sharing adjustments in IDA were not merely about bargaining games between rising powers and declining powers within the US-centred Western hemisphere, but also deeply shaped by power struggles between the hegemon and its geopolitical rivals.

Second, the degree of hegemonic influence at the World Bank was not simply a direct reflection of the US relative financial contribution, but was also more profoundly determined by two underlying forces:

---

[30]  Pfeffer (1978).

(a) the structural dependence of other IDA donors upon the hegemon, and (b) the legitimacy of the hegemon's power exercise perceived by other IDA donors. As other donors were more structurally dependent upon the hegemon for military protection against the Soviet Union and market access for economic recovery, so they had to tolerate a preponderant US influence at the World Bank even when the US financial contribution was flagging. Yet, as the hegemon skewed the contribution-to-influence disparity to the tipping point by consistently amplifying its undue influence while cutting its share of financial contributions, other donors opted to challenge the legitimacy of US power by refusing to embrace the hegemon's policy initiatives.

In a nutshell, the hegemon's contribution-to-influence nexus is far from a linear relationship, but is, rather, subject to a threshold effect. The hegemon can enjoy predominant influence incommensurate with its contribution for a sustained period of time at the World Bank if other donors are highly structurally dependent upon the hegemon in the broader international system. Yet, as other donors alleviated their structural dependence upon the hegemon, thus lowering their tolerance threshold of the US contribution-to-influence disparity, the hegemon could suffer from an imminent loss of influence in the wake of illegitimate US power exercises at the World Bank even when its share cuts were very mild.

In this book we will look into IDA replenishment history to grasp the core driving forces behind changes in burden shares and donor influence at the World Bank. Below are the essential questions and lines of inquiry.

## I.4.1 Why Did Cuts in the US Burden Share Sometimes Lag Far Behind Decline in Its Relative Economic Capabilities?

Imminent geopolitical threats could temporarily arrest US share reduction in IDA when the waning hegemon aspired to deploy IDA to preserve its hegemonic status. The US-centred Western international system was once embedded in a confrontational bipolar world order with developing countries on the margins. At times the communist East and the united South could pose serious threats to the US hegemonic status. When the perceived external threats were looming large, the US deployed the World Bank-IDA as a crucial geopolitical instrument for containing the external threats. The US overarching objective was to expand total IDA resources in order to counter the threats emerging outside the Western hemisphere. By doing so, the United States could either win a competitive edge in aid-giving contests with the Soviet Union in peripheral states, or accommodate the Third World's demand for development assistance so as to dissuade developing countries from demanding a radical overhaul of the US-centred international economic order. In order to foster the internal Western solidarity to augment total IDA resources, the hegemon was willing to stand by its traditional shares so as to encourage its Western allies to give as much aid as possible. Thus, in the face of imminent threats from the East in the late 1960s and the South in the mid-1970s, the hegemon was willing to maintain its traditional burden shares despite its relative economic decline. By contrast, as external threats faded away, the hegemon vigorously sought substantial share cuts, even when its Western allies were not willing to offset its shortfall.

In sum, to counter impending geopolitical threats from the East and the South, the United States was willing to maintain its traditional burden share in spite of its relative economic decline.

### I.4.2  Why Did a Significant Lag Exist for a Sustained Period of Time between Reductions in the US Burden Share and Deterioration in the Hegemonic Influence in the World Bank?

An intriguing counterintuitive phenomenon in IDA replenishment history is that the hegemonic influence endured and even amplified despite its diminishing financial contribution. The most striking change in IDA burden-sharing patterns is a precipitous fall in the US share from an unassailable position of over 40 per cent in 1960 to a modest 11 per cent in 2010. But throughout the first four decades of IDA history (from 1960 to 2000), the US policy influence at the World Bank hardly diminished at all. This runs contrary to the conventional wisdom that donors would lose their political influence as they cut their financial contribution to IOs.

There are two main reasons why the decline in the hegemonic influence lagged far behind the cut in its financial contribution.

A primary reason why other donors not only compensated for the US share cuts but also ceded influence to the United States was that they were so structurally dependent upon the hegemon for military protection and market access that they tolerated a preponderant hegemonic influence at the World Bank. For instance, in the early 1970s, even though other donors resented the undue US influence attempt to skew resource allocations in both IBRD and IDA to repair the damage in Indo-China inflicted by the United States during the Vietnam War, they still ceded influence to the United States in IDA-4 due to their heavy reliance on US military protection against the Soviet threat. Thus, the more structurally dependent rising powers are on the hegemon in other international arenas, the longer time lag between when the hegemon cuts its share and when the hegemon loses its influence at the World Bank.

Another counterintuitive reason for the enduring hegemonic influence is that pursuing fairness by secondary states in a rigid manner became a boost to, rather than a constraint on, US influence. The fairness concern is rooted in the belief that a donor's financial contribution should be commensurate with its political influence in IOs. As the United States amplified its influence but cut its burden share in the 1970s and 1980s, the influence-to-contribution disparity was widening to the tipping point that other donors could not tolerate any further cut in the US burden share. To preserve their sense of fairness, secondary states proportionally cut back on their cash contributions to avoid any slightest fall in the US burden share throughout the 1990s. While this punitive measure was originally designed to urge the United States to honour its 'fair' share so as to redress its influence-to-contribution discrepancy, the rigid pursuit of the fairness principle paradoxically augmented the US systematic financial leverage since the US dollar contribution effectively determined the total size of IDA replenishment. As the then Bank President James D. Wolfensohn put it, 'for every dollar cut by the US, IDA could lose a total of five dollars – as other nations reduce their contributions proportionally [given a fixed US share of about 20 per cent]'. As a result, Bank Management had a strong incentive to accommodate the US policy demands. Take IDA-12, negotiated in the late 1990s, for example: the United States achieved resounding success in pushing through a wide range of policy reforms across the whole World Bank, including implementing a transparent rule-based aid allocation system (known as 'Country Policy and Institutional Assessment' [CPIA]), despite the initial severe opposition from top Bank managers, and establishing a clear private sector development strategy for the IBRD, IDA, IFC, and MIGA. Hence, the rigid pursuit of fairness by secondary states can augment the US systematic financial leverage (i.e., the impact of the US contribution level upon others' willingness to contribute), thus boosting US influence.

In summary, the contribution-to-influence disparity can be attributed primarily to the structural dependence of other donors upon the hegemon in the broader international system. Other donors were more tolerant of the disproportionate US influence in the World Bank if they were more structurally dependent upon the hegemon for military defence against the Soviet Union and market access in international trade.

### 1.4.3 Why Has the Legitimacy of Hegemonic Power Exercises Played an Instrumental Role in Explaining a Sudden Fall in the Hegemonic Influence Despite a Mild Drop in the US Burden Share?

As we learnt earlier, the US contribution-to-influence discrepancy could last for a prolonged period of time when other donors were heavily structurally dependent upon the hegemon. Yet the 'unfair' disparity between the US influence and financial contribution would not persist forever. As soon as this discrepancy reached a tipping point in the aftermath of salient US violations of the 'fairness' principle (i.e., the hegemon unilaterally leveraged its financial strength to seek influence in line with its own values and interests, but failed to honour its financial commitments), the hegemonic legitimacy would be contested by other donors, substantially undermining the hegemonic influence.

The new millennium witnesses that hegemonic legitimacy began to erode in the wake of the hegemon's power initiatives that other IDA donors regarded as illegitimate.

In IDA-13, negotiated in the early 2000s, the United States unilaterally attached policy strings to its financial contributions but failed to honour its commitments despite Bank Management's compliance with its prescribed conditionality. Consequently, other donors began to openly question the US leadership. They severely doubted the Bush Administration's initiative of converting half of IDA resources into grants (as opposed to traditional loans) and even openly challenged the US initiative. Consequently, despite a mild US share reduction of

0.74 per cent, the hegemonic influence was openly questioned by other donors.

In IDA-14, other donors even took a step further to challenge the US leadership. They unanimously opposed the US proposal to appoint external candidates rather than high-level Bank officials to chair IDA replenishments. Furthermore, other donors decided to finance a bigger IDA, even though this decision would result in a precipitous fall in the US burden share (the USA, mired in the 'War on Terror' after the 9/11 event, could not afford its traditional share). Hence, getting rid of the rigid pegging practice would vitiate the systematic US financial leverage, once enjoyed by the hegemon throughout the 1990s when other donors insisted upon no further US share cut. Hence, neglecting the importance of legitimacy of its power exercises, the United States became a victim of its own success – unilateral pursuit of its short-term influence has undercut its hegemonic influence over the long run.

The rise of China has further eroded the hegemonic influence, as lack of voice opportunities at the US-centred Bretton Woods Institutions has driven China to take a leadership role in establishing new multilateral institutions with no US participation.

In IDA-15, negotiated in 2007, China decided to become a new IDA donor in order to vie for influence from within. The primary motivation for China's decision to become a new IDA donor was to redress a severe disparity between policy influence and financial contribution in World Bank governance. On the influence front, the voice of developing countries (IDA recipients and IBRD borrowers) was marginalised in World Bank governance, as IDA replenishment negotiations under the informal IDA Deputies group enabled donors to bypass the legal governance body of the Board of Executive Directors (where client countries have formal representation) and to capture a de facto decision-making power extending their policy influence well beyond IDA and across the whole World Bank Group. On the contribution front, China and other IBRD borrowers have reluctantly made indirect welfare transfers to IDA via IBRD net income transfers (which could have been used to reduce the borrowing cost of IBRD borrowers), because they do not have enough voting rights on the Board to counterbalance the G-7 countries' influence on revenue allocations. Accordingly, China was so resentful of being 'a quasi-donor without rights' that it aspired to seek 'influence from within' by winning a 'voice' opportunity at the IDA replenishment negotiation table.

Despite its attempt to gain influence from within, China gained much more profound policy influence by creating outside options to put competitive pressure on the World Bank. Impatient with the slow progress in gaining its desired policy influence, China has proactively adopted a two-track ('two-leg') strategy by establishing new multilateral financing arrangements to speed reform in existing international financial institutions. The founding of the AIIB is one quintessential example of China's quest for influence. In response to competitive pressures from China's rise as a development financer, the World Bank has made some adjustments in its development ideas and policies. For instance, China is spearheading a leaner and faster approach to development financing, compelling the World Bank to streamline procedures in order to cut down project preparation time. Another example is that the World Bank decided to relax its stringent rules on debt sustainability, which originally stipulated that IDA recipients had to bear a cut in the Bank's assistance if they borrowed 'non-concessional' loans at such a larger volume that breached the standard benchmark of debt sustainability prescribed by the Bank, as China's rapidly growing development finance with fewer strings attached provided LICs with an alternative source of financing, thus rendering the Bank's threat to cut its own assistance ineffective. Hence, China gained more influence via its leverage derived from newly created multilateral arrangements as an outsider than via its direct influence efforts as an insider.

What has enabled China to take the contestation of the hegemon's legitimacy further is that the US–China relationship was more characterised by complex interdependence than by asymmetrical dependence. Unlike past ascending powers, China does *not* depend upon the United States for military protection. Rather, the United States has relied on China's abundant foreign reserves to service its debt, whereas China has counted on US consumption to sustain its export-oriented growth. To sum up, the World Bank is heading towards a turning point where *financing and governing the World Bank-IDA would not require the US leadership as before.* Other donors not only decided to finance IDA without full US participation (as they no longer rigidly conditioned their contribution levels upon US cash contributions), but also resisted ceding influence to the United States even in the face of strong US opposition. The erosion of the US hegemonic influence has been further accelerated by ascending

China's decision to establish alternative multilateral development institutions without US participation.

In conclusion, hegemonic transition is a far cry from a smooth process where shifts in relative economic capacities would trigger corresponding changes in relative financial contributions to IOs and hence political influence in IOs on a commensurate scale. Burden-sharing adjustments are not simply driven by shifts in material capability, but also shaped by East–West/North–South power struggles. The hegemonic influence is not merely a linear function of the US financial contribution, but is also profoundly conditioned by the structural dependence of other IDA donors upon the United States as well as the legitimacy of US power exercises perceived by other donors at the World Bank.

## I.5 The Roadmap of the Book

The book proceeds as follows.

Chapter 1 first presents the intriguing puzzle about IDA burden-sharing patterns – that is, adjustments in burden-sharing have not matched with shifts in material capabilities. It then explains the limitations of the mainstream burden-sharing literature in resolving this compelling puzzle. Finally, it elaborates how IDA is financed and governed, and conceptualises the nature and role of 'influence' in IDA replenishment negotiations.

Chapter 2 synthesises central features of three recurring power plays throughout the history of IDA replenishments, namely (a) how the hegemon deploys IDA as a geopolitical tool for containing external threats from the East and the South; (b) how ascending powers wield IDA contributions to induce the hegemon and waning powers to cede voting rights both within and beyond IDA; and (c) how the fairness concern among secondary states about the hegemon's exercise of power in controlling Bank Management affected their willingness to contribute to IDA and to cede influence to the hegemon. This lays the ground for empirical chapters which contextualise these key insights and refine them with historical contingencies.

Chapters 3–7 offer a historical account of IDA replenishments by decade. These chapters are structured by decade because each decade shares, at it happens, similar historical context: intense bipolar rivalry in the 1960s, détente and oil crises in the 1970s, debt crises in the

1980s, the end of the Cold War and the arrival of 'the unipolar moment' in the 1990s, and the rise of emerging powers in the 2000s.

Chapter 8 focuses on China's decision to become a new IDA donor. China deserves a new chapter because it is analytically distinct from ascending Japan and Germany in the past: China needed to decide whether to step into the US-centred international institutions in the first place. The future of international development financing now hinges on the role of China in the ongoing hegemonic transitions.

The Conclusion goes back to the central theme of hegemonic transition and world order by distilling lessons from IDA replenishment history to look ahead.

# 1 | *IDA Burden-Sharing: The Unresolved Puzzle*

This chapter first presents an intriguing puzzle about IDA burden-sharing patterns – that is, that adjustments in burden-sharing are not always driven by shifts in material capabilities – and explains why the mainstream burden-sharing literature offers only partial answers in resolving this compelling puzzle. The chapter then provides essential background knowledge about the institutional settings of the World Bank-IDA in order to better understand the politics of IDA burden-sharing negotiations, and finally illustrates what kinds of influence donors pursue by making financial contributions to IDA.

## 1.1 The Central Puzzles of IDA Burden-Sharing

To better grasp the power dynamics of IDA replenishment history, we categorise donors into four groups:

First, the United States is treated as a '*Hegemon*' in a category of its own, not only because it possessed unrivalled power capabilities, but also because it played a leadership role in establishing IDA. In the hierarchical international system, other donors are secondary states. No matter how the US economy was weakening or strengthening, it still stood at the pinnacle of world power.

Second, '*Ascending Powers*' and '*Waning Powers*' are used to refer to the other four major donors, namely Japan, the UK, Germany,[1] and France. Their economic capabilities waxed or waned in relation to the United States over time. For instance, Japan was an ascending power in the first three decades of IDA replenishment history, but prolonged economic recession beginning in the early 1990s relegated Japan to a waning power. The principal protagonists in the tugs-of-war of IDA

---

[1]    From IDA-1 to IDA-9, Germany refers to West Germany; from IDA-10 onwards, Germany refers to the Federal Republic of Germany after German reunification in October 1990.

burden-sharing are the top five donors – the *Hegemon, Ascending Powers*, and *Waning Powers*. Collectively they provided more than 60 per cent of overall IDA resources.

A third category is small-/medium-sized donors. Some earned a reputation of being 'generous',[2] giving aid for altruistic development objectives rather than selfish donor interests,[3] and hence becoming known as 'like-minded donors' (e.g. Nordic countries, Canada, and some other small European donors).

A final category is new donors, including some former IDA recipients that graduated from LICs. They are analytically different from traditional donors because the first question for these emerging nations is whether to start contributing to IDA as they grow richer. Among new donors, '*Emerging Powers*' refers to oil-producing countries in the 1970s and China in the new millennium. Unlike other fast-growing economies, their spectacular ascendancy was claimed to pose challenges to the US-dominated international economic order.[4]

Figure 1.1 shows that burden shares of the top five major donors have undergone profound changes since IDA's inception in 1960. The most striking change is a precipitous fall in the US share from an unparalleled position of more than 40 per cent in 1960 to a modest 11 per cent in 2010.

What explains these changes? The World Bank's official account is that 'adjustments [in burden-sharing] have been made for changes in relative economic strength [or, shares of Gross National Product (GNP)]'.[5] This official explanation accords with the normative 'capacity-to-pay' principle that states should assume more burden as they grow richer. A cursory glance appears to lend credence to this argument – the steady decline in US share fits well with the popular narrative of 'hegemonic decline', whereas Japan's 'economic miracle' accompanied its share increase.

---

[2]  In 2011 only five donors (Denmark, Luxembourg, the Netherlands, Norway, and Sweden) reached the UN target of committing at least 0.7 per cent of their GNP to ODA. See Organisation for Economic Co-operation and Development (OECD), *Net Official Development Assistance from DAC and Other OECD Members in 2011*, 2012, www.oecd.org/investment/stats/50060310.pdf (accessed 1 May 2013).

[3]  Berthélemy (2006: 179–94).

[4]  Gosovic and Ruggie (1976: 309–45); Halper (2010).

[5]  World Bank (1982: 5).

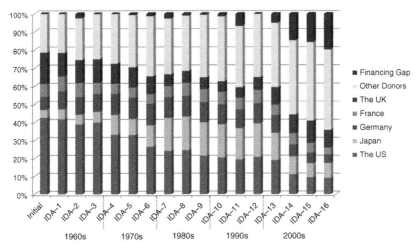

**Figure 1.1** Changes in Major Donors' Burden Shares in IDA
Sources: IDA Replenishment Agreements from IDA-1 to IDA-16.

A closer examination, however, reveals that adjustments in burden shares did *not* always match shifts in economic capabilities. The picture given by the official view is that hegemonic transition is a smooth, technocratic process where the declining hegemon would alleviate some of its burdens and rising powers would make a commensurate increase in its contribution to the World Bank-IDA. But this official explanation did not match with observed trends.

In-depth investigation is needed to solve the intriguing puzzle of why changes in burden shares did *not* always correlate with shifts in relative economic capabilities. Throughout the history of IDA replenishment, the most striking anomalies are as follows:

1. During the 1960s, from IDA-1 to IDA-3, IDA burden-sharing was fairly stable, despite the relative US economic decline and rapid post-war economic recovery of Japan and West Europe.
2. During the 1970s, from IDA-4 to IDA-6, the United States made steep share cuts, mainly offset by share increases from Japan and Germany, although these ascending powers' economic engines slowed down in the aftermath of oil crises.
3. During the 1980s, from IDA-7 to IDA-8, debt crises perpetuated sluggish economic growth of all major donors, which would predict a stable burden-sharing pattern. But significant burden-shifting

occurred in IDA-7 – the United States cut its share by 2 per cent and the UK cut its share by a third, whereas Japan boosted its share by more than a half. By contrast, the United States did no more than maintain its share in IDA-8, despite its economic revival in the late 1980s.

4. During the 1990s, from IDA-9[6] to IDA-12, the imminent collapse of the Soviet Union heralded the arrival of 'the unipolar era' – the United States enjoyed an economic boom, whereas Japan suffered from the 'lost decade' of economic recession. But the economically strengthening United States did not boost its share, whereas the ailing Japan maintained its then established share. In fact, the US share even fell by 14 per cent in IDA-9 (FY 1991–93), with no compensating share increase from other major donors.

5. After the new millennium, from IDA-13 to IDA-16, major donors all fared badly in sustainable economic growth; as a group they were rapidly being matched by emerging economies, especially China. Yet the sea change in IDA burden-shifting occurred not between Western donors and emerging powers, but within the Western donor group. After a precipitous fall in its IDA-14 (FY 2006–08) share, the United States ceded the No. 1 donor status to the UK in IDA-15 (FY 2009–11). While the waning UK successively increased its share, it was not sufficient to fill a huge fall in the US contribution. Consequently, the 'financing gap' – which occurs when share reductions are not fully offset by share increases – spun out of control.

In a nutshell, shifts in burden shares were *not* always driven by rises and falls in economic fortunes. This first-order puzzle manifests itself in the three disparate (even sometimes countervailing) subtypes of puzzles that occurred at different chronological stages (see Table 1.1 for exemplary historical episodes):

**Puzzle 1:** *Hegemonic Lag* – why the hegemon maintained its shares regardless of rise or fall in its economic status.

**Puzzle 2:** *Challenger Inertia* – why ascending powers were slow to assume greater burden despite their economic ascendancy.

---

[6] While IDA-9 was negotiated in 1989, the Soviet Union was on the verge of collapse. Thus, its historical background is closer to the ensuing replenishment rounds in the post–Cold War era.

**Table 1.1** *Summary of the Three Subtype Empirical Puzzles*

| Periods | Replenishment Round | P1: Hegemonic Lag | P2: Challenger Inertia | P3: Accelerated Burden-Shifting |
|---|---|---|---|---|
| 1960s (IDA1-3) | IDA-3 | √ [A *constant* US share despite relative economic *decline*] | √ [Japan and West Europe maintained or cut their shares despite economic rise] | – |
| 1970s (IDA4-6) | IDA-4/-6 | – | – | √ [US cut its contributions by a third, *largely* compensated for by ascending Japan and Germany's share increases] |
| 1980s (IDA7-8) | IDA-7 | – | – | √ [US made a share cut of 2%, and the UK cut its share by a third; ascending Japan increased its share by more than half] |
| | IDA-8 | √ [A *constant* US share despite economic *revival*] | – | – |
| 1990s (IDA9-12) | IDA-9 | – | – | √ [The US share fell by about 14% with *no compensating* share increases from other major donors] |
| | IDA11-12 | √ [A *constant* US share despite economic *revival*] | – | – |
| 2000s (IDA13-16) | IDA-14 | – | – | √ [An ever-largest fall in the US share *partially* offset by the waning UK's share increase] |

*Note:* Episodes of *Accelerated Burden-Shifting* are approximately identified when the ratio of change in burden share to change in GNP share is above the threshold of 1.2.

**Puzzle 3:** *Accelerated Burden-Shifting* – why significant burden-shifting occurred at a much greater scale than shifts in economic weight.

## 1.2 The Mainstream Literature on Burden-Sharing: Insights and Gaps

In this section, we first draw on insights of the mainstream burden-sharing literature, namely the collective good model and the joint-product model, and then elaborate on why the conventional approach is of limited use in explaining IDA burden-sharing dynamics.

### 1.2.1 The Collective Good Model[7]

The burden-sharing literature originated from the collective action theory of the 1960s.[8] The first theoretical endeavour to explain variations in burden-sharing patterns was made in Olson and Zeckhauser's seminal paper in 1966.[9] This pioneering study addresses the puzzle of why the United States devoted a larger percentage of its national income to common defence than did its smaller NATO allies (i.e. the US burden share was larger than its GNP share, known as the 'the small exploits the big' thesis).

Olson and Zeckhauser argue that asymmetric economic size is the principal cause. The rationale is that larger nations put a higher valuation on the alliance output than smaller nations, but cannot free-ride on smaller nations to provide the collective goods.

The above hypothesis is derived from a formal model with two strict assumptions. First, the alliance output is a 'collective good' in a sense that (a) no allies can be excluded from gaining benefits, and that (b) each ally's consumption of the good will not detract from another's enjoyment. Second, relative economic size determines a nation's valuation of the collective good provision.

Although Olson and Zeckhauser claim that their model is 'relevant' to any IO that nations establish to further their common interests,[10]

---

[7] Collective goods differ from public goods, for the former may offers benefits to the exclusive club rather than the general public.
[8] Olson (1965).     [9] Olson and Zeckhauser (1966: 266–79).
[10] Olson and Zeckhauser (1966: 266).

a preliminary application indicates that its prediction runs contrary to empirical evidence – even if at IDA's inception the United States was the largest donor with a share of about 40 per cent, this share still fell far below its GNP share (i.e. the hegemon did not take a 'disproportionate' burden in the context of IDA).

Yet this does not mean that the theory should be discarded. Instead, it encourages modifying its strict assumptions to widen its application while keeping its core insights. While the rigid assumption helps to conduct a neat statistical test that a nation's valuation of the total good provision solely depends on its national income, it rarely holds in reality. This raises the question of what other factors may shape a nation's valuation of the total aid provision. In Chapter 2, we will build on the collective good model presented above to introduce the central feature about the geopolitical power play between the US-led donor group and external threats from the Soviet Union and the united Third World.

## 1.2.2  The Joint-Product Model

The limitations of the collective good theory have stimulated new endeavours to extend the basic model. In the 1970s, the United States was increasingly reducing its burden in NATO, which seems to indicate the declining explanatory power of the collective good model.[11]

In a series of influential papers, Sandler and his co-authors relaxed the previously strict assumption that the alliance output is a pure collective good. They argue that *states are motivated to take on greater burdens, if their contributions are necessary to gain country-specific interests.*[12]

This theoretical insight helps solve the puzzle of 'notable changes' in NATO burden-sharing in the 1970s, where the group of European countries began to take on more burden shares. Sandler and his colleagues argue that the driving force behind this burden-shifting was 'a structural shift' in NATO's strategic doctrine from 'deterrence' to 'defence' in the late 1960s.[13] Hence, no longer could smaller European

[11]  Russett (1970).
[12]  Sandler (1977: 443–60); Sandler and Cauley (1975: 330–48).
[13]  Murdoch and Sandler (1984: 85). Yet Oneal and Elrod (1989) refute this argument by questioning whether there was a real shift in NATO's doctrine. Oneal (1990b) proposes an alternative explanation that greater interdependence

nations rely on nuclear deterrence for their own security; failure to increase national defence expenditures would invite conventional aggression from the Soviet Union in their own territories. In other words, 'the nature of the good' had changed from a 'pure' collective good to an 'impure' one. They thus coined the term 'joint product' to include purely collective, impurely collective, and purely private interests.[14]

In sum, the joint-product model emphasises that it is feasible to implement the 'benefit' principle of 'who benefits, who pays', because 'free-riders' can be excluded from obtaining country-specific interests if they fail to bear greater burdens.

The joint-product model should be applicable to IDA burden-sharing. Empirical research shows that aid-giving is driven not simply by humanitarian concerns but also by donors' strategic, political, and commercial interests,[15] and that influential donors skew aid allocations in IOs to serve their national interests.[16]

To sum up, the mainstream burden-sharing literature uses statistical analysis to test whether collective efforts can be viewed as a pure collective good (with the concomitant problem of free-riding) leading to 'the exploitation of the big by the small', or whether contributions can provide country-specific benefits, mitigating free-riding problems.[17]

### 1.2.3 Three Blind Spots in the Conventional Wisdom

Despite their enlightening insights, the mainstream burden-sharing literature overwhelmingly focuses on one particular type of burden-sharing arrangement that is fundamentally distinct from IDA.[18]

---

had increased coordination among European countries to foster a more equal burden-sharing among this subgroup.

[14] Sandler and Forbes (1980).

[15] Alesina and Dollar (2000); Neumayer (2003).

[16] The literature is vast, so I only list items related to the World Bank-IDA (Andersen, Hansen, and Markussen 2006). The most recent research shows that the United States uses foreign aid (including from the World Bank) to buy votes of poor countries in the UN Security Council (Vreeland 2014).

[17] The focus on the mainstream literature is not intended to capture every single perspective or approach. For a critique of interest-based analysis in the mainstream literature, see Thielemann (2003a); for bureaucratic politics, see Bennett, Lepgold, and Unger (1994); for game-theoretical approach, see Cornes and Sandler (1984: 367–79).

[18] Olson briefly touches upon this typology. See Olson (1971).

Table 1.2 *A Typology of Burden-Sharing Arrangements*

| | | Implementation Agencies | |
| --- | --- | --- | --- |
| | | National Agencies | IOs |
| *Contribution Decision-Making* | Bilateral Decisions | Type I: *NATO's main alliance forces* | Type III: *United Nations High Commissioner for Refugees (UNHCR)* |
| | International Negotiations | – | Type II: *Multilateral Development Banks (e.g. IDA)* |

Table 1.2 presents three ideal types of burden-sharing arrangements. The mainstream literature focuses on Type I where (a) nations agree in principle to cooperate for some specified purposes and then make contribution decisions *separately*, and (b) national agencies rather than IOs are responsible for providing the good. A common example is burden-sharing of NATO's main alliance forces.[19] In this case, contributors do not have a clear idea of their own burden shares until all contributors make their contributions separately to make the calculation of the actual sum possible. Only then are they able to calculate their relative contributions in relation to the actual sum.

By contrast, the IDA burden-sharing arrangement falls into the understudied category of Type II where (a) states negotiate their burden shares while simultaneously making collective decisions on the target total and other policy issues, instead of making bilateral contribution decisions separately; and (b) IOs, rather than national agencies, use common-pool resources to deliver goods. In this case, since the target total is collectively decided, donors can adjust their cash contributions to keep (and even target) their burden shares at a specified level.

Type III burden-sharing differs from Type II in that IOs directly raise voluntary contributions from each donor on an ad hoc basis as opposed to international negotiations. For instance, the UNHCR launches appeals throughout the year to seek donations from donor

---

[19] In addition, NATO burden also covers a small element (less than 1 per cent) of common NATO infrastructure that fits with Type II (to be discussed next).

governments.[20] Hence, burden shares are *revealed* after each donor makes separate contribution decisions to enable the calculation of the actual sum.

An overwhelming focus on the loose Type I scheme means that the standard explanations suffer from three blind spots when it comes to IDA burden-sharing dynamics.

Firstly, contribution decisions are not necessarily voluntary as described by the joint-product model (i.e. donors exchange aid for private interests); rather, intra-alliance relationship can be so hierarchical[21] that secondary states can be coerced by the hegemon into assuming a greater burden.[22]

Secondly, rather than making isolated contribution decisions, states collectively engage in strategic bargaining with each other, which opens up the possibility of deploying financial contributions to seek desired influence such as voting rights in IOs.

Finally, 'the nature of the good' cannot be taken for granted (e.g. assuming it is a public good in the case of the collective good model or private interests are exogenously determined in the case of the joint-product model).[23] Rather, states strive to control IOs to shape 'the nature of the good' in their favour. Delegating tasks to IOs confronts states with the risk of IOs being 'unfaithful agents'.[24] IOs may also be manipulated by strong states at the expense of weak ones.[25]

Focusing on the single case of IDA may raise the question of the extent to which empirical findings about IDA can apply to other IOs. As discussed earlier, IDA represents a typical but understudied burden-sharing arrangement. The aid windows of RDBs followed the footprint of IDA in designing their own replenishment procedures (i.e. negotiated contributions and collective decision-making). Thematic trust funds, such as the Global Environmental Facility (GEF), also adopt a similar fund-raising model. Hence, it is reasonable to expect that insights gained from the case of IDA can help to illuminate the international diplomacy behind donor financing of IOs similar to IDA.

---

[20] UNHCR, 'Fund-Raising', www.unhcr.org/donors.html#_ga=1.113513090 .44535290.1469093268 (accessed 4 August 2012).

[21] For alliance dependence, see Reisinger (1983: 143–55).

[22] Bennett, Lepgold, and Unger (1994).

[23] The collective good model presumes it is a 'collective good'; the joint-product model assumes that it is determined by 'exogenous factors' such as technology and geography in the context of NATO. See Sandler and Hartley (2001: 879).

[24] Hawkins et al. (2006a).       [25] Gruber (2000).

To sum up, the mainstream burden-sharing literature neglects the possibility that donors strategically deploy their financial contributions to pursue influence both within and beyond IDA. To better understand these power dynamics, we have to equip ourselves with essential knowledge of how IDA was financed and governed and what kinds of influence donors pursued.

## 1.3 Financing and Governing the World Bank's Aid Window

As power shifts, the questions of whether and how the patterns of burden-sharing and influence-sharing might change in the World Bank-IDA become relevant. Tackling this task requires us to master the essential knowledge of how IDA is governed and financed, and what kinds of influence donors pursue by making financial contributions to IDA.

### 1.3.1 Governing the World Bank-IDA

Understanding how IDA was positioned in the broader institutional setting of the World Bank is crucial to understanding the power dynamics within the World Bank Group.[26]

Legally, IDA has its own Articles of Agreement, so it appears to be an independent institution from its parent institution – the International Bank for Reconstruction and Development (IBRD), established in 1944 to help Europe recover from the devastation of World War II and then, with a redirected mission, to provide middle-income developing countries with development financing and ideas.[27]

In practice, however, IDA is no more than a trust fund of the World Bank that mobilises donations (or, taxpayers' money) from donor countries (known as 'Part I members') and disburses aid to recipient countries (known as 'Part II members'). Membership in IDA is

---

[26] The World Bank Group is a family of five institutions, including the International Bank for Reconstruction and Development (IBRD) created in 1944, International Finance Corporation (IFC) established in 1956, IDA founded in 1960, International Centre for Settlement of Investment Disputes (ICSID) founded in 1966, and the Multilateral Investment Guarantee Agency (MIGA) created in 1988. In this book, I use the term 'World Bank' or 'Bank' to refer to IBRD and/or IDA.

[27] Alacevich (2009).

conditional on membership in IBRD. Eligibility for IDA support depends first and foremost on a country's relative poverty, defined as GNI per capita below an established threshold. Some IDA-eligible recipient countries can also be IBRD borrowers (known as 'blend countries'), if they are creditworthy for some IBRD borrowing. IDA and IBRD are operated by the same Bank Management (including the Bank's president and professional staff). Furthermore, IDA and IBRD share the same Board of Executive Directors, for Executive Directors and Alternates of the IBRD serve ex officio as Executive Directors and Alternates of IDA. No wonder scholars have asserted that IDA is a 'legal fiction' and 'simply a fund administered by the World Bank'.[28]

At first glance, the Board of Executive Directors sets IDA policies and operations. Yet a close examination reveals that representatives from donor countries (known as 'IDA Deputies') grasp the actual decision-making power.

How did the term 'IDA Deputies' originate? When IDA ran out of its initial endowment of financial resources in 1962, the World Bank President proposed that Executive Directors formally embark on replenishment deliberations. Yet this procedure lasted only through the initial two replenishments. From IDA-3, replenishment meetings of donors only were directly arranged by Bank Management and chaired by high-level Bank officials. Given the geopolitical significance of IDA at the height of the Cold War, donor governments initially sent high-level deputy ministers of responsible agencies (Ministry of Finance or International Development) as negotiators. Later the rank of negotiators became lower as the role of IDA diminished over time. But the term 'IDA Deputies' was retained to refer to representatives from donor countries participating in negotiation meetings.[29]

The informal donor deliberation forum has created a governance conundrum for the World Bank, since IDA Deputies can wield paramount financial leverage upon Bank Management to shape IDA policies and operations outside the legal governance body of the Board of Executive Directors where IDA recipient countries had formal representation.

---

[28]  Libby (1975: 1065–72).

[29]  In the early years, representatives from donor governments were referred to variously as 'Part I representatives', 'delegates', and informally, 'IDA Deputies'.; beginning with the IDA-5 Replenishment Agreement in the mid-1970s, the term 'Deputies' was referred to more frequently (IDA 2001).

The governance conundrum has been further exacerbated, as donor-driven Bank policies (e.g. environmental and social safeguards) have been applied by the same Bank Management to IBRD borrowers – a group of middle-income countries (MICs) who do not receive any aid from donors but who have to accept the same conditionality as IDA recipients.[30] In principle, it is defensible to apply two distinct sets of operational policies, since IDA and IBRD are legally independent institutions. In practice, however, it is difficult to justify why IBRD borrowers ought to adhere to less stringent safeguard policies than IDA recipients. As a result, IBRD borrowers have to comply with the same policy conditionalities as IDA recipients did, only with few exceptions.[31]

In summary, IDA replenishment negotiations provide a golden opportunity for unpacking who owns the World Bank in practice.

## 1.3.2 Financing the World Bank-IDA

IDA is financially dependent on donor governments, for its concessional financing (known as 'soft loans') is far below market interest rates. Thus, if donors fail to reach agreement on burden-sharing, IDA operations will go into hiatus, thereby cutting off the lifeblood of aid-dependent recipients.

Given IDA financial dependence upon donor governments, a timely conclusion of IDA replenishment negotiations became a high priority for those who had high stakes in the continuation of IDA operations. Timing was the key. Take IDA-1 (FY1965–68), for example. In order to ensure that IDA could continue to operate for the next three years starting from the Bank's fiscal year (FY) 1965 (1 July 1964–30 June 1965), agreement had to be reached no later than the summer of 1963 so as to allow at least one year for donor governments to complete domestic ratification.

---

[30] It is worth noting that policy influence between IBRD and IDA also went the other way around. For example, in early years of IDA operations, Bank Management intentionally applied the rigorous IBRD standards to IDA in order to prevent IDA's 'soft loans' from tarnishing its creditworthiness in international capital markets.

[31] For example, at the urgings of the United States, ratings of 'Country Policy and Institutional Assessment' for IDA recipients were made public from 2000; due to persistent resistance of IBRD borrowers, however, their ratings have not ever been disclosed.

To hammer out IDA Replenishment Agreements, IDA Deputies have to go through successive negotiation meetings, usually taking a whole year to reach consensus on the size of an overall increase in IDA financial resources (the target total), the distribution of the increase among donors (burden-sharing), and other issues.

To grasp the dynamics of replenishment negotiations, it is important to understand how the target total, burden shares, and cash contributions are intrinsically interlinked.

First, donors had to reconcile differences to reach collective decisions on the total target. Focusing on burden shares does not imply that donors did not care about the target total. In fact, donors often disagreed with each other about the appropriate growth rate of total IDA resources. Where disagreement arose, donors had to make a collective decision on the basis of consensus.[32] Such a compromise is not simply determined by a majority view of 'how large an increase in total IDA resources should be over the next three years', but is also shaped by concerns among secondary donors about 'how appropriate the size of US burden shares ought to be'. Indeed, coining the term 'burden-sharing' indicates a conscious effort among contributors to compare efforts for the purpose of 'equity' or 'fairness'. For the sake of fairness, once the United States put a cap on its dollar contributions, other donors might have to agree upon a much lower target total than they desired in order to keep the US burden share above a certain floor. Hence, most donors could not join a collective agreement on the target total unless the US clarified its position on its dollar contributions.

Second, the size of a compromise target total had implications for change in burden shares. On the one hand, burden shares of donors, large and small alike, were fiscally conditioned by how much cash contribution they could afford in a given fiscal year. For example, a donor might be able to maintain its burden share of a relatively lower target total, but had to make a share cut if a higher target total was collectively agreed. On the other hand, donors could proactively

---

[32] Consensus decision-making did not rule out the fact that big donors might have a larger say given their preponderant financial clout. Yet collaboration among small donors could enable them to achieve a numerical majority that could shape the 'sense of meeting'. Indeed, many small-/medium-sized donors enjoyed an independent voice in the informal donor forum, even though they did not have an appointed seat and had to compromise their views with other members sharing one elected seat on the Board of Executive Directors.

adjust their cash contributions to target their burden shares at a specified level, since their burden shares were determined by their cash contributions divided by the ex ante collectively agreed target total (rather than the ex post actual sum). Hence, even in times of budgetary constraints, donors would generally stretch their budgetary resources to keep their traditional shares if they had a strong incentive to honour their shares as a symbol of their commitment to international responsibilities.

Last but not least, burden shares of donor contributions were negotiated among donors in the context of certain principles and norms. Donors generally embraced the 'capacity-to-pay' principle that claims for share reductions should not be justifiable unless donors suffered from a sustained decline in their overall economic capabilities.[33] Meanwhile, it was generally recommended that the total burden should be *fully* shared by all donors – any share reduction by some donors had to be compensated for by commensurate share increases by other donors.[34] This norm of 'the 100% total' aimed not only to embody the spirit of multilateralism (i.e. sharing the burden of collective efforts), but also to deter potential share cuts. Why? If donors faithfully followed this norm, any 'uncompensated' share reduction could jeopardise the successful conclusion of IDA replenishment negotiations. Accordingly, if no commensurate share increases were secured, donors who claimed share reductions might refrain from cutting their shares to avoid blame for ruining an IDA replenishment. Yet over time this norm of 'the 100% total' substantially eroded largely because the United States failed to honour its traditional shares even though no corresponding share increases were secured. Consequently, a yawning 'financing gap' – the difference between the target total and the actual sum – made its appearance.

Table 1.3 ('IDA Replenishments in Dates') presents changes in the target total from IDA-1 negotiated in early 1960s to IDA-16 negotiated in 2010. A clear pattern emerges that IDA enjoyed rapid expansion in the 1960s and 1970s with an average annual growth rate of over 70 per cent, but stagnated in the 1980s and 1990s. The new millennium

---

[33] Despite this widely recognised principle, donors never reached an agreement on 'universally applicable criterion or formula' to decide their burden shares (more details can be found in Chapter 4).

[34] IDA, 'Discussion Paper on Burden Sharing in IDA', IDA/RPL/78–1/1, 22 May 1978, 2, from the World Bank Archives.

Table 1.3 *IDA Replenishments in Dates*

| | Period | Negotiation Period | US Presidency | World Bank Presidency | Target Total (USD million) | Actual Sum (USD million) | Financing Gap |
|---|---|---|---|---|---|---|---|
| IDA-1 | FY 1965–68 | Mid-1962 – Sep. 1963 | Kennedy/ Johnson | G. Woods | 742.72 | 742.72 | 0.00% |
| IDA-2 | FY 1969–71 | Jul. 1966 – Jun. 1968 | Johnson | G. Woods | 750.00 | 750.00 | 0.00% |
| IDA-3 | FY 1972–74 | Dec. 1969 – Jun. 1970 | Johnson/ Nixon | R. McNamara | 1170.48 | 1170.48 | 0.00% |
| IDA-4 | FY 1975–77 | Dec. 1972 – Sep. 1973 | Nixon | R. McNamara | 2400.00 | 2400.00 | 0.00% |
| IDA-5 | FY 1978–80 | Sep. 1975 – Mar. 1977 | Nixon/Carter | R. McNamara | 4500.00 | 4500.00 | 0.00% |
| IDA-6 | FY 1981–83 | Sep. 1978 – Dec. 1979 | Carter/Reagan | R. McNamara | 7637.85 | 7586.19 | 0.68% |
| IDA-7 | FY 1985–87 | Nov. 1982 – Jan. 1984 | Reagan | A. W. Clausen | 12000.00 | 11838.56 | 1.35% |
| IDA-8 | FY 1988–90 | Jan. 1986 – Dec. 1986 | Reagan | B. Conable | 9000.00 | 8754.30 | 2.73% |
| IDA-9 | FY 1991–93 | Feb. 1989 – Dec. 1989 | Bush Senior | B. Conable | 11500.00 | 11387.68 | 0.98% |
| IDA-10 | FY 1994–96 | Jan. 1992 – Dec. 1992 | Bush Senior | L. T. Preston | 11679.00 | 10911.36 | 6.57% |
| IDA-11 | FY 1998–99 | Sep. 1994 – Mar. 1996 | Clinton | Preston/ J. D. Wolfensohn | 13000.00 | 11947.90 | 8.09% |
| IDA-12 | FY 2000–02 | Feb. 1998 – Nov. 1998 | Clinton | Wolfensohn | 5050.77 | 4578.69 | 9.35% |
| IDA-13 | FY 2003–05 | Feb. 2001 – Jul. 2002 | G. W. Bush | Wolfensohn | 8649.95 | 8088.57 | 6.49% |
| IDA-14 | FY 2006–08 | Feb. 2004 – Feb. 2005 | G. W. Bush | Wolfensohn/ P. Wolfowitz | 10020.00 | 9389.43 | 6.29% |
| IDA-15 | FY 2009–11 | Mar. 2007 – Dec. 2007 | G. W. Bush | P. Wolfowitz | 14129.76 | 12062.64 | 14.63% |
| IDA-16 | FY 2012–14 | Mar. 2010 – Dec. 2010 | Obama | R. B. Zoellick | 19943.00 | 16187.98 | 18.83% |

*Note:* In FY1984 and FY1997 IDA was replenished by special donor contributions from other donors outside the normal burden-sharing framework, because the United States decided to clear its arrears first before entering a new round of IDA replenishment.

reversed the negative trend of IDA contraction and witnessed an average increase of 28 per cent in the target total. Yet donors fail to fully commit their resources to reach the target, resulting in a widening financing gap of nearly 20 per cent.

Focusing on core donor contributions to IDA does not imply that we neglect alternative sources of financing IDA. Indeed, investigating IDA replenishment negotiations helps to better explain a dramatic increase in trust funds administered by the World Bank outside the traditional IDA burden-sharing framework since the early 1990s. The proliferating trust funds coincided with a stagnant growth of regular donor contributions to IDA. In contrast to traditional donor contributions with no strings attached, trust funds are earmarked by donors for particular countries and development issues; in effect, the Bank was hired as 'a service provider'. After a substantial expansion in the 1990s, donor contributions to Bank-administered trust funds have surpassed contributions to IDA since IDA-13 (FY03–05) on a flow basis.[35]

As seen in later empirical chapters, a primary reason why other donors increasingly shifted their aid money from IDA contributions to trust funds was that they deployed 'exit' and/or 'voice' options to redress the skewed contribution-to-influence equity line as the United States amplified its policy influence in the World Bank but failed to keep its financial commitments to IDA. On the contribution side, other donors insisted that the US burden share should not fall below a certain floor given its enormous economic capabilities and preponderant influence in the Bank. But the United States often put a cap on its dollar contributions, thus unable or unwilling to keep its burden share of a target total supported by a majority of donors. To preserve their sense of fairness, other donors proportionally cut back on their own cash contributions in order to keep a constant US burden share and then diverted their surplus funds to the Bank-administered trust funds or elsewhere. On the influence side, other donors strategically deployed trust funds as 'a unique tool' for gaining bottom-up influence by piloting development programmes, demonstrating success, and then mainstreaming them into the Bank's core business.[36]

In sum, the World Bank's trust fund portfolio mushroomed from the 1990s outside the traditional IDA burden-sharing framework, partly

---

[35] IEG (2011: 10).    [36] Clegg (2014: 259–74, 261).

because other donors reacted to the predominant US influence in the World Bank by diverting their aid money away from IDA to preserve their sense of fairness.

### 1.3.3  Buying What Kinds of 'Influence'?

At the heart of IDA replenishment negotiations is the exercise of relational power[37] in an effort to seek influence both within and beyond IDA.[38] For the purpose of this study, influence is defined as changes in the target's behaviours[39] as a result of the exercise of relational power: influence-seeker A's ability to get target B to do what B would otherwise not do.[40]

With a clear definition of influence in mind, we move to the next question of how to measure influence. For the purpose of this study, what matters is not simply actual influence but also perceived influence. To explain IDA burden-sharing patterns, we need to understand what determined donors' contribution decisions. In coming to their contribution decisions, decision-makers in donor governments consciously

---

[37]  Power analysis is at the centre of the inquiry of international relations. Researchers define 'power' differently depending on their research purposes. Broadly speaking, there is a basic distinction between power as resources and power as control over outcomes. For the purpose of conceptual clarity, I use the term of 'influence' to refer to control over *desired outcomes*, as opposed to 'power' as *material capabilities* (Hart 1976: 289–305; Cox and Jacobson, 1974).

[38]  The scope of influence in this study focuses on donor influence attempts related to IDA replenishments without encompassing all ad hoc influence attempts in the Bank's daily operation. The justification for this choice is two-fold. First, my primary interest lies in the bargaining power of donor governments while negotiating burden shares. Second, it is difficult, if not impossible, to systematically gather data on every single instance of behind-the-scenes donor influence.

  While scholars have used statistical analysis to assess the informal US influence on the World Bank's lending, it risks equating correlation with causation. See Fleck and Kilby (2006); Kilby (2013).

[39]  Behaviours here refer not simply to the target's specific actions, but also encompass agenda-setting and preferences. See Bachrach and Baratz (1962); Lukes (1974).

[40]  Dahl (1957); Baldwin (1980). In addition, critical perspectives indicate that power can be exercised through social relations rather than specific actors to shape beliefs and interests, such as 'productive power' (Barnett and Duvall 2005). Given my primary focus on donor governments' contribution decisions and influence attempts, I focus on relational power between specific actors.

make counterfactual analyses[41] – *how the target would have behaved, had donors not exerted threats or promises via IDA contributions.*

Measuring the degree of influence perceived by donors themselves defied a single objective benchmark. First, changes in the target's behaviours can be attributed to alternative means of influence (such as formal voting rights, power of persuasion, ad hoc influence on Bank staff) and multiple sources of influence attempts (such as non-governmental organisations, NGOs). Second, verifying the degree of success in gaining influence is plagued with uncertainty, because change in the target's behaviours usually occurs after contribution decisions are made. For instance, Bank Management implements policies after IDA replenishments are concluded. Finally, a target can deliberately hide its genuine preferences, thus deluding donors into making more financial contributions in exchange for a behavioural change that the target would have made even in the absence of donors' influence attempts.[42] Hence, we aim to unfold the full story by conducting in-depth interviews and archival research to gauge the degree of perceived donor influence.

Equipped with the definition and measurement of influence, we would like to have a better idea of what kinds of influence states aspired to by making financial contributions to IDA.

Voting power is the most obvious source of influence that donors seek. History reveals that donors have leveraged their IDA financial contribution to vie for voting power not only in IDA but also in IBRD and even IMF.

At first glance, some may argue that formal voting rights are of little significance since the boards make decisions by consensus and seldom resort to voting. Yet, in fact, strong states with greater votes have a larger say in shaping the outcome. Moreover, voting rights in international financial institutions (IFIs) symbolise relative economic status of member states. Hence, distributive consequences are severe when the pecking order in the shareholding is shifted.

Some may argue that there is no need for donors to expend IDA contributions to 'buy' voting rights in IFIs, since IFIs largely distribute voting rights among members in line with their capital subscription (unlike the 'one country, one vote' UN). These are known as 'weighted'

---

[41] Fearon (1991); Lebow (2010).      [42] Jervis (1976).

voting systems, which grant more voting rights to economically power-ful countries.[43]

Yet voting right adjustments in IFIs are far from an automatic process, since institutional rules stipulate that a member's voting right cannot be changed without its consent (referred to as 'pre-emptive rights'). Hence, adjustments in voting rights often lag far behind shifts in relative eco-nomic capabilities, which compels donors to deploy their financial leverage in IDA to speed voting rights adjustments in IFIs.

To better grasp how voting rights are distributed and redistributed among donors, we need to understand how institutional rules shape the power struggles over voting rights.

In the IMF, members use a quota formula to help assess each mem-ber's relative economic position, normally at five-year intervals (known as 'General Quota Review'). But actual voting-rights readjustments depend upon political negotiations: apart from the pre-emptive rights mentioned earlier, any changes in quotas must be approved by an 85 per cent majority of the total voting power. Hence, actual voting-rights adjustments in the IMF often lag far behind shifts in their relative economic positions in the world economy.

In IBRD, members initially decided to periodically readjust their voting rights in line with changes in negotiated IMF quotas (known as the 'parallelism principle'). This arrangement probably traces back to the incentive to reduce negotiation costs of prolonged and conten-tious voting-rights adjustments, since the scope of membership was almost the same in IBRD and the IMF.[44] But this parallelism principle was suspended in the mid-1980s, which encouraged donors to deploy their financial contributions to IDA to speed shareholding adjustments in IBRD.

In IDA, initial subscriptions in 1960 were proportional to the IBRD shareholding based on relative economic positions in 1945 despite the rapid economic recovery of Western Europe and Japan. The original rules of the game stipulated that additional resources donated to IDA would *not* carry voting rights unless they were made available in the form of 'subscriptions' (rather than 'contributions'). So donors initially did not gain an increase in their voting rights in IDA, even though they made additional financial contributions to IDA. This original rule of

---

[43] To mitigate this inequity, each member is entitled to certain 'basic votes'.
[44] To become a member of the Bank, a country must first join the IMF.

making contributions without gaining voting rights was modified under the pressure from rising powers in IDA-3 in the late 1960s.

The pace of voting-rights adjustments in IDA, IBRD, and the IMF is much slower than shifts in relative economic capabilities, leading to seesaw power struggles between rising powers and declining powers. Financial contributions to IDA – a global development institution – become a useful tool of statecraft for voting-rights struggles. Rising powers can promise to boost their financial contributions to IDA if they obtain more voting rights in IFIs, or threaten to cut their contributions if they fail. Rising powers might also donate to IDA on a sustained basis as an investment to demonstrate their readiness to bear international responsibilities, hence warranting their desired influence in terms of voting rights in these IFIs.

Apart from seeking formal voting rights, donors actively engage in exerting informal influence upon Bank Management to shape development policies and practices via the IDA Deputies forum rather than the formal Board of Executive Directors. Unlike voting rights struggles only among donors themselves, donors' influence attempts to shape the Bank's operation could incentivise Bank Management to play an independent role in defence of its autonomy. Bank Management may play one donor against another when donors hold diverse views about what the Bank should do. Bank Management may also signal mock compliance by inserting donors' demands in the IDA Replenishment Agreement, but do little to implement them. Yet Bank Management essentially depended upon donor contributions to keep IDA afloat, so it had a strong incentive to accommodate demands from donors to secure their financial support, especially faced with fierce competition in the international aid market. Hence, donors with preponderant financial leverage were likely to call the shots. But this does not mean that financial leverage was the only means of influence. In fact, when it came to influence upon development policies (as opposed to skewing aid allocations to their favoured countries), the power of persuasion played a more crucial role in garnering support for the proposed change.

It is worth noting that donor influence upon development policies and practices goes far beyond IDA, reaching across the whole World Bank and even with spill-over impacts upon the entire international development community. IDA is far from a stand-alone institution, since it is run by the same Bank Management as the IBRD. Policy conditionalities attached to IDA credits set by IDA Deputies were often applied to IBRD loans. Hence, for donors, IDA became a 'back-door' means of controlling the World Bank. More importantly, the World Bank has been viewed as a role model of the 'best' development ideas and practices to set the example for other development agencies to follow. For example, once the United States insisted on Bank Management adopting a transparent performance-based aid allocation system to reward 'good performers' and punish 'bad performers' using a standard benchmark of 'CPIA in IDA-12 of the late 1990s, RDBs then followed the World Bank's lead to establish similar performance-based aid allocations. While this was partly due to consistent US pressures in replenishment processes of these RDBs, it was also attributed to the fact that pressure was mounting for conformity with the 'best' practices demonstrated by the World Bank.

The nature of donor influence upon Bank Management is far from black-and-white.[45] Donors seek to influence a wide range of issues, including the terms of IDA credits, allocation of financial resources, policy conditionalities, and development ideas. Their motivations are mixed. Donors may be driven by narrow national interests to skew resource allocations in both IBRD and IDA to serve their short-term strategic and commercial interests, thus encroaching upon the Bank's professional independence. Donors may diligently and genuinely exercise stewardship to hold international bureaucrats accountable to improve development effectiveness, since their financial contributions to IDA are taxpayers' money. Donors may be also eager to promote the 'best' development ideas and policies informed by their own domestic development experiences, which might lead to counterproductive development outcomes in recipient countries no matter how well-intentioned donors are.

In sum, donors deploy their financial leverage in IDA to seek formal voting rights as well as informal influence upon IDA's policies and operation with spill-over effects upon IBRD and other development agencies, hence projecting their power far beyond IDA. While financial contributions alone do not necessarily guarantee donors' desired influence, a track record of IDA contributions can demonstrate donors' willingness to take on international responsibilities, thereby persuading

---

[45] For the motivations of aid-giving, see Lumsdaine (1993); Morgenthau (1962); Rodrik (1995).

others to grant their desired influence. Meanwhile, donors expect those with greater say in governing IDA to contribute more to IDA to warrant their influence.

## 1.4 Conclusion

To conclude, the intriguing puzzle about IDA replenishment history is that changes in burden shares were not always driven by shifts in relative economic capabilities of donors. The mainstream burden-sharing literature has overwhelmingly focused on military alliances whose burden-sharing arrangements are distinctive from IDA's, which falls short of explaining IDA burden-sharing dynamics. Resolving this puzzle requires us to unpack the three layers of power play – that is, (1) the US-led Western donor group versus the Soviet Union and the Third World; (2) voting rights struggles within the donor group; and (3) the informal donor influence upon Bank Management. The next chapter will elaborate on the central features of the three power plays to help us better to decipher the politics of IDA burden-sharing.

# 2 | *Three Power Plays behind the Politics of IDA Burden-Sharing*

The World Bank-IDA offers us a unique angle for exploring how power transitions shaped the US-led hegemonic world order. We have seen that the cost of financing IDA was not always redistributed in line with changing relative economic fortunes. Resolving this intriguing puzzle requires us to delve deeper into three layers of power plays at the heart of IDA replenishment negotiations – namely, (a) the US-led Western donor group versus the Soviet Union/Third World; (b) the internal donor struggle over voting rights between ascending powers and the hegemon/waning powers; and (c) the informal donor influence upon Bank Management.

This chapter will look into the three layers of power plays in turn. In each section, we will not only crystallise central features about these power plays emerging from in-depth case studies, but also illuminate how these observations have built upon and further extended existing theoretical insights. We will also point out complementary analytical factors which help us to grasp the full picture of IDA burden-sharing dynamics.

## 2.1 Structural Causes: External Threats from the East and the South

At the first layer of power play, involving the dynamics of the US-led donor group and the external threats on the boarder geopolitical chessboard, a recurring pattern is that *the hegemon was more likely to maintain its burden share, as the hegemon-centred Western world order faced looming external threats from the East and the South.* What we observe in case studies is that the United States honoured its burden share whenever the Soviet Union or the united Global South posed an imminent threat to the Western world order, but sought steep share cuts whenever these external threats faded.

To make sense of the above pattern, we need to understand that foreign aid is a geopolitical instrument for security competition in a broader confrontational international system. In an anarchical international system states have little choice but to engage in security competition for the ultimate end of survival.[1] States form alliances to balance against an external threat.[2] As the external threat looms larger, it is in the interests of each member to expand the total collective good provision in an effort to contain the common rival.

As a rational player, the hegemon pursues dual objectives of maximising influence while minimising cost. On the one hand, the hegemon seeks to maximise the total aid provision in order to contain its geopolitical rivals such as the Soviet Union and the united Global South. On the other hand, it desires to reduce its burden share by pressing its allies to bear greater aid burdens. Yet, while secondary states share a common interest in checking the external opponent, they tend to take a free ride on the hegemon. This echoes the basic insight in the 'collective good' model, as illustrated in Chapter 1.

To counteract its allies' free-riding incentive, the hegemon has to resort to coercion (or threats) to force its allies to assume more burdens. The hegemonic coercion stems from the ascending powers' structural dependence upon the hegemon. It often takes two forms: military dependence and economic dependence.[3] Accordingly, the hegemon can threaten to cut off military assistance or close off its market to 'free riders', unless they do their 'fair' share.

A greater external threat would render hegemonic coercion less credible. In an intense bipolar rivalry contest, carrying out coercive measures would hurt the hegemon as much or more than its allies which serve as the bulwark against the adversary pole.[4] In anticipating that the hegemon lacks the resolve to materialise threats, ascending powers are able to resist the hegemonic coercion. Hence, the success of hegemonic coercion largely depends on whether

---

[1] For core assumptions of structural realism, see Mearsheimer (2013). One major limitation of structural realism is that it explains away 'real and substantial' differences between foreign policy-makers in response to external threats. See Khong (1993: 309). I will address this drawback by paying due attention to how American decision-makers *perceived* the Soviet threat in empirical case studies.
[2] Walt (1987).
[3] For operationalisation of the two variables, see Lake (2009: 68–76).
[4] Gowa (1989); Snyder (1984); Waltz (1979).

threats are credible, which in turn hinges on how much damage materialising these threats would inflict on the hegemon itself.[5]

In view of its inability to coerce ascending powers to take on greater burdens, the hegemon has to balance the trade-off between its aspirations for total aid expansion and its desire for its own share reduction. Why this trade-off? If the hegemon insists on cutting its own share, it could trigger a downward spiral of contagious share cuts by its allies, thus defeating its principal goal of expanding the total aid. Therefore, the hegemon would prioritise total aid expansion over its own share reduction in an effort to contain its geopolitical rivals.

Conversely, as geopolitical confrontations recede, the hegemon is able to coerce ascending powers to compensate for its own steep share cut,[6] because the hegemonic coercion gains more credibility. As external threats subsided, materialising its threats inflicts less damage on the hegemon. Thus, we would expect that the hegemon makes substantial share cuts, made good by share increases of structurally dependent ascending powers.[7]

Along this line of reasoning, as geopolitical rivals collapse, the hegemon would no longer have any incentive to spend political capital to press for share increases from ascending powers. Since the external threat vanishes, the hegemon's traditional geopolitical rationale becomes obsolete. Accordingly, we would expect to see a sharp drop in the hegemon's share (without any compensation from ascending powers), if not an outright exit.

In a nutshell, the structural cause of external threats – the intensity of external threats perceived by the hegemon – matters in deciding whether the hegemon is willing to honour its own burden share in order to expand IDA.

## 2.2 Challenger Power Play: Quid Pro Quo between Burden Shares and Voting Rights

The second layer of power play lies in power struggles within the donor community between waning powers and ascending powers for voting

---

[5] Schelling (1960).

[6] Theorists have drawn our attention to variations in the credibility of coercion depending on the intensity of external rivalry within the bipolar structure of the Cold War (Martin 1992: 787).

[7] Keohane (1989b).

rights in IOs. A recurring pattern emerging from case studies is that *if the hegemon and waning powers desired to expand total IDA resources, they were likely to cede voting rights to ascending powers in exchange for financial support.*

To appreciate the insight behind the above observation, it is crucial that we equip ourselves with the necessary background knowledge about the rules of the game in IFIs. As mentioned in Chapter 1, while IFIs largely distribute voting rights among members in line with their capital subscription (known as 'weighted' voting systems), an automatic link between financial contributions and voting rights is *not* necessarily guaranteed. In IDA, originally additional resources donated to IDA did not carry voting rights. In IBRD, the practice of periodically readjusting IBRD shareholding in line with changes in negotiated IMF quotas (known as the 'parallelism principle') was terminated in the mid-1980s. In IMF, a member's voting rights cannot be changed without its consent (referred to as the 'pre-emptive rights' principle), which means that a member state can always step up its financial contribution in proportion to that of its challenger so as to avoid diluting its own voting rights. This pre-emptive principle also applies to IDA and IBRD. Consequently, voting-rights adjustments in IFIs often lag far behind shifts in economic status, since rising challengers cannot simply buy additional voting rights at will unless waning powers offer seals of approval. This echoes the theoretical insight of historical institutionalism that 'institutional stickiness' means that it is hard to alter institutional arrangements when they become settled.[8]

Power transition is far from a smooth and automatic process – as power shifts, ascending powers assume greater burden shares and gain more voting rights, while waning powers bear a lesser burden and enjoy less influence. In practice, waning powers are reluctant to cede influence, whereas ascending powers are hesitant to assume additional burdens. Consequently, ascending powers and waning powers engage in a perennial seesaw battle over the right balance between contribution (burden shares) and influence (voting rights).

For waning powers, the best option is to maintain or even amplify their influence while seeking share cuts (as justified by their relative economic decline); their second best option is to cede their influence

---

[8]  Pierson (2004: 11).

corresponding to their reduced contribution; and their worst option is to keep on bearing a constant burden while losing influence.

For ascending powers, the best scenario is to gain voting rights in line with their enhanced economic status without making any additional contribution; their second best scenario is to raise their voting rights commensurate with their increased contributions; and their least attractive option is to shoulder a heavier burden in return for no increase in voting rights.

The seesaw battle between waning powers and ascending powers can lead to a range of bargaining outcomes. This analysis of the seesaw battle between waning power and ascending powers can also be extended to power struggles between the hegemon and ascending powers. Similar to the advantaged waning powers, the hegemon enjoys the privilege of veto power in the Bretton Woods Institutions.

At one end of the spectrum, the hegemon and waning powers can cut burden shares but retain voting rights. As elaborated earlier in the section on structural cases (see Section 2.1), ascending powers may be coerced into carrying a greater burden without gaining commensurate influence because they are structurally dependent on the hegemon to counter a looming external threat.

At the other end of the spectrum, ascending powers can gain voting rights without assuming more burden share. Perhaps the hegemon and waning powers rely on ascending powers' cooperation in other areas of vital importance to their core interests; thus, they are compelled to cede voting rights in IOs in order to secure support from ascending powers in other areas.

The focal point of analysis here lies in between the above two extreme scenarios – quid-pro-quo deals with trading between burden shares and voting rights. Since this study empirically focuses on explaining change in IDA burden-sharing, we examine *under what conditions waning powers cede voting rights in exchange for ascending powers' increased burden shares.*

A prolonged disparity between economic capabilities and voting rights would provoke ascending powers to deploy their financial contributions to vie for voting rights. Foreign aid is an instrument of statecraft[9] and can be strategically used to promote foreign policy goals.[10] Ascending powers thus can wield 'carrot' (promise of share

---

[9] Baldwin (1985).    [10] Knorr (1975).

increases) and/or 'stick' (threat of share cuts or exit) in order to speed up the voting-rights adjustment process to better reflect their newly gained economic weight. Ascending powers' financial leverage is potent when financial contributions to international aid organisation are voluntary as opposed to mandatory (e.g., assessed contributions to the UN). Under these conditions, ascending powers are at liberty to withhold their contributions if they fail to achieve their desired influence.

Accommodate or resist? Initially, waning powers would prefer to resist ceding voting rights, not only because making concessions would undermine their reputation for resolve, thereby provoking additional aggression in the future,[11] but also because voting rights in IOs symbolise their international status.

Yet two grim consequences would follow if waning powers persist in clinging on to more voting rights than their current economic status would warrant. First, IOs' financial resources would be severely constrained, since ascending powers are unwilling to take up a greater burden whereas waning powers are unable to sustain their financial support. Second, it would undermine the legitimacy of IOs, so ascending powers may opt for outside options or create new ones if they lack ownership of the existing institution.[12]

To avoid the above gloomy prospects, waning powers would opt for accommodation if they have a strong interest in the total aid provision by the focal international aid organisation. At first glance, threats by ascending powers to cut the financial contribution to an international aid organisation may appear harmless to waning powers, since it is recipient countries that will be victimised by any cut in aid. Yet this view neglects the possibility that donors not only harvest donor-specific interests from greater aid disbursements by IOs, but also steer IOs to serve their long-term strategic objectives, such as countering their geopolitical threats. Thus, as de facto principal beneficiaries, waning powers would try their best to avoid severe share cuts by ascending powers.

In addition, the hegemon and waning powers would be more likely to cede voting rights to rising challengers when the following contributing factors are in place.

---

[11] Treisman (2004: 345).    [12] Stone (2011).

First, if the hegemon and waning powers anticipate greater preference congruence with ascending powers on substantive policy issues, they are more likely to agree upon shared leadership.

Second, if the hegemon and waning powers are confident of retaining strong informal influence over IOs, they are more willing to cede formal voting rights for the sake of maintaining the IO legitimacy.[13]

Last but not least, if voting-rights readjustments entail fewer distributional consequences, the hegemon and waning powers would be less hesitant to cede voting rights. For instance, if a shift in voting rights involves no disturbance in shareholding ranking, it helps to clear the blockage in the way of a potential quid pro quo between burden shares and voting rights.

In essence, if the hegemon and waning powers have a stake in IDA expansion, they are more willing to cede voting rights in IFIs in exchange for increased financial contributions to IDA from ascending powers.

## 2.3 Controlling IOs: Fairness and Legitimacy

The third layer of power play goes beyond formal influence of voting rights and extends our analysis into the informal donor influence upon Bank Management. In contrast with voting-rights struggles with distributional conflict among states themselves, IOs have the potential to play an independent role in protecting their autonomy and resisting informal donor influence.

The recent literature on IOs has emphasised that it is 'impossible' to understand how IOs actually work by focusing on formal rules alone.[14] Indeed, states regularly use informal means of influence (such as wielding financial contributions to set the agenda, appointing key personnel, persuading other states and Bank Management to support their initiatives) rather than formal voting rights to control IOs.[15] IDA Deputies bypass the formal Board of Executive Directors to strengthen their grip on Bank Management. In brief, while seeking voting rights is the most obvious means of controlling IOs, it is vital to examine donor control on IOs' policies and operations via informal means in order to grasp the full picture.

---

[13] Stone (2011).     [14] Kratochwil and Ruggie (1986: 755).
[15] For a special issue on informal influence, see Stone (2013).

When it comes to international aid organisations, deploying financial leverage to control IOs is particularly potent for two reasons. First, donor contributions come from taxpayers' money; thus, donor governments must diligently exercise stewardship to hold IOs accountable. Second, unlike the OECD Development Assistance Committee (DAC) that serves as a policy coordination platform among donors, international aid organisations manage a reservoir of financial resources to implement programmes and projects with significant financial leverage upon aid-dependent recipient countries. Hence, donors are more tempted to engage in unilateral influence contests to advance their own interests and values.[16]

A conventional approach to studying informal influence in IOs focuses on material leverage – donors increase their contribution to 'buy' more influence, but reduce their contribution if they lose influence. As the principal-agent literature has pointed out, 'principals [states] can punish agents for undesired actions and reward agents [IOs] for desired actions'.[17]

Yet 'buying influence' is merely the tip of the iceberg. Controlling IOs is not merely a matter of sheer material weight. Rather, it is mediated by certain 'principled beliefs' that specify criteria for distinguishing right from wrong and just from unjust.[18]

Fairness matters in governing IOs.[19] First, the fairness concern is 'necessary to the realization of a more durable and robust world order'. States demand 'reciprocity, equitable treatment, and procedural and distributive legitimacy'.[20] Second, the fairness principle can play 'an instrumental role' in guiding and facilitating international negotiations, with the same analytical standing as hard-core interests.[21]

The notion of burden-sharing implies a conscious effort among contributors to achieve 'equity' and 'fairness'. Donors expect that those who call the tune should pay the piper. This in effect creates an implicit 'equity line' between influence and contribution. Any egregious disparity is likely to induce countermeasures to restore the equity line. Thus, it is reasonable to expect that the fairness concern in controlling IOs is essential to a better understanding of IDA burden-sharing dynamics.

---

[16] Urpelainen (2012).　　[17] Hawkins et al. (2006b: 30).
[18] Goldstein and Keohane (1993: 10).　　[19] Keohane (1989a).
[20] Kapstein (2005: 88, 97).　　[21] Albin (2001: 35).

The fairness concern applies especially strongly to the hegemon. Endowed with preponderant material powers, the hegemon has stronger temptations to go it alone, to act in its narrow self-interest, and to shirk obligations.[22]

The question becomes how to discern how far the hegemon strays from the fairness principle. The contribution-to-influence equity line serves as a useful benchmark.

On the contribution side, donors are expected to do their 'fair' share and to honour their financial commitments under multilateral agreements. Thus, if donors claim 'unjustifiable' share reductions and/or incur overdue obligations, they run the risk of aggravating the fairness concern. While it is politically controversial to agree upon what constitutes 'equitable' burden-sharing, donors generally embrace the basic 'capacity-to-pay' principle. Hence, claims for share cuts are viewed by secondary states as 'unjustifiable' if the hegemon attempts to cut its burden share far below its GNP share.

On the influence side, what matters is not simply *how much* influence donors have upon IOs, but rather *for what purposes* and *with what means*. The equity line is skewed most severely when the hegemon unilaterally wields financial leverage to seek its private interests (e.g., the US may use Congressional threats to cut its financial contribution to IDA to force Bank Management to disburse more aid to countries of strategic importance to the United States). By contrast, the hegemon's influence attempts have least practical impact upon the fairness concern when it uses multilateral deliberation (such as persuasion) to convince others to follow its initiatives for the sake of collective interests. In short, the distributional consequences of donor influence depend on the *purpose* and *means* of influence attempts, and the sense of 'unfairness' is most acute when the hegemon seeks private interests with unilateral means.

The next question, then, is what happens if the hegemon chases privileges but shirks due obligations, thus widening the discrepancy between influence and contribution. Two broad options are open to secondary states to redress this disparity – 'exit' and 'voice'.[23]

---

[22] Patrick (2002: 9); Malone and Khong (2003: 424).

　　The analysis here does not rule out the possibility that the hegemon may pursue long-term goals by strategically binding itself in international institutions in order to send credible assurance to weak states (Ikenberry 2011).

[23] Originally, Hirschman used the concepts of 'exit' and 'voice' to examine how customers/clients can deploy these 'recuperation mechanisms' to reverse the

Exit involves the 'contribution' side of the equation.[24] Apart from an outright withdrawal from IOs (which is rare in the case of the World Bank), exit includes a wide range of possibilities. In order of severity from the lightest to the harshest, it encompasses: (a) refusing to compensate for the hegemon's 'unwarranted' share reduction (thus resulting in a 'financial gap'); (b) avoiding legitimising any further share cuts by the hegemon (and hence could lead to *'Hegemonic Lags'*);[25] (c) diverting money elsewhere from hegemon-dominated IOs; and/or (d) creating new alternative IOs excluding the hegemon.

Voice is associated with the 'influence' side of the equation – secondary states can (a) resist ceding influence to the hegemon, and/or (b) take initiatives to compete for more influence against the hegemon.

The above observation echoes the insight of the literature which emphasised the constraining effect of legitimacy upon the exercise of hegemonic power.[26] A hegemon is perceived as legitimate if it acts in accordance with the generally acceptable norms or rules.[27] Otherwise,

> deterioration in organisational performance (Hirschman 1970). Here I apply his core insights to analyse how secondary states can take countermeasures to redress the disparity between influence and contribution as a result of the hegemon's norm violations. Hence, I need to define 'exit' and 'voice' in this specific context. It is worth noting that 'exit' and 'voice' are not an either/choice. Rather, they are complementary and mutually reinforcing. For example, an ever-present 'exit' threat can strengthen effective 'voice' opportunities (Hirschman 1974).

[24] For the role of outside options in shaping the burden-sharing pattern, see Fang and Ramsay (2010).

[25] In IDA-type burden-sharing arrangements, donors collectively decide on the total target. Hence, secondary states can adjust the level of the total target so as to prevent the US burden share from falling below its minimum 'fair' share if the United States puts a cap on its dollar contribution.

[26] For the constraining effect of legitimacy, see Hurd (1999); Clark (2005); Franck (1990); Luck (2002).

> It is worth noting that scholars question whether legitimacy poses 'a structural constraint' upon the hegemon and contend that the hegemon is 'capable of using its preponderance to maintain and shape legitimacy'. See Brooks and Wohlforth (2008: 172).

[27] This is derived from the Constructivist definition that 'legitimacy is the normative belief held by an actor that a rule ought to be obeyed' (Hurd 1999: 381).

> An alternative definition of legitimacy 'hinges on whether its constituent members see it [the hegemon-led international order] as acceptable or better than any possible alternatives'. Thus, this definition does not necessarily imply 'fair procedures' or 'fair substantive outcomes'. While this working definition may be useful for certain research purposes, it does not fit my research purpose to explore how the hegemon's violation of the normative principles held by

losing legitimacy increases the costs of translating capabilities into desired outcomes in the short run,[28] and undermines its hegemonic leadership[29] and the hegemonic order in the long run.[30] Thus, the hegemon needs to heed the fairness concern in order to avoid breaching the tolerance threshold of secondary states.

In summary, a recurring pattern in the informal donor influence upon Bank Management throughout IDA replenishment history is that *if the hegemon violated the 'fairness' principle by shirking obligations but unilaterally pursuing undue influence, secondary states were likely to take 'exit/voice' measures to restore the implicit contribution-to-influence equity line.*

Yet IDA replenishment history shows that the hegemon seems to be able to cut its burden shares but retain or even amplify its influence in the World Bank.[31] We may be tempted to jump to the conclusion that the hegemon is so powerful that it can breach the fairness principle with impunity.[32] Yet a closer examination reveals that there is a considerable *time lag* before secondary states actually carry out their countermeasures.

This brings about the question of under what conditions secondary states postpone their 'exit/voice' countermeasures. Case studies tell us that *secondary states would postpone their 'exit/voice' measures if they were structurally dependent upon the hegemon and/or lack viable outside options.*

One reason for the time lag is that secondary states are so structurally dependent upon the hegemon that they have to tolerate unfairness in a specific international aid organisation in return for the hegemon's support in other domains. For instance, if they rely on the hegemon's military and economic tutelage against a common enemy, they would be more willing to bear a larger share of aid burden even without gaining commensurate influence in the focal IO.

Another reason for the time lag is the lack of viable outside options. Outside options are viable *if* they enable states to better achieve their objectives than via the existing focal IO. It has been argued that

---

secondary states impacts their willingness to contribute to IOs. See Brooks and Wohlforth (2008: 173); Stone (2011: 18).
[28] Clark (2005: 233).     [29] Reus-Smit (2004: 102).     [30] Cronin (2001): 113.
[31] Woods (2006; 2003); Gwin (1997).
[32] This perspective is commonly associated with the realist tradition. See Walt (2002).

a superpower can exploit its ability to use outside options to achieve favourable outcomes in multilateral bargaining more than secondary states can since the latter have fewer outside options.[33]

At first glance, the argument about 'outside options' appears irrelevant when it comes to bargaining in international aid organisations. The reason is that almost every donor, large and small alike, has their own bilateral aid agency. But this overlooks two crucial facts that help rediscover the analytical value of viable outside options.

First, bureaucratic politics and international obligations incentivise decision-makers to disburse all available aid money; thus, the paucity of viable outside options would delay the 'exit' option. Bureaucrats in government agencies seek to maximise their budget; they would want to increase or at least maintain the previous year's aid budget.[34] International obligations can amplify the effect of the disbursement imperative, as in the case of the UN General Assembly resolution stipulating that 'economically advanced countries' should devote at least 0.7 per cent of their GNP as ODA.[35] Meeting this UN target signals donor commitment to international development. This reputation concern may hold donors back from opting for exit if no viable outside options are available to help donors to disburse their planned spending in order to preserve their overall 'aid performance'. Hence, such a disbursement imperative may discourage donors from diverting their money back to their national coffers, even if they are dissatisfied with the disparity between influence and contribution in the focal IO.

Second, bilateral aid agencies have such a limited implementation capacity that a swift shift from international aid organisations to bilateral aid channels may turn out to be impractical within a certain time span. The availability of alternative multilateral aid channels, on the other hand, can facilitate shifts in donors' aid portfolios.

To sum up, structural dependence and outside options help to define the tipping point where secondary states decide to put their counter-measures into action.

---

[33] Voeten (2001).     [34] Mueller (1979).

[35] In 1970, the 0.7% ODA/GNI target was first agreed and has been repeatedly re-endorsed at the highest level at international aid and development conferences. See OECD, *The 0.7% ODA/GNI Target – a History*, www.oecd.org/investment/stats/the07odagnitarget-ahistory.htm (accessed 22 June 2010).

## 2.4 Complementary Analytical Perspectives

This section discusses complementary analytical factors to help us to navigate the complex dynamics of IDA replenishment negotiations. While we have mainly focused on the three layers of power plays at the international level, it is important to take into account domestically driven factors.

First, it is relevant to consider the relative autonomy of the executive branch from the legislative branch. Unlike the European parliamentary systems, the US government is 'divided', because one party controls the White House and another party controls one or both houses of the US Congress, thus leading to Congressional gridlock.[36] Hence, European donors have less difficulty in obtaining the legislative ratification of their financial contributions to IOs, whereas the US Administration has to spend much more political capital to get the stamp of approval from Congress at the both ratification and disbursement stages. This means that Congress may play an influential role in shaping US participation in IDA.[37]

Second, political will plays a crucial role in shaping donors' willingness to contribute. The succession of ruling political parties or high-level officials can shift priorities from multilateral aid to bilateral aid, or even to an anti-aid stance. These shocks can substantially undermine donors' willingness to contribute to IDA.

In empirical case studies, we will pay due attention to domestic factors to grasp donors' ability and willingness to contribute before entering strategic interactions on the international level to grasp the implications of power transitions for a US-led hegemonic international system.

## 2.5 Conclusion

To recap, this chapter has crystallised key insights behind the three layers of power plays – namely, the US-led Western donor group versus external threats from the East and the South; the internal donor power struggles about voting rights redistributions; and the informal donor influence upon Bank Management. Table 2.1 summarises the core

---

[36] Fiorina (1996).　　[37] Lavelle (2011).

Table 2.1 *Salient Historical Patterns of the Three Power Plays*

| Power Plays | Analytical Factors | | Empirical Outcomes |
|---|---|---|---|
| Structural Causes: external threats from the East and the South | The intensity of perceived external threat | High | *Hegemonic Lag*: the hegemon maintains its share |
| | | Low | *Accelerated Burden-Shifting*: the hegemon makes substantial share cuts compensated for by rising powers' share increases |
| Challenger Power Play: quid pro quo between burden shares and voting rights | The interest of the hegemon and/or waning powers in expanding total IDA resources | High | *Accelerated Burden-Shifting*: the hegemon and/or waning powers cede voting rights in exchange for ascending powers' share increases |
| | | Low | *Challenger Inertia*: no quid-pro-quo deals emerge |
| Controlling IOs: fairness & legitimacy | Scale of the hegemon's violations of the 'fairness' principle | High | Secondary states take 'exit/voice' measures |
| | | Low | No countermeasures taken |
| | Structural dependence/ viable outside options | High/ Fewer | Secondary states *postpone* countermeasures |
| | | Low/ More | Secondary states *accelerate* countermeasures |

empirical patterns of the three power plays emerging from in-depth case studies. They include:

1. Structural Causes: external threats from the East and the South

    a) The hegemon was more likely to maintain its burden share, as the hegemon-centred Western world order faced looming external threats from the East and the South;

2. Challenger Power Play: quid pro quo between burden shares and voting rights

    a) If the hegemon and waning powers desired to expand total IDA resources, they were likely to cede voting rights to ascending powers in exchange for financial support;

3. Controlling IOs: fairness and legitimacy

    a) If the hegemon violated the 'fairness' principle by shirking obligations but pursuing undue influence, secondary states were likely to take 'exit/voice' measures to restore the implicit contribution-to-influence equity line;

    b) Secondary states would postpone their 'exit/voice' measures if they were structurally dependent upon the hegemon and/or lack viable outside options.

With the above central features in mind, we can better navigate complex strategic interactions of IDA replenishment negotiations to grasp the central theme of how the US-centred international system has adapted to power transitions. Meanwhile, probing these power dynamics in further cases helps us appreciate how historical contingencies have enriched and refined the three core patterns.

# 3 | IDA *in the 1960s: Hegemonic Leadership amid Bipolar Geopolitics*

This chapter reviews the emergence of *Hegemonic Lag* and *Challenger Inertia* in IDA burden-sharing through the first rounds of replenishment negotiations, and explores the factors that contributed to the emergence of these dynamics.

The first decade after IDA's inception in 1960 witnessed considerable shifts in relative economic capabilities among major Western donors: Germany, France, and Japan enjoyed 'miraculous' post-war economic recoveries, rapidly catching up with the United States;[1] the waning UK lost its second largest economy status, overtaken first by Germany and then by Japan.[2]

Yet despite these dramatic economic shifts, IDA burden-sharing was fairly stable in terms of both donor ranking and percentage changes: (a) the pecking order was almost constant among the top donors – the USA, the UK, Germany, France, Canada, and Japan in the descending order;[3] (b) after initial modest share reductions, the USA even maintained its share in IDA-3.

This poses the intriguing puzzle of why changes in IDA burden-sharing lagged far behind shifts in relative economic weight among major donors.

This chapter proceeds as follows: first, it explores why the hegemon honoured its share despite its relative economic decline (*Hegemonic Lag*); second, it examines why ascending powers were slow to bolster their shares despite their economic ascent (*Challenger Inertia*); third, it takes a step further to discuss the balance of power in World Bank

---

[1] Japan enjoyed a spectacular annual average growth rate of about 10%, in sharp contrast with 4.7% in the United States and 2.9% in the UK. See World Bank, *World Development Indictors (WDI)*: http://databank.worldbank.org/data/rep orts.aspx?source=world-development-indicators (accessed 28 June 2013).

[2] *The Maddison Project Database*, www.ggdc.net/maddison/maddison-project/ data.htm (accessed 25 July 2013).

[3] Germany and France tied for third place in the initial subscription.

governance; finally, it summaries key findings that the intensifying Soviet threat in a confrontational bipolar international system compelled the USA to honour its burden share for IDA expansion so as to counterbalance the communist influence in the Third World.

## 3.1 Hegemonic Lag: The Soviet Threat Fosters US Leadership in IDA

This section explores what motivated the USA to sustain its financial support for IDA although its economy was in relative decline.

### 3.1.1 Deciphering US Vital Interests in a Bipolar International System

As the principal architect, the USA took the leadership in founding IDA as a vital geopolitical instrument for accommodating the Third World's demand for aid to counter the Soviet threat. This grand strategy was deeply rooted in the US belief that Western economic assistance played a pivotal role in promoting growth, economic liberalism, and liberal democracy to win minds and hearts in the Third World; economic stagnation in developing countries would lead to social revolution, hence spreading Communism.[4]

In the wake of unprecedented decolonisation movements, newly independent developing countries had been vigorously campaigning for a sizeable international development fund. As early as 1953, a specific proposal for a Special United Nations Fund for Economic Development (SUNFED) was proposed by an expert group commissioned by the UN Secretary General. Developing countries called upon rich industrialised countries to step up their aid efforts to compensate for damage inflicted upon poor countries in the dark colonial era of wealth extraction. Meanwhile, they insisted that this multilateral aid fund be under the 'one country, one vote' UN control so as to mitigate vast power asymmetries between strong Northern donors and weak Southern recipients.[5]

Initially the USA dismissed the Third World's proposal for a UN development fund. The Eisenhower Administration turned a blind eye to the poor countries' appeal because it was reluctant to relinquish its

---

[4] Ruttan (1996: 7).    [5] Mason and Asher (1973: 380–83).

control over financial resources to the UN where both the Soviet Union and recipient countries could have a significant voice.[6]

The looming Soviet threat, however, compelled the United States to shift its stance. In the late 1950s, the Soviet Union intensified its economic assistance as 'a political weapon' to cement close ties with developing countries.[7] As the Soviet penetration was deepening beyond Europe into the non-aligned periphery areas, the 'Less-Developed Countries' (LDCs) took on more and more importance on the geopolitical chessboard.[8] To prevent the spread of the Communist influence, economic aid contests with the Soviet Union began to dominate US foreign policy.[9] Ultimately the USA – at the initiative of Congress – made an important political shift and assumed the leadership in establishing IDA under the aegis of the US-dominated World Bank.[10] The US Congress had played a key role in reaching this point and strongly supported the initiative of taking advantage of the World Bank as a dispenser of aid to developing countries in the face of a looming Soviet threat.[11]

The foundation of IDA marked a North–South compromise in their power struggles for influence. IDA was established as the 'soft-loan' window of the World Bank in 1960, with an initial donor subscription of about $750 million over five years.[12] Although developing countries would have preferred an aid agency under UN control, they went along with IDA because they recognised that it was their only hope of funds on such lenient terms. (India actively supported the World Bank answer as a practical, fast start-up option).[13] Proponents claimed IDA served

[6]  Baldwin (1961: 91).      [7]  Valkenier (1983: 4).

[8]  From a US National Security Council memo, see Schweitzer (1990: 76).

[9]  Ruttan (1996: 69–75).

[10]  As the largest shareholder, the USA enjoyed the privilege of the veto power in the World Bank. The Bank President was always an American citizen nominated by the USA. During the Cold War, the Soviet Union was not a member of the World Bank.

[11]  IDA was originally proposed in a Senate Resolution by Democratic Senator Mike Monroney; a vote was passed in favour of the establishment of IDA in 1958. See Kapur, Lewis, and Webb (1997: 1127–28).

[12]  IDA's initial subscriptions were divided into two categories: the subscriptions of Part I members (developed countries or donors) were payable in full in gold or convertible currencies, whereas 10% of the subscriptions of Part II members (developing countries or recipients) were payable in gold or convertible currencies, with the balance being payable in a member's own currency. See International Development Association, 'International Development Association', Press Release No. 1, 26 September 1960.

[13]  Kapur, Lewis, and Webb (1997: 1127).

as 'living proof' that the international power structure is responsive to persistent peaceful pressure.[14] Opponents lamented that IDA 'strengthened the role of the Bank at the expense of the UN',[15] laying the ground for the imposition of donor-driven conditionality on recipient countries.

By linking IDA to the World Bank rather than the UN, the United States strived to accomplish dual objectives, namely: (a) maximising its influence upon its bipolar rival by expanding IDA's total aid supply to the Third World; and (b) minimising the cost by eliciting its Western allies to bear more aid burden via IDA burden-sharing arrangements.[16]

The following sections explore the history of IDA's early years to discover how the USA interacted with secondary states to achieve its dual goals, thereby shaping IDA burden-sharing dynamics.

### 3.1.2 IDA-1 (FY1965–68):[17] Geopolitical Imperatives Trump the US Desire for a Share Cut

In the early 1960s, the United States was horrified by the intensifying Soviet penetration in LDCs. Cold War tensions mounted with the construction of the Berlin Wall in 1961. The Soviet threat was further exacerbated by ideological rivalry. The Soviet Union denounced Western domination in the Third World that relegated poor countries to the role of raw material producers. It proclaimed that Soviet aid offered a viable alternative to the LDCs by helping to build up independent national economies.[18] The USA perceived that the Soviet Union was promoting a rival development model to achieve the 'ultimate objective' of 'the downfall of the West'.[19]

To counter the Soviet threat, the USA pressed its Western allies to step up collective aid efforts. President John F. Kennedy asserted that the 'Soviet threat is worldwide',[20] and declared in 1961 that America

---

[14]  Mason and Asher (1973: 380).      [15]  Shaw (2005: 44).
[16]  Baldwin (1961: 91).
[17]  IDA-1 covered the period of fiscal year (FY) 1965–67/8, negotiated between fall 1962 and summer 1963.
[18]  Valkenier (1983: 7).
[19]  Quotation by Douglas Dillon, Under Secretary of State, from US Department of State, *Communist Economic Policy in the Less Developed Areas* (Washington, DC: Government Printing Office, 1960), foreword.
[20]  Ruttan (1996: 77).

was willing to 'pay any price, bear any burden' to stifle the spread of Communism.[21]

As IDA-1 kicked off, the United States led the drive for an ambitious total target of $1.5 billion at three-year intervals (three times the initial donor subscriptions on a yearly basis). Despite support from small donors (e.g., Scandinavian countries), major donors (especially the UK and France, which were still in colonial financing mode) were reluctant to put their bilateral aid money into a multilateral institution in which they did not have full control.[22]

What made the other major donors less forthcoming in supporting an enlarged IDA fund was that the USA vigorously sought a share reduction. The USA justified its claim for share reduction on two grounds: (a) that 'as other donor nations grow financially stronger', they should 'assume a greater share of the burden of providing development finance'; and (b) that since the USA bore a disproportionate burden of collective defence of the 'free world', its military allies ought to shoulder more of the aid burden.[23] The Kennedy Administration also alluded to Congressional pressure for a more 'equitable' burden-sharing.[24]

This led to a head-on clash between the USA and other major donors over 'fair' burden-sharing in IDA. Other major donors contended that the hegemon was not putting up as much as its productive capacity would indicate – even though the USA accounted for more than half of total world output, it only carried about 40 per cent of the burden.[25]

As persuasion alone proved futile, the USA resorted to coercion to press ascending powers to pay their 'fair' shares. Germany was the No. 1 target to assume a greater proportion of aid burden, since its

---

[21]  Kissinger (1994: 19).

[22]  Statement of Douglas Dillon, Secretary of the Treasury, from Hearings from the US Senate Committee on Foreign Relations, *Amendments to Inter-American Development Bank and International Development Association Acts*, 88th Congress, 1st Session, 15 November and 4 December 1963, 17–18.

[23]  Statement of Hon. David M. Kennedy, Secretary of the Treasury, from Hearing before the US Senate Committee on Foreign Relations, *Increased Resources for International Development Association*, 91st Congress, 1st Session, 16 April 1963, 4.

[24]  Hearing before the House Committee on Banking and Currency, Expanding the Resources of the International Development Association, 88th Congress, 1st Session, 3–16 December 1968, 53.

[25]  Ibid., 50.

'economic miracle' was in full swing. President Kennedy put direct pressure on the German Chancellor by threatening to demand reimbursement for the US troops should Germany not step up its aid efforts.[26] France, Japan, and Italy were also subject to intense US pressures, given their dependence upon the USA for collective defence and market access.[27]

Yet it turned out that the hegemonic coercion was less credible as the Soviet threat intensified. In the aftermath of the Cuban Missile Crisis in October 1962, in order to strike a posture of determination to keep NATO strong, President Kennedy publicly assured West Europe of no troop withdrawals. Rather than making a large cutback in the US force, Kennedy steadily strengthened the American military presence.[28] Accordingly, ascending powers anticipated that the United States would not leave them helpless should the Soviets invade. They took advantage of the US imperative of assisting Western Europe and Japan as a vital bulwark for holding Communism at bay; thus, they resisted share increases.[29]

Consequently, the IDA replenishment was mired in arduous negotiations. The negotiation process involved a strict deadline.[30] Donors were compelled to seal a deal; otherwise, IDA would suffer from a hiatus in its operations when it ran out of resources. This would risk undermining the collective donor interest in containing the Soviet threat. To avoid this worst-case scenario, donors had to find ways to settle their differences regarding the target total and the burden-sharing.

At this critical juncture, the USA decided to prioritise its aspirations for IDA expansion over its desire for its own share cut. Otherwise, if the USA had taken a hard line on its share cut, it 'would only have reduced the total funds being made available'

---

[26] Lancaster (2007: 172).

[27] At this time, the USA led the founding of a Development Assistance Group (DAG) to establish a common benchmark for measuring aid efforts in order to press its Western allies to share more aid burdens. The DAG then became the Development Assistance Committee (DAC), within the OECD, under US Chairmanship for the following four decades. See OECD (2006).

[28] Raj (1983: 215–17).    [29] Lunn (1983: 2).

[30] To ensure IDA-1 could start operating in FY1965 (*1 July 1964–30 June 1965*), donors had to reach agreement by the summer of 1963 to allow at least one year for donors to complete domestic ratification.

through IDA.[31] Here was a fundamental trade-off in the US Cold War policy: any 'unjustified' US share reduction in IDA could trigger a domino effect on other donors' willingness to contribute, thus undermining US leadership for an ambitious expansion of IDA.

Finally, the USA refrained from claiming a substantial share reduction in exchange for other donors' support for a higher target total. The USA settled for a modest share cut of 0.74 per cent. In return, other donors collectively supported a much higher total target of $750 million. While it fell short of the original US goal of $1.5 billion, it surpassed the initial annual donor subscriptions by two-thirds.

In a nutshell, the intensifying Soviet threat rendered the hegemonic coercion less credible, because materialising the US threats would have undercut its core interests as much as, if not more than, they did to its allies. Accordingly, the US geopolitical imperative (i.e., maximising total aid provision to contain its bipolar rival) triumphed over its desire for share reduction to minimise financial cost.

### 3.1.3 IDA-2 (FY1969–71):[32] 'No Participation without Share Reduction'

By the mid-1960s, Congress was calling for a substantial US share cut in IDA, largely provoked by a deteriorating US ability to pay. Mired in the costly Vietnam War, Congress cut foreign aid expenditures to a historic low, complaining bitterly that aid spending was 'mainly responsible' for ever-increasing inflation, deficit spending, balance-of-payments deficits, and the continuing loss of gold reserves that vitiated the strength of the dollar as the international reserve currency.[33]

The new Johnson Administration was tempted to cater to Congress, which held the purse strings, since the Soviet threat was less imminent after the Cuban missile crisis in 1962 (known as 'post-Cuban détente').[34]

---

[31] Statement of Douglas Dillon, 33.
[32] IDA-2 covered the period of FY1969–71, negotiated between mid-1966 and March 1968.
[33] Congress, *Congressional Quarterly Almanac 1968* (Washington, DC: Congressional Quarterly Service), 604.
[34] Spencer (1990: 35).

Subsequently, the United States threatened that it would not participate in IDA-2 unless it achieved a share reduction.[35] Yet other donors
contended that the US claim for share reduction was 'unjustifiable', as
IDA should not be victimised by short-run fluctuations in donors'
ability to pay.

What upset other donors more than the US claim for share reduction
was that the United States sought a privilege of tying its financial
contribution to IDA procurement benefits to relieve its balance-of-
payments difficulties. As of FY1967, the US poor procurement performance had exacerbated its current account deficit.[36]

This undue US influence attempt was strongly resisted by both
Bank Management and other donors. So far, the World Bank had
adhered to the principle of open competitive bidding to ensure
equal opportunity for eligible bidders from all member countries.
Accommodating the US demand would have two consequences.
First, it would force IDA into allocating procurement benefits in
proportion to burden shares, if others followed suit to seek the
same privilege. Second, it would tarnish the Bank Management's
independence, thus adversely shaping the attitude adopted by
developing countries towards IDA as an international lender of
paramount importance to them.[37]

But the United States was adamant in its position, insisting that 'an
essential condition for US participation ... would be adequate balance
of payments safeguards'.[38] This thorny issue resulted in a severe delay,
throwing IDA into a funding crisis.[39]

To break the stalemate, a compromise was finally reached. On the
one hand, other donors made a one-off accommodation, allowing the
USA to *defer* draw-down of its contribution if its procurement gains

[35]  IDA, 'Discussion Paper on Burden Sharing in IDA', 3.
[36]  'Table 4: IDA Items Affecting US Balance of Payments', from the US National
      Advisory Council on International Monetary and Financial Policies (NAC),
      *Special Report to the President and to the Congress of the Proposed
      Replenishment of the Resources of the International Development Association*,
      April 1968.
[37]  Medley-Miller (Treasury), 'A draft paper on IDA-2 Replenishment',
      28 October 1966, from the UK National Archives.
[38]  NAC, Special Report to the President and to the Congress of the Proposed
      Replenishment of the Resources of the International Development Association,
      20.
[39]  IDA-2 was initially intended to cover FY1968–70 starting from July 1967, but it
      did not enter into effect until July 1969 – a two-year delay.

(inflows) could not offset its contribution (outflows) only during the period of IDA-2.[40] On the other hand, the USA accepted the desirability of maintaining the principle of open competitive bidding, thus dropping its proposed 'tied aid' string.

Nevertheless, the undue US influence undermined its leadership for a target total of $1 billion per annum. A majority of donors viewed this target as 'unrealistic'.[41] Finally donors settled on a total size merely at the level of $400 million per year – less than half of what the USA aimed for.[42]

What further thwarted the US leadership was that no one wanted to make good the US share cut. The USA's stubborn claim for share reduction triggered a bandwagon effect – Australia and South Africa also took a hard line of 'no participation without share reduction'.[43] But other major donors refused to make up these shortfalls; they resented that the USA sought an unwarranted privilege.

To avoid any further delay, 'like-minded' donors (Canada, Sweden, the Netherlands, Denmark, and Finland) decided to make 'supplementary contributions' outside the burden-sharing framework to close the 'financing gap'. Since 'basic' burden shares implied quasi-obligations taken as the starting point in future replenishment negotiations, they insisted that their generosity be a *one-off* accommodation so as to avoid inflating others' expectations on their future contributions.

To conclude, as the Soviet threat subdued, the erosion in the USA's ability-to-pay provoked it into taking a hard line on a share cut, leading to a smaller IDA. And the US attempt to seek privileges also undercut its leadership for IDA enlargement.

---

[40] This concession was confined to IDA-2 only, 'without prejudice to any arrangements in connection with subsequent replenishments'. See IDA, *Additions to IDA Resources: Second Replenishment* (IDA-2 Replenishment Agreement), 8 March 1968, para. 22.

[41] UK Ministry of Overseas Development (ODM), 'Her Majesty's Treasury: IMF/ IBRD Twenty Fourth Annual Meeting – IDA Resources and Lending Policy', 24 September 1969, from the UK National Archives, *Policy on Third Replenishment*, OD 9/272.

[42] US Senate, *Increased US Participation in the International Development Association*, 90th Congress, 2nd Session, Report No. 1670, 11 October 1968, 4.

[43] IDA, 'Discussion paper on burden sharing in IDA', 3.

### 3.1.4 IDA-3 (FY1972–74):[44] US Imposes Self-Restraint to Achieve an Ambitious Total

In the late 1960s, the Soviet threat was looming large. The Soviet-led Warsaw Pact invasion of Czechoslovakia in 1968 sparked 'an earthquake effect' in the Western alliance.[45] The Czech crisis was a wake-up call for the United States.

The Third World took advantage of the intensifying East–West confrontation to press for a link between Special Drawing Rights (SDRs) and aid in order to expand automatic resource transfers from rich Western countries to developing countries.[46] Unlike conventional foreign aid, the proposed new scheme would guarantee a predictable and sustainable flow of financial resources to poor countries, rather than being at the discretion of donor governments. Hence, Western donors felt that a decently large IDA-3 was necessary to persuade developing countries to forgo this compelling demand.[47]

These geopolitical forces created the conditions for strong hegemonic leadership as demonstrated in IDA-1, but the US domestic situation augured badly for its support for an ambitious total for IDA-3.

Congress vigorously urged a substantial share cut. It complained that, as the federal deficit and balance-of-payment deficits lingered on, donations abroad would further deteriorate domestic economic difficulties. Congress further lamented that IDA did not serve US interests well.[48] On procurement benefits, the USA gained only 19 per cent of IDA-financed contracts, far below its burden share of 40 per cent as of the end of 1970.[49] Congress lamented that the USA contributed much more than it could earn back. On aid allocations, the lion's share of IDA credits went to India and Pakistan.

---

[44] IDA-3 covered the period of FY1972–74, negotiated between December 1969 and June 1970.

[45] NATO Communiqué, October 1968. See Spencer (1990: 38).

[46] Bird (1976).

[47] 'Note of a Talk on 24 November 1969 between Mr. R.B.M. King, Ministry of Overseas Development, and Mr. P.M. Reid, Executive Directors of IBRD/IDA for Canada, Guyana, Ireland and Jamaica, 27 November 1969', from the UK National Archives, *Policy on Third Replenishment*.

[48] US Senate Report, *International Development Association Third Replenishment*, 92nd Congress, 1st Session, Report No. 92–396, 14 October 1971.

[49] Ibid., 8.

A Congressman ironically commented that IDA should stand for 'India-Pakistan Development Association'.[50] Yet despite the strong Congressional urging for allocating more aid to the Western hemisphere, the share of Latin American countries in IDA allocations shrank from more than 8 per cent in 1961–65 to 3 per cent during 1966–70.[51]

Despite the growing Congressional hostility, however, the new Nixon Administration swung towards renewed hegemonic leadership for an expanding IDA to counter the Soviet threat.

To create a strong momentum for IDA-3, the United States shifted towards a greater reliance on multilateral institutions.[52] A strong case was made by the Treasury – the department responsible for the US participation in the World Bank – that multilateral aid was superior to bilateral aid in achieving the maximum contributions from its Western allies to achieve the US geopolitical objective.[53]

To sustain the US-led momentum, the new World Bank President McNamara inspired a clarion call for action: the far-reaching *Pearson Report* urged that rich countries should reach the UN target of 0.7 per cent of GNP for ODA by 1975 and channel 20 per cent of their ODA via multilateral institutions. More particularly, it espoused that 'contributions to IDA should reach the order of $1.0 billion annually in 1972 and $1.5 billion by 1975'.[54]

At the early stage of negotiations, the United States took the lead in proposing a $1 billion per year target total. Meanwhile, the United States voluntarily imposed self-restraint on two fronts. First, it pledged to honour its traditional share of 40 per cent.[55] Second, it decided to forgo the privilege of deferring its disbursements until its balance-of-payment constraints ameliorated. The rationale behind such self-restraint was that the United States anticipated that seeking share-reduction and undue privilege

---

[50] Mason and Asher, (1973: 401).    [51] Ibid.

[52] US Task Force on International Development (1970).

[53] Hearing before the Senate Committee on Foreign Relations, *Increased Resources for the International Development Association*, 92nd Congress, 1st Session, 20 October 1971.

[54] Pearson Commission on International Development (1969).

[55] IDA, 'Discussion Paper on Burden Sharing in IDA', 4.

would discourage other donors from pledging their maximum levels.[56]

Despite support for the US position on the ambitious target total from small donors, France and Germany formed an alliance to campaign against the US proposal and set an upper limit of $600 million per annum.

To defeat the 'unholy alliance', Bank Management adopted a 'divide and conquer' strategy – outflanking Germany by making a secret deal with France. A quid pro quo was made between Bank Management and France – senior Bank Management succeeded in soliciting share increases by small donors to allow for a French share reduction of about 1.5 per cent in return for the French support for a $1 billion target total.[57]

Yet Germany was reluctant to maintain its burden share of a target total that was greater than $800 million. Despite the intense US pressure, Germany was able to resist the hegemonic coercion, because the looming Soviet threat compelled the United States to declare that it was 'imperative' to promptly bring American combat units in Europe up to full strength.[58] Hence, the US threat of withdrawing troops from the German frontline was hollow.

Subsequently, the United States had to yield to a lower total target of $800 million due to persistent German resistance. Had the United States insisted upon the original target of $1 billion per year, it would have had to elicit share increases to fill 'a German shortfall' – Germany made it clear that, with such an ambitious target, it would not stand by its traditional share.

What made a potential German share cut more troublesome was that should Germany fail to honour its traditional share, the UK would seek to cut its share.[59] Why did the UK tolerate a French

---

[56] E.g., the UK made it clear that it would cut its contribution if the United States continued to tie its contributions to procurement. See Minute from N. B. J. Huijaman to Mr Williams on the Preparation for IDA-3 Negotiation, 17 January 1969, from the UK National Archives, OD 9/272.

[57] Interview with Sir Denis H. F. Rickett (IDA-3 Chairperson), from the World Bank's Oral history Programme, 20 August 1986, 3–4.

[58] Congressional Record, vol. 114, Part 22, 29277.

[59] ODM, 'International Development Association: Third Replenishment and Related Issues: Brief for Initial Discussions with Sir D. Rickett', 24 October 1969, from the UK National Archives, OD 9/272.

share cut but refuse a German one? This question finds an answer in another power game beyond IDA. The UK had ceded voting rights to Germany in the 5th IMF General Quota Review; the UK thus urged Germany to shoulder an increased burden in IDA to justify its newly gained influence in the IMF.[60]

Eventually the US leadership paid off – the total size of replenishment in IDA-3 doubled that of IDA-2, reaching a record-high total of $2.4 billion for the three years, as compared with the initial target of $3 billion for FY1972–74.

Fortunately, three new sources – Ireland, Spain, and Yugoslavia – supported IDA-3. Their contributions were outside of the burden-sharing framework because it was agreed in IDA-1 that new IDA resources should be provided entirely by economically advanced countries (or, 'Part I' members) and that developing countries (or, 'Part II' members) had no obligation to contribute.[61] In order to sell IDA to Congress, the US Administration presented its share against the grand total to demonstrate progress towards a more 'equitable' burden-sharing.[62]

In conclusion, as the Soviet threat intensified, US geopolitical goals trumped its desire for share reductions in an effort to expand IDA to counter the Soviet threat. Hence, the USA maintained its share, despite its eroding ability to pay and declining specific short-term interests.

## 3.2  Challenger Inertia

In explaining the stable IDA burden-sharing pattern, the other side of the same coin was why ascending powers lagged behind in assuming greater burden shares. Germany and Japan dragged their feet over boosting their financial contributions, sticking to

---

[60]  ODM, 'Note of a Meeting with Mr. R.S. McNamara in the ODM on 12 November 1969', 13 November 1969, from the UK National Archives, OD 9/272.

[61]  NAC, Special Report to the President and to the Congress of the Proposed Replenishment of the Resources of the International Development Association, April 1968, 10–11

[62]  US Senate Report, *International Development Association Third Replenishment*, 92nd Congress, 1st Session, Report No. 92–396, 14 October 1971, 6.

third and sixth place, respectively, in the donor ranking. France even successively cut its share.

The preceding section indicates that the intensifying Soviet threat rendered the hegemonic coercion less credible, enabling ascending powers to resist US pressure for share increases. Yet grasping a full picture of *Challenger Inertia* requires investigating the motives of ascending powers.

### 3.2.1 France: Flagging Commitment to the 'Anglo-Saxon' IDA

After a slight share increase in IDA-1, France cut its shares by 0.21 per cent in IDA-2 and 1.85 in IDA-3. This stood in contrast with Germany and Japan, which increased or at least maintained their shares. This section explores what accounted for the flagging French support for IDA.

Ability-to-pay fares poorly in explaining the consecutive French share cuts. France was enjoying an economic boom, with an annual average growth rate of over 5.5 per cent.[63] Buoyant government revenue enabled France to dramatically boost its aid budget. By the end of 1960s France became the second largest Western donor after the United States.[64]

Yet enhanced capacity did not strengthen French support for international aid organisations. Why? France's core interests were to retain its influence upon its former colonies after unprecedented decolonisation. France held that bilateral aid was superior to multilateral aid, not only because it enhanced the visibility of donors, but also because it strengthened political and economic ties with its former colonies. Thus, France viewed the US urge for more multilateral aid with great suspicion because diverting aid to international agencies would weaken imperial links with its former colonies.[65] Thus, only 7 per cent of French aid went to multilateral institutions.[66]

Among international aid organisations, IDA was at the bottom of the French priority list because IDA did not serve the French national

---

[63] Source: WDI.      [64] Source: DAC Aid Statistics.

[65] The US Department of the Treasury, 'Future US Reliance on International Financial Institutions (WB, ADB, IDB): Opinion Paper', 8 February 1973, from the US National Archives, Chronological files of the Treasury, 1973–1975.

[66] Lancaster (2007: 147–48).

interests well. France was resentful of the 'distorted' IDA aid allocations. More than two-thirds of IDA credits went to India and Pakistan
(former UK colonies), whereas Francophone African countries merely
got a tiny slice. Consequently, French firms lacked any natural advantage in winning IDA-financed contracts, resulting in a drain of
$34 million on its balance-of-payment account up to FY1967.[67]

Moreover, over time France came to believe that the prospect of
shaping IDA aid allocations to its favour was bleak. France had pressed
strongly for more IDA assistance to French-speaking Africa,[68] and had
strong discontent over the slow progress. France felt that the Bank was
'too much under the thumb of "les anglo-saxones" and, therefore, not
an organization France was eager to support'.[69]

What facilitated the French diversion of its aid away from IDA
was that it had viable outside options. In 1961 France elevated its
bilateral aid agency to the status of a Ministry for Co-cooperation
responsible for assistance to (mainly African) developing countries.
Apart from its capable bilateral aid channel, France could direct
multilateral aid via the European Development Fund (EDF), first
launched in 1959, where France was a dominant power.[70] This
Fund was financed by the six founding members of the European
Economic Community (EEC)[71] and allocated aid to the eighteen
Associated States, of which fourteen were ex-French territories.
France's influence was 'predominant' in deciding aid allocations.
For instance, of $800 million in EDF-2 (which ran from 1964 to
1970), 91.25 per cent ($730 million) was for the former French
colonies, far greater than the French burden share of 33.75
per cent.[72]

Finally, what enabled France to resist the strong hegemonic pressure
for share increases was that France was less militarily dependent upon
the USA than Germany and Japan. In April 1966, during IDA-2 negotiation, France announced its withdrawal from NATO's integrated
military structure, because it felt that NATO was dominated by the

[67] Table 7: Estimated Effect of IDA Operations on Balance of Payments of Part
I Countries, from IDA, 'Amount of the Fourth Replenishment', IDA/RPL/72–2,
20 November 1972, from the World Bank Archives.
[68] Mason and Asher (1973: 403).    [69] Lancaster (2007: 148).
[70] The UK did not become a fully-fledged member of the EEC until 1973.
[71] They were Belgium, France, Italy, Luxembourg, the Netherlands, and West
Germany.
[72] Hayter (1966: 212).

USA. France desired to 'recover, in her territory, the full exercise of sovereignty'.[73] Hence, France had reduced its structural dependence upon the USA.

In summary, IDA's failure to satisfy French national interests was the major factor in explaining the French *Challenger Inertia*, which was further facilitated by the availability of viable outside options and less structural dependence upon the hegemon.

### 3.2.2 *Japan: An IBRD Rising Star Contrasts Sharply with an IDA Laggard*

Japan remained in the position of sixth-largest IDA donor, although it spectacularly rose to be the second largest economy in the world by the late 1960s. How, then, to account for Japan's slow pace in assuming a greater IDA burden despite its ascending economic status?

Was it because that Japan failed to realise its country-specific interests? It turns out that this was far from the truth. Japan was a principal beneficiary of IDA-financed procurement contracts – it won more back than it put in. By FY1969, Japan earned a lucrative net benefit of over $90 million.[74] Since the World Bank adhered to open competitive bidding, Japan's procurement advantage largely depended on the competitiveness of Japanese firms. Hence, an increase in Japan's burden share was not a precondition for winning more procurement benefits.

A closer look at the history reveals that Japan could have successfully achieved its desired influence – IBRD voting rights – without any need for assuming a corresponding IDA burden. In the 1960s, IBRD voting rights were periodically re-adjusted in line with negotiated changes in IMF quotas (known as the 'parallelism' principle).

Thanks to the 'parallelism' principle, Japan's IBRD shareholding position had been progressively enhanced: Japan had been lifted from its initial ninth position to being the eighth, seventh, and then the fifth largest IBRD shareholder through Selective Capital Increases (SCIs)[75]

---

[73]  Raj (1983: 112–16).
[74]  Table 7: Estimated Effect of IDA Operations on Balance of Payments of Part I Countries, from IDA, 'Amount of the Fourth Replenishment'.
[75]  In the IBRD, there are two kinds of 'capital increase' – General Capital Increase (GCI) and Selective Capital Increase (SCI). GCIs allocate shares *pro rata* to all members, aimed to strengthen the IBRD's financial position. By contrast, SCIs aim to adjust relative voting rights in order to reflect changes in relative economic position.

in 1959, 1965, and 1970 respectively. This had substantially increased Japan's influence in World Bank governance, for as one of the five largest shareholders Japan was entitled to an *appointed* seat (as opposed to an *elected* seat often shared with other constituencies) in 1971.[76] Thus, Japan could articulate its own voice with no need to compromise its positions with other constituencies.[77]

Yet this IBRD rising star was denounced as 'an IDA laggard'. This criticism was particularly strong from those who were losers as a consequence of Japan's rising status in the IBRD shareholding.[78] During the same period Japan slightly increased its IDA burden share by 1.07 per cent and 0.46 per cent in IDA-1 and IDA-2, and even stuck to its traditional share in IDA-3 at the height of the US hegemonic leadership. Even though Japan had surpassed Canada in the IBRD shareholding ranking, it still kept its No. 6 donor position behind Canada in IDA burden shares. In the face of international pressure, Japan turned a blind eye and insisted that its enhanced IBRD voting rights were warranted by its ascending economic status. In short, the overarching Soviet threat rendered hegemonic coercion less credible, which enabled rising Japan to resist share increases.

In sum, Japan lagged behind in assuming its 'fair' burden share, because it could obtain its desired influence via IBRD voting rights with no need for boosting its IDA contributions.

### 3.2.3 Ascending Powers: 'No Burden-Sharing without Influence-Sharing'

This part focuses on a revealing case of the quid pro quo between the waning UK and ascending Japan/Germany in their struggles over the right balance between influence-sharing and burden-sharing. History reveals that ascending powers might have even cut their shares further, resulting in greater *Challenger Inertia*, had waning powers not decided to cede IDA voting rights.

From a practical point of view, IDA voting rights might not all be that important. As mentioned earlier, the composition of the Board

---

[76] Gyohten (1997: 292).

[77] When Japan joined the IBRD, it gained an elected seat on the Board shared with Thailand, Burma, and Ceylon (Sri Lanka). Ibid., 279.

[78] Canada, Netherlands, and Belgium were surpassed by Japan.

depended on IBRD shareholding. Moreover, the Board made decisions by consensus and seldom resorted to formal votes.

But the 'symbolic significance' mattered. IDA voting rights are a symbol of representation in IOs and status in the international arena, so IDA members devoted 'considerable efforts' to set up and review the IDA voting-rights system.[79]

IDA's Articles of Agreements originally stipulated that 'additions to resources' other than subscriptions 'shall not carry voting rights'.[80] Up to IDA-2 none of the financial resources provided by donors, except for the initial subscriptions, carried voting rights because they had been made available in the form of 'contributions' (rather than 'subscriptions'). Hence, the relative voting power among donors remained the same despite changes in their relative financial contributions. This led to a wide discrepancy between burden shares and voting shares by the late 1960s, since the waning UK had substantially cut its burden share but retained its voting rights.

In IDA-1, the UK made a substantial share cut of over 4 per cent to bring its burden share more in line with its weakened economic position. At the stage of institutional design of IDA, the United States proposed that donors' initial subscriptions should be proportional to the IBRD shareholding based on relative economic position in 1945 in order to avoid prolonged burden-sharing negotiations. Yet this was severely out of line with new balances of economic power in late 1950s – after the breakup of its colonial empire, the UK was a weary titan suffering from a seemingly irrevocable economic decline. But the United States imposed a 'take-it-or-leave-it' option. The UK yielded by accepting a disproportionately greater burden share than accorded with its then economic standing, since exclusion from IDA was a price too high to take.[81] But as soon as IDA-1 negotiations kicked off, the UK was determined to achieve equity with Germany and France in IDA burden-sharing to mitigate its acute sense of unfairness. While ascending powers initially resisted peer pressure from the UK, they finally yielded some ground to

---

[79] World Bank (1982: 7).
[80] IDA's Articles of Agreement, Article VI, Section 3(a).
[81] Mason and Asher (1973: 390).

mounting US pressure and modestly increased their shares to fill the UK gap to seal a deal on time.[82]

Ascending powers initially tolerated the discrepancy between financial contribution and formal influence because they had to increase their IDA burden shares under US pressure. Waning powers also dismissed ascending powers' complaints on the grounds that contingent voting-rights adjustments in proportion to donor contributions would dilute voting rights of recipient countries. This would exacerbate the criticism that IDA was simply a tool of Western powers for controlling weak developing nations, eroding IDA's legitimacy and undermining the common donor interest in containing the Soviet threat.

Rising stars, however, could no longer accept the bleak prospect of perpetuating an 'unfair' status quo – the permanent divorce between financial contributions and voting rights. As early as in IDA-2, in November 1967, Japan made it clear that its government would 'not consider a contribution which is not accompanied by an increase in voting power'.[83] The German Governor also made a credible 'exit' threat in the 1969 Bank/IMF Annual Meeting, announcing that an essential precondition for Germany's participation in IDA-3 would be an adjustment of voting rights commensurate with new contributions.[84] Ascending powers formed a coalition demanding immediate measures to redress the unfairness inherent in IDA voting-rights system.

Yet the waning UK initially refused to cede influence, thus provoking rising challengers to escalate their threats. The lack of swift adjustments in voting rights motivated Japan to propose providing IDA with trust funds where Japan could have full control over both aid allocation and procurement benefits. If others followed suit, this would inevitably lead to unilateral influence contests, portending the end of multilateralism.[85]

---

[82] Hearing before the House Committee on Banking and Currency, *Expanding the Resources of the International Development Association*, 88th Congress, 1st Session, 3 and 16 December 1963, 96.

[83] IDA, 'Possible Changes in the Methods of Replenishment', IDA/RPL/69–2, 24 November 1969.

[84] Opening Address by Hon. Karl Blessing, Governor of the Bank for Germany, in *1969 Annual Meeting of the Boards of Governors: Summary of Proceedings*.

[85] From J. L. F. Buist to Mr King, 'Forms of Contributions to the Next Replenishment of IDA Funds', 8 October 1969, from the UK National Archives, OD 9/272.

Consequently, the imminent threats from ascending powers confronted the UK with a key strategic question of *whether to cede voting rights to ascending powers*.[86] Intensive deliberations took place within the UK government to weigh up the advantages and disadvantages of the two options – *retain* or *cede* voting rights. Finally, the conclusion was reached that 'despite the fact that it was to Britain's short-term advantage to retain a greater share in the IDA voting power than was warranted by the money she had put in', it was 'in Britain's interest to have IDA planning, financing and management firmly established on a defensible basis' which would induce ascending powers to 'put in more money than they are now doing'.[87]

What, then, motivated the UK to cede voting rights in return for ascending powers' financial support? In the mid-1960s the UK realised that it was the 'principal beneficiary' of winning IDA-financed procurement contracts.[88] In formulating the UK negotiating stance on IDA-3, decision-makers succinctly highlighted that the UK won back more than it put in,[89] which constituted 'a definite advantage' from the balance of payments point of view in an official memorandum. The memo went on to make a strong case for IDA expansion, 'as long as procurement pattern continues as at present, the UK is likely to gain in foreign exchange through increased total contributions to IDA'.[90]

The key question faced by the UK was whether its procurement advantage would endure in the future. At first glance, the answer appeared to depend on the relative competitiveness of British firms, since the World Bank adhered to the principle of open competitive bidding. Yet this view ignored the fact that donors had 'natural advantages' in securing contracts from certain regions where they had former

---

[86]  From D. Williams (UK Delegation to Bank/Fund Meeting), 3 October 1969, ibid.
[87]  From Buist to Mr King, 'Forms of Contributions to the Next Replenishment of IDA Funds', ibid.
[88]  'IDA Replenishment', official memorandum from G. W. Wilson to Sir Alan Dudley, 14 October 1966, from the UK National Archives, *The Second IDA Replenishment*, OD9/202.
[89]  The UK secured 25.4% and 20.6% of the total value of foreign procurement contracts under IDA credits in FY1967 and FY1968 respectively, in contrast to its then IDA burden share of about 12%. Minute from N. B. J. Huijaman to Mr Williams on the Preparation for IDA-3 Negotiation, 17 January 1969, ibid.
[90]  'IDA Replenishment', 14 October 1966.

colonial ties. For instance, France fared well in West Africa whereas Japan scored well in Southeast Asia. Among all eighteen IDA donors, the UK was the biggest winner of procurement benefits, because its two former colonies (India and Pakistan) had received over 70 per cent of all IDA credits committed during 1960–65.[91] Thus, the UK's future procurement benefits largely hinged on the likely pattern of IDA aid allocations.

To formulate its negotiating stance on whether to support IDA expansion, the UK needed some confidence that the present pattern of IDA aid allocations would continue to favour the UK's former colonies. This brought about the question of who decided how to ration IDA credits. So far, Bank Management had full liberty in deciding regional and country allocations, which opened up the possibility of informal donor influence. Indeed, the UK was fully aware that other major donors had strongly pressed Bank Management to divert more aid away from the 'Asian Big Four' (India, Pakistan, Bangladesh, and Indonesia) and towards their favoured client recipients during the informal donor consultation process. Meanwhile, recipient countries in Africa and Latin America had advocated a 'fairer' distribution of funds or distribution on a wider geopolitical basis.[92] Yet despite these mounting pressures from both giving and receiving ends, Bank Management was eager to disburse credits and thus favoured countries that were ready with projects of a familiar type.[93] Hence, while IDA credits were more evenly spread since IDA-2, there was a tacit agreement between senior Bank officials and the UK that the India share would not fall below a floor of 40 per cent. Since it took time for other recipients to develop project preparation capacity, it gave the UK confidence that the current pattern of IDA aid allocations would probably endure in the foreseeable future.[94] It further calculated that even if the worst-case scenario occurred – 'our contributions equalled the amount of business we obtained from IDA operations'[95] – IDA was still superior to alternative bilateral aid channels in securing procurement benefits.[96]

---

[91] Medley-Miller (Treasury), 'A draft paper on IDA-2 Replenishment', 28 October 1966, from UK National Archives, *The Second IDA Replenishment*, OD9/202.
[92] Mason and Asher (1973: 403).    [93] Ibid.
[94] 'IDA Replenishment', 14 October 1966.    [95] Ibid.
[96] While bilateral aid was 'tied' to the purchase of goods and services from donor countries, there was inevitable local cost financing. Hence, the UK could gain 80% of their bilateral aid in terms of procurement benefits. See ibid.

Therefore, the UK had a strong incentive to encourage others to contribute more to IDA.

Ultimately the UK decided to make a one-off concession to ascending powers by accepting under IDA-3 that IDA voting rights would be adjusted to reflect cumulative donor contributions.[97] This was made without amending IDA's Articles of Agreement by allowing donors to make additional 'subscriptions' to ensure that their shares of total subscriptions were equal to their shares of total financial contributions to IDA. This precedent has essentially been followed in subsequent IDA replenishments. The rationale behind this system was that a prolonged 'anomaly' between voting rights and burden shares would provoke ascending powers to turn their back on IDA, thus undermining IDA long-run financial sustainability.[98]

In sum, the waning UK ceded voting rights in exchange for more financial support to IDA from ascending powers because, as the principal beneficiary of IDA procurement, the UK had a strong interest in IDA expansion.

## 3.3  Who Runs the World Bank? The Role of Bank Management

This section explores the independent role of Bank Management in shaping the IDA burden-sharing dynamics in order to grasp the full picture of IDA replenishment history.

### 3.3.1  Institutional Interests Matter

On the surface, Bank Management is often cast in two stereotyped images: a puppet of powerful member states, or a corporation of technocrats free of political influence. Yet neither view captures the nuanced perspective that Bank Management could be an independent actor with its own institutional interests.

During the formative period of IDA, Bank Management shifted its attitude from opposition to support as it redefined its core institutional

---

[97] Safeguards were also provided to preserve the general voting balance between Part I and Part II members.

[98] World Bank, 'Study by Executive Directors on the Means for Providing Additional Resources to the Association and of an Adjustment of Voting Rights', para. 20.

interests. When the idea to establish IDA as an affiliate of the IBRD initially began to circulate in Congress and catch on in the US Administration, Bank Management had strongly opposed this proposal because it was concerned about the potentially negative effect of 'soft loans' (below market interest rates) on its AAA status on international capital markets.[99] Later on, Eugene Black, the then Bank President, came round to make a strong bid to host this new concessional financing facility in order to strengthen the Bank's position vis-à-vis the UN system.[100] This shift in position largely stemmed from the recognition that newly independent poor countries were not ready to become IBRD clients because they could not afford to pay back the conventional IBRD loans without jeopardising their indebtedness. So, the senior Bank Management realised that its client base would be shrinking rapidly as industrialised countries graduated from IBRD after successful post-war reconstruction. Thus, control of IDA was 'a matter of survival' for the Bank because its loss would mean the loss of a major Bank clientele.[101]

### 3.3.2 *Maximising Resource Mobilisation*

One overarching goal of Bank Management was to maximise total donor contributions. To advance this objective, it developed its own initiative to formulate negotiating strategies, cultivate burden-sharing norms to constrain potential share cuts, and even use its own institutional money to leverage more donor contributions.

First, Bank Management deployed negotiation tactics to expand IDA. Since Bank Management naturally had congruent interests with developing countries in expanding IDA resources, it proactively solicited developing countries to put bilateral pressure upon major industrial countries in order to maximise their financial contributions.[102]

Sometimes Bank Management even bypassed the multilateral negotiations process to solicit support from the largest contributor in order to enlarge IDA. To boost IDA-2 as high as possible, George Woods, the then World Bank President, adopted a negotiation procedure of 'multilateral giving, but bilateral asking',[103] by first holding intensive

---

[99] Weaver (1965: 28).     [100] Kapur, Lewis, and Webb (1997: 1120–21).
[101] Libby, 'International Development Association', 1072.     [102] Ibid., 1070.
[103] Mason and Asher (1973: 409).

bilateral consultations with the United States to win the largest donor's support and then approaching other donors for their assent. But this strategy did not pay off. Indeed, it turned out to be counterproductive. When Bank Management announced its ambitious bidding figure of $1 billion per annum for IDA-2, quadrupling the size of IDA-1, other major donors dismissed this unrealistic figure as 'out of the hat'.[104] Furthermore, other donors were so 'piqued' by being left in the dark for so long[105] that they suspected that some behind-the-scenes deal might be done to afford the United States informal influence over IDA operations. Eventually IDA-2 suffered from a severe delay, ending up with a much more modest total target of $400 million per annum.

Second, Bank Management served as norm-setter by defining what qualified as 'justified' share reductions in order to deter donors from making share cuts triggered by negative exogenous factors (e.g., domestic budgetary constraints, shifts in political priority from multi-lateral aid to bilateral aid). Practically, Bank Management promoted the norm that donors should maintain their traditional shares, unless claims for share reductions could be justified by a sustained decline in economic status. Moreover, Bank Management tried its best to prevent any donor from opening up burden-sharing negotiations, because it feared that politically contentious negations risked jeopardising a successful and timely IDA Replenishment Agreement. For instance, in IDA-2 the UK decided not to initiate 'fair' burden-sharing debates, partly because it anticipated that Bank Management always 'deprecated' such discussion.[106]

Finally, Bank Management acted as a 'quasi-donor' to deploy its institutional money (i.e., IBRD net income) to leverage more donor contributions. The US Congress had consistently demanded the Bank should transfer more of its own income to IDA, and even conditioned US contributions upon matching funds from the IBRD.[107] In response to strong donor pressures, Bank Management proposed transferring IBRD net incomes to IDA to the Board and was able to facilitate the

---

[104]   ODM, 'Multilateral Aid and the Aid Ceiling', 15 September 1965, from the UK National Archives, OD9/202.

[105]   Mason and Asher (1973: 409).

[106]   'Sir A. Cohen's conversation with Mr. Woods', from A. A. Dudley to Mr Mark, 9 February 1966, from the UK National Archives, OD 9/202.

[107]   Hearing before the US Senate Committee on Foreign Relations, *To Provide for Increased Participation by the United States in the International Development Association*, 91st Congress, 1st Session, 16 April 1969, 16–18.

acceptance of this proposal in the face of strong opposition from IBRD borrowers in 1964. Latin American representatives bitterly complained that many Latin American governments should be classified as 'Part III' members of IDA since they were neither donors ('Part I') nor recipients ('Part II'). This group of MICs opposed IBRD transfers to IDA, not only because these resources could have been used to reduce their borrowing cost in IBRD, but also because they derived 'almost no direct benefit' from such transfers.[108]

### 3.3.3 Autonomy Flourishes under Hegemonic Leadership

The other overarching goal of Bank Management was to maximise its autonomy. This led to an 'inevitable' tension between the institution's appetite for autonomy and the donors' demands for accountability. Unlike the IBRD, which raised funds from capital markets, IDA was replenished by donations from donor governments' domestic budgets. Hence, as the steward of taxpayers' money, donor governments should have the legitimate right to hold IDA accountable – as they as governments were accountable – for the use of public money.[109] In parallel, donors also desired to exert political influence upon the Bank's policies and operations in direct conflict with Bank Management's aspirations for professional independence.

In the 1960s, Bank managers and staff alike enjoyed an 'extraordinary degree of freedom' vis-à-vis the Board of Executive Directors.[110] The Bank President had the agenda-setting power, since it was up to the President to propose projects and policies for the Board approval. While the Board did have the power to deny the Bank's proposals, the Bank President often deployed the 'divide and conquer' strategy to influence Board members to change their views.[111]

Bank Management also enjoyed considerable autonomy vis-à-vis IDA donors. The prevailing norm was that IDA replenishment

---

[108]  Mason and Asher (1973: 402–3).

[109]  Kapur, Lewis, and Webb (1997: 1133).

[110]  Martijn Paijmans, vice president in charge of the institution's administrative and organisational planning, chosen by Robert McNamara in early 1979, ibid., 1191.

[111]  Interview with Robert McNamara, from the World Bank's Oral History Programme, 16 May 1990, 10.

negotiations should be strictly confined to how to finance IDA rather than how to govern IDA. This norm was proactively promoted and cultivated by Bank Management. Burke Knapp, the then Vice President who chaired the replenishment meetings, made it crystal-clear in his opening remarks that 'the management of IDA was responsible to Executive Directors', and therefore it would not be appropriate for Bank Management to engage in discussions of changes in IDA policies in any 'inter-government forum' other than IDA's own Board of Executive Directors.[112]

The norm of keeping policy discussions outside the informal donor forum was generally accepted by donors in principle.[113] For instance, in IDA-3 when the UK IDA Deputy called for discussion of IDA policies on geographical distribution and other issues, the Netherlands immediately replied that such matters should be left to the Executive Directors to consider.[114] This was the prevailing rule, evidenced by the fact that, throughout the 1960s, IDA Replenishment Agreements did not give any prescription on policy issues.

However, the formal acceptance of the principle that IDA Deputies should not intervene in policy issues did not rule out the possibility that they could exert informal influence upon Bank Management. Such informal donor influence was particularly intense when it came to the issue of IDA aid allocations. Unlike the IBRD, which could expand the envelope of funds by borrowing money from capital markets to mitigate the distributional conflict, IDA relied on scarce donor donations with a fixed total amount so that financing an IDA project in country X would inevitably reduce the amount of IDA funds available elsewhere.[115] Major donors took advantage of Bank Management visits to their capitals to press senior Bank officials to reveal the likely course of IDA's future lending in order to ensure that any policy change was in their favour.[116] Yet Bank Management skilfully used vague hints in order to preserve its freedom of action.

---

[112]  Shihata (2000: 565).
[113]  IDA, 'The IDA Deputies: An Historical Perspective', November 2001.
[114]  'IDA Third Replenishment: Summary of the Results of the First Meeting of Deputies', from the UK National Archives, *Policy on Third Replenishment, 1967–1969*, OD 9/273.
[115]  Mason and Asher (1973: 396).
[116]  R. E. Radford, 'Visit of Mr. Burke Knapp (vice president of the World Bank)', 27 October 1966, from the UK National Archives, OD 9/202.

Despite the informal donor influence, Bank Management enjoyed considerable discretion in how to allocate IDA credits across regions and sectors. In designing the IDA charter, a 'rational' allocation system – in which IDA would allocate credits based on a pre-determined formula – was proposed but rejected by members. Thereby, the heavy responsibility of how to ration money was placed upon Bank Management, which inevitably took the Bank into 'the realm of political judgments'.[117] Such liberty allowed the Bank to make behind-the-scene deals with major donors to meet their demands in exchange for financial support.

In a nutshell, the balance of power in World Bank governance was clearly tilted in favour of Bank Management. This was largely due to two factors: the hegemonic leadership, and the lack of viable outside options.

First, the USA prioritised its long-term geopolitical objectives over its short-term specific donor interests, thus largely refraining from claiming privileges. As elaborated in Section 3.1, the hegemon maintained its share for the purpose of IDA expansion despite erosion in its tangible short-run interests. Faced with a looming Soviet threat, American policy-makers pursued grand geopolitical objectives which did not have to be 'justified in terms of close calculation of strategic or economic advantage'.[118]

Second, IDA was the pre-eminent multilateral concessional lending agency in the 1960s. IDA was the only game in town, which strengthened Bank Management's bargaining power vis-à-vis donors. As several concessional funds of RDBs were established in the early 1970s, the balance of power began to shift away from Bank Management. This shift will be explored in the next chapter.

In sum, under the hegemonic leadership, Bank Management successfully achieved its dual objectives of maximising both resources and autonomy – total IDA resources surged, more than quintupling from $150 million per year in initial subscriptions to $800 million per year in IDA-3. The Bank's policies and operations were largely at its discretion.

---

[117] Interview with Burke Knapp, from the World Bank's Oral History Programme, October 1981, 31–32.
[118] Ruttan (1996: 7).

## 3.4 Conclusion

Through the 1960s, although relative economic capabilities of major Western donors underwent significant shifts, burden-sharing arrangements remained relatively stable.

Eroding ability-to-pay and US donor-specific interests did provoke Congress into urging share cuts. IDA-2 was a case in point. Under mounting Congressional pressure, the Johnson Administration insisted upon no participation without share reduction. But conventional explanations are of little help in explaining why the hegemon maintained its share in IDA-3 despite continued deterioration in capacity and interests.

A growing Soviet threat largely explains the *Hegemonic Lag*. The United States deployed aid as a weapon to address the perceived security threat of spreading Communism. As bipolar rivalry intensified in the late 1960s, IDA became such a powerful piece, like the 'white queen' in the geopolitical chessboard, that the United States could not make credible threats to coerce ascending powers to assume greater aid burdens. Accordingly, the United States exercised its hegemonic leadership by refraining from claiming share reduction. By doing so, the United States successfully expanded IDA to counter the Soviet threat.

An intensifying Soviet threat largely accounts for the *Challenger Inertia*, since the looming Soviet threat rendered the US threats of share cuts less credible, thereby enabling ascending powers to resist the hegemonic pressure for share increases. Two additional factors help to further enrich our understanding. First, failure to align with France's national interests helps to explain successive French share cuts in IDA, for West African countries only received a small slice of IDA credits. Second, automatic IBRD voting-rights adjustments in line with newly negotiated IMF quotas enabled ascending powers to gain IBRD voting rights without assuming greater IDA burden shares.

A quid pro quo between burden shares and voting rights did occur, when waning powers had a strong incentive to expand total IDA resources. In the late 1960s Germany and Japan threatened to 'exit' from IDA unless IDA voting rights were re-aligned with financial contributions. Ultimately, the waning UK decided to cede voting rights in order to arrest any further share cut by ascending powers because the UK had a strong interest in enlarging IDA to maximise its procurement benefits.

Finally, the fairness concern among secondary states about US power exercises in World Bank governance did not come to the fore in the 1960s. The US hegemonic interest of containing the Soviet Union took precedence over its short-term interests, mitigating its impulse for unilateral influence attempts. Moreover, IDA was the pre-eminent international aid organisation, facing little competition and thus enjoying a strong bargaining position vis-à-vis donor governments.

The next chapter will uncover why IDA burden-sharing underwent sea changes in the 1970s despite mild shifts in relative economic capabilities among major donors.

# 4 | *IDA in the 1970s: A Turbulent Era with* Accelerated Burden-Shifting

This chapter addresses the puzzle of what drove *Accelerated Burden-Shifting* from the hegemon to ascending powers in IDA-4 and IDA-6: the US made substantial share cuts, mainly compensated for by share increases from Japan and Germany in the early and late 1970s. Meanwhile, it opens up new horizons by exploring why the hegemon honoured its shares in IDA-5, negotiated in the mid-1970s, despite a meteoric rise of new emerging powers (oil-producing countries).

The second decade in IDA history witnessed a turbulent world economy. Oil crises in 1973 slowed down the economic engines of all major donors. Contrary to the rapid 'catching up' with the United States by Japan and Western Europe in the 1960s, relative economic positions among major Western donors remained largely intact.

In contrast to the fairly stable burden-sharing of the 1960s, however, IDA experienced significant burden-shifting in the early and late 1970s. The United States made dramatic share cuts, dropping by a third from 40 per cent to 27 per cent, mainly compensated for by share increases from Japan and, to a lesser extent, Germany. Consequently, major donor rankings were overturned: Japan and Germany surpassed the UK and tied for the second largest donor status.

Nevertheless, this *Accelerated Burden-Shifting* was arrested in IDA-5 (covering FY1978–80, negotiated between September 1975 and March 1977), where the hegemon and most other major donors maintained their traditional shares. At first glance, this is not puzzling, given the little change in relative economic weights within the Western donor group.

Yet the constant US share in IDA-5 demands further explanations if emerging powers are brought into the picture. In the mid-1970s the Western bloc was economically weakened by the skyrocketing of oil-producing countries. Despite their massive earnings from the oil price hike, however, only a few oil-producing countries began to make (modest) contributions to IDA *outside* the traditional burden-sharing framework.

The present chapter is organised by resolving each empirical puzzle in chronological order. It concludes with the extent to which conventional explanations and the three central features of power plays – the structural cause of external threat; the quid pro quo between burden shares and voting rights; the informal donor influence upon Bank Management – help to solve the puzzles.

## 4.1 IDA-4 (FY1975–77): *Accelerated Burden-Shifting* for the First Time

IDA-4 (FY1975–77, negotiated between December 1972 and September 1973) marked a sweeping change in IDA burden-sharing, wherein the United States accomplished a substantial share reduction of 6.67 per cent, fully offset by share increases from Japan (5 per cent) and Germany (1.67 per cent).

In the early 1970s, the US capacity-to-pay was deteriorating further. The persistent balance-of-payments deficits compelled the Treasury to formulate foreign economic initiatives to try to stop the flow of US capital abroad.[1] The prolonged Vietnam War put a strain on the US fiscal position. Domestic economic imperatives compelled President Nixon to unilaterally close the 'gold window' in 1971, portending the breakdown of the post-war international monetary regime.[2]

The bleak economic situation provoked Congress to demand further share cuts. Contrary to the strong bipartisan support at IDA's inception, Congress aired their grievances against a fast-growing IDA contribution over which it had less control than bilateral aid. Congress had dragged their feet in authorising US participation in IDA replenishments so that the United States was 'late three out of three times'.[3]

As seen in the previous chapter, the Nixon Administration resisted Congressional pressure for share cuts in order to expand IDA to

---

[1]   Memorandum from the US Executive Director of the IMF to the Under Secretary of the Treasury for Monetary Affairs, from *Foreign Relations of the United States, 1969–1976*, Volume III, Foreign Economic Policy; International Monetary Policy, 1969–1972.

[2]   Gowa (1983).        [3]   Mason and Asher (1973: 419).

counter the growing Soviet threat in the late 1960s, thus maintaining its share in IDA-3.

Would the US sustain its hegemonic leadership in IDA-4?

The geopolitical shift boded ill for the US leadership in terms of IDA expansion. As Soviet–American relations thawed (known as 'détente') in the early 1970s, IDA's geopolitical significance was diminishing. The Nixon Administration placed IDA lower down on its priority list and attempted to appease vigorous Congressional claims for a progressive share reduction in order to save political capital for other compelling priorities. Therefore, the United States no longer felt compelled to push for an IDA-4 as large as possible.[4]

Yet the US still held an interest in a sustained growth in total IDA resources in order to keep the Western competitive edge over the Soviet Union in the Third World. While détente was dominant, American–Soviet relations were characterised as a mix of 'competition and cooperation' throughout the 1970s.[5] The US Central Intelligence Agency (CIA) assiduously compiled information on the scale of the Soviet assistance and estimated an increase of some 70 per cent in the first part of the 1970s.[6] While the aggregate scale of the Soviet aid was nowhere near the Western total, the Soviet Union targeted a select number of key LDCs to achieve more influence than it would otherwise deserve.

To sum up, the receding Soviet threat resulted in a shift in US priorities from IDA expansion to its own share reduction – it no longer strived to expand IDA, although it still preferred a modest growth in total IDA resources.

After prioritising its own share reduction over IDA expansion, the Nixon Administration faced the strategic question of *how far the US planned to go in cutting its share in IDA*.

Why couldn't the United States simply seek to cut its share as much as possible? The answer was that contribution and influence went hand in hand – IDA burden share symbolised the US willingness and ability to take international leadership; should the United States shed its burden far below other donors' expectations about its minimum 'fair' share, others would be less willing to support the US leadership. This

---

[4]  Memorandum of Conversation (31 May 1973), *Foreign Relations of the United States, 1973–1976*, Volume XXXI, Foreign Economic Policy, Document 40.
[5]  Garthoff (1994: 627–28).    [6]  Becker (1987: 74–75).

boiled down to the questions of *to what extent the United States counted on others to achieve its objectives.*

In the early 1970s, the Nixon Administration put a premium on international monetary and trade reforms. The stakes were too high for the United States to do less than was required in development assistance.[7] As the pre-eminent international development institution, its IDA burden share symbolised its commitment to multilateralism. Hence, a steep share cut would project 'an isolationist stance', thus undermining the US leadership in securing cooperation from other industrialised countries in parallel monetary and trade negotiations.[8]

The question then became how the United States gauged its minimum 'fair' share. Of course, this ultimately depended on iterative negotiations to sound out others' reservation points. In formulating the US negotiating strategies, an internal official memorandum tentatively set one-third as 'a nominal floor', because it feared that other donors would question its entitlement to its 34 per cent IMF voting rights if it cut its share below this threshold.[9] This illustrates that IDA burden shares justified donor influence well beyond IDA itself.

The above deliberations within the US government set the tone for IDA-4 negotiations. At the first Paris meeting in December 1972, the US IDA Deputy – John Hennessy, Assistant Secretary for International Affairs of the Treasury Department – urged Japan and Germany to increase their shares to compensate for a substantial US share reduction, framed as a necessity for Congressional acceptance of US participation. Meanwhile, the US poured cold water on the range for the target total proposed by Bank Management – $1.2–1.8 billion per annum. The IDA-4 Chairman, Sir Denis Rickett, Vice President of the Bank, justified the lower bound as maintaining the value of IDA-3 ($800 million) in real terms. But

---

[7]   Statement by Hon. George P. Schultz, Secretary of Treasury, from Hearing before the US Senate Committee on Foreign Relations, *US Participation in ADB and IDA*, 93rd Congress, 1st Session, 19 November 1973, 10.

[8]   Statement by Hon. George P. Schultz, Secretary of Treasury, from Hearing before the House Committee on Banking and Currency, *To Provide for Increased Participation by the United States in the International Development Association*, 93rd Congress, 1st Session, 11 June 1974, 2–3.

[9]   The US Department of the Treasury, 'Future US Reliance on International Financial Institutions', 8 February 1973, from the US National Archives, General Records of the Department of the Treasury, Chronological files, 1973–75.

the United States bluntly viewed this figure as 'unrealistic', despite the 'general sympathy' from a majority of donors.[10] Such a passive US attitude gave Bank Management a sober warning that it 'no longer had the whole-hearted support of the US Treasury, still less of the Congress, and everything had to be fought for at great length'.[11]

In the absence of US leadership, Bank Management took a strategy of lining up as many donors as possible behind a higher target total in order to put maximum pressure on the United States. Chairman Sir Denis Rickett conducted intensive lobbying activities in donor capitals. Yet many donors qualified their support for fixing a target total of $1,650 million upon the condition that the United States would take up its traditional share of 40 per cent.[12]

Yet other donors' expectations on the 'appropriate' US share turned out to be wishful thinking. The United States strategically deployed the Congressional constraint to threaten a share cut. Chairman Passman from the House Appropriation Subcommittee demanded no increase in the US contribution in nominal terms from IDA-3 ($320 million per annum), and a share reduction of 15–20 per cent (below the traditional 40 per cent).[13]

After credibly establishing the disturbing baseline of its contribution level, the United States disclosed its terms for a compromise at the second London meeting in March 1973. It signalled that it could go above the lowest bound if others met the following conditions:

1. abolish the Maintenance of Value (MOV) obligations;
2. use substantial IDA and IBRD resources for Indo-China reconstruction;
3. establish an independent audit unit.[14]

These conditions had profound distributive consequences:

[10] Telegram on 'IDA Fourth Replenishment: First Meeting of Deputies', 21 December 1972, from the UK National Archives, *IDA Fourth Replenishment*, OD 33/198.

[11] Interview with Sir Denis H. F. Rickett, from the World Bank's Oral History Programme, 20 August 1986, 8.

[12] Minute from Overseas Development Administration to Treasury, 'IDA Fourth Replenishment', 7 March 1973, from the UK National Archives, *IDA Fourth Replenishment*, OD 33/199.

[13] UK Treasury Minute, 'IDA: Fourth Replenishment', 9 March 1973, ibid.

[14] IDA, 'Memorandum of Meeting on IDA Fourth Replenishment: Held in London on 13 March 1973', IDA/RPL/73–7, 4 April 1973, ibid.

MOV obligations were originally aimed at protecting IDA's financial strength from exchange rate fluctuations. Its abolition would help the United States to avoid making additional payments to IDA, if the US dollar steadily weakened. However, strong-currency countries (such as Germany and Japan) would stand to lose since such a change would remove their right of reimbursement from IDA each time their currency went up. Bank Management strongly opposed this because such vagaries would add complexities to Bank operations, running the risk of over-committing its resources.

On aid allocation, the United States aimed to divert a substantial proportion of IDA and IBRD funds away from India to Indo-China to repair the damage incurred by the Vietnam War. Skewing the Bank resources to serve US foreign policy interests was a compelling priority, because Congress began limiting US bilateral aid for Indo-China.[15] But this US influence attempt would set a bad precedent of overtly leveraging its IDA contributions to exert political influence upon both IDA aid allocation and IBRD loan distribution.

Regarding the independent audit unit, the United States targeted Bank Management, aiming to restrain its authority and to enhance its accountability for the use of public money. Prior to IDA-4, the US Administration, pressed by Congress and its audit arm – the US General Accounting Office (GAO) – had already tried to persuade the senior Bank officials to establish an autonomous evaluation unit for both IDA and IBRD. However, the Bank Management was unwilling to sacrifice its autonomy.[16]

An acute sense of unfairness among other donors was aroused by these undue US influence attempts and its relentless claim for a share cut. Other donors were tempted to opt for countermeasures. For instance, European donors convened a private meeting to coordinate their policy positions against an assertive United States. Meanwhile, the UK took this opportunity to 'secure a united front in opposing the American attempt to reduce the US percentage'. It argued that nine European donors were 'in a good position to preach the Americans on

---

[15] ODA, 'Note Comparing Various Levels of the 4th IDA Replenishment with Alternative Uses of Funds and Changes in Shares of IDA Contributions', 21 February 1973, ibid.

[16] US Senate Committee on Foreign Relations, *US Policy and the Multilateral Banks: Politicization and Effectiveness* (Washington, DC: US Government Printing Office), May 1977, 11–12.

burden-sharing', since their combined burden shares represented some 38.6 per cent, higher than their collective GNP shares of 34 per cent, whereas the United States bore only 40 per cent of the total burden, far below its GNP share of 48.5 per cent.[17]

But the United States was adamant in seeking a precipitous share cut. If no compensating share increases were secured, this could result in a catastrophic failure to reach agreement on IDA-4.

Why might a sharp 'uncompensated' US share cut lead to a fiasco of reaching no agreement at all? As mentioned in the previous chapter, IDA burden-sharing negotiations adhered to the principle that any share cut be fully compensated for by share increases. In other words, 'a 100% total' was regarded as a benchmark for a 'successful' IDA replenishment. The burden-sharing negotiations were thus structured in such a way that any 'uncompensated' US share cut would not simply imply a reduction in the United States' own financial contributions, but also jeopardise a timely conclusion of IDA replenishment negotiations. Other donors wished to avert this worst-case scenario because it would undermine the collective donor interest in counterbalancing the Soviet influence in the Third World.

The US threat of a substantial share cut was credible in the eyes of other donors. President Nixon's second inaugural address in January 1973 raised the prospect of a new 'isolationism' as the Soviet threat subdued.[18] Moreover, since the early 1970s, Congress had become more assertive in US foreign policy making.[19] In view of these intensified domestic political difficulties, the Nixon Administration carried out much closer consultation with a belt-tightening Congress from the preliminary stages in order to secure Congressional support.[20]

Should other donors resist ceding influence to the United States, they would have to figure out how to fill 'a US shortfall' as large as 20 per cent, as demanded by Congress. Ascending powers resisted peer pressure to substantially boost their shares. Japan was the No. 1 target, because Japan only contributed a share of 6 per cent – less than

---

[17]  Minute from ODA to Treasury, 'IDA Fourth Replenishment: First Meeting of Deputies', 2 January 1973, from the UK National Archives, OD 33/198.
[18]  Minute from Williams to Buist, 22 January 1973, ibid.
[19]  Kegley and Wittkopf (1996: 424).
[20]  Statement of Hon. George P. Schultz, 9.

half of its GNP share.[21] But Japan was reluctant to double its burden share. Germany came next. While the German burden share was only mildly below its GNP share of about 10 per cent, it was under peer pressure from the UK to increase its share because Germany had out-stripped the UK in GNP performance.[22] But the German Deputy refused to switch the donor ranking with the UK.[23] Accordingly, most IDA Deputies realised it could not seal a successful deal unless the United States agreed on a much more modest share cut.

The strategic decision faced by other donors was whether they would cede influence to the United States in exchange for a milder US share cut.

What made other donors less forthcoming in ceding influence to the hegemon was that the USA refused to clarify its position on its contribution level. Subsequently, the negotiations reached an impasse – no further advance could be made until the position of the United States had been clarified. Consequently, donors failed to reach a timely agreement as it reached the deadline in July 1973.

In order to give assurance to other donors, Henry Kissinger, the President's National Security Advisor, recommended that President Nixon make 'a direct intervention' with Chairman Passman at the House Appropriation Committee to obtain an increase in the US dollar contribution to IDA-4. In a confidential official memor-andum, Kissinger gave the rationale behind the US backing: the IDA replenishment was 'necessary' not only to support the United States' 'general objective of assisting economic growth' in 'priority countries' to work against Soviet penetration, but also to give the USA 'leverage' in getting the World Bank to 'play a major role in funding Indo-China reconstruction'.[24]

---

[21] IDA, 'IDA Fourth Replenishment: Table on Comparative Indicators for Part I and Selected Other Countries', IDA/RPL/73–4, 15 February 1973, from the UK National Archives, OD33/198.

[22] Minute from ODA (R. Browning) to Mr King (UK IDA Deputy), 'The Fourth Replenishment of IDA', 26 February 1973, from the UK National Archives, OD 33/199.

[23] ODA, 'Visit to Bonn, 1 March 1973', 26 February 1973, ibid.

[24] Memorandum From the President's Assistant for National Security Affairs (Kissinger) to President Nixon on International Financial Institution Funding, 8 August 1973, *Foreign Relations of the United States, 1973–1976*, Volume XXXI, Foreign Economic Policy, Document 243.

At an extra meeting in Nairobi in September 1973, in parallel with
the annual meeting of the Board of Governors, the United States finally
showed its hand by stating that it would be willing to raise its annual
contribution from the lower bound ($320 million) to the upper bound
($500 million), thus providing one-third of a replenishment total of
$1.5 billion if other donors accommodated the US policy proposals.[25]

Despite their resentments about undue US political influence and its
attempt to cut its share far below its GNP share, other donors yielded to
all US policy demands in exchange for a US contribution going from the
lower bound to the agreed upper bound.[26]

1. On the MOV, while donors in principle maintained that the MOV
   should be continued, they conceded that IDA-4 contributions
   should not be subject to any MOV obligation.[27]
2. On lending to Indo-China, the Bank reprogrammed IDA lending so
   as to provide about $100 million per year for Indo-China, begin-
   ning in 1974, plus some ordinary World Bank funding when
   feasible.[28]
3. On the independence audit unit, Bank Management accepted the
   concept of autonomy for its operations review group through
   a formal action by its Board of Executive Directors in October 1974.[29]

Meanwhile, ascending powers fully compensated for the US share
cut from 40 per cent to 33.3 per cent: Japan pledged to increase its share
from 6 per cent to 11 per cent, overtaking Canada and France and
becoming the third largest donor; Germany boosted its share from

---

[25] Testimony by John Hennessy, Assistant Secretary of the Treasury for
International Affairs, from Hearing before the Senate Committee on
Appropriation, *Foreign Assistance and Related Programmes 1975*, 93rd
Congress, 2nd Session, 28 May 1974, 611.

[26] Telegram from Treasury to Foreign and Commonwealth Office, 'IDA 4th
Replenishment: Meeting of Deputies, Nairobi, 22 September 1973',
22 September 1973, from UK National Archives, *Negotiations for the Fourth
Replenishment of the International Development Association*, T 317/1834.

[27] IDA, *Fourth Replenishment of IDA Resources* (IDA-4 Replenishment
Agreement), 30 October 1973, para. 13, from the World Bank Archives.

[28] George P. Shultz, 'Memorandum from Secretary of the Treasury Shultz to
President Nixon', 25 June 1973, *Foreign Relations of the United States,
1973–1976*, Volume XXXI, Foreign Economic Policy, Document 242.

[29] World Bank, *Operations Evaluation: World Bank Standards and Procedures*,
1976, 8.

9.76 per cent to 11.43 per cent, surpassing the UK as the second largest donor.[30]

In summary, the United States managed to cut its burden share but amplified its influence, thus widening the disparity between contribution and influence.

Why did ascending powers boost their shares to offset the US gap?

Was it because they made additional contributions to gain more country-specific interests? As indicated in the previous chapter, procurement benefits and aid allocations hinged on multilateral decision-making rules and international bargaining. Thus, there was no straightforward link between share increases and enhanced donor interests. Evidence shows that (a) procurement benefits of Germany actually deteriorated in the early 1970s – its previous surplus dropped to a deficit of $20 million in FY1972, and (b) there was no boost in the Japanese procurement benefits.[31] Thus, amelioration of country-specific interests is of little help in explaining share increases by ascending powers.

Instead, high structural dependence upon the hegemon was a crucial factor in understanding why ascending powers made good a US share cut 'unwarranted' by the capacity-to-pay principle.

The arrival of détente left Japan and Europe more worried about abandonment than domination by the United States, and they actively sought to ensure US commitment to protecting them against an over-hanging Soviet threat.[32]

Japan was concerned about a weakening US commitment to Asian security, especially when Moscow–Tokyo peace talks were mired in impasse in 1973.[33] Moreover, Japan was asymmetrically dependent upon the US market for export-led growth. To secure US military protection and market access, Japan began to resort to pledges to increase its ODA to meet US demands for greater security contribution in Asia and to forestall US urging to revalue its currency to reduce its trade surplus.[34] Under US pressure, Japan promised in September 1971 to increase its foreign aid budget.[35]

---

[30]  ODA Submission to UK Ministers, 'IDA Fourth Replenishment: Third Tokyo Meeting', 18 April 1973, from the UK National Archives, OD 33/199.

[31]  IDA, 'Amount of the Fourth Replenishment', IDA/RPL/72–2, 20 November 1972, from the World Bank Archives.

[32]  Kegley and Wittkopf (1996: 146).    [33]  Swearingen (1978: 87–88).

[34]  Orr (1990: 109).    [35]  Arase (1995: 211).

Germany remained concerned about Soviet intentions despite the arrival of détente. Willy Brandt, the Chancellor of Germany, feared that the mighty Soviet military capabilities could inflict damage on German territory.[36] As the Soviet threat abated, Congress urged the withdrawal of troops from Germany.[37] In the 'Year of Europe' initiative of 1973–74, Kissinger reminded the European allies 'in blunt realistic language' that 'they owed the US more economic cooperation in return for the provision of US military protection'.[38] Moreover, Germany took more heat in NATO than in IDA, since the 'Nixon Doctrine' compelled its allies to shoulder responsibility for their own security as a result of the US military retrenchment.[39] Precluded from obtaining its own national nuclear deterrent after being defeated in World War II, Germany succumbed to the hegemonic pressure and took on greater burdens in collective defence and development assistance.[40]

By contrast, Sweden opted for an 'exit' – a share cut of 0.25 per cent – to express its grievance against the United States' attempt to tarnish the Bank's independence to serve its short-sighted foreign policy goals. The Swedish exit was a notable exception, since most small-/medium-sized donors maintained their traditional shares. What expedited the Swedish 'exit' action? Sweden was less structurally dependent upon the United States – it adhered to its tradition of non-alignment and thus was not pursuing NATO membership.[41]

A lack of viable outside options was another primary reason for the delay in secondary states' execution of countermeasures.

In the early 1970s few viable alternative options were available. Apart from IDA, the *Inter-American Development Bank* (IDB) founded a *Fund for Special Operations* (FSOs) in 1959 which provided aid for poor Latin American countries. The United States provided 80 per cent of the FSOs' initial dollar resources and enjoyed veto power.[42] Thus, diverting funds to FSOs would be a reward rather than a punishment for the United States. The European Development

---

[36] Schweitzer (1990: 245, 257).      [37] Raj (1983: 288).
[38] Wallace (2002: 147).      [39] Litwak (1984).      [40] Hanrieder (1992: 197).
[41] Sweden used to be a wholehearted IDA-supporter and made substantial special 'supplementary contributions' outside the burden-sharing framework. At the early stage of replenishment negotiations, Sweden pledged to honour its share and supported a high total target. Hence, this evidence rules out the possibility that the Swedish share cut was incentivised by deterioration in capacity-to-pay.
[42] White (1972: 160).

Fund (EDF) was another option, but it was only open to the six donors in the EEC.[43] The UK, not yet a member of EEC, contemplated initiating a new fund for South Asian countries, mobilising EEC donors to agree upon a much smaller IDA-4, or even allowing IDA to collapse. This move would be triggered if aid allocation to India substantially declined and if the United States cut its share below one-third of a total smaller than $1,400 million.[44] Yet such an initiative turned out to be a non-starter. The set-up cost of such a new fund was too high, given the limited time frame.

In addition, newly founded aid windows of RDBs were not a viable option for most donors. It was recipient countries rather than secondary states that initiated RDBs as 'an act of political resistance against the developed countries' hegemony in the world economy'.[45]

*The African Development Bank* (AfDB) campaigned for a 'genuinely' multilateral soft fund 'financed by developed countries, but controlled by the bank itself' as early as 1966. While *the African Development Fund* (AfDF), founded in 1972, granted donors formal voting rights on the Board,[46] major donors, such as France, still regarded the Bank with 'no more than tolerance' (although donors withdrew their earlier outright opposition).[47]

*The Asian Development Bank* (AsDB) was not founded until the United States shifted its position to endorse an initiative from the UN's Economic Commission for Asia and the Far East (UNECAFE). President Johnson desired to escape the trap of the Vietnam War through a speedy settlement, and thus supported the foundation of AsDB. The United States was a dominant shareholder from the beginning.[48] Thus, despite its strong interest in Asia, the UK pledged only a moderate initial subscription. France refused to participate.[49]

---

[43] They were France, West Germany, Italy, Belgium, Luxembourg, and the Netherlands. France did attempt to form coalition with other EEC members to push for a much smaller IDA in order to save money for the Fourth EDF Replenishment (*FY1975–1980*). Minute from ODA to Treasury, 'IDA Fourth Replenishment: First Meeting of Deputies'.

[44] ODA, 'Note Comparing Various Levels of the 4th IDA Replenishment with Alternative Uses of Funds and Changes in Shares of IDA Contributions', 21 February 1973, from the UK National Archives, OD33/198.

[45] White (1972: 28).

[46] AfDB was founded in 1964 and originally excluded non-regional countries from membership to meet local desires for self-determination and autonomy. Ibid., 117–20.

[47] Ibid., 118.　　[48] Ibid., 40–51.　　[49] Ibid., 47.

*The Asian Development Fund* (AsDF) was not established until 1973.[50]

In a nutshell, with the dissipating Soviet threat, the United States shifted its priority from IDA expansion to its own share reduction. The receding Soviet threat made hegemonic coercion more credible. Thus, the United States successfully coerced ascending powers to compensate for its share cut. Meanwhile, the sense of unfairness among secondary states was exacerbated as the USA overtly deployed its financial leverage to seek undue political influence. Yet, due to high structural dependence and lack of viable outside options, most donors postponed their 'exit/voice' countermeasures – they accommodated the US policy demands and made good the US share cut.

## 4.2 IDA-5 (FY1978–80): Resurgent Geopolitical Threat Renews the *Hegemonic Lag*

Burden-sharing tugs-of-war took on a new dimension in IDA-5 (FY1978–80, negotiated between September 1975 and March 1977 and spanning as long as eighteen months), for traditional donors urged that newly rich oil-producing countries – the Organization of Petroleum Exporting Countries (OPEC) members – contribute to IDA from their windfall incomes in order to lessen the crushing debt burden of the LDCs incurred by the oil price spike in October 1973.[51]

But these emerging powers maintained that it was the entrenched injustice of the Western-dominated international system that was the root cause of the LDCs' misery. In fact, they were victims of this unfair system – their concerted effort to control oil production was a self-defence remedy for the irresponsible US dollar devaluations evaporating their hard-earned foreign reserves.[52] Thus, new players saw little reason why their enhanced capacity should lead to increased contributions to IDA – a Western-dominated institution – thereby allowing the West to shirk its obligations.

---

[50] AsDB's special funds started operation in 1966.
[51] Developing countries were overloaded with a crushing debt burden, growing by more than 80% between 1972 and 1975 and reaching $165 billion in 1975. See Hearing before the Senate Committee on Foreign Relations, *International Financial Institutions*, 95th Congress, 1st Session, 9–10 March 1977, 89.
[52] The oil embargo was also used by the OPEC as a geopolitical tool for punishing the USA due to its support for Israel in the 1973 Arab–Israel war (Ciro 2012: 22).

This posed an unprecedented challenge to the IDA burden-sharing framework. Unlike the previous replenishments where traditional donors had a basic consensus on the shared burden (despite their ad hoc bargaining on upward or downward share adjustments), the sticking point of IDA-5 was whether contributions from potential new donors should be *within* or *outside* the traditional burden-sharing framework.

On the one hand, traditional donors insisted that contributions from emerging powers should be an *integral* part of the total, for any division between the old and the new would detract from the multilateral basis of IDA.[53] On the other hand, OPEC members contended that their contributions should be *additional* to those of traditional donors, for their voluntary donations should not enable traditional donors to shirk their obligations.[54]

At the heart of this bargaining was a power struggle. Waning powers pressed newcomers to bear the maximum burden without ceding their core influence, whereas emerging powers aspired to enhanced influence without bearing excessive burden.

This boiled down to the politically divisive question of *what was fair burden-sharing*. Traditional donors tactically proposed using international reserves as an alternative yardstick (rather than GNP shares) for burden-sharing, since oil-producing developing countries enjoyed windfall oil revenues despite their poor GNP performance. But emerging powers contended that GNP shares were more appropriate, since this traditional criterion implied that rich industrialised countries should bear the bulk of the burden.[55]

Parallel with these burden-sharing battles were struggles for influence-sharing – emerging powers insisted distribution of IDA voting rights give more weight to new contributions than in the past, whereas waning powers desired to maintain the status quo of according voting rights in line with cumulative financial contributions.[56]

---

[53] IDA, 'IDA Fifth Replenishment: Chairman's Report on First Meeting of Deputies, Held in Paris on 24–25 November 1975', IDA/RPL/75-5, 12 December 1975, 10, from the UK National Archives, *Negotiations for 5th Replenishment of IDA*, OD36/348.

[54] Ibid., 7.

[55] 'IDA V Replenishment: Fourth Meeting of Deputies: Kyoto, 12–13 October 1976', Brief for the UK IDA Deputy, 8 September 1976, from the UK National Archives, *Negotiations for 5th Replenishment of IDA*, OD36/252.

[56] Ibid.

Consequently, the negotiation reached an impasse – traditional donors refused to take a penny out of their purses unless new players made a concrete indication of significant contributions, while potential new donors awaited an assurance that traditional donors would substantially increase their contributions in real terms.[57]

To break this deadlock, Chairman Cargill, the then Vice President of the World Bank, proposed that traditional donors take the lead in order to 'induce the OPEC members to take a positive position'.[58] This Bank Management strategy was necessitated by the distinct possibility that protracted negotiations would force IDA to suspend its operation as it could soon run out of resources.

The question then became whether major traditional donors were willing and/or able to take the lead.

Bank Management first looked to the United States for leadership. Yet the Republican Ford Administration took a passive stance. The geopolitical significance of IDA was diminishing in the thawing US–Soviet relationship. Congress was more hostile to IDA,[59] demanding that average burden shares of the US contributions to the MDBs be cut to 25 per cent.[60] After an unprecedented initial vote-down of IDA-4 in January 1974, Congress stretched out its IDA-4 contributions over four years rather than the normal three.[61] This necessitated heavier drawings on others than was warranted by the originally negotiated multilateral agreement on IDA burden-sharing.[62]

Yet the prospects of gaining leadership were even bleaker when Bank Management turned to Germany – the second largest donor. Germany had cut back on government expenditures, and the aid budget bore the

[57]  Letter from I.P.M. Cargill (the World Bank Vice President for Finance) to Dick King (UK IDA Deputy), on 30 April 1976, from the UK National Archives, *Negotiations for 5th Replenishment of IDA*, OD 36/251.
[58]  Ibid.
[59]  Due to the delay in Congressional appropriations of the first instalment of IDA-4, the US 'could not agree to positive statements on contributions to IDA-5'. Source: Memorandum from Secretary of the Treasury Simon to President Ford on Jamaica Meetings of Interim and Development Committees, 13 January 1976, *Foreign Relations of the United States, 1973–1976*, Volume XXXI, Foreign Economic Policy, Document 128.
[60]  Hearing before the Senate Committee on Foreign Relations, *International Financial Institutions*, 95th Congress, 1st Session, 9–10 March 1977, 27.
[61]  *Congressional Quarterly Almanac*, 1975–77.
[62]  Minute of Bank of England, 'Potential Contributions to IDA-V', 2 October 1975, from the UK National Archives, OD36/348.

brunt of the cuts with a severe reduction of about 15 per cent.[63] Worse, public opinion confirmed the unpopularity of development aid. Thus, as the general election was approaching in October 1976, 'a huge multilateral aid item' would be 'extremely embarrassing' amidst domestic austerity.[64]

Japan even took a more recalcitrant stance because it resented the discrepancy between its IDA burden share and its IBRD voting rights. Japan shouldered 11 per cent of the IDA burden, but enjoyed only 6.24 per cent of IBRD voting rights.[65] Such a disparity was viewed as 'unfair' by Japan because it still ranked below France in the IBRD shareholding list even though it had surpassed France to become the fourth largest donor in IDA. To speed up IBRD voting-rights adjustments, Japan threatened to cut its IDA burden share.[66]

Bank Management then counted on France to take a more generous attitude than Japan, since in August 1976 France pledged to reach the UN target of allocating 0.7 per cent of GNP as ODA by 1980.[67] But such enhanced capacity did not prove a blessing to IDA. Rather, France claimed a share reduction because it had lost IMF voting rights in the Sixth General Quota Review (GQR-6) in 1976. Specifically, it insisted on a cut in its IDA share from 5.63 per cent in IDA-4 to 4.92 per cent – equal to its reduced IMF quota share to achieve parity between contribution and influence.[68] What further motivated France to reduce its contribution was that it felt that IDA aid allocations continued to discriminate against Francophone Africa.[69]

[63] Dick King (UK IDA Deputy), 'Note for Record: Meeting with Mr. McNamara', 8 January 1976, ibid.
[64] Ibid.
[65] IDA, 'The Fifth Replenishment of IDA: Comparative Indicators', January 1976, from the World Bank Archives.
[66] P.M. Newton (First Secretary of British Embassy in Tokyo, Japan), 'IDA: 5th Replenishment', 20 February 1976, from the UK National Archives, *Negotiations for 5th Replenishment of IDA*, OD36/250.
[67] C.W. Fogarty to Sir Richard King, 'French Aid Policy', 26 February 1976, ibid.
[68] 'Briefing Paper: France and IDA-5', 31 August 1976, from the World Bank Archives.
[69] During IDA-3 (*FY1972–74*), only 8.4% of IDA credits went to West Africa, whereas South Asia gained 48.9%, East Asia 13.3%, East Africa 16.2%. See IDA, 'The Fifth Replenishment of IDA: Note on the Geographic Distribution of IDA Credits', IDA/RPL/76–9, 13 February 1976, the UK National Archives, OD36/250.

The last hope of Bank Management rested on the UK. Traditionally, the UK had been a strong supporter of IDA since it was a principal beneficiary of IDA-financed procurement. Although its procurement performance had been deteriorating since the early 1970s, IDA was still a better means of gaining commercial interests than alternative aid channels – its benefit-to-cost ratio in IDA was still as high as 67 per cent, even higher than the estimated procurement return from bilateral aid of about 60 pence per £1 spent.[70] Thus, the UK had a stake in the achievement of a target total 'as large as possible'. But it simultaneously aimed to bring its share down to a level 'as small as respectably possible'[71] in order to hedge against potential losses in its procurement benefits. This risk was looming large, since the United States exerted political influence on IDA aid allocations to the detriment of the UK (as shown in IDA-4, above).

In order to grasp this last glimmer of hope, Chairperson Cargill privately assured the UK of 'a generous share to India' and underlined that the United States would not oppose this in view of an ameliorated US–Indian relationship.[72] Since British firms had a natural advantage in winning contracts in India, the UK was assured that its procurement performance would not deteriorate to the tipping point where IDA was inferior to its bilateral aid.

Accordingly, the UK took the lead to bring together a coalition of donors, including Nederlanders, Scandinavians, Canadians, and Kuwaitis, to press for a total target for traditional donors of $7.2 billion – equal to IDA-4 in real terms based on the World Bank calculation.[73] Although this diplomatic effort helped secure 'a numerical majority' (i.e., the number of donors) in favour of this target total, it was unrealistic without support from big players (especially the United States). Otherwise, there would be a huge 'financing gap' that small-/medium-sized donors could not make good, even if the burden was spread as thinly as possible among the remaining small donors.

---

[70] Brief from J. M. M. Vereker (ODM), 'IDA Fifth Replenishment: Brief for the UK Representative at the First Meeting of Deputies: Paris 24–26 November 1975', from the UK National Archives, OD36/348.

[71] Ibid.

[72] IDA, 'The Fifth Replenishment of IDA', IDA/RPL/75–1, 29 October 1975, ibid.

[73] Official Memorandum of the UK ODM, 18 February 1976, from the UK National Archives, OD 36/250.

To sum up, the United States was no longer willing to exercise leadership as the Soviet threat receded, and all other major donors except the UK pressed for share reductions due to erosion in capacity and/or interests. This portended a breakdown in replenishment negotiations.

The North–South power struggle heralded a turnaround. Developing countries formed a united front for a bigger say in decision-making on international economic and political issues as well as more equitable returns for their contributions to the world economy, calling for a 'New International Economic Order' (NIEO) in the 1974 and 1975 special sessions of the UN General Assembly.

Emerging powers strategically strengthened this Third World solidarity so as to fortify their bargaining power vis-à-vis Western powers.[74] The OPEC turned down the original US proposal to hold an international energy conference in mid-1975 on the grounds that energy could not be isolated from other North–South economic issues.[75]

By linking issues on as wide a front as possible, LDCs hoped to force donors to make concessions which would not otherwise have been possible. Thus, far from condemning the OPEC as the 'villain' of their distress, LDCs hailed their fellow oil-producers as 'heroes':

The action of the OPEC countries was a break-through in the efforts of the third world to correct the massive dominance of the industrialized countries in the world market for raw materials. It set the stage for the creation of a new economic order through co-operation between the developed and the developing countries on the basis of equality.[76]

Subsequently, Western donors had to yield to link oil with other North–South issues, for the oil shock had made industrialised countries realise their vulnerability – a complete cut-off in the oil supply would bring their economies to the brink of collapse. Thus, they agreed to set up four commissions covering *energy, raw materials, development, and finance* at a Conference on International Economic Co-operation,

---

[74] Shihata (1978: 8).

[75] Statement of Hon. Richard N. Cooper, Under Secretary of State for Economic Affairs, from Hearing before the Subcommittee on International Economics of the Joint Economic Committee, *Issues in North-South Dialogue*, Congress of the United States, 95th Congress, 1st session, 21 June 1977, 3.

[76] UN Seventh Special Session, 1975, 37.

beginning in December 1975, in Paris (proposed by France and running over more than a year) between nineteen developing countries (known as 'G-19') and seven industrialised countries plus the EEC.[77] The G-19 seized this opportunity to call for fundamental reforms in international economic relations:

1. On raw materials, the G-19 pressed for 'indexation' schemes linking the prices of raw materials exported by developing countries to the prices of manufactured goods produced by the developed countries.
2. On finance, the G-19 aimed for a *general* debt relief scheme to mitigate the acute external debt burdens of *all* developing countries rather than *case-by-case* debt restructuring.
3. On development, the G-19 castigated the erosion of ODA in real terms and urged developed countries to reach the UN target of channelling 0.7 per cent of their GNP as development assistance.[78]

These demands encountered strong opposition from Western powers, especially the United States. Given the NIEO's blatantly anti-American and pro-Socialism overtones, the United States feared that Third World solidarity would result in 'the breakdown of the old order',[79] thus threatening the US hegemony.[80] Led by the United States, Western industrialised nations maintained that 'the primary emphasis on the North–South dialogue should be on improving rather than restructuring the international economic system'.[81]

The heightened North–South power struggle compelled traditional donors to accomplish a decently large total size of IDA-5 in order to pre-empt more radical approaches such as the NIEO.[82] For instance, unlike the conventional case-by-case approach, a generalised debt relief would open up insatiable demands for additional aid to meet debt service requirements across the board.[83] Therefore, to buy the goodwill of the South, major traditional donors pledged their support for IDA-5

---

[77] Overseas Development Institute (ODI), 'The Paris Conference on International Economic Co-operation', ODI Briefings, August 1976.
[78] Ibid.      [79] Renninger (1976: 39).      [80] Abbott (1982: 215).
[81] Statement of Hon. Richard N. Cooper, 3.      [82] Bergsten (1980: 11).
[83] HM Treasury, 'Note of a Meeting in the Treasury at 3.00 p.m. on 12 November 1976 to Discuss the Proposal Made by the EEC Commission that There Should be a Supplementary IDA Replenishment', November 1976, from the UK National Archives, OD 36/252.

in the hope that the G-19 would forgo their call for automatic means of resource transfers.

Bank Management took advantage of this momentum to encourage traditional donors to increase their contributions in real terms 'with none of them breaking ranks [maintain their traditional shares]'.[84] Otherwise, prolonged burden-sharing negotiations would risk a 'breakdown' that would be seen badly in the North–South dialogue.[85]

Given their common stake in a constructive North–South dialogue, major donors at last relented in the final replenishment meeting in March 1977. A newly elected Democratic Carter Administration, which coincided with a Democratic Congress, brought a distinct move forward in the US position. The United States expressed its deep commitment to 'playing a full role', but qualified its support for a $7.2 billion total upon: (a) no other major traditional donor reducing its IDA-4 share; and (b) a substantial contribution from new donors.[86] Germany, Japan, and France shifted away from their previously passive stance by agreeing to maintain their traditional shares in support of a target total of $7.2 billion – a substantial increase in real terms over IDA-4, based on their calculation.

Ultimately, the North–South power struggle motivated traditional donors to subordinate their internal discord on 'fair' burden-sharing to their collective interest in dissuading the Third World from pressing for the NIEO. Otherwise, the erosion in their capacity and/or interests would have provoked substantial share cuts.

How about contributions from emerging powers? Although Bank Management actively reached out many OPEC members, only two became new donors – Saudi Arabia and the United Arab Emirates (UAE). Moreover, they insisted that their contributions should be *outside* the traditional burden-sharing framework so that their contributions should not induce traditional donors to shirk their historical responsibility.

---

[84] 'Informal Meeting of European Contributions to IDA: Paris, 12 November 1976: Brief for the United Kingdom Representative', from the UK National Archives, OD 36/252.

[85] Ibid.

[86] IDA, 'The Fifth Replenishment of IDA: Chairman's Report on the Sixth Meeting of Deputies', IDA/RPL/77–8, 22 April 1977, from the UK National Archives, *Negotiations for 5th Replenishment of IDA*, OD 36/254.

This raises the question of why emerging powers contributed much less to IDA than their enhanced capacity would have predicted. The OPEC's collective aid efforts skyrocketed to $8 billion in 1976, accounting for nearly two-fifths of the total ODA from both traditional donors and emerging powers.[87] Yet emerging powers only contributed 5.72 per cent of the grand total in IDA-5.[88]

Two fundamental reasons underlay the OPEC disinterest in IDA. First, the emerging powers believed that their obligations should be fundamentally different from those of traditional donors. Their wealth was derived from 'depletable natural resources' rather than 'industrial power';[89] the latter was partly derived from the exploitation of the Third World. Hence, they maintained that there was no case for 'sellers' (OPEC) to compensate 'buyers' (including LDCs) for every significant price rise, unless it was assumed that such a price spike would last forever.[90] Thus, they insisted that their contributions be outside the traditional burden-sharing framework in order to prevent traditional donors from shedding their historical duty.

Second, IDA aid allocations were not in line with OPEC's priorities. Arab countries were their top priorities – about two-thirds of the OPEC's bilateral aid went to the Arab world in 1976, despite a widening geographical distribution after the oil spike.[91] But IDA only disbursed 11.8 per cent to Arab countries during FY1972–74.[92] They saw no immediate prospect of reallocating IDA aid allocations to their favoured countries because that would put them at loggerheads with the powerful incumbents. Especially after their aspirations for more voting rights were dismissed by traditional donors, they concluded that the prospect of a swift shift in influence-sharing was gloomy. Hence, the OPEC members mainly channelled their funds through outside options – their own bilateral and newly created multilateral agencies[93] – to fulfil their objectives.

---

[87] Data on OPEC aid comes from OECD and World Bank estimates, from Shihata and Mabro (1978: 2, 12–13); Data on DAC donors from OECD Aid Statistics.

[88] This even included an extra contribution from Kuwait – a traditional donor – beyond its basic share.

[89] Shihata and Mabro (1978: 1).        [90] Ibid., 8.        [91] Ibid., 2, 6.

[92] IDA, 'The Fifth Replenishment of IDA: Note on the Geographic Distribution of IDA Credits', IDA/RPL/76–9, 13 February 1976, from the UK National Archives, OD36/250.

[93] Bilateral development agencies include the Kuwait Fund for Arab Economic Development (founded in 1961), UAE's Abu Dhabi Fund for Arab Economic Development (1971), and the Saudi Fund for Development (1974). Newly

In a nutshell, the emerging powers of the 1970s did not have a shared sense of common burden with traditional donors and had little voice in the US-dominated international institutions. Hence, they played a marginal role in financing IDA.[94]

To conclude, the North–South power struggle renewed the hegemonic support for IDA as the United States sought to preserve its hegemonic international economic order.

## 4.3 IDA-6 (FY1981–83):[95] *Accelerated Burden-Shifting* Resumes

This section first explores why the United States not only resumed its priority of share reduction over IDA expansion in the late 1970s, but also deployed its financial leverage to control Bank Management. It then examines the internal donor power struggle over 'fairness' as Congress unilaterally deployed financial leverage for narrow US national interests. Finally, it explores how ascending powers engaged in peer competition for IBRD voting rights, thus boosting their financial contributions to IDA-6.

### 4.3.1 *Renewed US Passion for Share Reduction*

In the late 1970s, the Third World's united front for the NIEO began unravelling, partly due to political and ideological divisions among developing countries coupled with uneven economic progress, thwarting their concerted efforts.[96] It also reflected that OPEC lacked a genuine commitment to using its oil weapon on behalf of general demands for a more equal international economic order, since their primary objective was confined to

created multilateral development finance institutions include *Special Arab Aid Fund for Africa* (1973), *The Arab Bank for Economic Development in Africa* (1975), *The Islamic Development Bank* (1975), *The OPEC Fund for International Development* (1976), *The Arab Authority for Agricultural Investment and Development* (1977), *The International Fund for Agricultural Development, or IFAD* (1977), etc. See Neumayer (2002).

[94] Their annual IDA contribution accounted for less than 2% in their overall aid efforts. Shihata and Mabro (1978: 12–13).

[95] IDA-6 covered FY1981–83, negotiated from September 1978 to December 1979.

[96] Wickes (1984: 86, 92).

preventing the West from lining up other developing nations against them.[97] Yet a more fundamental reason was the weak power position of Third World countries, for they were highly vulnerable to external adversities but rarely powerful enough to command monopoly in commodities other than oil.[98] Consequently, their demand for aid was not taken so seriously by donors as before.

Alongside the receding North–South geopolitical struggle was the continued easing of West–East tension. The United States established diplomatic relations with the People's Republic of China in January 1979.[99] Two years earlier, President Carter had stated that 'being confident of our own future, we are now free of that inordinate fear of communism'.[100]

The geopolitical shift diminished the significance of IDA's geopolitical role in accommodating Third World demands and countering the Soviet threat. Thus, the United States was no longer willing to exercise hegemonic leadership for IDA expansion and, as in IDA-4, resumed its passion for share reduction.[101]

What further exacerbated the prospects for IDA-6 was that the second oil shock in December 1978 plunged donor countries into economic recession. Amidst budgetary constraints, aid ministries began to look increasingly to commercial benefits rather than development effectiveness. To secure their short-run interests, donors believed that their objectives could be better assured under bilateral than multilateral auspices. Consequently, the tide was rising against multilateral aid.[102]

To achieve a successful IDA-6 in the face of exogenous adversity, Bank Management proactively made a strong case for a substantial increase in IDA-6 resources. First, President McNamara initiated an *Independent Commission on International Development Issues* (known as the 'Brandt Commission'), calling for a large-scale

---

[97] Ibid., 79–80.    [98] Amin (1984: 86, 301).    [99] Ali (2005).

[100] *Presidential Documents*, vol. 13 (30 May 1977), 774.

[101] As happened in IDA-4, the USA still preferred a modest increase in total IDA resources since it was estimated that the Soviet Union made a noticeable increase in its aid flows to LDCs in the latter half of the 1970s. See Machowski and Schultz (1987: 126).

[102] World Bank, 'The Bank's Competitive Position in the ODA "Market"', 1984, from the World Bank Archives.

transfer of resources to developing countries.[103] Second, the World Bank launched the *World Development Report* in 1978, making a convincing case that 'additional concessional resources would be required to achieve both higher rates of growth in the poorest countries and greater progress in poverty alleviation'.[104]

Building on the above positive momentum, Bank Management initially proposed a doubling of IDA's resources to $15 billion. Yet this bidding figure received a cold reception from major donors.

The United States argued that the Bank's bidding figure was 'clearly inconsistent with the donors' domestic constraints'.[105] The economic downturn had compelled Congress to tighten the budget, intensify the fight against inflation, and reduce the government budget deficit. Consequently, Congress not only put a cap on the cash contribution – no increase in real terms – but also was determined to bring the US share down to the lowest possible level.[106]

At the initial replenishment meeting, the United States claimed a sharp share reduction and urged Germany and Japan to make compensating share increases.[107] To justify its claim, the United States argued that IDA development assistance was a kind of 'collective good' to help build a peaceful and prosperous free world from which all Western nations benefited. Thus, as Japan and Germany were rising economically, they should assume additional responsibilities for promoting international development. Otherwise, they would become 'free riders' on the system while the United States shouldered a heavier burden in providing collective defence and maintaining an open liberal economic order. Thus, the United States put maximum pressure on Japan and Germany to offset its shortfall.[108]

---

[103] Independent Commission on International Development Issues, *North-South, A Programme for Survival* (Cambridge, Mass.: MIT Press, 1980).

[104] IDA, *Sixth Replenishment of IDA Resources*, 15 January 1980, para. 15, from the World Bank Archives.

[105] NAC, Special Report to the President and to the Congress on the Proposed Replenishment of the Resources of the International Development Association, 1980, 13.

[106] Statement of Hon. C. Fred Bergsten, Assistant Secretary of the Treasury, from Hearings before House Committee on Banking, Finance and Urban Affairs, *International Development Association Sixth Replenishment and African Development Bank Membership*, 96th Congress, 2nd Session, 26–27 March and 16 April 1980, 99.

[107] Statement of Hon. G. William Miller, Secretary of the Treasury, ibid., 22.

[108] Telephone interview with the former US Treasury official, 11 April 2012.

In formulating its negotiating strategy, the United States was prepared to settle for a smaller IDA in the absence of a more 'equitable'
burden-sharing. Why this trade-off? Since the United States attempted
to make a steep share cut, this would motivate ascending powers to
push down the total target in order to minimise their costs of filling
a US gap. This stood in stark contrast with the previous US stance in the
1960s that prioritised IDA expansion over its own share reduction at
the height of the bipolar rivalry.[109]

Conventional explanations based on deteriorating country-specific
interests are of little help in understanding what motivated the United
States to seek share cuts in the 1970s. As will be shown later in this
section, there is little evidence showing deterioration in the US country-
specific interests; instead, the US parochial national interests were
enhanced via unilateral Congressional threats to be shown later.[110]

To conclude, as external threats receded, the United States resumed
its passion for share reduction even at the expense of a larger total size
of replenishment.

### 4.3.2  *The US Seizes Control over Bank Management via the Informal Donor Forum*

Apart from a claim for share reduction, the US IDA Deputy made
a more systematic effort to deploy its financial leverage to seek policy
influence, including:

1. Expanding IBRD/IDA Energy lending to ease upward price
   pressure;
2. Continuing to strengthen IDA's major thrust in reaching the poor;
3. Improving supervision and evaluation of IDA projects.[111]

---

[109]  Ibid.
[110]  Here I do not use the indicator of formal voting record on aid allocation to
gauge how successfully the USA achieved its country-specific interests in aid
allocations. While the formal US opposition votes were usually ineffective, it is
too hasty to conclude that the USA failed to gain its country-specific interests
for two reasons. First, loans that the USA really opposed seldom passed the
screening to come to the Board for a vote. Second, the US 'no' votes helped the
US Administration to make 'a public statement' to domestic audience that it
disfavoured certain loans (but it did not oppose them privately). See Brown
(1992: 243).
[111]  Statement of Hon. G. William Miller, 42–43.

Regarding the substance of the US influence attempts, policy preferences of other donors were more aligned with those of the United States than had been the case in IDA-4. Hence, no major policy debates occurred in IDA-6.[112]

Yet procedurally, accommodating the US demands would have far-reaching implications for World Bank governance in the long run. Instead of confining IDA replenishment to financial issues, the United States consistently demanded that Bank Management prepare discussion papers on IDA policies and operations to enable IDA Deputies to give policy guidance. The effect of this procedural change set the precedent that could unleash a profound shift in the decision-making power from the formal Board of Executive Directors to the informal IDA donor forum.

So far, Bank Management had resisted donor contributions 'with strings attached' on the grounds that it would hurt Bank's independence and tilt the balance of power against IDA recipients and IBRD borrowers. Since client countries had no voice in the exclusive donor forum, relegating the formal Board would undermine the legitimacy and effectiveness of the World Bank.

While donors in principle embraced Bank Management's resistance against informal donor influence, IDA-6 witnessed an emerging acquiescence among donors in the practice of using IDA contributions to seek policy influence for two reasons.

First, budgetary austerity had intensified domestic legislative scrutiny over IDA's polices and operations. IDA contribution was such a 'big ticket' item that it was facing increased legislative questioning.[113] Thus, donor governments were compelled to demonstrate influence upon IDA commensurate with their contribution.

Second, the global aid 'market' was becoming so competitive that the World Bank had to be more receptive to donor demands in order to secure scarce resources. In the late 1970s, the Bank's historically pre-eminent position became more exposed to competitive challenge.[114] Among emerging competitors were newly established aid windows of RDBs. Dissatisfied with the Western-dominated World Bank, developing countries believed that they would have more leverage over regional

---

[112] Telephone interview with the former US Treasury official, 11 April 2012.
[113] World Bank, 'The Bank's Competitive Position in the ODA "Market"'.
[114] Ibid.

institutions.[115] Yet, over time developing countries had to compromise their initial aspirations for self-determination in order to secure more financial support from donors.[116]

Therefore, power struggles over policy influence in IDA-6 was less about tussles within the donor group and more about battles between the United States and Bank Management.

The United States resented that Bank Management had excessive discretionary power without adequate Board supervision. For instance, as IDA moved from project to country programming to disburse its fast-growing resources under the leadership of President McNamara, the US senior official complained that it was 'done solely' by Bank Management 'without Board involvement or even in many cases Board awareness'.[117] Thus, the United States aimed to leverage its IDA contribution to redress the unbalanced power relationship between major shareholders and Bank Management.

Accommodate or resist? These were stark options faced by Bank Management.

As the largest donor, the United States possessed preponderant financial leverage, much larger even than its own dollar contribution would have indicated. This was largely due to the fact that other donors conditioned their financial support upon US participation for the sake of 'equitable' burden-sharing.

First, at the ratification stage, IDA replenishments could not come into force unless donors authorised more than 80 per cent of their total pledges. Since the United States was the single donor contributing more than 20 per cent, the US Congressional authorisation committees enjoyed 'veto power' in deciding whether IDA could keep running or fall into a hiatus.

Second, at the disbursement stage, other donors introduced the 'pro rata' rule in IDA-6 – they were entitled to withhold their payments in proportion to any US shortfall.[118] This responded to a new demand from the United States that qualified its participation upon *annual* Congressional appropriations rather than *three-year* authorisations.

---

[115]   White (1972: 28).     [116]   Krasner (1981).

[117]   Statement of Charles Cooper (the former Assistant Secretary of US Treasury), from Hearing before the Senate Committee on Foreign Relations, *International Financial Institutions*, 95th Congress, 1st Session, 9–10 March 1977, 105.

[118]   IDA, *Sixth Replenishment of IDA Resources*, para. 60.

Such a device was used by the Carter Administration to assure Congress of more control over the US contribution to IDA.[119]

Intensified competition in the international aid market was another compelling reason for Bank Management to accommodate the biggest shareholder's demand. To secure its share of multilateral aid,[120] the World Bank had to make swift adjustments to demonstrate its 'ability of responding flexibly to the most pressing priorities and problems of the time, addressing donors' concern with the poorest, and enhancing effectiveness in delivery'.[121]

Ultimately Bank Management accommodated the US demand for desired policy influence. Otherwise, a cut in the US contribution would have triggered a domino effect upon other donors' contribution levels.

First, on energy lending, the Board of Executive Directors approved an expansion of the IBRD/IDA energy programme in January 1979 amid IDA-6 negotiations to step up its energy efforts up to at least 15 per cent ($8 billion) of total Bank lending within five years.[122]

Second, in response to US demand for reaching the poor, the Bank would steadfastly expand lending to agricultural and rural development in order to directly benefit the poor and to increase food production.[123]

Third, as to the US demand for improved supervision and evaluation of IDA projects, Bank Management presented a paper detailing the

---

[119] NAC, Special Report to the President and to the Congress on the Proposed Replenishment of the Resources of the International Development Association, 16.

[120] IDA-6 negotiations (negotiated from September 1978 to December 1979) were overlapped with AsDF-2 (negotiated from January 1978 to December 1978), AfDF-2 (negotiated from January 1979 to December 1981), and the First Replenishment of newly founded *International Fund for Agricultural Development* (negotiated between September 1978 and December 1979).

[121] The Bank's share of multilateral aid rose from 26% in 1970 to 38% in 1978/82. See World Bank, 'The Bank's Competitive Position in the ODA "Market"'.

[122] Statement of Hon. G. William Miller, 14, 17.

[123] As the US Agency for International Development (USAID) began to restructure its programme to emphasise meeting basic human needs, the MDBs began cautiously to shift the composition of their lending programmes in the same direction. Statement of Hon. Paul A. Volcker, Chairman, Board of Governors of the Federal Reserve System, from Hearing before House Committee on Banking, Finance and Urban Affairs, *International Development Association Sixth Replenishment and African Development Bank Membership*, 123.

During the period 1975–80, about 46% and 30% of IDA and IBRD lending, respectively, flows to the agricultural sector, up from 37% and 11% in the early 1970s. Statement of Hon. G. William Miller, Secretary of the Treasury, ibid., 16.

expanded procedures to ensure the United States was 'fully satisfied that resources provided to IDA were being efficiently and effectively utilised'.[124]

In summary, as the geopolitical threats subdued, the United States proactively deployed its financial leverage to strengthen its control over Bank Management via the informal donor forum. This means of influence increasingly gained legitimacy among donors.

### 4.3.3 The 'Equity Line' Skews Further

At first glance, the fairness concern should have been mitigated among secondary states in IDA-6 compared with IDA-4, since the US Administration's influence attempts created much less distributional conflict and other donors acquiesced in the usage of the informal donor forum for policy influence.

A closer examination, however, reveals that the equity line was inordinately skewed because Congress unilaterally imposed its will upon Bank Management to serve US foreign policy interests.

Since the early 1970s, a growing conflict between the legislative and executive branches occurred on the question of 'which branch shall determine US policy towards MDBs'.[125] Generally speaking, it was the President and the Treasury Department that were responsible for the US participation in the World Bank. But it was Congress that held the power of the purse, thus deciding the terms of the United States' involvement. Yet Congress was far from a single actor. Securing funds for IDA required a stamp of approval from four relevant committees – that is, two authorising committees (House Banking Committee and Senate Foreign Relations Committee) and two appropriating committees (House/Senate Appropriation Subcommittees on foreign operations).[126] Authorisation occurred every three years, while appropriation took place annually. This offered Congress ample opportunities to add strings as 'Amendments' in their legislation in an

---

[124] NAC, Special Report to the President and to the Congress on the Proposed Replenishment of the Resources of the International Development Association, 15.

[125] Brown (1992: 171).

[126] These committees frequently held different views about the US participation in IDA (Sanford 1982: 110–26).

effort to tighten Congressional grip on the US participation in the MDBs.

In the early 1970s, Congress began to play a more significant role after the erosion of the executive leadership in US foreign policy-making in the wake of the Vietnam War and the Watergate scandal. By contrast, in the 1960s, US Administrations had enjoyed paramount discretion in formulating the US policy towards the World Bank-IDA, as shown in the previous chapter.

President Carter initially stood firm against Congressional earmarking on the grounds that the World Bank as a multilateral institution was not legally allowed to accept any funds with strings attached. To placate Congress, President Carter once promised to instruct the US Executive Directors in the MDBs to oppose and vote against any loans to Vietnam.[127] But it turned out to be insufficient to pacify Congress: an initial agricultural loan to Vietnam was approved by the Board because the other Executive Directors would vote 'yes', forming a majority necessary for the loan's approval (despite the 'no' vote by the US Executive Director). Some Congressmen furiously complained that any further loans from the Bank would free up money for the Vietnamese government to pursue war with its neighbours.

As the foreign aid appropriations bill for FY1980 was debated in the House Appropriations Committee in 1979, the Carter Administration seemed unable to resist a roaring sentiment among a large majority of Congressmen that an amendment needed to be added to prohibit the use of US contributed funds for MDB loans for Vietnam. This position contrasted with that in IDA-4, where the Nixon Administration deployed its financial leverage to skew the Bank lending for reconstruction in South Vietnam. This shift stemmed from the recent political change: the government of South Vietnam had fallen in April 1975, replaced by the socialist North Vietnam. Especially after Vietnam invaded Cambodia in September 1979, the Congressional sentiment was too strong for President Carter to forestall legislative strings of US contributions.

At this critical juncture, President McNamara took the unusual step of meeting with a group of Congressmen to assure them that no further Bank or IDA loans to Vietnam were contemplated. But this oral assurance did not satisfy the hard-liners in the House. On 1 November 1979,

---

[127]   Brown (1992: 187).

McNamara took a step further by signing a letter directly to Congress in order to make a written assurance.

The Congressmen celebrated this letter as 'a great victory', since it committed the Bank not to use *anyone*'s money for loans to Vietnam whereas the proposed amendment would have only restricted the use of US contributed funds.[128]

But the unilateral Congressional influence upon the Bank received a severe reprimand from the Board of Executive Directors. William Clark, the then Vice President for External Relations of the World Bank, described it as follows:

Then the storm burst. The Bank's Board of Executive Directors – long disturbed by American attitudes – joined *unanimously* to protest both the bypassing of the Board and the clear breach of the established practice that the President of the Bank dealt only with the executive authorities of member governments; to them McNamara's action underlined the determination of the United States to *politicize* the multilateral institutions. The episode really shook the confidence of the Board in their chairman's capacity to defend them against what they perceived as a hostile America. To make matters worse, even after McNamara's personal reassurance, Congress did not appropriate new funds for IDA and did not do so during the remainder of his term of office. (emphasis added)[129]

The US politicisation of the Bank was aggravated in IDA-6, since Congress unilaterally 'subjugated' the Bank to serve American foreign policy goals but failed to honour the US financial commitments on time.

Furthermore, the Vietnam case was by no means a one-off exception, but, rather, a quintessential example of growing unilateral Congressional influence. Evidence showed that Congress intensified its interventions to forestall the Bank's assistance for commodity production that generated competitive pressures on American producers.[130]

To sum up, in the 1970s the United States successfully leveraged its preponderant financial weight to pursue parochial national interests, which stood in contrast with its hegemonic self-restraint in seeking narrow national interests in the 1960s. Consequently, the equity line between influence and contribution was skewed further in IDA-6, because other donors were full of indignation that (a) the United States sought a substantial share cut and even accumulated overdue

---

[128] Ibid., 188     [129] Clark (1981: 181).     [130] Sanford (1982: 37–38).

obligations of $485 million (about a third of its due amount for IDA-4),[131] but (b) Congress unilaterally encroached upon the Bank's independence to serve short-term commercial and strategic interests.

The growing fairness concern culminated in a special donor meeting held in June 1978 to deliberate on fair burden-sharing criteria before the IDA-6 negotiations started.

The meeting represented a conscious donor effort to search for a benchmark for gauging 'equitable' burden-sharing in order to facilitate smooth burden-sharing adjustments to reduce negotiation costs. But it turned out to be futile. Ultimately, donors conceded that 'no universally applicable criterion or formula could be found',[132] because each donor intentionally selected indicators that put the heaviest burden on others and put itself in the best possible light.

But most donors generally agreed (a) that GNP shares (adjusted for income per capita) should serve as an indicative point of reference for 'fair' burden-sharing,[133] and (b) that donors should maintain their basic burden shares in the previous replenishment round unless justified by erosion in relative economic capabilities.

The US fell short in paying its 'fair' share in the eyes of other donors, especially Japan and Germany, who were pressed by the United States to offset its shortfall.

Japan and Germany maintained that the US claim for share reduction was 'unjustifiable'. First, the United States contributed far below its GNP share.[134] Second, the United States shirked its leadership role in preserving a liberal economic order. The international monetary system was in disarray: after the Nixon Administration defaulted on

---

[131] *Congressional Quarterly Almanac, 1975–77.*

[132] IDA, *Sixth Replenishment of IDA Resources*, para. 30.

[133] The formula for calculating adjusted GNP shares is as follows:

$$Adjusted\ GNP\ share\ =\ g_i = \frac{GNPpc_i * GNP_i}{\sum_j GNPpc_j * GNP_j}$$

It takes three steps: first, standardise the weight of GNP per capita of a given donor ($GNP_{pci}$) with the USA as the benchmark; second, multiply its GNP by its standardised GNP per capita; third, repeat step 2 for all donors to get the sum and then calculate the share of the given donor of the sum.

Source: IDA, 'IDA-8 Size and Burden Sharing', 1986, 12, from the World Bank Archives.

[134] Letter from Mr Matthofer (Germany) to the World Bank President McNamara, 16 January 1980, from the World Bank Archives.

obligations of the dollar to gold, the real value of the dollar reserves held by the UK, Germany, France, and Japan in terms of commodities shrank by around 60 per cent in the 1970s.[135]

But despite their discontent, Japan and Germany substantially increased their shares to make good on the US share cut due to their high structural dependence upon the hegemon.

Japan was horrified by increasing Soviet Pacific force levels in the mid-1970s.[136] In Japan's fourth post-war White Paper on Defence, published in July 1978, it underlined 'apprehension' over the Soviet Union and expressed 'serious reservations' over President Carter's plan to withdraw ground combat forces from Asia.[137] Ko Maruyama, Japan's Defence Agency vice minister, considered the Soviet Union to be 'a direct threat'.[138] Worried about being abandoned by the United States, Japanese leaders requested closer defence consultations with them.[139] Moreover, Japan relied more on the US market to re-ignite its export-led growth in the aftermath of the oil crises.[140] By contrast, the United States depended much less on the Japanese market, since the United States enacted a domestic fiscal stimulus before the 1976 election to fuel growth.[141] Hence, the United States took advantage of the Japanese structural dependence. The hegemon threatened that if Japan did not increase its IDA shares, the United States would be tougher on both military and economic fronts.[142] In response to the US pressure, Japan announced an ambitious objective of 'doubling ODA in five years' in 1977. Prior to Prime Minister Fukuda's meetings with President Carter in May 1978, Fukuda decided to shorten the period of doubling ODA from five to three years as 'an important manifestation of Japan's increasing willingness to play a greater role in burden sharing'.[143]

While Germany proactively reduced its economic dependence upon the United States, it remained militarily dependent upon it. To reduce its reliance upon the USA in international monetary affairs, Germany took the lead in establishing the European Monetary System (EMS) to

---

[135]  Yu (2013: 6).     [136]  Tōgō (2005).     [137]  Swearingen (1978: 220).
[138]  Ibid.     [139]  Auer (1991).     [140]  Lake (2009: 89).
[141]  Japan was asymmetrically dependent upon the US market to sustain its export-led growth – over 30% of total Japanese exports went to the US market, whereas only 10% of the US exports went to Japan. See Sperling (1992: 174–75).
[142]  Telephone interview with the former US Treasury official, 11 April 2012.
[143]  Orr (1990: 111).

insulate their currencies from the vagaries of the dollar. This move was perceived by Congress as 'a direct assault on America's reduced leadership'.[144] Moreover, Germany's trade was steadily 'Europeanised' – exports to Europe accounted for more than 70 per cent of its overall exports, compared with less than 10 per cent to the US. However, Germany had to count on US nuclear deterrence against Soviet attack. Helmut Schmidt, the then Chancellor of Germany, believed that Soviet offensive military capability could be employed to achieve political goals at any time.[145] Hence, the US made 'periodic threats' to reduce American troops if Germany failed to meet US demands in international economic issues.[146]

In summary, the intensifying unilateral Congressional influence and overdue US obligations further exacerbated the sense of 'unfairness' among secondary states; however, ascending powers delayed their exit options and continued to compensate for the 'unjustified' US share cut because they were structurally dependent upon the hegemon.

### 4.3.4 Peer Competition among Ascending Powers for IBRD Voting Rights

As seen in the previous chapter, ascending powers deployed their financial contributions to vie for IDA voting rights. This section broadens the analysis to uncover how Japan and Germany engaged in peer competition for IBRD voting rights, thus boosting their financial contribution to IDA-6. As explained in the previous chapter, IBRD voting rights carried more significance than IDA voting rights because IDA and IBRD shared the same Board, whose seats were determined by IBRD voting strength rather than IDA voting strength.

Japan made its first demand to 'harmonise' IDA burden shares with IBRD voting rights in IDA-5 (negotiated in the mid-1970s). Yet Japan's claim was not heard by other countries. Due to high stakes in the North–South power struggle in the mid-1970s, Japan only made a token share reduction of 2 per cent in IDA-5, simultaneously offset by its own supplementary contribution. Japan persistently used

---

[144] Hearing before House Committee on Banking, Finance and Urban Affairs, International Development Association Sixth Replenishment and African Development Bank Membership, 109.
[145] Schweitzer (1990: 245).    [146] Hanrieder (1992: 219).

'check-book diplomacy' to speed up the IBRD voting-rights adjustment in IDA-6 by wielding both 'stick' and 'carrot'.[147]

Yet neither the declining hegemon nor the waning UK were willing to cede their voting rights to accommodate this rising star's demand, since they no longer strived to expand IDA. As elaborated earlier, the USA assigned low priority to IDA expansion since the geopolitical threats subdued. The UK no longer had as strong an interest in enlarging IDA as before, because its procurement benefits were eroding to the tipping point where its bilateral programme fared better than IDA. Moreover, it showed 'no real signs of regaining the position it held in the early 1970s'.[148] Hence, the UK lost interest in augmenting IDA and sought a share reduction to hedge against further loss of procurement benefits.[149]

In contrast to the passive stances adopted by the USA and the UK, Bank Management welcomed Japan's intention to increase its share-holding in IBRD in the hope that this could secure a substantial increase in Japan's IDA contribution. Since Japan pledged to double aid (in dollars) by 1980, the Bank desired to secure a fat share of the Japanese burgeoning aid budget.[150] Hence, the Bank proposed a SCI by granting Japan 4,000 *unallocated* shares.[151] Allocating unallocated shares required only a simple majority; thus, it would help mitigate potential

---

[147]  Arase (1995: 209).

[148]  A major factor behind this erosion was that procurement contracts won by recipient countries had increased from 10 per cent in the early 1970s to above 40 per cent in the late 1970s. Procurement was awarded in recipient countries in order to encourage local business and in cases where the nature of the contract would make international competitive bidding unsuitable. See ODA, 'Notes for Supplements: IDA-6: Draft Speaking Notes for Mr. Hurd (The Under-Secretary of State for Foreign and Commonwealth Affairs)', February 1981, from the UK National Archives, *IDA: sixth replenishment, UK Parliamentary authority*, OD 108/28.

[149]  'Table 3: GDP Indicators, from IDA, "Burden-Sharing: Selected Statistics"', IDA/RPL/79–3, 15 February 1979, from the World Bank Archives.

[150]  'Burden-Sharing Arrangements in IDA6', from I. P. M. Cargill to Mr Edward Fried (Executive Director for the US), 12 January 1979, the World Bank Archives.

[151]  'Unallocated' shares are those that have already been authorised by the Board of Governors but not yet taken up by members, so they incur no dilution in others' absolute shares and might have mild repercussions on ranking close to those calling for an increase in voting power. World Bank, 'Technical Note: Past IBRD Capital Increases', SecM87-1039, dated 22 September 1987, Annex, 6.

distributive battles by avoiding prolonged negotiations on a SCIs that required 75 per cent of voting power to approve it.

Japan's pioneering efforts to gain additional IBRD voting rights via its IDA contribution stimulated Germany to make competitive bids in order to secure its third largest shareholder position. This was a necessary move for Germany for two reasons. First, the traditional mechanism of automatically adjusting IBRD shareholdings in line with the seventh IMF General Quota Review failed to realise Germany's aspiration for an enhanced IBRD shareholding.[152] Second, Japan had surpassed Germany as the second largest economy and aspired to wield its IDA contribution to ascend to the second largest IBRD shareholding position; thus, Germany had to match Japan's IDA contribution – a symbol of their willingness to take responsibility – in order to justify its IBRD voting rights. Accordingly, Germany 'declared its readiness to increase its [basic] share from 10.9 per cent to 12.0 per cent' to achieve parity with Japan[153] in the hope of a 'return' (IBRD voting rights) to its increased IDA contribution in the future.[154]

However, the above increases in basic shares were not adequate to compensate for potential share reductions to close the financing gap. Subsequently, IDA-6 negotiations reached a critical stage – how to induce donors to make supplementary contributions to close the remaining financing gap so as to bring the negotiations to a successful conclusion. Yet major donors withheld their purses unless others matched their generosity. To break this stand-off, Bank Management visited Germany's capital in December 1979 in order to informally encourage Germany to pay up for its expected influence.[155] Ultimately, Germany made an additional contribution of 0.5 per cent

---

[152] Germany was dissatisfied about the discrepancy between its IDA burden share (10.91% in IDA-5) and its IBRD voting rights (7.7% among all contributions and 5.4% among all members) after the 1979 SCI. See Resolution No. 335, 'Special Increases in Certain Subscriptions to Capital Stock', adopted 30 April 1979; Table 7 'Current Shares in IBRD Capital and in IMF Quotas', from IDA, 'Burden-Sharing – Selected Statistics', from the World Bank Archives.

[153] Letter from Mr Matthofer (Germany) to the World Bank President McNamara, 16 January 1980, from the World Bank Archives.

[154] Ibid.

[155] 'Visit to Bonn', from Moeen A. Qureshi (Vice President for Finance) to Mr Robert S. McNamara, 4 December 1979, from the World Bank Archives.

so as to pull up an additional Japanese supplementary contribution of 2.65 per cent.

Thus, for the first time the combined shares of Germany (12.50 per cent) and Japan (14.65 per cent) exceeded the US share (27 per cent).[156] The USA celebrated this 'more equitable burden-sharing' as a 'success'.[157]

In summary, while Japan and Germany compensated for the US share cut mainly due to their structural dependence upon the hegemon, ascending powers' willingness to increase their shares partly reflected their competition for IBRD voting rights.

## 4.4 Conclusion

What insights can we gain from a close look at IDA burden-sharing dynamics in the 1970s?

As we learnt from the previous chapter, deterioration in ability-to-pay did incentivise the United States to cut its share. Eroding capacity provoked Congress to urge further share cuts throughout the 1970s. Congress even threatened to refuse to authorise the US participation in a new round of IDA replenishment unless the executive branch achieved a share reduction. Such growing Congressional difficulties stood in sharp contrast with its initial leadership in establishing IDA.

The conventional explanation of country-specific interests fares badly in understanding *Accelerated Burden-Shifting* where substantial US share cuts were largely compensated for by share increases from Japan and Germany. The United States' narrow interests were enhanced rather than being eroded, whereas procurement benefits of ascending powers did not enjoy a noticeable boost. Hence, it is of little help in understanding the US share reductions and the ascending powers' share increases.

Below we look into the three layers of power plays to see how they help us to resolve the puzzles of *Accelerated Burden-Shifting* in IDA-4/-6 and *Hegemonic Lag* in IDA-5.

---

[156] NAC, Special Report to the President and to the Congress on the Proposed Replenishment of the Resources of the International Development Association, 1.

[157] Hearing before House Committee on Banking, Finance and Urban Affairs, International Development Association Sixth Replenishment and African Development Bank Membership, 15.

At the first layer of power play between the US-led donor group and external threats, the fading Soviet threat largely explains the steep US share cuts in the early and late 1970s, whereas the growing menace from the united Global South resolves the puzzle of a constant US share in the mid-1970s.

The receding Soviet threat is of great help in understanding *Accelerated Burden-Shifting* from the hegemon to ascending powers in IDA-4 and IDA-6. Upon the arrival of détente, the US shifted its priority from IDA expansion to its own share reduction.[158] The receding Soviet threat rendered US hegemonic coercion more credible, since its Western allies were terrified that the US military retrenchment would leave them alone to combat Soviet invasions in their own territories. Hence, the United States successfully coerced Japan and Germany to compensate for its share reductions. By contrast, in the late 1960s the intensifying Soviet threat held the United States back from cutting its share in order to expand IDA to counterbalance the Soviet influence in the Third World.

By contrast, the intensifying external threat from the Global South helps us to comprehend why the United States kept its share in IDA-5 in the mid-1970s. The Third World formed a united front to demand the NIEO, which posed an imminent threat to the US-led international system. To pre-empt an overhaul of a West-dominated international system, the USA led traditional major donors to maintain their shares to augment total IDA resources in order to accommodate the Third World's demand. Thus, the North–South power struggle arrested the general trend of *Accelerated Burden-Shifting* in the 1970s.

At the second layer of power play about the internal donor struggle for voting rights, the declining interest of the hegemon and the waning UK in IDA expansion helps to explain why ascending powers were less successful in 'buying' IBRD voting rights. The United States no longer had the imperative to enlarge IDA due to the diminishing Soviet threat; the UK lost its procurement advantage and thus had no interest in augmenting IDA either. Accordingly, while Japan adamantly wielded both stick and carrot, it failed to change the pecking order in the IBRD shareholding.

---

[158] In the absence of a genuine US leadership, IDA experienced a much more modest increase of about 4% in real terms – well below average increases in earlier rounds of replenishment of 8%.

Even in the absence of quid pro quo between voting rights and burden shares, peer competition among ascending powers boosted their financial support for IDA-6. This underlines the symbolic value of IDA burden shares – contributing to the World Bank, the pre-eminent international development institution, enabled donors to demonstrate their willingness to take responsibility to justify their bids for influence well beyond IDA. The next chapter will uncover how Japan finally realised its aspiration of becoming No. 2 in the IBRD shareholding by making a quid-pro-quo deal with the UK.

At the third layer of power play about the informal donor influence upon Bank Management, the concern with fairness among secondary states began to gain significance in the 1970s. In contrast to the hegemonic self-restraint displayed in the 1960s, the United States not only proactively deployed its financial leverage to unilaterally seek political influence upon the Bank's policies and operations, but also claimed share cuts and, moreover, accumulated arrears.

Although the contribution-to-influence equity line was further skewed in IDA-6, however, secondary states largely delayed their 'voice/exit' option, largely due to their high structural dependence upon the United States and the lack of viable outside options. Hence, the United States managed to achieve substantial share cuts but augmented its policy influence, which runs contrary to the conventional wisdom that donor influence would diminish as their contribution declined.

Detailed case studies also help us to realise that the delay in secondary states' execution of the 'voice' option was also attributed to the systematic US financial leverage. As the largest donor, the United States carried more weight than its dollar contribution would have indicated: (a) the United States was the single major donor that contributed more than 20 per cent; hence, IDA replenishment could not come into effect without US participation; (b) the newly introduced pro rata rule entitled other donors to make proportional cuts in case the US failed to make payments on schedule, which potentially multiplied the US financial leverage. This helps to understand the counterintuitive finding that the United States managed to amplify its influence while cutting its share.

The next chapter will move to IDA burden-sharing in the 1980s to uncover (a) what led to the first-ever uncompensated US share cut in IDA-7; (b) a subsequent *Hegemonic Lag* (a constant US share) in IDA-8 under the same Reagan Administration; and (c) what drove *Accelerated Burden-Shifting* from the UK to Japan in IDA-7.

# 5 | IDA in the 1980s: The Rise and Retreat of the 'Reagan Revolution'

This chapter aims to resolve the following puzzles: (a) why the United States made a first-ever *uncompensated* share reduction of 2 percentage points in IDA-7 in the early 1980s;[1] (b) why the US economic revival in the later years of the 1980s did not translate into a reversal of its previous IDA share cuts in IDA-8; and (c) what accelerated a significant burden-shifting from the UK to Japan in IDA-7.

## 5.1 Empirical Puzzles

In the first half of the 1980s, major donors suffered from sluggish economic growth amidst debt crises.[2] Yet despite the fairly stable relative economic positions, IDA-7 witnessed significant burden-shifting – the US reduced its share from 27 per cent to 25 per cent, and the UK cut its share by a third: from 10.10 per cent to 6.70 per cent; Japan substantially increased its share by more than one-half: from 12 per cent to 18.70 per cent.

In the latter half of the 1980s, the United States enjoyed economic rejuvenation. Yet the hegemon lagged behind in boosting its share in IDA-8.[3]

In sum, the baseline capacity-to-pay explanation cannot explain the *Accelerated Burden-Shifting* in IDA-7 and the *Hegemonic Lag* in IDA-8.

---

[1]  As we learnt in the previous chapter, in IDA-4 and IDA-6 the United States tried to ensure that Japan and Germany made compensating share increases to largely offset the US share cuts.

[2]  The United States experienced an annual average growth rate of about 3%, compared with 4% in Japan and 2% in Germany, France, and the UK. Source: WDI.

[3]  Due to rapid economic growth and the appreciation of the US dollar, the US GNP share went up dramatically, from 32.49% to 41.27%, but its burden share remained 25%. See IDA-7 and IDA-8 Replenishment Agreements.

124

This is even more puzzling if we apply historical insights on how the intensity of external threat shaped IDA burden-sharing dynamics. As seen in the previous chapters, the hegemon was willing to honour its traditional share in order to underpin IDA expansion when external threats intensified in the 1960s (a looming Soviet threat in IDA-3) and the mid-1970s (an imminent threat from the South in IDA-5), whereas it was ready to seek substantial share cuts when external threats dissipated as in the early and late 1970s (IDA-4/-6).

If the above historical insights hold water, we would expect to see that (a) the United States should have maintained its share in IDA-7, since the decade-long détente gave way to a renewed East–West confrontation after the Soviet intervention in Afghanistan in December 1979;[4] and (b) the United States should have had a strong incentive to shirk its burden in IDA-8, as the Soviet threat faded away in the late 1980s.

Yet empirical evidence runs contrary to the above predictions: the United States made a substantial share cut in IDA-7, but maintained its traditional share in IDA-8. Hence, the first layer of power play between the US-led donor group and the external threats seems to be of little help in resolving the puzzles in the 1980s.

This chapter will apply an analytical eye to history for further explanation of the three outstanding puzzles: (a) a substantial uncompensated US share cut in IDA-7; (b) the *Hegemonic Lag* in IDA-8; and (c) the *Accelerated Burden-Shifting* from the UK to Japan in IDA-7.

## 5.2 IDA-7 (FY1985–87): The Rise of the 'Reagan Revolution'

This section first explores what triggered the anti-IDA 'Reagan Revolution', provoking a 'funding crisis' in FY1984; it then examines how the US managed to make a unilateral share cut down to 25 per cent but simultaneously amplify its policy influence not only in IDA but also in IBRD; and, finally, it considers how secondary states opted for a mild exit in response to the widening disparity between US contribution and influence.

---

[4] Garthoff (1994: 1082).

## 5.2.1 A 'Funding Crisis' in FY1984: A Traumatic Start

President Ronald Reagan came to power in January 1981, portending a radical departure from the traditional US stance towards IDA. Previously, the United States had pursued its vital survival interest of expanding IDA in order to counter the Soviet threat in the 1960s. Even though this geopolitical driver slowed down upon the arrival of the détente in the 1970s, the United States still consistently increased its dollar contribution and urged ascending powers to make share increases to achieve a steady growth in IDA's total resources. However, the Reagan Administration not only sought to cut its dollar contribution, it also strived to amputate total IDA resources.

Was the anti-IDA stance driven by deterioration in the US national interests? This speculation was far from the truth. An internal study, conducted in 1982 by the Treasury to evaluate the US influence in the MDBs, found that the World Bank-IDA had served US interests well.[5]

A closer look at the US decision-making process reveals that a dramatic shift in political will occurred as the Republican Reagan Administration succeeded the Democratic Carter Administration. This bred an anti-IDA stance.

First, ideologically the Reagan Administration held a deep conviction that the magic of free markets was the road to economic prosperity for rich and poor nations alike, and thus cast severe doubt on IDA's 'overtly statist and redistributive' approach to poverty reduction.[6] It took the critical view that the World Bank was undermining private enterprise and promoting socialism.[7] By contrast, previous Administrations held that IDA's development assistance was pivotal to prosperity and democracy in the Third World as a firewall against the Soviet threat.

Second, the imperial impulse of the new Administration induced the United States to turn its back on multilateral institutions, reversing a decade-long stance in favour of multilateral aid.[8] President Reagan resorted to direct military intervention to destroy pro-Soviet Third World governments and built massive defence forces to destroy the 'evil empire' of the Soviet Union.[9]

The negative US attitude towards IDA was further reinforced by severe budgetary cuts. Fiscal austerity hit foreign aid hardest, because

---

[5] US Department of the Treasury (1982: 95–96).     [6] Feinberg (1987: 149).
[7] Silk (1981).     [8] Lancaster (2007: 81–82).     [9] Feinberg (1987: 148).

rampant aid fatigue in public opinion exacerbated the Congressional antagonism towards foreign aid.[10]

To sum up, a shift in political will and fiscal austerity augured badly for US participation in IDA.

It was rumoured that the Reagan Administration would renege on the US pledge to IDA-6 negotiated by the previous administration. In September 1981, Beryl Sprinkel, Treasury Undersecretary, for the first time ever left open the possibility that the United States might end its contributions to IDA when its present commitments ran out.[11] This risk loomed large after the lame-duck Congress failed to pass the bill proposed by the Carter Administration that authorised US participation in IDA-6 in December 1980.[12]

To other donors' relief, President Reagan later decided to honour US commitments, but unilaterally decided to back-load its payment schedule to delay the bulk of its contributions to the last fiscal year of IDA-6.[13]

Congress was mired in deep divisions regarding the US contribution to IDA. Traditionally, Congress could achieve a reasonable consensus to authorise the US participation via a stand-alone law. Yet the growing Congressional hostility necessitated bundling the unpopular IDA bill with other must-pass bills in the 'safe vehicle' of an omnibus act in order to ratify the US participation in IDA-6. Furthermore, Congressional proponents and opponents of IDA could not get their act together so, as a compromise, they decided to stretch out the disbursement over four years (rather than the usual three years).[14]

---

[10] 'Aid Fatigue', *The Washington Post*, 19 April 1983.    [11] Rowen (1981).

[12] UK Foreign and Commonwealth Office (FCO), 'Prime Minister: IDA: 6th Replenishment: Bridging Arrangements', 13 February 1981, from the UK National Archives, *International Development Association (IDA): Sixth Replenishment*, OD108/27.

[13] The proposed schedule was $540 million (16%) in FY1981, $850 million (26%) in FY1982, and $1,850 million (57%) in FY1983, in contrast to the originally agreed schedule of 29%, 33%, and 38% respectively. See IDA-6 Replenishment Agreement, para. 59; Hearing before the House Committee on Banking, Finance, and Urban Affairs, *International Development Association*, 98th Congress, 2nd Session, Agreement No. 98–981, 10 August 1984, 4.

[14] Statement of Hon. Donald T. Regan, Secretary of the Treasury, from Hearing before the House Committee on Banking, Finance and Urban Affairs, *US Participation in the International Development Association Seventh Replenishment*, 98th Congress, 2nd Session, 29 February and 1 March 1984, 139.

The unilateral US decision to spread disbursements over four years sowed the seeds of a funding crisis in FY1984. By 1982, the United States had accumulated overdue obligations of over $1 billion (almost equal to its annual contribution to IDA-6). Subsequently, it announced that it would clear its arrears as a first order of business before entering IDA-7 negotiations.[15]

This created a predicament for secondary states – whether to embark on IDA-7 without the United States; or, if not, how to finance IDA in FY84. A consensus emerged that a premature start of IDA-7 would further skew 'fair' burden-sharing, letting the United States off the hook.[16] Yet if they insisted upon US participation to preserve their sense of fairness, this would entail a precipitate shutdown in IDA's lending programmes. Since other donors were eager to reconcile their sense of fairness with their desire to avert a breakdown in IDA operations, they chose a middle ground by providing additional special contributions for FY1984 *outside* the traditional burden-sharing framework.[17]

Two alternative options were proposed. Initially, France, Canada, and the Netherlands took the lead to propose 'a Special Fund' that restricted US access to procurement benefits, because they felt that the United States should not benefit from a fund to which it made no contribution.[18] This 'punishment' provoked the United States into threatening to cease its IDA contribution forever.[19] Horrified by the US exit threat, Bank Management proposed a more amenable alternative – an 'FY84 Account' that entitled the United States to win procurement contracts while according secondary states with voting rights in proportion to their contributions.[20]

---

[15] IDA, 'The Status of Contributions Released under IDA6 and Options for Augmenting IDA's Commitment Authority in FY83–84', IDA/RPL/82-7-1, 1982, 8, from the World Bank Archives.

[16] Ibid., 4.

[17] IDA, 'Arrangements for Special Contributions', IDA/R82-117, 8 October 1982, 2, from the World Bank Archives.

[18] IDA, 'A Technical Note on Alternative Approaches for Supplementing IDA Commitment Authority for FY82–86', IDA/RPL/82-6, 4 May 1982, from the World Bank Archives.

[19] Interview with Percy Mistry, Senior Advisor to Senior Vice President for Finance in the World Bank, 10 August 2012, Kingham, UK.

[20] Ibid.

Eventually, a majority of donors decided to avoid irritating the hegemon, despite their acute sense of 'unfairness'. Accordingly, most channelled their special contributions – equivalent to one-third of their IDA-6 contribution – through the 'FY84 Account' rather than the 'Special Fund'.[21]

The traumatic start put severe strains on the 'fair' burden-sharing relationship between the United States and secondary states. Initially to vindicate American good faith in FY81,[22] other donors had voluntarily waived their pro rata rights (i.e., other donors were entitled to withhold their payments in proportion to any US shortfall at the disbursement stage).[23] However, the reckless US action in FY84 irritated other donors, especially Germany and Japan, once pressed hard by the US into bearing larger shares. Hence, in FY82 and FY83 some donors exercised their pro rata rights as a protest against the US 'breach' of the international agreement.[24] This led to the blunt criticism by the new World Bank President Clausen that the US had 'amputated' the IDA programme.[25]

## 5.2.2 A Unilateral US Share Cut

The dramatic shift in political will translated into the top US negotiating priority in IDA-7 (FY1985–87, negotiated between November 1982 and January 1984): a substantial cut in the US absolute contribution in order to shrink IDA.[26]

A shrinking IDA could help to achieve the Reagan Administration's predominant purpose – '[to] bring developing countries into the Western economic system on a permanently self-sustaining basis'.[27]

[21]  19 donors out of 26, accounting for 68% of the total special contributions for FY84, had decided to make their contribution through the FY84 Account rather than the Special Fund. See IDA-7 Replenishment Agreement, paras. 2.10, 2.11.

[22]  FCO, 'Prime Minister'.

[23]  IDA, 'Meeting of IDA Deputies, Washington, DC, 27–29 September 1981: Chairman's Summary Note', from the World Bank Archives.

[24]  'Views Clash on World Bank Agency', *The New York Times*, 8 September 1982.

[25]  'Clausen: World Economic Situation "Grim"', *The Washington Post*, 7 September 1982.

[26]  US Treasury, United States Participation in the Multilateral Development Banks in the 1980s.

[27]  US, Assessment of US Participation in the Multilateral Development Banks in the 1980s: Consultation Draft, 21 September 1981, from the World Bank Archives.

A diminishing IDA would accelerate graduation of recipient countries, hence moving towards 'greater reliance on market forces' and 'reduced government intervention'.[28] Otherwise, a growing IDA would post-pone weaning countries off official financing, thus thwarting the United States' primary goal of establishing free markets globally.[29] A scarcity of IDA resources would also 'reinforce a more selective approach' to policy conditionality, thus enhancing rather than impairing IDA's leverage over recipient countries in enforcing pro-market economic reforms. The rationale was that most recipients primarily relied on IDA for external financing, as private financing dried up amidst debt crises.[30] Thus, the United States set a ceiling of $750 million on its annual dollar contribution, down from $1,080 million in IDA-6 – a reduction of nearly a third.

Meanwhile, the United States continued to seek a further share cut. It aimed to negotiate a reduction from 27 per cent to 25 per cent.[31] To demonstrate its resolve, it resorted to the Congressional guideline that the US share in future IDA replenishments should not exceed 25 per cent.[32]

As seen in the previous chapter, the United States consciously avoided going too far in share cuts in order to preserve its core influence. This had been previously exemplified in IDA-4, where the Nixon Administration kept the US burden share above a third in order to prevent others from challenging its equivalent IMF voting rights. This was also reflected in IDA-6, where the United States did not cut its share sharply down to 25 per cent as stipulated by Congress. The then US IDA Deputy, C. Fred Bergsten, reasoned that if the United States had gone too far in cutting its shares below the threshold of the mini-mum 'fair' share perceived by other donors, it would have potentially undermined the US influence.[33] To probe how far other donors could tolerate a US share cut, Bergsten based his judgement on how many

---

[28]  Ibid., 103.        [29]  Ibid., 9.
[30]  Statement of the Honourable Beryl Sprinkel (Under Secretary of the Treasury for Monetary Affairs), from Hearing before the House Committee on Banking, Finance and Urban Affairs, 15 June 1982, 6.
[31]  Statement of Hon. Donald T. Regan, 140.
[32]  Public Law 95–481 for FY1979 Appropriations, 18 October 1978.
[33]  Statement of C. Fred Bergsten, from Hearing before the Senate Committee on Foreign Relations, *International Development Association: Funding for the US Contribution to the Seventh Replenishment*, 98th Congress, 2nd Session, 27 March 1984, 57, 59.

share increases he could secure from ascending powers. It turned out that Japan and Germany would not boost their shares any further to offset a bigger US share cut. Hence, the United States resisted the temptation to make a 'unilateral' share reduction (i.e., without being compensated for by corresponding share increases). Bergsten argued that the incumbent Reagan Administration was 'short-sighted', and that the United States should make a higher contribution even at the risk of some arrears in the future.[34] The rationale was two-fold: (a) contributing far below others' expectations of the US 'fair' share would put the US influence in jeopardy; and (b) a precedent of 'uncompensated' US share cut would undermine IDA's burden-sharing principle that any share reduction be fully offset by share increases, hence weakening the deterrent effect on potential share reducers and risking a spiral of 'unjustifiable' share reductions.[35]

During Congressional consultations by the Reagan Administration, Congress also shared the same concern that a precarious US share cut would undercut the US leadership in the World Bank:

Over the long run the US cannot simultaneously maintain its influence in the MDBs and reduce its share of financial contributions. The US must come to terms with this reality. Two courses are open. The US can seek to maintain its influence by sustaining a commensurate level of financial participation. Alternatively, the US can accept some decline in its own influence, while seeking to work closely with other donor nations.[36]

But the new Reagan Administration took a different view on whether a sharp unilateral share reduction might undermine its influence: it anticipated that a progressive reduction in its IDA share would not incur any imminent threat to its influence upon either Bank Management or recipient countries. In principle, it acknowledged the possibility that 'if other significant actors perceive the US is no longer willing or able to continue to play a major financial and leadership role in the MDBs, they may be less likely to be supportive of US policy initiatives in the banks'.[37] In practice, however, Donald Regan, the new

---

[34]  Ibid., 62.      [35]  Ibid., 57.
[36]  Quoted from a report published in 1982 by the House Subcommittee on International Development Institutions and Finance, entitled 'The Future of Multilateral Development Banks'.
[37]  US Treasury, United States Participation in the Multilateral Development Banks in the 1980s, 5.

Treasury Secretary, confidently believed that contributing below international expectations would not 'hurt the US leadership'. Regan maintained that both LDCs and developed countries were structurally dependent upon the US supreme market power for 'their own economic salvation' in the aftermath of the debt crises that erupted in August 1982 (not to mention its Western allies' enduring dependence upon US military protection against a more aggressive Soviet Union), so while others might 'regret' a steep fall in US contribution, they could do nothing but 'recognise' US leadership.[38]

In summary, the shift in the US political will and economic ideology precipitated a dramatic fall in both its absolute and relative contribution to IDA-7, resulting in an unprecedented unilateral share cut of 2 per cent.

### 5.2.3 The Fairness Concern Surges

In parallel with its readiness to shirk its burden, the United States vigorously pursued sweeping policy influence, including shifting IDA resources away from India and China to Sub-Saharan Africa (SSA).[39] This was aimed to achieve its broad goal of accelerating the graduation of recipient countries with access to alternative sources of external capital.

To advance its goal, the Reagan Administration had already exerted influence via both the Board and periodic pressures upon the senior Bank officials since it took the helm in January 1981. During IDA-6 (FY1981–83), the share of SSA had progressively risen to 31.9 per cent, up from 23.7 per cent in IDA-5. Correspondingly, the Indian share had consistently dwindled from a traditional share of 40 per cent since IDA-2 to 34 per cent in IDA-6.[40]

However, the United States was unsatisfied with this slow pace in gaining influence, urging 'further progress in IDA-7 in maturing India into hard window borrowing'.[41] It anticipated that the 'progress'

---

[38] Statement of Hon. Donald T. Regan, 146.

[39] Hearing before the House Committee on Banking, Finance and Urban Affairs, *US Participation in the International Development Association Seventh Replenishment*, 202.

[40] IDA-7 Replenishment Agreement, 'Table 2.3: FY81-83: Allocation of IDA Resources'; 'Table 2.5: IDA's Lending by Region'.

[41] US House, *International Development Association*, 98th Congress, 2nd Session, 10 August 1984, 8.

would be even slower in IDA-7 if the United States did not take any proactive action. The reason was that it perceived that Bank Management and several major donors (especially the UK and Japan) had 'a strong commitment' to maintaining a sizeable IDA programme in both India and China – a new IDA recipient.[42] Thus, the United States deemed it necessary to wield its financial leverage to accelerate the shift in IDA aid allocations from India–China to SSA.

This foreshadowed contentious negotiations on aid allocations, since distributive conflicts were exacerbated by the assumption of member-ship by the People's Republic of China (hereafter referred to as China) in the World Bank in May 1980.[43] After embarking on its reform and opening-up policy, China began to seek external capital. This presented a golden opportunity for the World Bank. Driven by the prospect of extending the Bank's support to a country with a billion people, World Bank President McNamara took personal charge of the membership negotiations with China.[44] Since China's membership would legitimise the World Bank as a truly global institution and substantially widen its client base, the Bank promised that China would get an independent elected seat on the Board and eligibility for IDA's development assistance.[45] Since China joined the Bank after the IDA-6 deal was sealed, it was agreed that China would not get any slice of donor contributions, but would instead receive an amount equivalent to IBRD income transfers to IDA: 3.4 per cent of the total resources.[46] Hence, Bank Management expected China to become a fully-fledged borrower in IDA-7, justified by its 'legitimate needs' as 84 per cent of its vast population lived in extreme poverty.[47] An unspoken motivation

---

[42] Statement of Hon. James W. Conrow, Deputy Assistant Secretary of the Treasury, from Hearing before House Committee on Banking, Finance and Urban Affairs, *To Provide for a United States Contribution to the Special Facility for Sub-Saharan Africa Administered by the International Development Association*, 99th Congress, 1st Session, 18 April 1985, 22.

[43] P.R. China replaced the Republic of China (Taiwan) that initially joined the World Bank in 1945.

[44] World Bank Archives, 'Robert Strange McNamara', http://go.worldbank.org/44V9497H50 (accessed 6 December 2013).

[45] Interview with Percy Mistry, 17 May 2012, Kingham, UK.

[46] World Bank, 'Replenishing IDA Resources: Recent Events and Issues', Prepared for Board Seminar, 15 December 1982, from the World Bank Archives; IDA-7 Replenishment Agreement, 'Table 2.3: FY81-83: Allocation of IDA Resources'.

[47] Percy Mistry, 'Replenishing IDA Resources: Recent Events and Issues', Prepared for Board Seminar on 15 December 1982, from the World Bank Archives.

behind Bank Management's support for greater IDA aid to China was that there was a tacit agreement between China and the senior Bank Management that the ratio of China's borrowing from IDA to that from IBRD should be 4:6. In the high-interest-rate environment of the mid-1980s, China wanted to access relatively cheap IDA credits. Thus, China refused to borrow more money from IBRD unless it obtained a substantial amount of aid from IDA.

This led to a head-on clash between the United States and Bank Management on what counted as 'legitimate needs' – the US maintained that 'poor countries' without access to alternative financing should have 'first claim' on IDA resources,[48] whereas Bank Management, supported by the UK and Japan, contended that each human life had equal value and, thus, IDA should not bias against 'poor people' living in big countries with better performance. In fact, in terms of annual average per capita commitment, SSA countries had already been 'the largest recipients' in IDA-6, receiving \$3.75 compared to \$1.40 for India and \$3.22 for other countries.[49] Consequently, the China allocation question became mired in intense negotiations.

One way of meeting the demands from both big 'blend' countries[50] and SSA was to amplify the total size of the replenishment. Initially, Bank Management proposed that IDA-7 be no less than \$16 billion to maintain the real size of IDA-6. It took six meetings to reach a majority view that IDA-7 should be \$12 billion (equal to IDA-6 in nominal terms). This realistic level was largely compelled by severe budgetary situations in donor countries. Thus, all other donors confirmed their support for this target total *provided* that 'the US took up a share of 25 per cent'.[51] This implied an annual US dollar contribution of \$1 billion.

But the United States was adamant that its annual contribution level would be no more than \$750 million, with a maximum share of 25 per cent.[52] This cap on the US dollar contribution would dictate the total size of IDA-7: as low as \$9 billion if other donors refused to accept any further US share cut to below a quarter.

---

[48]   Statement of Hon. James W. Conrow, 31.
[49]   IDA-7 Replenishment Agreement, para. 2.12.
[50]   India and China borrowed from both IDA and IBRD; thus, they were called the 'blend' countries.
[51]   IDA-7 Replenishment Agreement, para. 3.18.     [52]   Ibid., para. 3.19.

In the hope that the United States could buttress a larger total, Bank Management facilitated a compromise between the United States and the UK/Japan in July 1983 that (a) the share of SSA would go up from 32 per cent in IDA-6 to at least 35 per cent in IDA-7, and (b) a ceiling had to be placed upon the share of India and China, but abrupt changes should be avoided.[53] The United States secured its position by inserting a prescription in the IDA Replenishment Agreement that SSA should receive 'the highest priority' in IDA aid allocations.[54]

Yet despite the concessions made by the UK and Japan, the United States still took an intransigent position on its capped contribution level. As a result, secondary states resented that the United States was a laggard in contributions but was in the vanguard of asserting influence.

On the contribution side, the United States contributed far below its GNP share of 32.49 per cent. Especially, the United States had unilaterally stretched out its IDA-6 contribution, creating a funding crisis in FY84. Thus, the US share of actual disbursements fell below 20 per cent, despite its nominal share of 27 per cent in total donor pledges to IDA-6.[55]

On the influence side, the United States used its privilege of personnel control to spread the free-market tenet known as liberalisation, privatisation, and deregulation in the Bank. In July 1981 the United States nominated Alden W. ('Tom') Clausen as the new World Bank President; he had a 'fundamental commitment to free markets, private flows of capital', was resolved to steer the Bank to focus substantial resources on working to 'free up' markets of developing countries, and 'championed increased structural and sectoral lending'.[56] Another key idea-control position was the Chief Economist. In September 1982, Anne Krueger, a well-known conservative economist, was appointed.[57] She led a series of the annual flagship *World Development Report* that emphasised the importance of getting the overall economic policy framework 'right': namely, opening up trade regimes, avoiding undue

---

[53] Statement of Hon. Donald T. Regan, 174.

[54] IDA-7 Replenishment Agreement, para. 3.6.

[55] IDA, 'Burden Sharing in IDA', IDA-7 discussion paper, 1982, 11, 37, from the World Bank Archives.

[56] World Bank Archives, Alden Winship ('Tom') Clausen, http://go.worldbank .org/DG1E29A900, (accessed 26 December 2012).

[57] Wade (2002: 237–38).

Table 5.1 *Possible Alternative Financing Scenarios for IDA-7*

|  | Scenario 1 | Scenario 2 |
| --- | --- | --- |
| US annual contribution (USD millions) | 750 | 750 |
| US cash contribution (three-year, USD billions) | 2.25 | 2.25 |
| US burden share | 18.75% | 25.00% |
| Total (USD billions) | 12 | 9 |

government intervention, etc.[58] Such one-sided emphasis on free markets was at odds with varieties of capitalism in Europe and Japan.

Eventually, the fairness concern surged as a consequence of a widening US contribution-to-influence discrepancy.

### 5.2.4 Secondary States Collectively Deploy the 'Exit' Option

The US cap on its dollar contribution presented other donors with a stark choice between (1) acquiescing in a much smaller IDA-7 of $9 billion, if they proportionally cut back their absolute contributions in order to avoid the US share falling below 25 per cent, or (2) accepting a much steeper US share reduction of 8.25 per cent (from 27 per cent in IDA-6 to 18.75 per cent in IDA-7), if they continued to support a higher target total of $12 billion (see Table 5.1).

Should the fairness concern play only a little role in IDA replenishment negotiations, secondary states would choose Scenario 1, tolerating a sharper US share cut for the sake of a larger IDA. Yet in IDA-7 the sense of unfairness was so acute that other donors could not tolerate any further US share cut below 25 per cent, let alone a precipitous fall.

Consequently, the fairness concern impelled secondary states to start to deploy the 'exit' option – other donors insisted upon no further US share cut even at the expense of achieving a larger total size of replenishment – in an effort to restore the contribution-to-influence equity line.

The only way to avoid this dispiriting Scenario 2 was to persuade the United States to raise the ceiling on its dollar contribution.

[58] Interview with Anne Krueger, 29 January 2010, from the World Bank's Oral history programme.

To encourage the United States to go above its stringent ceiling, Moeen Qureshi, the then Bank's Senior Vice President for Finance, managed to get many heads of state (e.g., the French President, the British Prime Minister, the German Chancellor, and recipient countries) to write directly to President Reagan to make a case for IDA. Unfortunately these diplomatic efforts proved counter-productive, for Treasury Secretary Regan was piqued by Bank Management bypassing him to go directly to the President.[59]

Pressure also came from the pro-IDA Congressmen who urged the Reagan Administration to reassess its contribution level, which had been pitched 'lower than necessary to achieve passage'.[60] They further argued that the Reagan Administration should not resort to Congressional difficulties as 'a convenient excuse' to defend its dogmatic position when it failed to defend its ideological bias in front of other donors.[61] Given the Reagan Administration's adamant position, Congress complained that the executive branch used ostensible Congressional consultations as 'one-way provision' of 'an early, firm decision' made by the Administration without regard for Congressional opinions.[62]

Despite these pressures from both outside and within the US government, however, the Reagan Administration refused to budge an inch. Consequently, donors settled for a total of $9 billion for the sake of the fairness concern.

The agreed total of $9 billion was deemed 'gravely inadequate' by most Deputies.[63] Yet the US IDA Deputy contended that the fundamental root causes of underdevelopment were not simply lack of resources; rather, the wrong policies were being pursued by developing countries.[64] Hence, the key to success was not simply to expand

---

[59] Interview with the former Senior Vice President for Finance, 27 September 2012, Washington, DC.
[60] Hearing before the House Committee on Banking, Finance and Urban Affairs, US Participation in the International Development Association Seventh Replenishment, 11.
[61] Ibid., 6.
[62] House Committee on Banking, Finance and Urban Affairs, 'International Development Association', Report 98–981, 98th Congress, 2nd Session, 10 August 1984, 7.
[63] IDA-7 Replenishment Agreement, para. 3.20.
[64] Statement of Hon. James W. Conrow, 26.

aid, but to leverage existing resources to promote 'sound' policy reforms.[65]

In summary, the fairness concern was further deteriorating to the point where secondary states insisted upon no further cut in the US share even at the expense of a larger IDA.

### 5.2.5 Postscript: Topping up IDA-7 with a Special Facility for Africa

IDA-7 reversed the traditional pattern of real growth at an average annual rate of about 8 per cent.[66] All donors except the United States agreed that 'additional resources' should be mobilised to bridge the gap between the agreed $9 billion and the generally embraced $12 billion.[67] This led to the question of how to supplement core IDA resources outside the burden-sharing framework.

Two alternative options were proposed: one was a *general* supplementary financing based on the conventional burden-sharing scheme; the other was a *separate* special fund earmarked for Africa on a voluntary basis.

The UK publicly proposed the first option. In January 1984 the UK announced that it would be prepared to take its share of a general supplementary financing scheme of $3 billion on the same burden-sharing basis as IDA-7 including the United States. Yet the latter's involvement was *not* a precondition for UK participation. However, the USA dismissed this proposal, because this initiative would highlight that the United States had singlehandedly dragged down the total size of IDA-7. Other donors did not want to offend the largest donor.[68] In addition, Germany and Japan opposed this UK proposal because they conditioned their participation upon the US contribution due to their acute fairness

---

[65] For instance, 75% of IDA projects with negative rates of return were in SSA with poor policy environment. See: Hearing before the House Committee on Banking, Finance and Urban Affairs, *US Participation in the International Development Association Seventh Replenishment*, 147.

[66] Mistry, 'Replenishing IDA Resources: Recent Events and Issues'.

[67] IDA-7 Replenishment Agreement, para. 3.20.

[68] Interview with the former Bank's Vice President for Finance, Washington DC, 2 August 2012.

concern.[69] Consequently, the idea of general supplemental financing was a non-starter.

An alternative proposal was then put forward by France, calling for the creation of a special assistance facility to provide SSA with fast-disbursing financing.[70] While Bank Management preferred the UK proposal of a general supplementary financing with no strings attached, it sensed that an earmarked separate fund might be a more realistic option. So, Bank Management proposed to establish the *Special Facility for Africa* (SFA) in September 1984.

While the United States took a permissive stance on other donors' participation, it refused to participate in the proposed SFA. Although the United States ardently supported the idea of more aid to SSA, it was concerned that Bank Management might attempt to use this initiative to justify allocating more *core* IDA-7 resources to India and China.[71] Thus, rather than investing in IDA, the United States boosted its support for the AfDF by increasing its cash contribution by half and raising its share in this African Development Bank soft window from 13.1 per cent to 15.4 per cent so as to avoid leaking a penny to India and China.[72]

But Congress opposed the Administration's decision of non-participation in the SFA, which they feared would be perceived as lack of US commitment to multilateral institutions,[73] with consequent exclusion from procurement opportunities generated by SFA operations.[74] Hence, Congress authorised $225 million for the SFA despite the vocal opposition of the US Treasury.[75]

With other donors, ideally they would put up their share of $3 billion in line with the publicly endorsed target total of $12 billion in IDA-7. However, it turned out that only 19 out of 32 donors contributed to the SFA, with total funding of about $2 billion. Five donors (the UK,

---

[69] Mr Timothy Raison, The Minister for Overseas Development, Testimony before International Development Association (Seventh Replenishment) Order 1984, 7 November 1984.

[70] World Bank, 'Toward Sustained Development in Sub-Saharan Africa: A Joint Program of Action', 1984.

[71] Statement of Hon. James W. Conrow, 23–25.   [72] Ibid., 8.

[73] Hearing before House Committee on Banking, Finance and Urban Affairs, To Provide for a United States Contribution to the Special Facility for Sub-Saharan Africa Administered by the International Development Association, 99th Congress, 1st Session, 18 April 1985, 23.

[74] US House, International Development Association, 11.   [75] Ibid., p. 11.

Germany, Japan, Saudi Arabia, and Belgium) lent their support via 'special joint financing' by simply earmarking already-planned bilateral programmes for Africa.[76] This was viewed by the United States as a sign of 'hypocrisy' on the part of other donors who had vowed to support a target total of $12 billion in IDA-7 but proved unwilling or unable to follow through on their promises.[77] Some donors indeed exploited the laggard position of the United States by publicly pledging to contribute more in order to win a reputation as 'generous' donors.[78] In the face of downward US pressure on the total size of IDA-7, other donors started a mild exit by topping up their basic contributions with a Special Facility for Africa.

To conclude, the rise of the 'Reagan Revolution' bred an anti-IDA stance due to a dramatic shift in political will and economic ideology. The Reagan Administration's top priority was to shrink total IDA resources; thus, it demanded a further share cut without ensuring compensating share increases. Meanwhile, the prevailing fairness concern compelled secondary states to initiate an 'exit' in order to avoid any further US share cut. However, they did not challenge the US influence, mainly because they structurally depended upon the hegemon.

## 5.3  IDA-8 (FY1988–90): The Retreat of the 'Reagan Revolution'

In the late 1980s, the United States would have claimed a further share cut and continued to put a cap on its cash contribution in IDA-8 (FY1988–90, negotiated between January and December 1986) had the Reagan Administration succumbed to budgetary constraints. In 1986, the US federal deficit had soared to more than US$ 200 billion, quintupling the annual average in the previous Carter Administration.[79] For the first time, the United States was legally bound to instigate across-the-board cuts to curb yawning budget deficits.[80] The axe would easily fall on IDA, since IDA had no 'strong national constituency to press for financing through the give-and-take'

---

[76]  World Bank Annual Report 1988, 36.
[77]  Statement of Hon. James W. Conrow, 22.
[78]  Interview with the former UK IDA Deputy, 16 March 2012, Oxford, UK.
[79]  Source: IMF, Government Finance Statistics.
[80]  It was known as the Gramm-Rudman Budget Act.

that characterised the US legislative process.[81] Indeed, Congress found it hard to justify any slight increase in the dollar contribution to IDA-8 over IDA-7. Meanwhile, anti-IDA Congressmen persistently pressed for a further share reduction, for they contended that Germany and Japan continued to 'free ride' on American generosity in the defence of the free world and thus should contribute more of their abundant surpluses to address the Third World debt problem.[82]

Yet contrary to the prediction of a passive US participation, the United States honoured its traditional share of 25 per cent and increased its dollar contribution by 28 per cent in IDA-8. This section examines what motivated the United States to buttress its financial support for IDA in this period.

In its second term, the Reagan Administration made a dramatic turnaround in its policy towards IFIs, for it came to appreciate their value for leveraging resources to combat international debt crises. A business-as-usual approach would have undercut the essential US interests: the imminent danger of debt defaults would bring the US banking system to the brink of collapse; and prolonged debt servicing difficulties had dried up the foreign reserves of developing nations, undercutting US exports.[83]

After an initial setback due to relying on IMF's emergency measures alone, the United States resorted to a growth-lifting strategy to fight debt crises in developing countries. The United States had led a campaign to increase the IMF funding to help indebted LDCs to meet short-term debt obligations. But such a short-term emergency measure proved inadequate to pull the developing world out of the debt trap. The United States saw that the crisis ran deeper, demanding a growth-lifting strategy. Accordingly, the newly appointed Treasury Secretary, James A. Baker III, initiated the 'Baker Plan' at the Annual World Bank/IMF Meetings in October 1985, aimed at using creditors'

---

[81] Statement of Hon. James A. Baker III, Secretary of the US Treasury, from Hearing before the US Senate Committee on Foreign Relations, *Multilateral Development Banks Authorization Requests*, 100th Congress, 1st Session, 25 February 1987, 17.

[82] Ibid., 40, 50.

[83] The US had the highest stake in resolving debt crises, for 40% of US exports went to LDCs compared with an average of 25% of OECD countries. Congressional Quarterly, *US Foreign Policy: The Reagan Imprint* (Washington, DC: Congressional Quarterly, 1986), 120.

financial leverage to promote market-oriented policy reforms in debtor countries to rejuvenate growth.[84]

To put the 'Baker Plan' into action, the United States assigned the World Bank a more important role in making the transition from fiscal austerity to renewed growth. The Bank was superior to its bilateral aid programmes in enforcing policy conditionality because the latter often subordinated policy conditionality to strategic security concerns.[85] Moreover, Congress precluded the US bilateral aid agency allocating substantial funding to heavily indebted developing countries, being wary of bailing out reckless commercial banks at the risk of breeding further rounds of imprudent lending. Hence, under strong pressures from Congress, the Reagan Administration had to count on IFIs to play the lead role in helping to renew growth in indebted developing countries.[86]

But inadequate funding had stalled the Baker Plan.[87] To leverage more resources, the United States had high stakes in augmenting the total size of IDA-8. While the major debtors of US commercial banks were located in indebted middle-income Latin American countries,[88] the Reagan Administration was concerned that official debt servicing problems in low-income African countries were so severe that they would declare default that might spread to other developing regions.[89]

After re-discovering IDA's value, the United States reverted to its traditional negotiating tactic of deploying its financial leverage for desired policy influence. In a confidential letter from Secretary Baker to the Bank's President Clausen, the United States strategically wielded both sticks and carrots to press for policy changes, mainly in IDA recipient countries.[90]

Dear Tom,
    The specific policy changes we are seeking are:

---

[84] James A. Baker III, 'Statement before the Joint Annual Meeting of the World and the International Monetary Fund', Summary of Proceedings, Seoul, South Korea, 8 October 1985.
[85] Feinberg (1987, 155).
[86] Gwin, 'US Relations with the World Bank, 1945–1992', 234.
[87] World Bank lending was constrained by capital inadequacy.
[88] A General Capital Increase for IBRD, endorsed by the US Treasury, was approved by the Board of Executive Directors in 1988.
[89] Rothchild and Raven (1987: 418).
[90] Letter from US Secretary of Treasury, James A. Baker III, to the World Bank President, Mr A. W. Clausen, 13 January 1986, from the World Bank Archives.

- Lending terms: a reduction of maturities and grace periods and an increase in interest charges;
- A lending program that emphasizes and supports directly the private sector;
- A larger proportion of the total lending program dedicated to policy based lending – particularly in Sub-Saharan Africa; a stronger push by the Bank to get major debtor countries to move toward market oriented economic policies, i.e., fair but strong conditionality which will not be compromised;
- A larger IDA share for Sub-Saharan Africa

With these policy changes, I believe a replenishment in the $9 to $12 billion range may be feasible.

We recognize some of these changes will not be easy; but they are essential.

A failure to act much more quickly could very well jeopardize the program that we have all agreed is needed.

Bank Management and other donors were by no means passive rule-takers. They exploited the US desire for policy changes by exaggerating how divergent their initial positions were from those of the United States in order to solicit a higher US contribution. For instance, the UK IDA Deputy internally proposed that the UK should 'exploit any element in the US position which exerts downward pressure on the total without showing ourselves to be simply their running dogs'.[91] In anticipation of others' tactics, the United States deliberately adopted a more extreme policy position in order to make others feel that they had achieved a good bargain with the USA.

Accordingly, the total size, burden-sharing, and policy changes were negotiated as a package, because Bank Management and other donors reserved their positions on policy changes unless the United States clarified its stance on the target total and its burden share.[92]

In proposing a negotiating range for the target total, Bank Management learnt lessons from IDA-7, where its ambitious bidding figure came out 'prematurely' and 'found itself in a confrontational position with the US'. In IDA-8, Bank Management adjusted its

---

[91] 'IFAD and IDA-8', from Rex Browning (IDA-7 UK Deputy) to Mr Buist (IDA-8 Deputy), 8 January 1986, from the UK National Archives, *International Development Association (IDA): Its Future Direction and the Eighth Replenishment*, OD57/15.

[92] IDA, 'IDA's Scale of Operations, Terms and Allocations in the Eighth Replenishment', IDA/RPL/85–4, 27–28 January 1986, para. 3.32, from the World Bank Archives.

negotiating strategy by indicating the lowest bound of the negotiating range at the level of $12 billion in order to maintain the real level of IDA-7 and the SFA combined,[93] and then gradually built donor support for a larger total.[94]

Other donors maintained that they would not increase their contributions to support the proposed target total of $12 billion unless the United States took its 'customary' share of 25 per cent.[95]

The prevailing fairness concern motivated other donors to insist upon no slightest US share cut. First, the United States had been contributing far less than its GNP shares[96] – 'the most acceptable' measure of 'ability-to-pay' in the eyes of most donors.[97] Second, the United States had asserted disproportionate influence on how to govern IDA, perceived by others to be disproportionately greater than its burden share. Since IDA-4 the United States had persistently cut its share but amplified its influence (with an exception in IDA-5, where the United States maintained its share and exercised self-restraint at the height of the North–South power struggles). Such a contribution-to-influence disparity was further exacerbated in IDA-6, where Congress unilaterally imposed its will upon Bank Management to serve its narrow foreign policy interests. Then, the discrepancy continued, deteriorating in IDA-7 where the United States adamantly claimed a substantial share cut and pushed through sweeping policy changes driven by its idiosyncratic economic ideology. Last but not least, the United States shirked its broader responsibility of maintaining a viable international economic system. On monetary policy, the United States had prioritised its domestic policy imperatives over its international responsibility for maintaining a stable exchange rate. To fight inflation, the United States had tightened money supply and boosted governmental

---

[93]  Ibid., 3.

[94]  'IDA Public Affairs Strategies', Office Memorandum, from Frank Vogl, IPA, to Moeen Qureshi, et al., 17 October 1985, from the World Bank Archives.

[95]  Interview with the former Bank Senior Vice President for Finance, 16 August 2012, Washington DC.

[96]  Due to the appreciation of the US dollar and rapid economic growth, the US GNP share went up dramatically, from 32.49% in 1981 to 41.27% in 1984. See 'Table 3.1 Revised Burden-Sharing Statistics' in IDA-7 Replenishment Agreement; 'Table 3.2 Selected Burden-Sharing Indicators' in IDA-8 Replenishment Agreement.

[97]  'Mr. Boehmer (German IDA Deputy)'s Request for Burden Sharing Indicators', Official Memorandum, 9 December 1985, from the World Bank Archives.

borrowing, pushing up interest rates. As a result, foreign investors flocked to the United States, driving up the value of the dollar and rendering international currency markets extremely volatile. But to the dismay of its allies, the United States resisted the pleas of the Europeans to intervene and advocated a hands-off approach to exchange rates.[98] On trade policy, in sharp contrast to the US generosity in providing market access to Europe and Japan in the past, the Reagan Administration provoked its allies into 'a trade war' by seeming to 'bully' them to pursue narrowly defined US interests.[99] In sum, secondary states demanded that the United States maintain its minimum 'fair' share of 25 per cent.

To achieve a successful IDA-8, the United States decided to refrain from claiming a share reduction. In the face of the vocal demands from other donors for a 25 per cent US share, Secretary Baker came to believe that if the United States was to 'continue to exercise leadership' in addressing debt crises, it must be willing to commit its 'fair' share.[100] Otherwise, the US zeal for share reduction would approach a tipping point where a further reduction would 'significantly' impair its ability to influence IDA's decision-making.[101]

Subsequently, the sticking point hinged on whether Bank Management and other donors would accommodate the US policy demands – (a) the terms of IDA credits, and (b) aid allocations – in exchange for US support for a larger total.

Regarding the terms of IDA credits, the United States aimed to harden the terms by (a) reducing maturities from 50 to 30 years, (b) shortening the grace period from 10 to 8 years, and (c) charging interest rates of around 3 per cent for blend countries, notably India and China.

Even though the United States justified its proposal on economic grounds, IDA interest-free and long-term credits were excessively cheap compared with commercial loans, due to a spike in market interest rates. But others perceived the United States to be motivated by dogmatic ideology. In particular, they felt that the US demand on the interest charge was an 'essentially political slogan' for the US Treasury to sell IDA to Congress, since Congress contended that it made little

---

[98] Congressional Quarterly, *US Foreign Policy*, 118.    [99] Cohen (1987: 134).
[100] Statement of Hon. James A. Baker III, 12.
[101] Hearing before the US Senate Committee on Foreign Relations, *Multilateral Development Banks Authorization Requests*, 36.

sense to plough IDA funds into the Chinese economy to augment its substantial international reserves.[102]

Other donors contended that the proposed changes were too harsh, with two potential repercussions: first, hardening the terms could worsen borrowers' debt servicing profile; second, this would hasten repayments to IDA – an effective substitute for new donor commitments in future replenishments. But they indicated they were willing to consider 'modest' hardening if there was a real prospect of an increase in the total size of IDA-8.[103]

What made others even less reluctant to cede concessions to the United States was that the United States refused to commit itself to any 'price tag' – how much additional contribution it was ready to make to 'buy' policy concessions from others. At the third replenishment meeting other donors reached a consensus on their reservation point – the grace period should *not* be shortened and *no* interest rates should be introduced. But other donors still reserved their position on whether to shorten maturities in the hope that the US could credibly promise to go above the lowest bound of the total size ($9 billion).

In parallel with negotiations on hardening the terms were deliberations over aid allocations. Specifically, the United States attempted to achieve two goals: (a) further moving away IDA credits from India and China to SSA; and (b) increasing Structural Adjustment Lending (SAL) with harsher conditionality by strengthening IMF–World Bank collaboration.

On geographical allocations, the United States had successfully increased the share of SSA from 31.9 per cent in IDA-6 to 35 per cent in IDA-7.[104] Taking into account the SFA, the SSA share would go up to 44 per cent. However, the United States was not content with this, complaining that progress was 'still too modest and not fully responsive to the IDA Deputies' recommendation in IDA-7 to accord highest priority to this region'.[105] While Bank Management attributed the slow pace to limited absorptive capacity in Africa, the United States

[102]  IDA, 'IDA Eighth Replenishment Meeting of Deputies, Paris, Monday and Tuesday, 27–29 January 1986: Chairman's Summary Note', 29 January 1986, from the UK National Archives, OD 57/15.
[103]  ODA, 'IDA 8 Negotiations, 27–28 January 1986, Paris', 31 January 1986, ibid.
[104]  Statement of James W. Conrow, Deputy Assistant Secretary for Developing Nations, from Hearing before the US House Select Committee on Hunger, *The World Bank in Africa*, 100th Congress, 1st Session, 23 July 1987, 19.
[105]  Ibid., 9

contended that the lack of progress was due to a strong commitment at the Bank and amongst the donor countries (especially the UK and Japan) to maintain sizeable IDA programmes in the two big giants.[106]

To secure its influence, the United States pushed hard to expand the authority of the informal donor forum and sought to specify *numeric targets* for credits allocated to SSA – 50 per cent of IDA resources should go to Africa – in the IDA-8 Replenishment Agreement. Such targets could effectively limit the autonomy of Bank Management and the power of the Board of Executive Directors where both India and China had an independent elected seat.

This proposed target received mixed feedback from donors. On the one hand, France wholeheartedly supported the United States as it was perfectly aligned with its priorities. Scandinavian countries were sympathetic to the US proposal, for African famines were in the headlines, arousing their humanitarian concerns. On the other hand, however, the UK and Japan persistently opposed the US attempt and maintained that allocations to the major blend countries in nominal terms should not be reduced.

Bank Management took advantage of the US desire for a greater SSA share by promising that the SSA share would be raised as the total size of IDA rose. On the other hand, a flat IDA-8 at the level of $9 billion would result in a stagnant African share.

On the SAL, the United States pursued the goal of more fast-disbursing loans with stronger policy conditionality, especially in SSA. It proposed that more IDA-8 resources be earmarked for SAL in conjunction with the IMF's Trust Fund reflows.[107]

As to the balance between the new SAL and traditional investment lending, most donors took a cautious approach to expanding SAL. They believed that the Bank's primary function was investment lending and that it should not become involved in quick-disbursing or lending too fast.[108] They also perceived that the United States was attempting

---

[106] Ibid., 22, 30.

[107] This proposal was first tabled in the IMF's Board discussion in September 1985 without any prior consultation. 'IDA-8: US Proposal for an IMF/Bank Program to Promote Economic Adjustment', from Ernest Stern (Senior Vice President for Operation) to Members of the Managing Committee, 16 September 1985, confidential OPS/MC85-53, from the World Bank Archives.

[108] Interview with the former Bank Senior Vice President for Finance, 16 August 2012, Washington DC.

to 'extricate the IMF from its arrearages problems with its poorest borrowers'.[109]

As to strengthening policy conditionality, Bank Management initially resisted US pressure, perceiving the strident US demands as a 'politically-oriented thrust'. If Bank Management was seen to pander to the United States, it would undermine its 'politically independent character'. That could prove counterproductive in bringing about right policy reform in recipient countries in the long run.[110]

Previously, Bank Management had pushed back against the US pressure through the Board of Executive Directors, in order to defend its independent professional judgement and ensure that the pace of adjustment was in line with political stability and laid the foundation for growth.[111]

But now Bank Management and other donors agreed to make policy concessions on SAL if the United States supported a larger total target of $12 billion. A discussion paper prepared by Bank Management maintained that the absolute level of project lending (mainly allocated to big blend countries) should be maintained, and proposed that an increase in adjustment lending could only be accommodated if there was an increase in the total size of IDA-8.[112]

Subsequently, the negotiations reached a climax: shortening of maturities, the SSA share, and the share of SAL all hinged on the US position towards the total size.

Eventually, the United States pledged its support for a 25 per cent share of a target total of $11.5 billion (with an annual contribution of $958 million, up from its threatened baseline of $750 million) in order to achieve its desired policy influence.

In return for an increased US contribution, other donors ceded the following policy influence and reached compromise with the US.

On the terms of IDA credits, other donors agreed to reduce maturities from 50 years to 40 years for the least-developed recipient

---

[109] 'Managing Committee: US Proposal for an IMF/Bank Program to Promote Economic Adjustment', 20 September 1985, from the World Bank Archives.
[110] World Bank, 'US Position on MDBs', from Moeen A. Qureshi (Vice President) to A. W. Clausen (President), 8 July 1985, confidential (declassified), from the World Bank Archives.
[111] Interview with the former Bank's Senior Vice President for Finance, 16 August 2012, Washington DC.
[112] IDA, 'IDA's Scale of Operations, Terms and Allocations in the Eighth Replenishment'.

countries (or, 'IDA only' borrowers) and to 35 years for others.[113] The more lenient terms for 'IDA only' countries were introduced because this was the only way to secure Nordic agreement to the deal. Although they were small donors, their voice counted because the IDA Deputies made decisions by consensus.[114]

On the SSA share, it was agreed that 'all efforts should be made by the Association [IDA] to allocate to countries in Sub-Saharan Africa 50 per cent of the resources available under IDA-8, if warranted by progress with their economic adjustment programmes, and at a minimum of 45 per cent of such resources'. Meanwhile, it was agreed that 'nominal allocations to the major blend countries not be reduced' and their share should be around 30 per cent.[115]

On SAL, donors agreed that 'increased emphasis should be given to the use of IDA-8 resources for adjustment lending'.[116] The IDA Replenishment Agreement stipulated that $3–3.5 billion of total IDA-8 resources might be used for adjustment support.[117] Thus, adjustment support as a proportion of total lending would increase from 14 per cent in IDA-7 to 25–30 per cent in IDA-8. Moreover, for many African countries, more than one-half of IDA-8 support was likely to take the form of fast-disbursing adjustment lending.[118]

But the $11.5 billion total was below the general will of $12 billion, because the US Administration feared that Congress would vote down a bill as high as $1 billion per annum (replaying the bad precedent it set in IDA-6). Given the heightened Congressional hostility amidst budgetary constraints, it would be 'foolish, if not suicidal' to come up with a billion-dollar request in Congress.[119]

Once again, the US downward pressure on the target total confronted other donors with a dilemma of whether they should support a higher total target of $12 billion entailing a US share reduction, or accept a lower total of $11.5 billion so as to avoid any slight US share cut. As in IDA-7, other donors tactically agreed to settle for a lower target total lest it legitimise any slight fall in the US share.

---

[113] IDA-8 Replenishment Agreement, para. 5.3.
[114] UK Steering Brief, 'IDA Deputies Meeting: Washington: 23–25 September 1986',1986, from the UK National Archive, OD57/12.
[115] IDA-8 Replenishment Agreement, para. 4.6.    [116] Ibid., para. 4.8.
[117] Ibid., para. 4.8.
[118] Statement of James W. Conrow, from Hearing before the House Committee on Hunger, *The World Bank in Africa*, 19.
[119] Statement of Hon. James A. Baker III, 39.

In summary, the US maintained its share to augment total IDA resources in IDA-8, partly because it rediscovered the value of IDA in tackling the debt crises, and partly because the fairness concern compelled secondary states to demand a 'customary' US share of 25 per cent.

## 5.4 A UK–Japan Quid Pro Quo Enables '*Accelerated Burden-Shifting*'

As learnt from earlier chapters, power struggles over voting rights between ascending powers on the one side and waning powers and the hegemon on the other side was a recurring theme in shaping IDA burden-sharing dynamics. A UK–Japan quid-pro-quo deal between voting rights and burden shares helps to explain *Accelerated Burden-Shifting* in IDA-7 in the form of a substantial UK share cut of 3.4 per cent, fully compensated by a Japanese share increase.

As seen in the previous chapter, Japan was the protagonist in wielding IDA contributions to gain IBRD voting rights. Yet Japan achieved only modest progress in the 1970s, because neither the hegemon nor the waning UK had an interest in IDA expansion. Hence, Japan had failed to realise its institutional aspiration to become the second largest IBRD shareholder. Moreover, Japan realised that the slow adjustment in the IMF governance structure meant that the conventional 'parallelism' between IMF quota shares and IBRD voting rights would fall short of its expectations. The IMF's GQR-8 was concluded in March 1983, keeping the traditional pecking order of the Group of Five (G-5) intact – while Japan was already the second largest economy, it remained the fifth largest IBRD shareholder, behind the UK, Germany, and France.

IDA-7 negotiations (from November 1982 to January 1984) became the critical battlefield for Japan to get its 'deserved' position in the IBRD. Its success crucially depended on whether the UK was willing to cede its seat as the second largest shareholder to Japan.

A radical overhaul of UK aid policy presented Japan with a golden opportunity to make a quid-pro-quo deal with the UK. The new Prime Minister Margaret Thatcher called for a radical shift from multilateral aid to bilateral aid. The shift in political will was based on the belief that bilateral aid served British national interests better. Thus, the

'Thatcher Revolution' necessitated a substantial UK share reduction in IDA-7.

Despite its determination to make a steep share cut, the UK had a strong incentive to seek out and target share increasers to make good its shortfall. Why?

First, a share cut would entail a political risk of undercutting the UK influence both within and beyond the World Bank, because its IDA burden share symbolised a commitment to international responsibility that justified the UK influence well beyond IDA. To mitigate this political risk, the UK desired to secure share increases from others to fill the UK gap.

Second, in the same vein, the UK wanted to avoid taking the blame for jeopardising the IDA replenishment. The '100% total' burden-sharing principle remained strong in IDA-7: any share reduction had to be fully compensated for by share increases; 'settling for an actual replenishment lower than 100% was simply a way of camouflaging an unsuccessful replenishment negotiation'.[120] In practice, the financing gap had to be kept under the ceiling of 5 per cent.

A bilateral deal with Japan on trading IDA burden shares with IBRD voting rights helped the UK to achieve a share cut without taking too much political risk.[121]

To mitigate the distributional conflict involved in ceding voting rights, the UK managed to gain assurances that it would preserve the second largest position in the IMF and retain its appointed seat on the Bank's Board, thus keeping its substantive influence intact. Furthermore, the UK felt that its preferences were largely in line with those of the Japanese, such as allocating aid to Asia. This helped the UK feel more comfortable in ceding formal influence to Japan. Ultimately, a swap between Japan and the UK was made.[122]

After striking a deal with the UK, Japan faced the next hurdle of gaining support from the United States. The Reagan Administration took advantage of Japan's ambition to become the second largest IBRD shareholder; hence, the United States pressed Japan hard to make

---

[120] Interview with Senior Advisor to Senior Vice President for Finance, Mr Percy S Mistry, 17 May 2012, Kingham, UK.

[121] Japan doubled its ODA budget in dollar terms within five years in order to maintain good relationship with the United States in other bilateral areas.

[122] Interview with the former UK Alternate Executive Director, Oxford, UK, 24 October 2012.

concessions in bilateral negotiations on the liberalisation of Japan's financial markets and internationalisation of the yen.[123] Initially, Japan resisted US pressure to make concessions on these economic issues in exchange for IBRD voting rights. But the United States blamed Japan for blocking a timely agreement on IDA-7.[124] In exchange for US support, Japan finally committed to certain financial liberalisation measures in April 1984, before the passage of the resolution on the 1984 SCI.[125]

Finally, a viable UK–Japan deal required a 'green light' from Germany and France, since each member in the World Bank enjoyed a 'pre-emptive right' – the liberty of increasing one's own subscriptions in order to preserve one's shareholding intact in the context of SCIs. Neither Germany nor France wanted to be negatively influenced by a switch of position between the UK and Japan.[126] The UK did not want to drop below France, because it would signal a decline in its international status vis-à-vis France. France boosted its burden share by 1.22 per cent to almost reach parity with the new UK burden share of 6.7 per cent in an effort to tie the fourth largest IBRD shareholding position with the UK. Germany cut its basic share by 0.5 per cent to express its grievance over the failure to gain an increase in its IBRD voting rights as it expected in boosting its IDA-6 contribution (as shown in the previous chapter). Japan boosted its share by 4.05 per cent in exchange for its desired No. 2 IBRD shareholder position. During the IDA-7 negotiations, it was ensured that the combined IDA burden share of the UK, France, Germany, and Japan was no less than it was under the previous replenishment.[127] Thus, the IDA-7 Report clearly stated that 'The [burden] share of France, Germany, Japan and the UK were based on understandings reached among these countries concerning their relative standings in the share capital of IBRD'.[128]

To conclude, the UK–Japan swap was largely driven by the UK desire to mitigate the political risk of a substantial UK share cut in IDA. It was

---

[123] Rapkin, Elston and Strand (1997: 176–77).
[124] 'Briefing for IMF/IBRD Annual Meeting in 1984', from UK National Archives, OD 57/19.
[125] Ogata (1989).
[126] 'Selective Increases in IBRD Capital Subscriptions, memorandum to the Executive Directors', 6 December 1983, from the World Bank Archive.
[127] Interview with the former UK IDA Deputy.
[128] IDA-7 Replenishment Agreement, para. 3.26.

also facilitated by synergistic interests between the UK and Japan. This highlighted the symbolic value of IDA burden shares in signalling donor commitment to international responsibility so as to preserve their influence well beyond IDA.

## 5.5 The 'Hidden' US–Japan Quid Pro Quo

Despite the breakthrough after the UK–Japan swap in 1984, Japanese officials regarded Japan's 'current status as an insufficient return for its contributions' to IDA.[129] Although Japan's economy had surpassed the German economy by a wide margin and was challenging the economic strength of the United States, its IBRD shareholding was only slightly above Germany and far behind the United States – the supreme shareholder with veto power.

Once again, Japan deployed 'cheque-book diplomacy' in IDA-8, seeking to secure a more solid No. 2 position. Japan used both 'sticks' and 'carrots' at the same time. On the one hand, it threatened to 'go back to 12 per cent' of IDA burden share if it could not achieve a further increase in IBRD shareholding to 8.5 per cent (an increase of 3 per cent).[130] Japan justified its claim for share reduction by arguing that this would yield the same ratio of IDA burden share to IBRD voting rights as Germany – i.e. a ratio of 2.2.[131] On the other hand, it promised to make a substantial additional 'supplementary contribution' if an increase in its IBRD voting rights materialised. Unlike the quasi-obligatory basic burden share that would be taken as the starting point of the negotiation in future IDA replenishments, a 'supplementary contribution' was a purely voluntary endeavour. Hence, Japan aimed to reduce the cost of its proposal by putting forward this one-off deal between IDA contribution and IBRD voting rights.

What made Japan's bid more compelling and credible was the favourable yen/dollar exchange rate. Through the 1980s, Japan's

---

[129] Rix (1987: 23).
[130] Meeting between Sir Crispin Tickell and Mr Qureshi, 9 June 1986, World Bank Archives.
[131] 'Informal Economic and Financial Affairs Council (ECOFIN) 19–20 September 1986; IMF/IBRD Meetings: World Bank Issues: IDA 8', September 1986, from UK National Archives, IDA: Its Future Direction and the Eighth Replenishment, OD 57/21.

national currency (yen) had appreciated significantly against the US dollar, in which IDA contributions were denominated. Japan could easily increase its contribution in dollar terms by more than 40 per cent with the same amount of its IDA-7 contribution in yen terms, thus incurring no additional budgetary cost. Moreover, Japan's aid budget was also booming.

Japan's bid was high, for the concession of 3 per cent of IBRD votes was hard to swallow for other major donors. Major donors made use of the Group of Seven (G-7) Tokyo Summit in May 1986 to sound out the reservation point of Japan. It was concluded that Japan would probably continue to maintain its 18.7 per cent IDA burden share if it could be guaranteed additional IBRD voting rights of 1.5 per cent.[132]

Accommodating Japan's aspiration thus hinged on whether the United States was willing to cede some IBRD voting rights in exchange for Japan's financial support for IDA-8. As mentioned earlier, the United States had rediscovered the value of the World Bank-IDA in tackling debt crises in developing countries, and was thus striving to enlarge IDA-8; yet the fairness concern of secondary states limited the total size of IDA-8 to $11.5 billion in order to keep a constant US share. Thus, the United States had a strong interest in playing on the Japanese desire to strengthen its international profile to urge a substantial increase in Japan's supplementary contribution.

Yet ceding IBRD voting rights of 1.5 per cent or more would threaten the US veto power. To preserve its core influence, the United States insisted on the amendment of the IBRD Articles of Agreement to increase the supermajority vote from 80 per cent to 85 per cent. Thus, even if the US IBRD voting rights dropped below 20 per cent, it could still retain its veto power. The US move revealed the unceasing power struggle in multilateral financial institutions: bids for more voting rights by any one member have to be 'accommodated' on the basis that 'the interests of other shareholders were not impaired'.[133] Accordingly, the United States signalled its willingness to cede voting

---

[132]  Ibid.
[133]  'Agreements of the Executive Directors of the Bank: Increases in Subscriptions of Certain Members to Capital Stock', Summary of Proceedings: 1987 Annual Meetings of the Boards of Governors, Washington, DC, 29 September– 1 October 1987, 246.

rights to Japan, if Japan would make a special contribution of around $1 billion to IDA above its basic contribution.[134]

What made the bargaining process more complicated was that Japan's bid for a further increase in its IBRD voting rights provoked associated bids from a number of other donors.

Japan's bid first provoked France to ask for more votes to take it above the UK in IBRD shareholder ranking. This was absolutely unacceptable from the UK perspective.[135] The UK took a hard line in IDA-8: it was non-negotiable for the UK to drop from the joint fourth place with France to a solitary fifth place. Due to strong opposition from the UK, France quit its bidding.

But this was not the end of the story. Italy was a third bidder in this power struggle. Unlike Japan, which had made a sustained and substantial IDA contribution in the past, Italy's bid for extra IBRD shares proposed only a one-off supplementary contribution of $250 million. This proposal was regarded at first as a case of wishful thinking and did not gain much support from other IDA donors. So far, Japan's cheque-book diplomacy had established an unwritten principle that IBRD voting rights should be adjusted to reflect a track record of cumulative IDA contributions. Italy's bid was not justified on a cumulative basis. Should it materialise, it would set a bad precedent – donors could use a 'one-off' supplementary contribution to buy a permanent increase in IBRD voting rights. (The increase in IBRD voting rights was permanent, because members have 'pre-emptive rights' to enable them to have control over future transfer of any of its shares and no one could take it away without the consent of shareholders concerned.)

What made the situation more complicated was that Italy's bid provoked a counter-bid by Canada, because Italy would jump up several places in IBRD shareholdings if it succeeded.[136] Italy hoped to raise its rank in the IBRD from No. 10 to No. 6, surpassing Canada, ranked ninth among IBRD shareholders.[137] Thus, Canada joined Italy

---

[134]  Talking Points for Discussion with Secretary Baker, IDA-8, confidential, from the folder entitled 'Financial Advisor: IDA – Deputies Meeting', 1986, from the World Bank Archives.

[135]  'Informal Economic and Financial Affairs Council'.

[136]  UK Steering Brief, 'IDA Deputies Meeting: Washington: 23–25 September 1986', September 1986, from the UK National Archive, *International Development Association (IDA): Its Future Direction and the Eighth Replenishment*, 1985–86, OD 57/21.

[137]  Ibid.

in expressing willingness to raise their shares in IDA in exchange for an increase in their IBRD shareholding.[138]

Donors were compelled to settle these competitive bids for IBRD voting rights in order to conclude the IDA-8 negotiation on time. Otherwise, IDA would run out of fresh money and stop committing new loans. The risk was that this complex IBRD voting-rights struggle would provoke endless bidding. Thus, donors tried to facilitate a deal which would give Italy and Canada parity.[139]

Timing was key. When IDA-8 negotiations had to be concluded in December 1986, the deal on IBRD voting-rights adjustment had not been fully settled. Thus, to mitigate the uncertainty of providing additional aid without gaining expected influence, these bidders withheld part of their IDA-8 contributions until they secured their desired voting rights. It was the first time that the linkage between the IDA contribution and IBRD voting rights was explicitly acknowledged in an IDA Replenishment Agreement.[140]

Finally, the United States ceded 2 per cent of its IBRD voting rights to Japan, Italy, and Canada.[141] In return, Japan made an additional supplementary contribution of $450 million. The total Japanese contribution to IDA-8 rose by more than half in dollar terms and 8 per cent in yen terms (see Table 5.2). In total, the actual sum of donor contributions to IDA-8 reached $12 billion.

In summary, the United States ceded its IBRD voting rights to Japan in exchange for Japanese financial support for IDA-8. It was a 'hidden' quid pro quo because Japan made a supplementary contribution outside the burden-sharing framework to 'buy' IBRD voting rights. The primary reason for this successful quid pro quo was that the United States held a strong interest in enlarging IDA.

## 5.6 Conclusion

What insights can be drawn from an analytical look at this period of IDA's history?

---

[138] 'Visit of Mr. Conable to Ottawa', Canada, 11–12 September 1986, from the World Bank Archives.
[139] Ibid.    [140] IDA-8 Replenishment Agreement, para. 1.3.
[141] Resolution No. 416, 'Increase in Subscriptions of Certain Members to Capital Stock', 13 April 1987.

Table 5.2 *Linkage between IDA Contributions and IBRD Voting Power Adjustments in 1986–87*[142]

| | IDA Contributions | | | IBRD Shareholding Adjustments | | |
| | IDA-7 Burden Share | IDA-8 Basic (B) *plus* Supplementary (S) Contributions | Change in Basic Burden Shares | Before | After | Change in IBRD Voting Power |
| --- | --- | --- | --- | --- | --- | --- |
| **United States** | 25% | 25% | 0 | 20.91% | 18.91% | –2.00% |
| **Japan** | 18.7% | 18.7% plus $450 m (S) | 0 | 5.19% | 6.69% | +1.50% |
| **Italy** | 4.30% | 5.30% plus $90.5 m (S) | + 1% | 2.87% | 3.20% | +0.32% |
| **Canada** | 4.50% | 5.00% plus $28.75 m (S) | + 0.50% | 3.02% | 3.20% | +0.18% |

[142] 'Share Reallocation in the Context of IDA-8', 20 August 1986, the World Bank Archives. In addition, the Netherlands and Korea also made share increases and/or supplementary contributions to gain additional IBRD voting rights. But their demands were accommo-dated via other sources of IBRD voting shares rather than from the USA.

The wax and wane of external threats in the middle and late 1980s lead us to expect that the United States could have kept its share in IDA-7 and made a steep share cut in IDA-8. Yet what we observed is exactly the opposite: a unilateral US share cut of 2 per cent in IDA-7 and a constant US share in IDA-8. Political will in domestic politics played a key role in resolving these puzzles, because it profoundly shaped the US willingness-to-contribute and hence its negotiating position at the international level. A dramatic shift in political will and economic ideology was the primary reason for the first-ever uncompensated US share cut in IDA-7. The new Republican Reagan Administration held a fundamental belief in free markets, which translated into its top priority of shrinking IDA. Hence, the United States put a non-negotiable ceiling on both its absolute and relative contributions. By contrast, in IDA-8 the Reagan Administration rediscovered the value of the World Bank in working to solve debt crises. Accordingly, the USA refrained from claiming a share reduction even in the face of vocal Congressional demand for share cuts, because it decided to meet the others' expectation on its minimum share in order to gain desired influence on policy fronts. This partly explains the *Hegemonic Lag* in IDA-8.

A US–Japan quid pro quo between voting rights and burden shares did occur, when the United States rediscovered the value of IDA in IDA-8 and thus desired to cede voting rights in IBRD to Japan in exchange for an increased Japanese financial contribution to IDA. Meanwhile, another quid pro quo took place between the UK and Japan in IDA-7, where the UK ceded its second largest IBRD shareholding to Japan in return for a boost in the Japanese burden share in IDA. A close look at history reveals that this quid pro quo occurred not because the UK had a strong interest in augmenting IDA, but because the UK desired to mitigate the political risk of its ideologically motivated share reduction in IDA.

When it comes to the informal donor influence upon Bank Management, the fairness concern gained much more significance in the 1980s because the Reagan Administration shirked its burden but amplified its policy influence. On the contribution side, the United States contributed far below its GNP share and unilaterally decided not to participate in the financing of IDA in FY84 due to the accumulation of unsustainable arrears. On the influence side, the USA used its privileged position to control high-level personnel positions (such as

President and Chief Economist) to spread the free market ideology and pushed through pro-market policy changes.

To restore the notional equity line between contributions and influence, secondary states started to deploy the 'exit' by agreeing upon a smaller target total in order to avoid any further US share cut. The exit was mild, because they simultaneously topped up IDA via a separate facility or supplementary contributions. Yet they delayed the 'voice' option, as evidenced by the fact that the United States gained most of its policy influence with far-reaching impact on the Bank's operations, because they were structurally dependent upon the hegemon for economic recovery amidst debt crises and for military protection against the hostile Soviet Union.

The next chapter will explore IDA burden-sharing in the 1990s in the wake of the collapse of the Soviet Union. The end of the Cold War was a watershed in IDA replenishment history, as no unifying external threat existed outside the Western bloc. Would internal donor struggles over fairness prevail in shaping IDA burden-sharing dynamics?

# 6 IDA in the 1990s: The Struggle for Power and Fairness in a Unipolar World

This chapter aims to address the puzzles of (a) what triggered a steep fall in the US share in IDA-9 without any compensating share increase from other major donors ('*Accelerated Burden-Shifting*'); and (b) why the US share stabilised at around 20 per cent in IDA-11/-12 despite its economic revival ('*Hegemonic Lags*'). It also examines whether the correlation between a mild drop in the US GNP share and a modest cut in the US share in IDA-10 was a causal relationship.

Here we organise the four replenishments (from IDA-9 to IDA-12) in one chapter because their common background was the zenith of the US hegemony. The imminent collapse of the Soviet Union heralded the arrival of the 'unipolar moment' where the US stood at the pinnacle of world power.[1]

## 6.1 Empirical Puzzles

In IDA-9 the US share dropped from 25 per cent to 21.61 per cent, but other major donors did not increase their shares to make good this substantial US shortfall.

A preliminary examination seems to show that the first layer of power play between the US-led donor group and the external threats explains the puzzle well. As the Soviet threat was fading away, the hegemon no longer had an interest in expanding IDA. Thus, it was quite likely that the United States would cut its share without bothering its allies to fill the consequent IDA funding gap.

Yet this substantial US share cut is puzzling from the 'fairness' perspective. As seen in the previous chapter, the fairness concern motivated secondary states to insist upon a 'customary' US share of 25 per cent in IDA-8. If fairness had been a persisting concern, we

---

[1] Krauthammer (1990: 23–33).

would expect that other donors would have refused to accept such a big US share cut in IDA-9.

Was it because the US participation in IDA demonstrated its self-restraint on a global strategic level, thus alleviating the acute sense of unfairness among secondary states? This appears plausible, as it is argued that its unrivalled power capabilities would incentivise the United States to bind itself in multilateral rule-based institutions in order to signal its strategic self-restraint to weak states.[2] More ground needs to be explored here to uncover why secondary states accepted a significant US burden-share deficit.

In IDA-10, the US share fell mildly, by 0.75 per cent. At first glance, it is not puzzling from the 'capacity-to-pay' perspective, given a mild decline in the US GNP share.

But this modest US share cut in IDA-10 poses a puzzle from the 'external threat' perspective. As explained above, as the Soviet threat vanished, the United States would be much more likely to have claimed a much steeper share cut (as it did during the decade of the détente in the 1970s). What held the United States back from seeking a much sharper share reduction?

In IDA-11/-12, the United States kept a constant share of 20.86 per cent despite its economic revival in the late 1990s. Here, the baseline 'capacity-to-pay' explanation would predict successive US share increases, leaving '*Hegemonic Lags*' unsettled.

The '*Hegemonic Lags*' are equally puzzling from the 'external threat' standpoint. The United States took a leadership role in founding IDA to accommodate the Third World's demand for aid and thus to help contain the Soviet Union. As IDA had successfully accomplished its original mission as envisaged by its chief architect, it is reasonable to expect that the United States would claim substantial share cuts, if not move to outright withdrawal.

Was it because the United States rediscovered the value of IDA as it did in IDA-8, hence sustaining its financial support? Or, was it because secondary states were again preoccupied with the fairness concern and thus refused to legitimise any US share cut?

The following sections tackle the three outstanding empirical puzzles. Section 6.2 examines why secondary states accepted a steep US share reduction in IDA-9. Section 6.3 explores why the United

---

[2] Ikenberry (2001).

States made a modest share cut in IDA-10. Section 6.4 uncovers what accounted for the '*Hegemonic Lags*' in IDA-11/12. Finally, the key findings are summarised.

## 6.2  IDA-9 (FY1991–93):[3] North–South Struggles Suspend the Fairness Concern

As George Bush senior came into office in January 1989, the United States was at the apex of world power, as the Soviet Union was on the verge of collapse. The Bush Administration reoriented its grand strategy towards the Bretton Woods Institutions. Instead of deploying IDA as a geopolitical tool against its bipolar rival, President George Bush senior laid out the new grand strategy of spreading the US core values of 'economic freedom and political freedom' worldwide at the annual meetings of the Boards of Governors.[4] Specifically, he highlighted the Bank's role as 'a fundamental tool' for enforcing policy conditionality in indebted developing nations as a precondition for receiving debt reduction.[5] Rather than dismantling IDA, therefore, the hegemon aspired to maintain 'an active leadership role' in the World Bank to integrate developing countries into a liberal-capitalist world order.[6]

But the renewed US aspirations for leadership in the World Bank did not automatically translate into a strong preference for augmenting total IDA resources. Rather, the United States believed that IDA could fulfil its new missions with no need to expand its resources. The lost decade of debt crises in the 1980s had deprived most recipient countries of external private financing, so they had no viable alternative financing other than Western aid. Thus, IDA had sufficient financial leverage to enforce conditionality on aid-dependent recipient countries. Therefore, the United States no longer led the drive to enlarge IDA. This stood in stark contrast with the US leadership for IDA expansion in the 1960s to

---

[3]  IDA-9 covered FY1991–93, negotiated between February and December 1989.

[4]  Opening Remarks by the Hon. George Bush, President of the United States, from *1989 Annual Meetings of the Boards of Governors: summary proceedings*, Washington, DC: World Bank, 1990, 1.

[5]  Ibid., 174.

[6]  Statement of Hon. Nicholas F. Brady, Secretary of the Treasury, from Hearing before the Senate Subcommittee on Foreign Operations, Export Financing, and Related Programmes Appropriations for FY1991, S. Hrg. 101–1093, Part I, 3 April 1990, 175.

win hearts and minds in the Third World in fierce aid contests with the Soviet Union.

The US leadership aspirations contrasted with its bleak budgetary constraints. President Bush inherited a burdensome deficit from the Reagan era that rocketed to over $166 billion in 1988.[7] A tight-fisted Congress was desperate to curtail budgetary deficits. And worse, dollar depreciation severely undercut US ability-to-contribute.

In short, the lukewarm support for IDA expansion and the eroding US capacity-to-pay help to predict a substantial US share cut.

But they are only partial explanations, for history indicates that such a substantial US shortfall would be pre-empted if the fairness concern continued to impel secondary states to insist upon a constant US share.

Why, then, did the fairness concern appear to have become subdued? Was it because the United States refrained from unilaterally seeking policy influence, thus alleviating the influence-to-contribution disparity?

A closer examination reveals that the fairness concern remained prevalent among secondary states. In fact, the discrepancy between the US contribution and its influence was widening.

On the contribution side, other donors complained that the United States contributed far below its 'fair' share. In a discussion paper entitled 'IDA-9 Burden Sharing', the United States emerged as the single major donor that failed to embrace the 'capacity-to-pay' principle, contributing less than half of its GNP shares (adjusted for income per capita).[8] Furthermore, other donors were upset by a repeated pattern of US failure to honour its financial commitments on time.

On the influence side, secondary states resented that the United States dominated World Bank governance to a degree far greater than its nominal burden share would warrant. A senior Canadian official complained that 'the US uses the World Bank as an instrument of geopolitics, and it reaps the whole benefit at a bargain price of $1 for every $4 spent [i.e., the US share of 25 per cent]'.[9]

What made secondary states feel even more resentful was that Congress unilaterally asserted its will upon Bank Management. Congress complained that the Bank consistently opposed

---

[7] IMF, *Government Finance Statistics.*

[8] IDA, *IDA-9 Burden Sharing*, IDA-9 Discussion Paper, (June 1989), 14–15.

[9] Solomon (1989).

US economic, political, or ethical interests as legislated by Congress – every US-opposed loan since 1977 had been approved by the Board. To reassert its authority, Congress threatened to deny any new funding to IDA.[10] In order to secure Congressional support to keep IDA afloat, Barber Conable, a long-serving and popular Republican congressman, was appointed as World Bank President. His assignment was to 'convince his former colleagues that the Bank was reforming itself and deserved continued funding by the American taxpayer'.[11] Hence, Congress enjoyed a convenient contact point to mould the Bank to its will.

The fairness concern remained prevalent so that secondary states should have good reason to insist upon no further US share cut. Why, then, did secondary states seem to have postponed their countermeasures?

As seen in the previous chapters, secondary states might delay their corrective measures if they were structurally dependent upon the hegemon and/or lacked viable outside options. Such delay in the 'exit/voice' option was exemplified in the 1970s when Japan and Germany compensated for substantial US share cuts and other donors ceded influence to the United States.

Yet it turned out that there was little reason for any further delay in IDA-9 (FY1991–93, negotiated between February and December 1989). First, as the Soviet Union was on the verge of collapse, Japan and Germany were less concerned about the threatened US troop withdrawal. They also diversified their export markets, lessening their economic dependence upon the United States. Second, more viable outside options became available to donors. This was reflected in Bank Management's anxiety to secure donor money in the face of competitors. An internal official memorandum warned that 'a sales talk about [financing] needs is likely to be counterproductive' because the real question was 'why money should be given to IDA'.[12]

In sum, secondary states should have not tolerated a substantial US shortfall, since less structural dependence and more viable outside options would have expedited their countermeasures.

Then why did secondary states seem to subordinate their fairness concern?

[10]  Tammen (1988).      [11]  Caufield (1997: 178).
[12]  'Proposed Schedule for First IDA9 Meeting', from Ernest Stern to Messrs Jaycox, Karaosmanoglu, and Rajagopalan, 2 December 1988, from the World Bank Archives.

A close look into the negotiation process uncovers that a North–South power struggle subordinated the internal donor struggle over fair burden-sharing, thus compelling other donors to accept a steep US share cut.

In the absence of a unifying Soviet threat, Western donors discovered a new common interest in gaining collective influence upon developing nations' environmental policies via the World Bank's financial leverage. As the stewards of taxpayers' money, donor governments were under mounting pressure from NGOs to improve aid effectiveness. Among burgeoning priorities, environmental protection was high on the agenda. While Bank Management had already taken initiatives to address environmental concerns, NGOs lamented that the progress was too modest and too slow.[13] Accordingly, NGOs mounted a lobbying blitz to urge donor governments to use IDA replenishment negotiations to press for further policy changes.[14]

IDA replenishment negotiations presented a superb opportunity to gain influence over Bank Management because donors could withhold contributions until policy reforms were done. By comparison, alternative means of influence seemed less effective. First, although donors enjoyed a lion's share of voting rights on the Board of Executive Directors, they were impatient with the slow progress in policy deliberation with recipients and borrowing countries which often got bogged down in polarising views. Second, unlike the regular three-year interval of IDA replenishment, the IBRD's General Capital Increases took place only sporadically, as it primarily raised funds from capital markets with much less financial dependence upon donors.

But developing countries strongly opposed donors usurping the power of the Board and using environmental concerns as 'a disguised instrument' to impose proliferating conditionality at the sacrifice of their economic development.[15] Their stance was informed by the lessons in the 1980s – a decade of debt crises where debtor nations had borne the brunt of adjustment burdens, because donors enforced harsh conditionality via IFIs.[16]

---

[13] Friedland (1987); Leighty (1989).    [14] Darst (1987).    [15] G24 (1989).
[16] Statement of Mailson Ferreira da Nobrega (Brazil), Governor of the Bank and Fund on behalf of the countries of Latin America and the Philippines, from *1989 Annual Meetings of the Boards of Governors: summary proceedings*, Washington, DC: World Bank, 1990, 55, 57.

This was not merely a battle between Western donors and IDA recipients, but, rather, a power struggle between industrialised nations and developing nations as a whole (including both IDA recipients and IBRD borrowers). IBRD borrowers suspected that rich countries were attempting to use IDA replenishments as a 'back-door' means of imposing undue environmental safeguards across the World Bank Group: IDA and IBRD were administered by the same management, so IDA's guidelines could easily extend to IBRD operations. In principle, policy conditionality for IBRD loans could differ from those for IDA credits, since they were legally independent institutions. In practice, however, the same Bank staff followed a single 'Operations Manual' that specified operational policies and Bank procedures. Therefore, developing nations, led by Brazil, India, and China,[17] insisted that no more environmental safeguards be imposed upon their national development projects unless Western donors offered additional financial assistance. They maintained that incorporating environmental safeguards into development projects involved additional costs – a trade-off should be balanced by a national decision-making process rather than being dictated by an external donor group. Furthermore, industrial countries had 'a major responsibility' for global environment problems, so they should take concrete action to redress the damage. Finally, it would be unfair for rich countries to exploit poor countries' financial reliance on the Bank to force them to bear 'disproportionate obligations'[18] since the Bank's leverage to check environmental damage by rich countries was limited.

In the face of such strong resistance from developing nations, Western donors could not afford to turn a blind eye, since IBRD borrowers were starting to access private capital (even though most IDA-only recipients were aid-dependent).[19] So, the donor group sensed

---

[17]  In 1989 Brazil was an IBRD borrower and became a new IDA donor in IDA-6 (*FY1981–1983*); India and China were 'blend countries' receiving both IDA and IBRD credits. Collectively, the three countries borrowed more than a quarter of total IBRD loans and IDA credits from 1982 to 1988. Source: World Development Indicators.

[18]  Statement of S. B. Chavan (India), Governor of the Bank and Fund, from *1989 Annual Meetings of the Boards of Governors: Summary Proceedings*, 96; Statement of Li Guixian (China), Governor of the Fund, 65; Statement of S. B. Chavan (India), 96.

[19]  IDA, *IDA in the Context of Multilateral Concessional Flows*, IDA-9 Discussion Paper, May 1989, from the World Bank Archives.

that if the total size of IDA-9 fell short of developing countries' expectations, the collective donor objective of enforcing environmental safeguards would be defeated. Hence, a well-funded IDA-9 was necessary to soften the firm position of developing nations.

Yet, as foreshadowed earlier, the erosion in the US fiscal capacity meant that the United States could not afford its traditional share of a decently large IDA-9 equal to IDA-8 in real terms – that is, SDR11.68 billion.[20] Wild dollar depreciation meant that the USA had to increase its dollar contribution by 30 per cent in order to barely stand by its traditional share. This was clearly politically infeasible in a belt-tightened Congress. Congress was increasingly hostile towards IDA because NGOs blamed the World Bank for aggravating chronic poverty in Africa and damaging the planet.[21] Such antagonism sabotaged the passage of stand-alone bills for authorising US participation in IDA replenishments throughout the 1980s. Consequently, the IDA bill had to be hidden into must-pass 'omnibus' bills to save the day.[22]

The United States' inability to support a larger total confronted other donors with the dilemma of whether they were willing to accept a US share reduction for the sake of a larger total. History tells us that other donors had collectively settled for a lower total in order to avoid legitimising any slight US share reduction in IDA-8. Had this practice persisted, IDA-9 would have resulted in a severe cutback in the total size of replenishment.

Initially, other donors were so reluctant to compromise their fairness concern that they insisted that the United States keep its traditional share of 25 per cent.

As pressures from developing countries built up, however, other donors had to prioritise achieving a larger total over preserving their sense of fairness. Otherwise, their common objective – leveraging aid for policy changes in developing nations – would have been thwarted.

Ultimately, donors supported a total target equal to IDA-8 in real terms and accepted a substantial US share reduction of as much as 3.39

---

[20] Since IDA-9, donor contributions were denominated in SDRs instead of USD to mitigate consequences of volatile dollar fluctuations.

[21] Hearing before the House Committee on Banking, Finance, and Urban Affairs, *The Ninth Replenishment of the International Development Association (IDA)*, 101st Congress, 2nd Session, 28 March 1990.

[22] The US Congress, *Congressional Quarterly Almanac* (Washington, DC: Congressional Quarterly Inc., various years).

per cent.[23] Furthermore, they promised to top up IDA-9 by establishing a special environmental fund (later known as the Global Environment Facility, [GEF]) – outside IDA and administered by the World Bank – to demonstrate their *additional* financial support for environmental protection.[24]

But no other major donors were willing to compensate for the 'unwarranted' US share cut. Germany even took a step further and made a token share reduction of 0.5 per cent (simultaneously offset by its own special supplementary contribution) to signal its indignation against the 'unjustified' US share cut.[25]

As a result, the 'financing gap' soared from less than 1 per cent in IDA-8 to over 6 per cent in IDA-9, largely due to the US gap. Bank Management solicited supplementary contributions and used 'creative accounting' to narrow the 'unallocated gap' down to 0.49 per cent in order to mitigate any negative impacts of the weakening '100% total' burden-sharing principle.[26]

The comparison between IDA-8 and IDA-9 illustrates how donors deliberated on the trade-off between accomplishing a larger total and protecting the sense of fairness in determining IDA burden-sharing dynamics. In both cases, the United States could not afford its traditional share against a total target that kept pace with inflation. In IDA-8, preserving the fairness principle took precedence over reaching a larger total, thus resulting in a *Hegemonic Lag*, whereas in IDA-9 the North–South power

---

[23] The US finally pledged $3,180 million, a 10% increase over its IDA-8 level in dollar terms, to reward Bank Management for making its desired policy changes, including: (a) more weight given to 'performance' in aid allocation criteria; (b) disclosure of environmental assessment information to the public; and (c) strengthened IDA-IMF collaboration in structural adjustment programmes. See Basil G. Kavalsky (Director of IDA's Resource Mobilisation Department) 'Possible Remarks for Mr. Stern for the Washington (5th) Meeting for your comments', 6 September 1989, from the World Bank Archives; Statement of Hon. Nicholas F. Brady.

[24] Telephone interview with the former director of IDA Resource Mobilisation Department, 15 September 2012.

[25] Ernest Stern (IDA-9 Chairman, Senior Vice President for Finance), 'Mobilizing Resources for IDA: The Ninth Replenishment', *Finance & Development* 27, no. 2 (1990): 23.

[26] By 'creative accounting', Bank Management granted additional credit to donors that accelerated their disbursements without incurring any additional budgetary cost. Telephone interview with the former director of the IDA Resource Mobilisation Department, 15 September 2012.

struggle compelled donors to give priority to achieving a larger total even though it entailed a substantial US share cut.

In summary, the fairness concern was temporarily downplayed by secondary states because their common interests in influencing environmental policies in developing countries necessitated a decently large total size of IDA-9. Hence, they accepted a substantial US share reduction, generating a significant case of '*Accelerated Burden-Shifting*'.

## 6.3  IDA-10 (FY1994–96): A Delicate Balancing Act between Contribution and Influence

The imperative to reach a larger size of IDA replenishment became more urgent in IDA-10, as the North–South power struggle culminated in the United Nations Conference on Environment and Development (known as 'Rio/Earth Summit') in June 1992. At the strong urging of developing nations, industrialised countries recognised the need to provide additional financial assistance to compensate for extra costs of integrating environmental needs into development projects.[27] Furthermore, the G-7 pledged to give additional financial support via IDA-10 in July 1992 in order to encourage developing countries to implement national action plans for environmental protection.[28]

Against this favourable background, Lewis T. Preston, the new Bank President, harnessed the momentum to urge 'a real increase' in IDA-10 (FY1994–96, negotiated between January 1992 and December 1992).[29] To solicit donor support, Bank Management strategically proposed two alternative funding scenarios for the target total – a low case of SDR13 billion to keep the real value of IDA-9, and a high case of SDR16.25 billion. To incentivise donors to support the high-case scenario, Bank Management promised that greater total donor contributions could 'stimulate both borrowers and staff to

---

[27] United Nations, *Agenda 21: United Nations Conference on Environment & Development, Rio de Janerio, Brazil, 3 to 14 June 1992* (accessed 24 February 2014).

[28] G7 Summit Communiqué, *Economic Declaration: Working Together for Growth and a Safer World* (Munich, Germany, July 6, 1992).

[29] Annual Address by Lewis T. Preston, President of the World Bank Group, Summary of Proceedings of Annual Meetings 1992, 17.

institutionalise more quickly their commitment to improving environ-mental quality'.[30]

But most industrial countries could not support a real increase in the target total of IDA-10 because they faced stringent fiscal constraints. The axe fell on aid budgets.[31] Countering this donor reluctance, Bank Management urged that it was important to 'maintain the practice of insulating multilateral concessional loan replenishments from short-term budgetary constraints to the maximum extent possible'. Otherwise, a flat IDA-10 would 'damage the credibility of the donors' commitment'.[32]

To divert pressures for a real increase, donors instructed Bank Management to explore how IDA reflows could be used to top up fresh donor contributions. This led to a contentious debate on whose money IDA reflows should be counted as. Historically, donor contri-butions were the principal source of IDA's financial resources, since the terms of IDA loans were so favourable (e.g., long maturity) that reflows did not accumulate in noticeable scale until IDA-9 (accounting for about 10 per cent of the grand total).[33] Bank Management viewed reflows as internal institutional money that 'no longer belonged to donors',[34] whereas donors maintained that reflows originally stemmed from past donor donations. Recipients of IDA could argue that reflows were partly attributed to their prudential financial management in making revolving funds viable. Indeed, as IDA reflows started to pile up in IDA-8, some senior Bank officials proposed that reflows should entitle recipients to more voting rights in order to address the democratic deficit in IDA's governance structure. But this proposal was a non-starter due to anticipated opposition from powerful shareholders.[35]

Under the spotlight of publicly declared recognition of additional financing, however, other donors felt more compelled to stretch their budgets to at least maintain IDA funding in real terms. Moreover, they

---

[30] IDA, *The Programme Implications of the Size of IDA-10*, IDA-10 Discussion Paper, June 1992, 15–16, from the World Bank Archives.
[31] IDA, *IDA-10 Size and Burden Sharing*, IDA-10 Discussion Paper, November 1992, 2, from the World Bank Archives.
[32] Ibid., 1–2.     [33] IDA-9 Replenishment Agreement, para. 35.
[34] IDA, *IDA-10 Burden Sharing*, IDA-10 Discussion Paper, 1 June 1992, 22, from the World Bank Archives.
[35] Interview with a former senior Bank staff member, 5 October 2012, Washington, DC.

promised to complete the first GEF replenishment (FY1995–98) earmarked for environmental protection as soon as the IDA-10 agreement was sealed.

Once more, other donors faced an unpleasant dilemma between accomplishing a larger total or preserving their sense of fairness, because deteriorating US fiscal ability again put a cap on the US dollar contribution. This was further exacerbated by continued dollar depreciation.

Eventually, as the North–South tensions intensified, donors were compelled to reach a decently large IDA-10. And, once again, other donors decided to subordinate their fairness concern to accept a substantial US share cut for the sake of a larger total.

But unlike IDA-9, where the United States acquiesced in its sharp share cut, the United States stretched its budgetary resources to avert a much steeper share cut in IDA-10. Since other donors became more lenient about a steep US share cut at the height of North–South struggle, the US burden share would have dropped by at least 4 per cent from 21.61 per cent to 17.69 per cent, assuming that it could at best maintain its dollar contribution in nominal terms. Yet it turned out that the United States found the budgetary resources to avert a much steeper share cut in IDA-10. It stepped up its dollar contribution by 18 per cent, and hence maintained its share above 20 per cent even in the face of growing discontent in a Congress that had instructed the Bush Administration to cut back on its dollar contribution.[36]

What motivated the United States to increase its cash contribution? Was it because it had made additional contributions in order to harvest donor-specific interests (e.g., a substantial boost in the US procurement benefits and/or aid allocations)? If yes, then was there a causal link between an increase in contribution and a boost in donor interests?

Regarding procurement benefits, the data shows that the United States registered a mere $18 million in procurement in FY1994, whereas its annual IDA contribution was as high as $1 billion.[37] As developing countries won more procurement contracts, major donors suffered a substantial loss in procurement benefits, which

---

[36] Hearing before the Senate Subcommittee of Appropriations, *Foreign Operations, Export Financing, and Related Programs Appropriations for FY1990*, S. HRG. 101–359, Pr. 1, 30 September 1990.

[37] World Bank, *Contract Awards under Bank-Financed Investment Projects*, http://go.worldbank.org/GM7GBOVGS0 (accessed 25 February 2014).

amounted to only a fraction of their financial contributions. As domestic development constituencies in donor countries vigorously pushed their governments to end the privilege of their national firms in winning procurement contacts of aid projects, donors generally put less emphasis upon procurement gains.[38] Had procurement benefits been the primary driving force behind donor contributions, the United States would have substantially cut its contribution.

In terms of aid allocations, since the mid-1980s the United States had consistently strived to raise the share of aid allocations to SSA. This was partly driven by the Reagan Administration's economic ideology of cutting off aid from big blend countries, and partly motivated by the demand from Congressional black caucus. The Bush Administration sustained this priority to realise its grand strategy of building a liberal-capitalist world order. But the share of SSA was fairly stable during this period, in the order of 45 per cent. Thus, the analytical factor of 'country-specific interests' offers little guide in explaining enhanced US support for IDA.

If tangible donor-specific interests fail to explain an increase in the US dollar contribution, then what else might have motivated the United States to buttress its support for IDA? As shown in the previous chapters, the United States boosted its contribution to reward Bank Management for its newly gained influence. The following section looks into replenishment negotiation processes to find out whether the United States succeeded in using money to buy more influence.

IDA-10 coincided with two high-profile events that severely tarnished the public image of the World Bank and eroded donor confidence in the credibility of Bank Management's implementation of donor prescriptions on the ground.

The first was India's Sardar Sarovar dam, viewed as a test case of the Bank's willingness to enforce its own environment and social safeguards. Although an independent review recommended that the Bank withdraw from this project due to violation of its own policies, the Board decided to continue funding the project, despite strong opposition from the US and another five Executive Directors in October 1992.

---

[38] These lobby efforts culminated in the untying aid agreement in 2001. See Development Assistance Committee (DAC), *Recommendation on Untying ODA to the Least Developed Countries*, April 2001.

The second was a far-reaching internal report by the Task Force on Portfolio Management (known as the 'Wapenhans Report'). It pinpointed that problems besetting the Sardar Sarovar project were 'more the rule than the exception'. It also highlighted that project quality was deteriorating because a deep-rooted 'culture of approval' rewarded the disbursement of new loans rather than effective management of existing projects. Moreover, the report found that the lack of borrowers' ownership had encouraged staff to take control of the project design process, hence the later reluctance to cancel bad projects.[39]

Consequently, international NGOs intensified their denunciations of the World Bank; its misuse of public money was contributing to further indebtedness, social inequity, and environmental destruction.[40] Furthermore, they stepped up their lobbying efforts to urge Congress to be the driving force for advancing efficiency, accountability, and transparency in the World Bank.

In response to these civil society demands, the United States was in the vanguard of pushing through sweeping reforms. It threatened to cut its cash contribution if it failed to achieve the following changes in the bank: (a) improving the quality of project implementation;[41] (b) establishing an independent appeals mechanism (later known as the Inspection Panel) to investigate claims of policy violations brought by people who had suffered adverse impacts of the Bank's projects; (c) comprehensively revising the Bank's Information Disclosure Policy to address the NGOs' complaints that the Bank failed to provide timely information; and (d) forcing China to graduate from IDA.[42]

Yet not all of these US proposals gained wholehearted support from other key stakeholders. First, IDA recipients and IBRD borrowers were sceptical about the motives behind the Inspection Panel because they feared that it might be manipulated as a process to pressure them into accepting conditionality not required under loan agreements. The Bank's senior staff also resisted the external pressure and argued

---

[39] World Bank (1992a).    [40] Pallas (2013).
[41] US General Accounting Office (GAO), 'Multilateral Development: Status of World Bank Reform', June 1994, 15.
[42] Statement of Hon. Lawrence Summers, Under Secretary for International Affairs, US Department of the Treasury, from Hearing before the House Committee on Banking, Finance, and Urban Affairs, *Authorizing Contributions to IDA, GEF, and ADF*, 103rd Congress, 1st Session, 5 May 1993.

that 'an *ad hoc* inspection capacity' would suffice.[43] Second, some major donors saw little rationale for pioneering transparency in the World Bank since their domestic executive branches did not disclose information to legislative branches on such an unprecedented scale.[44] Last but not least, Japan, supported by the Europeans, argued strenuously against graduating China from IDA on the ground that continued engagement with this giant borrower would support China's poverty alleviation and environmental improvements.[45]

Consequently, these US attempts at influencing the Bank's performance ended up with mixed results. A look at the record shows that the US:

1. Succeeded:
    - in inserting a provision in the Replenishment Agreement that called on the Bank to develop a reform plan to improve the quality of project implementation in response to the recommendations of the Wapenhans Report[46] (the Board approved an action plan in June 1993, with eighty-six time-bound actions);[47]

2. Partially Succeeded:
    - in reducing the share of 'blend borrowers' (receiving both IBRD and IDA loans) from 40 per cent to 30–35 per cent with the tacit agreement that China would bear the brunt of this cut. But it failed to force China to graduate.[48]

3. Failed (or left pending):
    - to establish an independent Inspection Panel;
    - to overhaul the Bank's Disclosure Policy.

Despite its failure to gain all its desired influence, the United States counter intuitively boosted its dollar contribution. Rather than cutting its dollar contribution as threatened by Congress, the Bush Administration

---

[43] Shihata (2000: 17).    [44] Statement of Hon. Lawrence Summers.
[45] Secretary Lloyd Bentsen, 'How can we Improve the Banks?', from Hearing before the Senate Foreign Operations Subcommittee of the Senate Appropriations Committee, *Multilateral Funding and Policy Issues*, 27 April 1993.
[46] IDA-10 Replenishment Agreement, para. 41.
[47] GAO, 'Multilateral Development: Status of World Bank Reform', 16.
[48] IDA-10 Replenishment Agreement, para. 56.

increased its cash contribution so that its share slipped by less than 1 per cent, thus keeping above 20 per cent.

What, then, held the US back from materialising its threat? The answer lies in its desire to preserve its 'Major Donor' status, as granted to donors whose basic burden share was greater than 20 per cent.

Why did the 'Major Donor' status matter?

Symbolically, the United States was the single donor entitled to the 'Major Donor' status, signalling its unrivalled and indeed preponderant influence. So far the United States had been the single donor enjoying this privileged status. Japan cautiously kept its *basic* share below the 20 per cent threshold to avoid challenging the predominant US position in IDA, even though it was fiscally capable of doing so. Successive doubling of its ODA targets took Japan in 1989 to the extraordinary position of overtaking the United States for the first time, thereby becoming the largest donor in the world. Indeed, the sum of the Japanese basic contribution (18.7 per cent) and supplementary contribution (3.91 per cent) in IDA-8 surpassed the threshold of 20 per cent. (It is worth noting that the symbolic value of IDA burden share was unique since IDA was the pre-eminent global development institution, outshining the RDBs. By comparison, Japan overtook the United States as the largest donor in both the AfDF and the AsDF.[49])

Substantively, the 'Major Donor' status endowed the United States with much more financial leverage than its absolute contribution would have indicated. First, the IDA Replenishment Agreement could not come into effect unless it received more than 80 per cent of total donor commitments; thus, the United States enjoyed a de facto 'veto power'. Second, the pro rata rule entitled other donors to reduce their contributions in proportion to any shortfall of the Major Donor's annual appropriation. Thus, a US threat of withholding funds could trigger a domino effect upon other donors.

Therefore, the United States felt compelled to keep its share above the crucial threshold in order to preserve its influence, both symbolically and substantively, in the long run.

In summary, the United States significantly increased its dollar contribution to avoid making a much steeper share cut in IDA-10,

---

[49] 'IDA9 Burden-Sharing', from Mary O. Smith (Chief Officer, FRM) to Ernest Stern and Joseph Wood, 14 September 1988, from the World Bank Archives.

despite the failure to gain all its desired influence, in a bid to keep its 'Major Donor' status intact so as to preserve its influence in the future.

## 6.4  IDA-11(FY1998–99)/IDA-12(FY2000–02): The Fairness Concern Renews '*Hegemonic Lags*'

In contrast to the successive share cuts in IDA-9/-10 negotiated in the late 1980s and the early 1990s, the US share stabilised at the level of 20.86 per cent throughout the mid-/late-1990s. What prevented any further US share cut?

One possible explanation is a shift in political will in favour of IDA. As seen from the previous chapter, the Republican Reagan Administration shifted away from its anti-IDA stance in IDA-8 (FY1988–90, negotiated between January and December 1986), hence maintaining the US traditional share in order to augment total IDA resources.

At first glance, this explanation appears plausible. The Republican Bush Administration was succeeded in 1992 by the Democratic Clinton Administration, which was in charge of the two successive replenishment negotiations. It is reasonable to expect that this new Democratic Administration, which coincided with a Democratic Congress, restored the democratic tradition of pro-multilateralism and thus buttressed US financial support for IDA.

However, this optimistic expectation of US leadership is at odds with reality. The US annual contribution to IDA-11 (FY1998–99, negotiated between September 1994 and March 1996) was reduced by about 36 per cent – an even sharper cut than that in IDA-7 when the most hostile Reagan Administration was at the helm. Meanwhile, the total size of IDA-11 shrank by more than two-fifths relative to IDA-10 on an annual basis.

It turns out that the Clinton Administration was mired in bureaucratic and Congressional politics to cut aid budgets to reduce the federal deficit. Congress frequently exercised its power of the purse by dramatically cutting the president's foreign aid requests and imposing proliferating conditions. From the president's point of view, this created 'inappropriate congressional micromanagement'. To mitigate 'excessive legislative interference in the conduct of America's foreign policies', the Clinton Administration in early 1994 attempted to eliminate Congressional earmarks and revamp the foreign aid programmes in pursuit of broad foreign policy goals.[50] It articulated the strategy of 'enlargement' aimed to help 'democracy and market economies take root', which in turn expanded and strengthened the wider Western democratic order.[51] But Congress was unwilling to 'relinquish its right to place a legislative imprimatur on American foreign policy'.[52] Amid the adverse environment of 'aid fatigue', the White House even opposed mentioning 'aid' in the president's speeches, let alone any administrative initiative.[53]

Historical insights inform us that secondary states insisted upon a customary US share if their fairness concern was acute, as happened in IDA-8 negotiated in 1986. This offers us a clue to whether the fairness concern prevailed again in explaining the '*Hegemonic Lags*'.

### 6.4.1 The North–South Power Struggle Recedes

As described above, North–South power struggles temporarily subordinated the fairness concern so that secondary states tolerated successive US share reductions in IDA-9/-10 in the late 1980s and the early 1990s for the sake of a decently large total size of replenishments.

Yet the trend of a declining US share was arrested in IDA-11/-12. Was it because the North–South power struggle subsided, so the fairness concern trumped the imperative for a larger total?

Close examination lends support to this inference. A key 'achievement' in IDA-10 (FY1994–96, negotiated between January and December 1992) was that donors had successfully institutionalised their newly gained influence upon environmental policies in recipient countries. To ensure that policy changes could translate into actual influence at the country level, donors collectively demanded that Executive Directors annually review Country Assistance Strategies (CASs) for each IDA recipient.[54] As an oversight mechanism, CASs would punish non-compliance with a substantial cut in aid.[55] This was strongly opposed by

---

[50] Kegley and Wittkopf (1996: 451–53).
[51] Quotation from National Security Advisor Anthony Lake: see Ikenberry (2002b: 134).
[52] Kegley and Wittkopf (1996: 451–53).    [53] Lancaster (2007: 85).
[54] IDA-9 Replenishment Agreement, para. 25.
[55] World Bank, *Country Assistance Strategies Translating IDA Priorities into Action*, IDA-11 Discussion Paper (April 1995), 10, from the World Bank Archives.

recipients due to their fear of one-way proliferating conditionality.[56] But the decision was made in an exclusive donor club (namely the IDA Deputies), and euphemistically called a 'Deputies' recommendation'. Effectively these recommendations turned into actual Bank policies (though procedurally requiring Board approval). Hence, as IDA-11 negotiations kicked off, donors anticipated that their influence upon aid-dependent recipient countries[57] could be self-sustaining even without a boost in fresh donor money.

The above analysis is revealing since it draws out the distinction between obtaining new influence and preserving newly gained influence in analysing the relationship between financial contribution and policy influence. To win influence over recipients in the face of full-swing bargaining power of developing nations in IDA-9/-10, donors strived to achieve a decently large total size of IDA replenishment. By contrast, after their influence was institutionalised and thus sustained without any need for a substantial increase in donor contributions, they no longer felt compelled to boost total IDA resources.

In sum, as soon as the North–South power struggle receded in the mid-1990s, it paved the way for a resurgent fairness concern within the donor group.

### 6.4.2  The Fairness Concern Resurges

A close look at history reveals that the equity line was skewed to breaking point as a result of two salient US violations of the 'fairness' principle: (a) it unilaterally deployed its legislative appropriation procedures to seek influence that it failed to obtain through multilateral IDA-10 negotiations; (b) its overdue obligations rocketed to an unsustainable level, creating a funding crisis in FY1997 as it did in FY1984.

---

[56]  World Bank, 'Country Lending Strategy', Office Memorandum, 17 March 1989, 3, from the World Bank Archives.

[57]  Despite a surge in private capital flows to developing countries in the early 1990s, this has largely bypassed the IDA countries other than China and India. IDA, *Prospects and Options for Effective IDA Lending*, IDA-11 Discussion Paper, January 1995, 8, from the World Bank Archives.

## Congress Unilaterally Calls the Shots

Congress intensified direct pressure upon the Bank to achieve US policy initiatives unfulfilled during the IDA-10 multilateral negotiations in 1992.

In the wake of IDA-10, NGOs waged unprecedented campaigns to lobby Congress to withhold IDA-10 funding unless the World Bank made key reforms on the Inspection Panel and Disclosure Policy.[58] The House Authorisation Subcommittee Chairman, Barney Frank, was receptive to NGOs' criticism towards the Bank and introduced an amendment to withhold the last tranche of the three-year IDA-10 contribution so that Congress could review progress before authorising it. Passionately driven by a mission to hold the Bank accountable, Chairman Frank even directly threatened key Bank staff to withhold full authorisation unless there was rapid change at the Bank.[59] This was hailed by the NGOs as a 'victory'.[60] Yet the Senate Authorisation Subcommittee attached more importance to honouring the US multilateral commitments and thus authorised the full share. As a result, the House and Senate authorisation committees failed to get their act together. Subsequently, they had to postpone the authorisation decision to the joint appropriation committees in September 1993. Later, Congress became even tougher in demanding that the Bank take rapid reforms before it would authorise and appropriate funds for IDA.[61]

Under this tremendous external Congressional pressure, the World Bank hastened the pace of reform.

On disclosure policy, President Lewis Preston made this 'a key priority', because 'if the Bank did not, there was real risk that external pressure would eventually force the bank to make changes which might go well beyond the institution's interest'.[62] In August 1993, the World

---

[58] Environmental Defence Fund, et al., 'International NGO Statement Regarding the Tenth Replenishment of the International Development Association (IDA)', January 1993.

[59] Pallas (2013: 65).

[60] 'Finance: Key Congressional Committee Cuts IDA Short', IPS-Inter Press Service, 22 September 1993.

[61] Senate Amendment 953, introduced and agreed on 23 September 1993, in *Foreign Operations, Export Financing, and Related Programs Appropriations Act, 1994*, Public Law No: 103–87, 30 September 1993.

[62] An internal memo dated 17 May 1993, from Mark Tran, 'World Bank Moves towards Openness', *The Guardian*, 29 June 1993.

Bank overhauled its Disclosure Policy to introduce the Project Information Document and created a Public Information Centre that had not existed previously.

On the Inspection Panel, the World Bank's Board decided to establish an independent Inspection Panel for the IBRD and IDA in September 1993, just before the US Congressional vote.[63] Previously, a majority of Executive Directors favoured an in-house Inspection Panel as a subsidiary body of the Operation Evaluation Department (OED) reporting to the Board.[64]

Despite the time delays in gaining these hard-won impacts,[65] the US Treasury celebrated them as 'ground-breaking initiatives'.[66] But NGOs lamented them as 'inadequate', arguing that the panel did not meet the most important concerns and needed more independence and more money to do a credible job.[67] Consequently, a widening perception gap emerged regarding how much influence the US had gained – NGOs set a high bar by focusing on what had *not* been achieved, whereas the US Administration emphasised what *had* been achieved in order to secure full Congressional support and avert further arrears eroding the US credibility and leadership.

Ultimately, Congress authorised only the first two years of funding and even cut the first-year appropriation for IDA-10 from $1,250 million to $1,024 million.[68] Since many new Congressmen were elected on a cut-the-deficit plank, it was politically convenient to use the NGOs' high-standard benchmark to blame the Bank's under-performance as a lofty excuse for cuts.

In summary, the United States unilaterally enhanced its power vis-à-vis other Bank members because it directly pushed through institutional reforms via its own legislative processes, bypassing both the formal Board and the informal IDA donor forum. Other members were upset by the fact that Congress directly flexed its money muscle

---

[63] 'Finance: World Bank Announces Inspection Panel', *IPS-Inter Press Service*, 23 September 1993.

[64] Shihata (2000: 24–27).

[65] The Inspection Panel became operational on 1 August 1994.

[66] Hearing before the House Committee on Banking, Finance, and Urban Affairs, World Bank Disclosure Policy and Inspection Panel, 103rd Congress, 2nd Session, 21 June 1994, 13.

[67] 'Finance: World Bank Announces Inspection Panel'.

[68] The US Congress, *Congressional Quarterly Almanac*.

via 'specific legislated mandates' to press for specific reforms that undermined the multilateral decision-making process.[69]

### The US Fails to Pay the Piper: Funding Crisis in FY97

As noted above, although the US Administration celebrated 'sweeping operational reforms' as a success,[70] Congress was so discontented with the actual influence that it severely cut its appropriations to IDA-10. Congress maintained it was hard to discern the true US influence on Bank Management's policies, let alone actual impacts on client countries. In fact, it suspected that the Treasury was biased to exaggerate the progress achieved in order to sell IDA to Congress. Influenced by eye-catching negative news reports, Congress had 'a general feeling' that policy reform had neither gone as far as it should have nor been complied with at the country level.[71] Consequently, the perceived failure to gain influence resulted in a sharp cut of $550 million in FY1996 (the last tranche of IDA-10). As a result, the US cumulative arrears reached $935 million, almost equal to its annual contribution.[72] As the only major donor that fell behind in its payments, the USA was 'castigated for not carrying its due share but demanding the rest of the world to follow its lead' on how to govern the World Bank.[73]

The mounting US arrears created a funding crisis in FY1997, because the USA decided to clear its arrearage first before entering a new round of IDA-11 negotiations. The rationale behind this decision was that it was vital to send a strong message that America would lead and fulfil its commitments.[74] As President Clinton urged, 'if America is to lead, those of us who lead America must find the will to pay our way'.[75] But this put

[69] Hearing before the House Committee on Banking, Finance and Urban Affairs, *Authorising Contributions to IDA, GEF, and ADF*, 103rd Congress, 1st Session, 5 May 1993, 49–50.

[70] Ibid.

[71] Remark by Chairman Castle, from Hearing before the House Committee on Banking, Finance, and Urban Affairs, *Authorisation for Multilateral Development Banks*, 105th Congress, 1st Session, 13 March 1997, 9.

[72] World Bank, *Funding Options for IDA-11*, IDA-11 Discussion Paper, November 1995, 3, from the World Bank Archives.

[73] Secretary Lloyd Bentsen, 'How Can We Improve the Banks?', from Hearing before the Foreign Operations Subcommittee of the Senate Appropriations Committee, *Multilateral Funding and Policy Issues*, 27 April 1993.

[74] The US Treasury, *International Programs: Justification for Appropriations*, FY1997, 1.

[75] Bill Clinton, 'State of the Union Address', 1993.

other donors in a similar predicament as in FY84, when the Reagan Administration decided not to contribute to IDA-7 until it cleared its arrears (after Congress stretched out its IDA-6 contribution over four years).

In the absence of the US participation, others had to decide how to finance the gap year. Two major options stood out: one was a general fund, and the other a special fund (that would deprive non-contributors of procurement benefits).

Historically, in FY1984 most donors had opted for the former option of a general fund because they were fearful of the US exit threat if they stripped the hegemon of procurement opportunities.

A decade later, however, other donors were less tolerant of the USA as the privilege taker – calling the shots without paying its due fee – since they were less dependent upon it for military protection. After the Cold War, US troops in Europe reduced to a third of their previous strength.[76] No threat existed to unite Western allies. For instance, Europeans never viewed the US concept of 'rogue states' as compelling; instead, they believed that the US 'conjured up implacable enemies to replace the lost Soviet threat'.[77] Thus, European allies saw the US as 'the world's lonely superpower' demanding that others pay for it to maintain its privileged position.[78]

Hence, secondary states unanimously decided to establish an Interim Trust Fund (ITF) that forbade the US to win procurement contracts. The ITF had a separate legal and accounting status, to be held in trust, managed and used by IDA. Credits financed by the ITF were made on the same terms and conditions as those of IDA credits, with two exceptions. First, eligibility for procurement under ITF credits extended only to nationals of countries that either contributed to the ITF or were eligible to borrow from the IBRD or IDA (thus in effect excluding American firms from bidding for ITF-funded projects). Second, ITF credits were approved by IDA's President after consultation with a committee of Executive Directors representing the donors and eligible borrowers (hence effectively excluding the US Executive Director from the decision-making process).[79] They aimed to incentivise the US to make a fair and timely IDA contribution.

---

[76]  Wallace (2002: 149).    [77]  Ibid., 151.    [78]  Ibid., 149–50.
[79]  IDA, 'Proposed Termination of the Interim Trust Fund', February 2001, 1.

The proposed punishment provoked Congress to threaten to truncate IDA funds or walk away from IDA forever. The stakes were so high that other donors held a special meeting to assess the situation. After long deliberation, other donors came to believe that: first, the US Administration would not go as far as to withdraw from IDA; second, should this worst-case scenario occur, the world would not blame them since they did the right thing – a hegemon should not assert influence without paying its fair share; and finally, if the United States did withdraw from IDA, they were prepared to accept the fact that the United States was no longer able or willing to play a leadership role in international development.[80]

Ultimately, the secondary states collectively decided to give priority to preserving the principle of fairness even at the risk of a permanent US exit.

Yet from the standpoint of the US Administration, it was counterproductive for other donors to impose restrictions on its access to procurement bidding opportunities as a means of inducing the United States to clear its arrearage. For a long time, the Treasury had tried to hide its poor IDA procurement performance since its primary objective was not to pursue commercial interests but, rather, to leverage US contributions to shape the World Bank's policies and operations. Hence, this punitive measure only provided 'ammunition for Congress to oppose IDA'.[81] Consequently, the US Administration 'had to direct much of our energy to persuade other donors to cancel these restrictions instead of being able to focus on pressing for policy reforms in the World Bank'.[82]

In sum, the equity line between influence and contribution was further skewed due to unilateral Congressional interventions and soaring US arrears. As a result, the fairness concern dominated the agenda, which set the tone for burden-sharing negotiations about the core IDA-11 funding for FY1998–99.

---

[80] Interview with the former German IDA Deputy, 25 August 2012, Cologne.

[81] Interview with the former US IDA Deputy, 25 September 2012, Washington, DC.

[82] Statement of William E. Schuerch (Acting Deputy Assistant Secretary of International Affairs, US Department of the Treasury), from Hearing before the House Committee on Banking, Finance, and Urban Affairs, *Authorizing Contributions to IDA, GEF, and ADF*, 4. It was not until Congress cleared all the arrears that other donors decided to remove these restrictions in February 1997.

### 6.4.3 Secondary States Take Countermeasures: Restoring the Equity Line?

In response to the widening discrepancy between the US influence and its contribution, secondary states strived to restore the equity line to preserve their sense of fairness.

**Expediting Real 'Exit' Options**

As in IDA-8, negotiated in 1986, secondary states could no longer tolerate any slight US share cut in IDA-11/-12 in the mid-/late-1990s.

The burden-sharing discussion paper in IDA-11 identified 'a degree of loss in the sense of fairness'.[83] It 'reaffirmed the principle that donors should increase their basic shares if they fell short of the burden-sharing indicators.[84] Among the top fifteen donors, the United States was the only donor that had 'major discrepancies' between its actual share and its 'appropriate' share.[85]

Many donors took a 'rigid' position on nominal burden shares because of their acute sense of unfairness. On the one hand, they set a floor for the US burden share and could not tolerate any slight reduction. On the other hand, they put a ceiling on their own shares because they were reluctant to fill 'a US gap'.[86]

This rigid approach to burden-sharing ruled out the possibility of taking a more flexible stance where warranted.[87] For instance, the extremely volatile exchange rate movements rendered the principle of maintaining donors' traditional shares unviable. Take IDA-9 (FY1993–95, negotiated in 1989), for example: keeping basic shares implied huge disparity in national budgetary efforts – donors that suffered from currency depreciation had to put up additional contributions of as much as 20 per cent (e.g., the United States), whereas those who enjoyed currency appreciation could easily bring as much as 15 per cent back to their national coffers (e.g., Japan).[88] Bank

---

[83]    IDA, *Burden Sharing in IDA Replenishments*, IDA-11 Discussion Paper, April 1995, 9, from the World Bank Archives.

[84]    Ibid., 15.

[85]    The US IDA-10 burden share was 20.86% – far below its GNP share and adjusted GNP share of 31.03% and 33.62% respectively. Ibid., 10–11.

[86]    It was also because they felt it was hard to justify any increase before their domestic parliaments, given their 'fairly stable' economic positions. Ibid., 7.

[87]    Ibid., 6–9.

[88]    IDA, *IDA-9 Burden Sharing*, June 1989, 6, 20, from the World Bank Archives.

Management proposed a modified burden-sharing approach in order to persuade all donors to make contributions that offset domestic inflation rates. In this way, burdens could be more evenly shared in the hope of future reciprocity. But such a flexible approach would entail a US share cut, so it never took off due to the fairness concern.[89]

And worse, this rigid approach to burden-sharing could amputate the total size of IDA replenishment when the United States could not maintain its traditional share of a decently large total. Due to Congressional hostility escalated by the procurement restriction in the ITF, the US annual contribution dropped from $1,250 million to $800 million, a reduction of more than a third. Exacerbated by further dollar depreciation, this direct pegging burden-sharing system resulted in a precipitous fall of 40 per cent in the total size of IDA-11.

But unlike the mild exit in the 1980s, few donors chose to top up their basic contributions outside the burden-sharing framework (with a special financing facility or voluntary supplementary contributions). Consequently, the 'financing gap' soared to nearly 10 per cent. Given the limited supplementary contributions, the 'unallocated' gap rose from about 1 per cent to more than 7 per cent.[90]

Consequently, other donors diverted more aid money away from IDA and into outside options. As a result, IDA's share of total donor contributions to multilateral aid organisations dropped from an annual average of one-third in the 1980s to one-fourth in the 1990s.[91]

To conclude, the acute sense of unfairness compelled secondary states to adopt a rigid position of zero tolerance towards a US share cut, which helps to explain the '*Hegemonic Lags*'.

### Delaying Voice Options: The Fairness Concern Amplifies US Influence

If the fairness concern resurged, did secondary states exercise the 'voice' option to refuse to cede policy influence to the United States?

A closer look at the negotiation processes reveals a counterintuitive finding that the US influence endured and even strengthened. Paradoxically, while the fairness concern was originally intended to restore the equity line between influence and contribution, in effect it

[89] IDA, *Burden Sharing in IDA Replenishments*, 9, from the World Bank Archives.
[90] IDA-11 Replenishment Agreement.    [91] OECD Aid Statistics.

amplified the US financial leverage, thus exacerbating the discrepancy. Below is an anatomy of the US influence in IDA-11/-12.

In IDA-11, negotiated in the mid-1990s, the United States pledged to increase its cash contribution from the baseline of $700 million (a realistic level based on the amount appropriated by Congress in FY1996) provided China graduated from IDA by the end of the IDA-11 period (FY1999). It justified this proposal on the grounds that China had access to international capital markets.[92] In fact, under US pressure, China's share in IDA's aid allocations had steadily declined, from 16 per cent in IDA-9 to 11 per cent in IDA-10 and a projected 4 per cent in IDA-11. Yet the United States had failed to achieve its ultimate goal of weaning China off IDA's assistance, as evidenced in IDA-10.

The US financial leverage was exponentially amplified in IDA-11, because the US dollar contribution effectively dictated the total size of IDA replenishment as other donors proportionately cut back on their own absolute contributions to keep a constant US share. Given the preponderant US financial clout, it was decided that China would be cut off from IDA's assistance in FY1999. Accordingly, the USA went above the baseline by $100 million. This increase in the US cash contribution in turn lifted the total size of replenishment by $500 million, given the US share of about 20 per cent.

In IDA-12, negotiated in late-1990s, the USA achieved marked success in provoking profound policy changes. The most notable one was to make the aid allocation system (known as 'performance-based allocation', [PBA]) more transparent and 'rule-based'.

At first glance, this proposal appears irrational: why did the largest donor proactively try to tie its own hands, since the existing opaque process could allow the USA to informally skew aid allocations with little public scrutiny? In fact, empirical studies have shown that the USA exerted just such political influence on IDA aid allocations.[93]

The following section investigates the underlying rationale behind the US influence attempt to make IDA aid allocations more transparent and formula-based.

---

[92] Hearing before the House Committee on Banking, Finance, and Urban Affairs, *Authorisation for Multilateral Development Banks*, 105th Congress, 1st Session, 13 March 1997, 46.

[93] Andersen, Hansen, and Markussen (2006: 772–94).

First, the US Administration suspected that Bank Management's disbursement imperative diluted the Bank's ability to influence policy changes in the recipient countries. While Bank Management had promised since the late 1980s to give increased emphasis to 'performance' in aid allocation criteria, the USA was sceptical about whether the World Bank was faithful in following donor instructions. The USA maintained that Bank Management had a perverse incentive to disburse money to recipients to protect the Bank's financial position from potential defaults, so the Bank could not rigorously insist on compliance with aid conditionality. The evidence showed that at least 40 per cent of the Bank's structural adjustment loans suffered from 'overt slippage'.[94]

Second, the USA believed that the problem ran deeper because opposition views from borrowers on the Board had diluted or even discarded Deputies' Recommendations made during IDA replenishment processes.[95] On the PBAs front, although IDA Deputies explicitly urged Bank Management to 'apply performance criteria in a transparent and consistent manner across regions and countries',[96] neither the methodology nor the result of 'performance' assessments had been disclosed, so it was hard to verify whether Bank Management actually rewarded 'good performers' while punishing 'poor performers'.[97] The limited awareness of precise benchmarks among recipients cast further doubt upon whether this PBA system actually provided an incentive to recipient countries to adopt concrete policy reforms to earn more IDA credits. Finally, this doubt was exacerbated by news reports on IDA allocations to countries riddled with appalling corruption and poor governance.[98]

To ensure its effective leverage on recipient countries, therefore, the USA strove to uncover the black box of IDA's aid allocation processes to make its criteria, methodology, and results more transparent. Moreover, it aimed to substantially increase the weight of 'governance'

---

[94] Mosley, Harrigan, and Toye (1991: 306).    [95] Ibid., 9–10.
[96] IDA-10 Replenishment Agreement, para. 54.
[97] Although Bank Management did provide IDA Deputies with information at the aggregate level to demonstrate how good performers received more aid on a per capita basis than poor ones. But the Deputies had good reasons to suspect that this might be 'reverse engineering' to justify aid allocation patterns that were driven by factors other than performance. Interview with the former US IDA Deputy, 3 October 2012, Washington, DC.
[98] Ibid.

in performance assessments by scaling back or stopping aid entirely to 'poor performers'.[99]

How did other donors react to the US proposal to make IDA aid allocations more transparent and rule-/formula-based?

While most donors embraced the principle of rule-based and transparent decision-making, they disagreed with the radical idea of disqualifying recipients from receiving aid on grounds of 'weak governance'. To persuade others to go along with its proposal, the USA tried its best to convince them that governance was a serious constraint to aid effectiveness. To incentivise recipient governments to enact the 'fundamental, yet painful reforms' that were a prerequisite for growth, IDA could use this carrot and stick approach to 'reward' those that reformed and 'deny' loans to those who did not.[100] But Nordic donors held that this argument wrongly assumed that the root cause of weak governance was lack of *intent* rather than constraints of *capacity*. In fact, many so-called poor performers were victims of chronic civil wars and historical legacy.[101] Thus, they argued to ring-fence a pot of money to assist countries with the potential for better performance to achieve a turnaround. The UK also persistently maintained that more emphasis should be given to 'need' and that poor people should not be punished for something out of their own control.[102] But the USA initially demurred on the grounds that this would create perverse incentives for recipients to count on drawing money from this 'exception' pocket rather than improving their 'governance'.

Furthermore, other major donors disagreed with the US on what counted as 'good' development policies and institutions and how to achieve them. First, Japan challenged the Bank's core ideas about the role of the state in development strategy, since the CPIA had a built-in bias in favour of the free market. Such a challenge had already been crystallised, but not resolved, in the Bank's publication *The East Asian Miracle: Economic Growth and Public Policy*.[103] Second, other donors maintained that the World Bank should engage with 'poor performers'

---

[99] Ibid.
[100] The US Treasury, *International Programs: Justification for Appropriations, FY1998*, 3.
[101] IDA, *IDA's Support for Poorly Performing Countries*, IDA-12 Technical Note, 29 April 1998, 2, from the World Bank Archives.
[102] Interview with the former UK IDA Deputy, 6 November 2012, Oxford, UK.
[103] Wade (1996).

to help them to improve their institutions; a complete cut-off of aid would stifle potentially productive initiatives helping them progress into 'good performers'.[104]

How, then, did Bank Management respond to this US influence attempt?

Bank Management strongly resisted a transparent formula-based aid allocation process on the grounds that it would tempt donors to exert political influence on both the aid allocation formula and actual aid allocation processes. In fact, the PBA system was originally the Bank's own invention in the early 1970s, aimed at 'rationalising' aid allocation process in order to build 'firewalls' to resist ad hoc donor influence.[105] But the formula was used only for internal planning purposes and was never disclosed to donors or recipients, let alone the public. Although donors had provided broad numeric guidelines on regional allocations since IDA-8, negotiated in 1986, Bank Management enjoyed substantial discretion on how to allocate aid across countries and sectors. Hence, Bank Management refused to make the formula-based aid allocation process transparent in order to protect its independent professional judgement.

Furthermore, Bank Management warned of the risk of 'imposing undue rigidities on IDA's assistance strategy'[106] where professional autonomy was required to tailor the Bank's response in each case with different circumstances.[107] In fact, the IDA-7 Replenishment Agreement reached in January 1984 clearly stated that 'there was no precise formula that could be applied in advance to derive the amounts to be allocated to any country ... considerable judgment would need to be used by management in determining actual allocations in any given year'.[108]

Despite its extreme reluctance to forgo professional autonomy, Bank Management finally had to yield because of the preponderant weight of the US cash contribution in deciding the total size of replenishment.

---

[104] Interview with the former UK IDA Deputy, 6 November 2012, Oxford, UK.
[105] Telephone interview with the former World Bank staff, 21 August 2012.
[106] IDA, *Country Performance and IDA Allocations*, IDA-12 Discussion Paper, September 1998, 9, from the World Bank Archives.
[107] IDA, *IDA's Support for Poorly Performing Countries*, IDA-12 Technical Note, April 1998, 3, from the World Bank Archives.
[108] IDA-7 Replenishment Agreement, para. 3.4.

Regarding the aid allocation formula, the Bank substantially revised its original performance assessment criteria (known as the 'Country Policy and Institutional Assessment', [CPIA]) by adding six newly developed 'governance' indicators.

Furthermore, the Bank adopted a punishment instrument (known as the 'governance discount') that reduced the overall performance ratings by one-third in the case of countries that scored very poorly in the 'governance' measure.[109] As a result, fifteen poor reformers were projected to have their aid cut to half of what would otherwise have been allocated.[110]

In addition, Bank Management had to compromise their professional judgement and merge four economic indicators into two in order to give space to accommodate other donors' concerns, such as gender equality and social inclusion.[111]

Eventually, the USA successfully restrained Bank Management's autonomy by granting donors the authority to devise an aid allocation formula to strengthen the effect of policy conditionality upon recipients.

As for transparency, the methodology of PBA was disclosed from 1999, although it was not until August 2000 that the Board agreed to disclose the results of performance assessments (relative ratings in quintile format) for IDA-eligible countries.[112]

For the first time, Bank Management presented country-by-country IDA lending projections to donors.[113] Thus, its autonomy was considerably constrained because it had to justify any 'exceptional deviations' from the planning allocations.[114]

Apart from its influence on aid allocation rules, the USA also accomplished a wide range of policy reforms, and the IDA-12 Replenishment Agreement explicitly extended the IDA Deputies' authority to the whole World Bank Group. Even though donor-driven IDA policies had been applied to IBRD borrowers as well (such as environmental

---

[109]  World Bank, Country Performance and IDA Allocations, 7.      [110]  Ibid., 9.
[111]  Interview with former World Bank staff, 16 August 2012, Washington, DC.
[112]  Operation Evaluation Department (OED), *Review of the Performance-Based Allocation System, IDA10-12*, 14 February 2001, viii, 10.
[113]  World Bank, *IDA-12 Lending Projections*, IDA12 Technical Note (May 1998), http://documents.worldbank.org/curated/en/1998/05/16613287/ida-12-lending-projections (accessed 18 March 2013).
[114]  World Bank, 'IDA Country Performance Assessments', from IDA-12 Replenishment Agreement, Annex A, para. 11.

and social safeguards), it was the first time in an IDA Replenishment Agreement that IDA Deputies directly prescribed policy reforms for the whole World Bank Group. In response to strong US urging, Deputies' Recommendations included: establishing a clear private sector development strategy for the World Bank Group during the course of 1999 to guide the work of the IBRD, IDA, IFC, and MIGA;[115] and instructing Bank Management to make a formal proposal on instituting an appropriate and independent inspection function for IFC and MIGA.[116]

To reward Bank Management for positive policy changes, the USA kept up its dollar contribution rather than amputating it as Congress had instructed. Thanks to the windfall of dollar appreciation, the total size of IDA-12 rose by 14 per cent. In contrast to IDA-11, the USA unexpectedly put upward pressure on other donors who had made their budgetary planning based on their past contributions in national currency terms.

Such a resounding hegemonic success in gaining influence begs the question of why secondary states delayed exercising their 'voice' option. This is puzzling, because they could have refused to cede influence to the USA and attempted to restore the equity line between contribution and influence, just as they had expedited the real 'exit' option (given the fact that they were less structurally dependent upon the USA and had more viable outside options). The answer boils down to two main factors: preponderant US financial weight, and voice opportunities of secondary states.

First, the USA enjoyed far greater financial leverage upon Bank Management than its own contributions would indicate. As most donors consciously pegged their contributions to that of the hegemon at a fixed burden-sharing position, the USA dollar contribution effectively determined the total size of replenishment. Moreover, the 'pro rata' rule introduced in IDA-6 multiplied the leverage of any delay in the US payment to IDA. This was succinctly described by the new Bank President James D. Wolfensohn: 'for every dollar cut by the US, IDA could lose a total of five dollars – as other nations reduce their

---

[115] International Finance Corporation (IFC) was founded in 1956; Multilateral Investment Guarantee (MIGA) was founded in 1988.
[116] IDA-12 Replenishment Agreement, paras. 63, 55, 77.

contributions proportionally'.[117] Thus, Bank Management was inclined to yield to the US demand to maximise the total size of replenishment.

Second, secondary states enjoyed ample 'voice opportunities' in IDA replenishment negotiations. Bank Management had incentives to accommodate each donor's concerns in order to secure their financial support. This resulted in proliferating agendas and priorities: the IDA-11 Replenishment Agreement was replete with thirty-four 'recommended action' under twenty-four themes,[118] and IDA-12 saw this number shoot up to forty-three actions. Moreover, IDA Deputies made decisions on a consensual basis, so the USA was willing to make concessions to make other donors' voices heard. For instance, the USA accommodated the UK and Nordic donors' demands to give more weight to 'need' in the aid allocation formula and acknowledged the necessity to assist countries that had poor policies but were adopting policy reforms.[119]

Hence, it was not necessarily a zero-sum game when donors sought policy influence upon Bank Management. The power struggle had more to do with the USA vis-à-vis Bank Management and less to do with the USA vis-à-vis secondary states. Because of relatively high donor preference alignment,[120] both the USA and other donors could simultaneously enhance their influence upon Bank Management.

In summary, as the North–South battle ebbed away, the fairness concern dominated the burden-sharing negotiations in IDA-11 and IDA-12 in the aftermath of two salient US norm violations: (a) the US unilateral influence upon Bank's institutional and policy reforms via Congressional threats, and (b) rocketing overdue obligations. Consequently, secondary states refused to legitimise any further share cut. Yet, paradoxically, this direct pegging practice amplified the

---

[117] Annual Address by James D. Wolfensohn, President of the World Bank Group, from *1995 Annual Meetings of the Boards of Governors: Summary Proceedings* (Washington, DC, 10–12 October 1995), 20.

[118] IDA, *IDA-11 Matrix: Implementing the IDA-11 Framework*, IDA-12 Background Note, April 1998, from the World Bank Archives.

[119] IDA-12 Replenishment Agreement, para. 37.

[120] The US policy proposals were seldom diametrically opposed by other donors, though donors disagreed with each other over priorities and means of how to improve development effectiveness. Interview with the former Belgian IDA Deputy, 2 October 2012, Washington, DC.

US financial leverage, hence preserving – or even enhancing – its influence.

## 6.5 Conclusion

The end of the Cold War marks a watershed in IDA replenishment history, for the first layer of power play between the US-led donor group and the Soviet Union has been marginalised and the third layer of power play about the informal donor influence upon Bank Management came into full play. As geopolitical threats faded away, the USA no longer had the imperative to expand IDA. Hence, no quid pro quo between voting rights and burden shares occurred during this period.

The collapse of the Soviet Union has diminished the importance of geopolitical threats in resolving IDA burden-sharing puzzles and brought the internal donor struggle over fairness to the fore. In the past, the existence of an overarching external threat compelled the hegemon to seek to foster internal donor solidity to expand IDA in order to counter their common enemy. Moreover, with this overarching goal in mind, the USA refrained from squandering its power in World Bank governance to secure short-sighted national interests. Hence, the fairness concern within the donor group was not a salient issue. By contrast, as the bipolar rival collapsed, the hegemon was tempted to tighten its grip on Bank Management to shape IDA's policies and operations in ways that reflect its interests and values. This aroused an acute sense of unfairness among secondary states, especially when they disagreed with the USA about how to govern the Bank, when the USA bypassed the deliberation within the donor group to leverage its Congressional threats to push through sweeping reforms in the Bank, and when the USA failed to honour its financial commitments despite its growing influence upon Bank Management. Hence, in the absence of a unifying external threat, donor solidarity was unravelling so that the fairness concern harboured by secondary states came to the fore.[121]

---

[121]  Scholars disagree with each other on whether unipolarity would incentivise the hegemon to rely on command or consent to make collective decisions with other constituent members in the hegemon-led world order. Ikenberry (2011) argues that a far-sighted hegemon should embrace an open and rule-based 'liberal' order in order to signal strategic self-restraint to weak states. Yet

Case studies revealed that the fairness concern among secondary states accounts for the '*Hegemonic Lags*' in IDA-11/-12 where the US shares were constant. The equity line between contribution and influence was skewed to breaking point in IDA-11 for two reasons: (a) the US Congress unilaterally threatened to push through profound institutional and policy reforms in the World Bank; and (b) escalating arrears created a funding crisis in FY1997. As a result, other donors proportionally cut back their own cash contributions, as they did in IDA-8, in order to avoid any further US share cut. To restore the equity line, secondary states accelerated their 'exit' options. Compared with the 1980s where other donors topped up their basic contributions to IDA, they actually took a harsher exit by diverting more aid money elsewhere. Consequently, we see an increasingly declining share of IDA in total donor contributions to multilateral aid organisations. This acceleration stemmed from two factors: (a) the end of the Cold War and economic diversification rendered other donors less structurally dependent upon the hegemon; and (b) multilateral aid channels were proliferating.

Yet a counterintuitive finding was that while the fairness concern of other donors was directed to restoring the balance between contribution and influence, it actually amplified the US financial leverage in IDA-11/-12 because in a direct pegging burden-sharing system the US dollar contribution dictated the total size of replenishments. Meanwhile, secondary states enjoyed new voice opportunities, thus tolerating more US influence with little distributional consequences upon themselves.

In addition, detailed case studies also revealed that historical contingencies and nuanced analytical angles can help us understand power dynamics behind replenishment negotiations in IDA-9 and IDA-10.

First, what triggered a substantial US share cut in IDA-9? The erosion in fiscal capacity and wild dollar depreciation meant that the USA was unable to afford its traditional share of a target total that offset inflation. Previously in IDA-8 (FY1988–90, negotiated

Lake (2012: 250) contends that unipolarity permits either an 'imperial' or a 'liberal' order to emerge and that which strategy a hegemon selects depends on many factors.

This study advances the debate by focusing on whether the hegemon would abandon self-restraint in World Bank governance as its bipolar rival collapses (with other factors held constant).

between January and December 1986), other donors proportionally cut back on their cash contributions to avoid any further US share cut in order to preserve their sense of fairness, when the US budgetary constraints and Congressional hostility made it impossible for the hegemon to honour its traditional share of a relatively larger target total. By contrast, other donors accepted a substantial US share cut in IDA-9. Why did other donors seem to downplay their fairness concerns in the context of a widening disparity between US financial contributions and its policy influence? In the late 1980s, the North–South battle over environmental protection trumped intra-donor dissonance over fair burden-sharing. Hence, other donors accepted a US share cut for the sake of a larger total size of replenishment. A decently large total size of IDA replenishment could help to persuade developing countries to incorporate environmental safeguards in their development projects, hence enhancing collective donor interests in protecting a sustainable planet.

Second, what drove the USA to make a substantial increase in its cash contribution, thus averting a much steeper share cut in IDA-10? While the hegemon would have cut its share sharply as the traditional geopolitical rationale was rendered obsolete, the USA set up a new US grand strategy of integrating developing countries into a liberal-capitalist world order. Thus, the USA cared about its leadership role in the Bank. But the US ability-to-contribute was further deteriorating due to severe dollar depreciation and fiscal austerity. This would have resulted in a much steeper US share cut, since other donors continued to feel compelled to achieve a decently large total size of IDA-10 at the height of North–South power struggles. Yet the USA stretched its budgetary resources to keep its share above the 20 per cent threshold in order to preserve its 'Major Donor' status. By contrast, the USA was prepared to accept a big share cut in IDA-9 as long as it did not trigger an imminent threat to its influence. In short, these two cases suggest that the relationship between relative contribution and influence is far from a simple linear one but, rather, a delicate balancing act: the hegemon tried its best to avoid a steeper share reduction if it perceived that a slight share cut might incur a substantial loss in influence. In IDA-11/-12, as the collective donor influence upon recipient countries' environmental policies was institutionalised in the World Bank, other donors no longer felt compelled to give priority to a large size of IDA replenishments. Accordingly, the fairness concern came to the fore.

The next chapter will examine IDA burden-sharing after the new millennium. In contrast to the constant US share in IDA-11/-12, IDA-14 witnessed the largest ever decline in the US burden share. Comparison of these two historical periods will allow us to understand these seemingly anomalous burden-sharing patterns.

# 7 | IDA *in the New Millennium: Leadership in Transition?*

This chapter explores the watershed in the IDA burden-sharing scenery in the first decade of the new millennium – after a precipitous fall in its share in IDA-14 (FY2006–08, negotiated from February 2004 to February 2005), the United States ceded the status of the largest donor to the UK in IDA-15 (FY2009–11, negotiated from March 2007 to December 2007).

As seen in previous chapters, IDA replenishment history witnesses a steady decline in the US share (halved from the initial two-fifths in the 1960s to the customary one-fifth in the 1990s). This declining trend was sporadically arrested by '*Hegemonic Lags*' – sometimes motivated by the overriding aim of the United States to counter looming external threats challenging a US-led hegemonic world order, and at other times provoked by the fairness concern among secondary states to avoid legitimatising any further US share cut.

At first glance, it may not come as a surprise to see another US share cut, given the overall pattern of a shrinking US share throughout the history.

Yet the steep fall of the US share in IDA-14 was unprecedented. For the first time the US share fell below 20 per cent, losing the 'Major Donor' status that it once strived to preserve, as seen in IDA-10 in the previous chapter. Consequently, the United States fell from its previously unchallengeable height to become just the first among equals in terms of IDA burden shares.

This chapter first explores what drove this *Accelerated Burden-Shifting* and then examines how this leadership transition impacted on World Bank governance (financial contributions to IDA were claimed to warrant influence in the World Bank, since they symbolised a donor's commitment to shouldering responsibility, encouraging other donors to endorse its initiatives).

## 7.1 Empirical Puzzles

The new millennium saw major Western donors as a group in relative economic decline, as emerging powers – especially China – were growing at an unprecedented pace and financial crisis erupted in the developed world in the latter years of the first decade.

Yet the significant burden-shifting in IDA did not occur from major Western donors to emerging powers, but within the Western group. The US basic share witnessed a largest ever drop of 7.17 per cent in IDA-14 (FY2006–08) down from 20.12 per cent in IDA-13 (FY2003–05) to 12.95 per cent in IDA-14, while the UK sharply boosted its share by 2.25 per cent from 12.14 per cent in IDA-14 to 14.39 per cent in IDA-15, surpassing the United States as the top donor in IDA-15 (FY2009–11).

The baseline explanation of shifts in relative economic positions fails to explain this US descent and UK ascent. First, the steep tumble in the US share was clearly a deviant case during this period, since its GNP share declined only mildly and at a roughly even pace. Second, the UK weakening economic status would predict successive share cuts.[1]

The dramatic US share cut is puzzling from the 'fairness concern' perspective. As seen in the previous chapter, secondary states refused to legitimise any slight US share reduction in IDA-11 and IDA-12 (negotiated in the mid-/late-1990s) in order to restore an equity line that had been skewed by a widening disparity between the expanding US influence and the shrinking US contribution. If this fairness concern had been sustained, other donors would have proportionally cut back on their own cash contributions to keep a fixed US share. Such a rigid stance would have resulted in constant US burden shares, as seen since the mid-1990s. Hence, the question arises as to why the direct pegging burden-sharing system seemed to collapse at the dawn of the new millennium.

The significant drop in the US share is even more puzzling, implying that the US seemed ready to relinquish its privileges as *the* 'Major Donor' (with a burden share above 20 per cent). The US was the single donor that enjoyed the special status of 'Major Donor', which entitled the hegemon to two unique leverages.[2]

---

[1] See WDI.

[2] The two provisions creating these leverages had been introduced to ensure that the USA – the largest donor – would meet its commitments on time, thus ensuring

The first was the 'veto power' over whether IDA could continue to operate, deriving from the provision that replenishment agreements could not come into effect unless IDA received at least 80 per cent of total donor contributions. Hence, IDA would enter a hiatus if Congress failed to authorise US participation in an IDA replenishment.

The second leverage was derived from the pro rata provision[3] under which donors could withhold their contributions in proportion to any shortfall in annual US appropriations. This could effectively magnify the US bargaining power, for any US shortfall could amputate the total resources by a factor of five (given its share of 20 per cent).[4]

As seen in the previous chapters, Congress had effectively used its unrivalled financial leverage to achieve sweeping policy and institutional reforms across the whole World Bank Group (even going far beyond IDA with spill-over influence upon RDBs).[5] Why, then, did the hegemon accept a precarious fall in its share from 20 per cent to 13 per cent, thus forgoing its 'Major Donor' status, if preserving this status played a crucial role in sustaining its predominant hegemonic influence?

In summary, the *Accelerated Burden-Shifting* (from the US to the UK) poses an intriguing puzzle that requires further investigation.

## 7.2 Explaining the Watershed in IDA Burden-Sharing

This section examines what caused a fall in the US share and a rise in the UK share by tracing IDA replenishment negotiation processes. Since

equitable burden-sharing. But their usefulness in encouraging timely contributions proved to be limited, as evidenced in accumulating US arrears. IDA, 'Additions to IDA Resources: Thirteenth Replenishment', 17 September 2002, 36.

[3] The pro rata provision was introduced in IDA-6.

[4] For instance, unpaid US contributions provoked some other donors to proportionately withhold contributions during IDA-12 and IDA-13. See Martin A. Weiss, 'The World Bank's International Development Association (IDA)', Congressional Research Service, Order Code RL33969, 18 April 2007, 5.

Although sometimes other donors might waive their right of withholding their contributions in proportion to the US shortfall in order to avoid disruption of IDA's operations, the existence of the possibility substantially amplified the US financial leverage beyond its dollar contribution.

[5] Woods (2003); Kapur, Lewis, and Webb (1997: 1145); Gwin (1997).

On the 'spill-over influence' on RDBs, one example was that RDBs adopted PBA to guide aid allocations after IDA piloted this US initiative.

these replenishments are contemporary, the data was primarily collected from elite interviews instead of archives.

### 7.2.1 The US Leadership in Question: A Traumatic Start in IDA-13 (FY2003–05)

As the Bush Administration came to power in January 2001, development was elevated to one of the three priorities of US foreign policy, alongside defence and promoting democracy abroad. Thus, President Bush committed a dramatic boost in US aid, arresting a decade-long slump.[6] This appeared to foreshadow triumphant US leadership in the World Bank.

One primary US objective in IDA-13 (FY2003–05, negotiated between February 2001 and July 2002) was a significant increase in grants as a new form of IDA assistance which would depart from the traditional concessional loans. This goal was first proposed by President Bush in July 2001, calling on the World Bank to convert 50 per cent of IDA's funding to grants to the poorest countries.

The United States justified its grant proposal on developmental grounds. First, grants were the best way to help poor countries make productive investments without saddling them with ever-larger debt burdens; thus, grant financing was pivotal to a long-term debt sustainability solution that could end the lending-and-forgiving cycle. Second, grants could endow donors with greater financial leverage over recipient countries than loans, which could help to ensure closer monitoring of programme implementation and tighter measurement of results.[7]

But the US grant proposal encountered overt opposition from other donors. So far, IDA extended grants only in exceptional cases, amounting to less than 1 per cent of IDA's total disbursements. Other donors were concerned that a radical shift from loans to grants would not only change IDA's nature as a revolving fund at the risk of overlapping the function of UN-affiliated aid bodies, but also jeopardise the financial discipline of borrowing countries cultivated by loans.[8] Clare Short, the UK Development Minister, publicly criticised the grant proposal as 'crazy' and threatened to divert funds from IDA if the United States

---

[6] Lancaster (2007: 91).    [7] Sanford (2002: 741).    [8] Salazar (2002).

got its way.[9] The UK even took the lead in mobilising support from other European donors and IDA recipients to block the US initiative.

The division between the United States and other donors ran deeper, because they distrusted the lofty motivations publicly stated by the United States. Such overt opposition stemmed from their suspicion that the United States was plotting a back-door means of depriving IDA of its future reflows from recipients, thus undermining its financial autonomy.[10] In IDA-12, reflows had already accounted for 38 per cent of IDA's total resources.[11] As IDA reflows were speeding up, the World Bank projected that IDA would not require fresh donor contributions possibly as early as IDA-15 (2009) and certainly by IDA-18 (2018).[12] Such an imminent prospect of complete IDA financial self-sufficiency did concern the United States because donors would lose a key point of influence over Bank Management. As the then US IDA Deputy argued, 'donor funding, even if it represents only a small portion of an institution's lending base, provides a powerful source of leverage over its policies and priorities'.[13]

Consequently, the fissure led to a gridlock between the United States and other donors. The following issues were in contention: (a) grants or loans – whether to introduce grants; (b) if grants, what would be an appropriate grant share; (c) grant compensation– whether donors should compensate IDA for its future loss in loan reflows.[14]

Both sides dug in their heels and refused to budge an inch. On the one hand, the United States persistently stuck to 50 per cent of grant share for IDA-only countries and opposed any compensation scheme because it argued that there was no guarantee that loans would be repaid. Moreover, the United States took a firm 'take-it-or-leave' stance by publicly declaring that its position was non-negotiable and that the

[9] Beattie (2002).   [10] Salazar (2002).

[11] IDA-12 Replenishment Agreement, vii.

[12] IDA, *Background Note on Prospects for IDA to Become Financially Self-Sustaining*, IDA-11 Technical Note, December 1995, 1, from the World Bank Archives.

[13] Hearing before the House Committee on Banking and Financial Services, *Authorisation for Multilateral Development Banks*, 105th Congress, 1st Session, 13 March 1997, 47.

[14] World Bank, *Grants in IDA-13*, IDA-13 Discussion Paper, September 2001, http://documents.worldbank.org/curated/en/2001/09/2481053/grants-ida13 (accessed 24 May 2012).

other donors needed to come around to the US position.[15] On the other hand, other donors, led by the UK, resisted introducing grants and argued for a compensation scheme in the case that grants were introduced.[16] With the clock ticking on the end-of-December 2001 deadline for a final agreement, this 'Grants vs. Loans' debate escalated into an ideologically divisive dispute whose resolution went beyond the usual give-and-take negotiations with a spirit of compromise.[17]

At this critical juncture, NGO advocacy helped to tip the balance in favour of the United States and put normative pressure on other donors to accept the introduction of grants. The Bush Administration formed a natural coalition with the Jubilee Debt Campaign that called for cancellation of the Third World debt.[18] With biblical inspiration, some civil society activists genuinely embraced the belief that 'lending at gain is evil, and borrowing at interest is slavery'. This enabled the Bush Administration to claim the moral high ground, although it stood alone among IDA donors. Faced with mounting pressures from their domestic NGOs, European governments felt it would be not defensible to reject the US grant proposal outright. Ultimately, they ceded the ground to the USA and agreed to introduce grants.[19]

The next outstanding issue was the appropriate grant share. As the harsh deadline of end-June 2002 (the planned start date of IDA-13) approached, major donors felt compelled to press for a quick resolution. Otherwise, IDA would suffer from a hiatus. A deal was ultimately sealed at the higher Ministerial level in the G-7 Summit on 15 June 2002, ending up with a fairly classical compromise – the parties split the difference and set grants share in a range of 18–21 per cent in IDA-13.[20]

---

15  Sanford (2002: 754).
16  Department for International Development (DFID), *Loans or Grants: IDA's Concessional Lending Role*, from the UK National Archives, 2002, http://web archive.nationalarchives.gov.uk/+/http:/www.dfid.gov.uk/news/News/files/bg _ida_grants.htm (accessed 25 June 2012).
17  Interview with Geoff Lamb, the former World Bank Vice President for Concessional Finance, World Bank Oral History Programme, 60–61.
18  Busby (2007: 247–75).
19  Interview with the senior DFID official involved, 30 January 2014, Oxford, UK.
20  'G-7 Finance Chiefs Agree on Grant Ratio in IDA Capital Boost', *Jiji Press Ticker Service*, 16 June 2002.
　　Due to the severe delay, donors collectively agreed to lower the trigger for IDA-13 effectiveness from 80 per cent to 60 per cent. Hence, the 'Major Donor' status no longer carried the 'veto power' regarding whether IDA Replenishment

The last sticking point was grant compensation. Due to the persistent UK stance supported by other Europeans, the United States conceded that it was necessary to compensate for the fall in reflows to IDA (grant costs). But the United States disagreed with Bank Management over these estimated costs: the Bank's figure went as high as $100 billion, whereas the US calculation was as modest as $15.6 billion.[21] To avoid any further delay cost, donors decided to postpone this pending issue to IDA-13's Mid-Term Review. In order to secure its desired objective, the UK decided to contribute an additional GBP100 million (SDR112.9 million), conditional on donors agreeing an appropriate compensation scheme.[22]

For the first time in IDA replenishment history, a US initiative was openly opposed by other donors. While the buoyant US aid budget could have amplified its bargaining power, it fell short of attaining its original negotiating objective of converting half of IDA disbursements to grants without any compensation. Moreover, the concession the United States secured from other donors had less to do with the hegemon's financial clout than moral pressure from NGOs.[23] This indicates the limitations of financial leverage as a means of gaining influence when the legitimacy of US leadership was in question. Little wonder that a seasoned researcher from the US Congressional Research Service (CRS) warned that this debate might 'presage' a shift in influence from the USA to European donors who were becoming more 'assertive' in their views and seeking a larger voice.[24]

In summary, the 'Grants vs. Loans' debate was a litmus test of US leadership in the World Bank, because it illustrated how much

Agreement could come into effect since IDA-13. See IDA-13 Replenishment Agreement, para. 118.

[21] Statement of Hon. Joseph A. Christoff, Director of International Affairs and Trade, General Accounting Office, from Hearing before the US House Committee on Financial Services, *Proposed Changes to both the World Bank-International Development Association and the North American Development Bank*, 107th Congress, 2nd Session, 2 May 2002.

[22] UK House of Commons, *Written Answers to Questions: International Development Association*, Foreign and Commonwealth Affairs, 23 July 2002, www.publications.parliament.uk/pa/cm200102/cmhansrd/vo020723/text/207 23w06.htm (accessed 24 March 2014).

[23] Interview with the former General Director of the UK Department for International Development (DFID), 26 November 2012, Oxford, UK.

[24] Sanford (2002: 757).

other donors mistrusted US motives and contested the legitimacy of US influence.

## 7.2.2 The Fairness Concern Surges: Paradoxes in the US Pursuit of Influence

Apart from the grant proposal, another major US objective in IDA-13 (FY2003–05, negotiated between February 2001 and July 2002) was to establish a Results Management System (RMS) to measure progress towards development outcomes.[25] It expected the World Bank to take 'a leading role' in establishing 'an accountability structure for standardizing and measuring a set of priority development results'.[26]

Despite a general donor consensus on the necessity for a RMS,[27] however, they could not agree on how to achieve it. First, some Deputies were concerned that the proposed RMS would overburden Bank Management with tonnes of additional paperwork. Second, some cautioned that a three-year period was too short a timeframe to evaluate many development projects that usually took ten years or longer to have effect. Last but not least, there was an 'attribution' issue – IDA should not be punished by outcomes that went beyond its control.[28]

To advance its desired policy change and secure Congressional support, the Bush Administration proposed a new form of contribution – 'incentive contributions' – whose release hinged on whether Bank Management met pre-determined performance benchmarks. Initially the USA tried to persuade others that the virtue of the RMS was to help make informed decisions based on the evidence of the effectiveness of targeted development interventions in areas such as health and education. Impatient with the slow progress, at a very late stage of IDA-13 negotiations the United States proposed that donors provide additional

---

[25] John Taylor, Undersecretary of the Treasury, 'Improving the Bretton Woods Financial Institutions', Washington, DC, February 2002, www.treasury.gov/press-center/press-releases/Pages/po996.aspx (accessed 26 May 2012).

[26] Remark by Paul O'Neill, the US Governor of the Bank and the Fund, from World Bank, 2002 Annual Meetings of the Boards of Governors: Summary Proceedings, 203–4.

[27] For instance, as early as IDA-11, Deputies urged Bank Management to formulate 'development impact indictors' to systematically assess achievements of IDA operations. See IDA-11 Replenishment Agreement, para. 31.

[28] Interview with the former UK IDA Deputy concerned, 6 November 2012, Oxford, UK.

'incentive contributions'[29] The thrust of its proposal was that it would contribute an additional $100 million and $200 million in FY2004 and FY2005 (the last two tranches of IDA-13) if Bank Management's performance met a set of 'triggers' defined by the United States.

What motivated the USA to propose this novel scheme of 'incentive contributions' was not only its strong desire to speed the reform process towards its desired direction, but also its genuine belief that a direct marriage between contribution and influence could help demonstrate US influence and thus enhance the domestic legitimacy of its IDA contribution in Congress.

Paradoxically, the US attempt to pursue policy influence and domestic legitimacy was questioned by other donors as 'illegitimate', because they were deeply concerned that this 'selective bonus' approach would trigger unilateral influence contests and hence undermine the multilateral principle. A counter-argument to this concern of other donors might be that the IDA replenishment model had already been transformed into a sort of 'bonus' approach, because donors reviewed IDA's performance every three years and then based their contributions on this assessment. But what distinguished the US proposal from this traditional approach was not simply that it would shorten the timeframe of IDA's monitoring and evaluation from three-year to one-year cycles; rather, it would tempt each donor into unilaterally incentivising Bank Management to adopt certain conditionalities, bypassing multilateral deliberation processes. Other donors warned of the peril of establishing this precedent by pointing out that 'IDA Deputies worked like a Parliament: legislators should not go directly to the executive level when they could not agree with each other'.[30] Therefore, no other donors opted for this incentive contribution, but they could not openly oppose it because it might be perceived as 'stopping others from offering additional aid'.[31]

But despite lack of support from other donors, the US still decided to go it alone by attaching specific strings to its contributions. Subsequently Bank Management agreed to do further work on how

---

[29] IDA, *Measuring Outputs and Outcomes in IDA Countries*, IDA-13 Technical Note, February 2002, 1, www.worldbank.org/ida/papers/IDA13_Replenishment/measuring%20outputs.pdf (accessed 27 March 2014).

[30] Interview with the former IDA Deputy, 6 November 2012, Oxford, UK.

[31] Ibid.

an RMS could be established over the course of IDA13 with milestones defined by the USA.[32]

What made US legitimacy more contested was that it failed to provide the second tranche ($200 million) of its unilateral incentive contribution. While Bank Management demonstrated that it had met the US conditionality, Congress was suspicious of the Bank's self-evaluation and insisted on an independent study, financed by the Bank's own resources, to assess whether the Bank had achieved its goal or not. Executive Directors viewed this US proposal as 'unfair'. Hence, they proposed that if the study showed that the Bank had achieved the goal, the United States should pay for the study; otherwise, the Bank would finance the study. But the United States opposed this middle-ground solution. Eventually, external consultants were financed by the Bank and a report was produced confirming Bank Management's compliance with the US requirements. But the United States still failed to honour its pledge of $200 million for the second tranche due to domestic divisions.[33]

In conclusion, while the USA claimed to take the lead in reforming the World Bank for better development effectiveness, the legitimacy of its power exercise was severely contested. Accordingly, the fairness concern surged because of both its unilateral means of seeking influence and its failure to honour its commitments. Hence, the USA put itself at risk of becoming a victim of its own success – gaining specific policy reforms via unilateral means could potentially undermine its influence in the long run.

### 7.2.3 *The UK Drive for IDA Expansion: Explaining a Steep US Share Cut*

Historical insights would lead us to expect that IDA-14 saw a fixed US share again, since the fairness concern surged in IDA-13 in the aftermath of salient US unilateral influence attempts and noticeable overdue obligations. As shown in the previous chapter, IDA-11 saw the emergence of a direct pegging burden-sharing system, because the United States unilaterally pushed through far-reaching institutional

---

[32] IDA, *Measuring Outputs and Outcomes in IDA Countries*, 1.
[33] Interview with the former Executive Director, 2 October 2012, Washington DC.

reforms but accumulated surging arrears (creating a funding crisis in FY1997).

In reality, however, we observe the largest ever US share reduction in IDA replenishment history. How, then, to explain this unexpected US shortfall?

Erosion in the US ability and willingness to contribute offers a first-cut analysis in explaining this significant US share cut. As happened in the Reagan Revolution in the early 1980s, the Bush Administration reignited US unilateralism. After the 9/11 terrorist attack in 2001, President Bush waged a costly and prolonged 'War on Terror' and displayed the US imperial impulse.[34] Turning its back on multilateral institutions, the United States channelled its buoyant aid via newly established bilateral channels such as *President's Emergency Plan for AIDS Relief* (PEPFAR) in 2003 and *Millennium Challenge Corporation* (MCC) in 2004. Accordingly, multilateral development cooperation fell to the bottom of its priority list, because it was more interested to pursue goals unilaterally and bilaterally. This bleak prospect was further exacerbated by severe dollar depreciation of as much as 16 per cent. Consequently, IDA-14 had to come to terms with the unpleasant political reality that the United States would at best provide a flat dollar contribution.

A passive US stance (manifested by a cap on its cash contribution) confronted secondary states with a dilemma between achieving a sufficiently large total (hence accepting a US share cut) and preserving their sense of fairness (thus accepting a much smaller total size of IDA replenishment due to their refusal to accept any further US share reduction).

As we see from the previous chapters, alternative burden-sharing scenarios would emerge, essentially hinging on how other donors weighed up one objective against the other (i.e., the total size of IDA replenishment *versus* the fairness concern). In IDA-9/-10 the North–South power struggle necessitated accomplishing a decent total; thus, the fairness concern was subordinated, and other donors accepted successive US share cuts. By contrast, in IDA-11/-12, with the North–South struggle subdued, the fairness concern came to the fore; hence, other donors insisted upon no further US share cut, and were ready to accept a lower IDA total as a consequence.

---

[34] Ikenberry (2002a).

The above analysis guides us to expect that a drive for IDA expansion might temporarily suspend the fairness concern among secondary states, which helps to explain the sharp US shortfall in IDA-14.

The new millennium saw the renaissance of the international development agenda after the dormant 1990s. World leaders rallied to the *United Nations Millennium Declaration* and pledged to finance time-bound targets to reduce extreme poverty (known as the 'Millennium Development Goals' [MDGs]). This helped to reverse aid fatigue and bolster political and public support for ODA, which gave rise to the landmark *UN International Conference on Financing for Development* in March 2002 that urged developed countries to deliver their promise of reaching the target of 0.7 per cent of GNP as ODA to developing countries.[35]

Bank Management seized the opportunity to create a positive momentum for IDA-14.[36] It tried its best to make the case that IDA was the most efficient way for donor resources to finance the MDGs. Yet Bank Management soon realised that moral suasion alone did not suffice to induce donors to support a large total – since the fairness concern was prevailing, secondary states insisted upon a fixed US share, portending a shrinking IDA.

A possible way out of the dilemma was to settle on a lower total size of basic contributions topped up by voluntary supplementary contributions, because this could avoid incurring a US share cut. The virtue of this approach was to enable other donors to avoid legitimising a permanent fall in the US basic share in the hope that the hegemon might restore its leadership in the future. This was exactly the strategy adopted by other donors in IDA-7, by establishing a supplementary *Special Facility for Africa* in the face of an adamant Reagan Administration that put a ceiling on its dollar contribution.

Yet the above approach proved unviable in IDA-14 because attractive outside options could likely motivate most donors to divert their saved funds away from IDA. Compared with IDA-7 in the early 1980s, the aid landscape was changing – a growing number of alternative aid mechanisms were competing for donor attention and funds.

---

[35]  UN (2003: para. 42).
[36]  IDA-14 covered FY2006–08, negotiated between February 2004 and February 2005.

First, trust funds (earmarked by donors for special purposes and administered by IOs) had begun to expand since the early 1990s and mushroomed from the early 2000s. Donors enjoyed more control over how to use trust funds. A World Bank study found that donors resorted to trust funds where 'bilateral aid is not an option' and 'there is a need to fill gaps' in the multilateral aid system. While donor contributions to trust funds amounted to far less than IDA contributions through the mid-1990s, Bank-administered trust funds surpassed donor contributions to IDA in IDA-13 (FY2003–05).[37]

Second, vertical funds (designed to address a particular thematic challenge) were also burgeoning, as this modality could more easily demonstrate visible outcomes and thus garner public support (e.g., the Global Fund to Fight AIDS, Tuberculosis and Malaria was created in 2002).[38] Thus, donors were prone to channel their money through these outside options.

After ruling out the traditional strategy of maximising the total size of IDA replenishment with 'supplementary contributions', Bank Management felt compelled to look to a lead donor to drive for an ambitious target total of basic contributions in order to overcome the US pessimism.

Among the top five major donors, the UK became an ideal choice because it aspired to assume the leadership in the field of international development after elevating its Overseas Development Administration to a Department for International Development (DFID) with a Cabinet-level Secretary of State. To advance its leadership role, the UK made global poverty reduction the centrepiece of the UK's European Union Presidency, forging a 'European Consensus on Development' in 2005.[39] Its aspirations were buttressed by its soaring aid budget even during a period of fiscal restraint (1997–2000). The UK multilateral aid spending had risen more sharply and looked set to continue to rise in absolute terms,[40] partly because its bilateral aid implementation capacity was constrained by limited staff (as the government aimed to reach efficiency targets in the civil service). Against

---

[37] IEG (2011: 5, 10–11).
[38] See the Global Fund's website at www.theglobalfund.org/en/ (accessed 26 March 2014).
[39] EU (2005).
[40] UK's multilateral aid share rose from 34% in 1999 to 39% in 2003. See DAC (2001: 1–6; 2006: 6).

this backdrop of a rapidly expanding aid budget, the UK boosted its share by 3 per cent in IDA-13, whereas all other major donors cut their shares.

The UK was ready to take the leadership role in achieving a total size of IDA-14 as large as possible. The UK Development Minister, Clare Short, embraced the idea that the main role of the UK's aid was to leverage more international resources into development and to influence the 'big players' (e.g., the World Bank) so that their strategies could contribute more to global poverty reduction.[41]

IDA-14 represented a superb opportunity for the UK to advance its overarching objectives, for two reasons. First, its own aid could leverage more aid from 'relatively less effective' bilateral aid agencies to 'the more effective' IDA, deemed to be 'the central instrument for policy dialogue and resource transfers to developing countries'.[42] Second, it could wield the leverage of IDA to shape development policies across the World Bank Group as well as the entire international development community, since the Bank had assumed an intellectual leadership role worldwide.

To drive for IDA expansion, the UK deliberated on whether it should bid high at the early stage of IDA-14 negotiations to overcome the pessimism generated by US unilateralism.

The upside of the 'bidding high' approach was to crowd in as much aid money as possible from many small-/medium-sized donors. The UK was informed by past experience that if the USA went for a low figure, everyone else would go low too in order to keep a 'fair' US share.[43] Thus, the UK anticipated that in the absence of 'a lead donor' this prevailing practice would probably endure, thus suppressing the total size of the replenishment. This would defeat the UK objective of enlarging IDA, because small-/medium-sized donors would divert their aid money elsewhere (even though they could fiscally afford their traditional shares of the high UK-proposed bidding figure).

Why was the UK confident that most small-/medium-size donors were inclined to maintain their traditional shares regardless of the total size of IDA replenishment? Past replenishment experiences informed the UK that small-/medium-sized donors pursued one overriding negotiating objective: honouring their traditional shares.

---

[41] Chhotray and Hulme (2009: 43).     [42] DAC (2001).
[43] Interview with the former UK IDA-14 Deputy, 18 May 2012, London.

These donors did not want their shares to slip an inch because they attached great importance to the symbolic value of IDA burden shares as witness to their commitment to multilateralism and international development. For instance, when Belgium could not afford its traditional share in IDA-9 due to unexpected currency depreciation, it had resorted to an innovative way of compensating for its own modest share cut by accelerating its payments to IDA. Thereafter, Belgium had stood by its traditional share.[44] Therefore, the most crucial determinant of small-/medium-sized donors' cash contribution was how large the target total would be, given their willingness to keep a fixed share.

Yet the UK 'bidding high' strategy was not free from risks. A major risk was that it would entail a steep US share cut which might in turn trigger a chain of share reductions by other major donors, especially Japan.[45] Japan had always kept its share below that of the USA, even by merely a narrow margin. For one thing, Japan did not want to challenge the USA's No. 1 donor status; for another, the disparity in influence-sharing dissuaded Japan from playing a greater role in burden-sharing, since Japan's IBRD voting rights lagged far behind those of the United States, which enjoyed the veto power.

After weighing up the pros and cons, the UK still decided to adopt the 'bidding high' strategy because the collective financial weight of small-/medium-sized donors was much greater than that of the United States. Collectively, small-/medium-sized donors carried about 40 per cent of the IDA burden, doubling the US basic share. Moreover, the UK anticipated that Japan should have the incentive to keep a reasonably 'appropriate' share to preserve Japanese influence gained in the past. This confidence stemmed from the fact that Japan strived to maintain its basic share throughout the 1990s despite its decade-long economic recession. For instance, Japan cherished the senior position of Executive Vice President in the World Bank's Multilateral Investment Guarantee Agency (MIGA), which had always been held by a Japanese citizen since MIGA was founded in 1988.[46] Therefore, the UK decided that it was much more important to crowd in more aid money from

---

[44] Interview with the former Belgian IDA Deputy, 6 August 2012, Washington, DC.

[45] Interview with the former UK IDA-14 Deputy, 18 May 2012, London.

[46] The Japanese managed to gain this MIGA senior position from the beginning partly because they made a behind-the-scenes deal with Bank Management

fiscally fit small-/medium-sized donors than to preserve a 'fair' share from the laggard United States.

Hence, the UK decided to 'bid high' at a much earlier stage than it would have done on other occasions. Normally, donors tended to wait for others to pledge first in order to avoid committing themselves to a premature position. But the UK declared itself ready to increase its burden share in support of an ambitious target total – a 40 per cent increase over IDA-13. In doing so, the UK tried to establish a higher benchmark for others to measure against, rather than allowing US pessimism to be the basis for setting the contribution levels of other donors.

Yet to rally a majority support for the high target total, the UK, together with Bank Management, had to persuade other donors to downplay their fairness concerns, thus dropping their insistence upon a minimum US 'fair' share.

One way to soften other donors' rigid position towards a fixed US share was to assure them that the US must/should be the largest donor despite a drop in its share. This assurance aimed to uphold their conviction that the United States ought to bear the greatest burden since it was the largest economy as well as the most influential donor. It also helped to dispel the fear that the United States would walk away from IDA and from multilateralism.[47] Thus, symbolism mattered; even if the United States was only marginally above the second largest donor, it could help to alleviate both the fairness concern and the fear of US unilateralism.

Another way to encourage other donors to take a more lenient view of the minimum 'fair' US share was to allow them more voice opportunities. This could help others hold out hope of redressing the imbalance between contribution and influence via the 'voice' option as opposed to the 'exit' option.

Empirical evidence shows that other donors did gain confidence in the prospect of resisting undue US influence in order to restore the equity line.

Regarding influence on the replenishment procedure, the selection of chairperson for IDA replenishment showed that the United States could

during the IDA-8 negotiations. Interview with former Senior Advisor to the Senior Vice President for Finance, 7 November 2012, Kingham, UK.

[47] Interview with the former Vice President for Concessional Finance and Global Partnerships (IDA-14 Chairperson), 25 June 2012, Washington DC.

not override other donors' objections to get its way. Traditionally, the senior Bank Management chaired the replenishment meetings. However, the United States insisted upon selecting an external independent chairperson for IDA-14,[48] complaining that Bank Management had institutional interests that biased a neutral discussion among donors. This US proposal was strongly resisted by the Bank President, James Wolfensohn, on the grounds that providing the IDA chairperson was 'the only venue' to ensure the Bank's influence on IDA policies to counterbalance undue donor influence when donors' proposals could not be justified from a developmental perspective or supported by experience.[49] This US initiative was also opposed by other donors, who maintained that an internal chairperson was important to ensure the IDA Deputies' policy recommendations were 'implementable' for the Bank's operational teams.[50] At strong US urging, however, a selection process was initiated where both an external candidate and an internal candidate were nominated. But it turned out that the US proposal encountered unanimous rejection – all Deputies (except the US Deputy) voted for the internal candidate. Hence, the United States failed to push through this procedural change, and the traditional practice was preserved thereafter.

Regarding influence on substantive policy issues, deliberations on grant allocation criteria and grant share restored small donors' confidence in the spirit of multilateralism. These matters had been 'divisive issues' in IDA-13.[51] Big donors sealed the deal in the G-7 Summit, and small donors had little say in the process. Hence, IDA-13 ended up with an 'arbitrary' system riddled with multiple special-purpose vehicles. To restore donor confidence in multilateral deliberation, Bank Management proposed shifting the focus from 'political bargaining without analytical grounding' to 'discussing about principles'. Accordingly, Bank Management prepared high-quality papers to make a convincing case for a new grant allocation system that linked grant allocation with ratings of recipients' debt sustainability. Such ratings would be professionally assessed by Bank Management. Thus,

---

[48] IDA-13 Replenishment Agreement, para. 107.
[49] Interview with a former senior Bank Management official, 5 October 2012, Washington DC.
[50] Interview with the former UK IDA-14 Deputy, 18 May 2012, London.
[51] Interview with the former Vice President for Concessional Finance and Global Partnerships, 25 June 2012, Washington DC.

the grant share would then be derived from this rational allocation system rather than being dictated by bargaining power. This basic proposal was further refined by incorporating feedback from donors, large and small alike. This helped to reach consensus, with IDA Deputies recognising that their suggestions had been reflected in the revised proposal. This case illustrates how Bank Management could play an independent role in guiding policy discussions and thus shaping replenishment dynamics. As a former World Bank Vice President recalled, 'Even though IDA Deputies have money – the power of the purse, Bank Management has the power of the pencil so that it can set the agenda and propose the issues to be discussed and the solutions to policy issues.'[52]

In short, allowing small-/medium-sized donors more voice opportunities in processes of policy deliberation helped persuade other donors to be less adamant about a minimum 'fair' US share.

One primary reason why secondary states, especially European donors, accelerated their 'voice' option to restore the equity line was that they were less structurally dependent upon the United States. For instance, the creation of the European Monetary Union at the beginning of 1999 and the later launching of the euro were seen as a major challenge to the USA and to the role of the dollar as the dominant reserve currency.[53]

To win a decisive victory in maximising the total size of IDA-14, the second hurdle was to persuade the USA to accept its share dropping below the threshold of 20 per cent and hence losing its 'Major Donor' status.

Initially, the United States seemed to be reluctant to accept a share cut. It pressed for a low-case funding scenario (a 20 per cent increase as opposed to the 40 per cent increase proposed by the UK) on the grounds that Bank Management unrealistically overestimated the financing requirements of recipient countries. This could be interpreted by others as a US attempt to avoid a precipitous fall in its share.

The senior Bank Management played a proactive role in persuading the United States to accept the loss of its 'Major Donor' status in order to make a successful IDA-14 possible. The Vice President for

[52] Interview with the former Vice President for Concessional Finance and Global Partnerships, 2 July 2012, Washington DC.
[53] Feldstein (1997: 60–73).

Concessional Finance approached the US Treasury to persuade it to be flexible with its traditional burden share; otherwise, 'it was not good for the US if it was seen to draw down the overall IDA replenishment'.[54] Bank Management thought that the USA might have been concerned about its public image, since the IDA-13 replenishment process inaugurated a new wave of unprecedented participation and transparency – selected borrower representatives were invited to attend the once closed-door IDA Deputies' meetings; wide-ranging consultations were held with NGOs, private sectors, and academia; all of the background policy papers as well as the summaries of the meetings were made available on IDA's website; and the Replenishment Agreement was disclosed for public consultations before finalisation.[55] This push for transparency in IDA replenishment processes was mainly driven by the increasing emphasis upon country-owned poverty reduction strategies in the broader international development community.[56]

The move towards public scrutiny of IDA replenishment processes had raised public expectations for an eye-catching headline of a record-high IDA-14 amidst the United Nations Millennium Campaign. A laggard USA might tarnish its image of global leadership, which could have repercussions in other international arenas where the United States counted on cooperation from other key players. Thus, Bank Management thought that the United States might see little sense in clinging to the old share and taking the blame for hindering the aspirations of others for a larger IDA.

A deeper reason why the USA was ready to forgo its 'Major Donor' status was that IDA's strategic significance was declining in the eyes of the Bush Administration.[57] First, the unilateral turn in US foreign policy devalued the symbolic role of its IDA burden share in signalling its leadership role in the World Bank. Second, IDA's traditional financial leverage was vitiated, as aid dependence of LICs had fallen sharply since 2000.[58] Thus, the United States had a declining interest in

---

[54]  Ibid.      [55]  IDA-13 Replenishment Agreement, para. 3.
[56]  Tony Faint, 'Selectivity and Accountability in IDA's Replenishments', IDA Replenishment discussion paper, from the World Bank Archives, 8.
[57]  Interview with the former Assistant Secretary for International Affairs, US Treasury, 31 May 2012, Washington DC.
[58]  Although aid has been burgeoning, aid dependency has been lessening because growth was rising faster, enabling countries to mobilise more resources

the World Bank. This stood in sharp contrast with the former Bush Senior Administration of the early 1990s, which stretched its budget constraint to preserve its No. 1 donor status and thus its leadership position. One useful indicator to capture this flagging US interest is the participation of US Presidents in the Annual Meetings of the World Bank Group and the IMF. From 1947 to 1999, every US president from Harry Truman to Bill Clinton took advantage of this gathering to address the world's finance ministers and central bank governors and to make a case for the American vision of how to enhance global prosperity. But George W. Bush had forgone this opportunity.

Ultimately, the UK leadership for IDA expansion bore fruit. Donors agreed upon a target of a 30 per cent increase in the total size of replenishment over IDA-13. Out of 41 traditional donors, 31 maintained or even increased their traditional shares. Hence, despite major share reductions of 7.17 per cent by the United States and of 4.25 per cent by Japan, the actual sum of donor contributions surged by about 25 per cent. This was celebrated as a victory.

With hindsight, the drive for IDA enlargement had largely neglected the reputational risk to IDA – setting a goal that was out of reach. The 'financing gap' doubled, rocketing to above 18 per cent. This gap was widening because total share increases amounted to only about 5 per cent, which fell short of offsetting total share reductions of about 15 per cent.

### 7.2.4  A Global Power Play? The UK Overtakes the US as the No. 1 Donor in IDA-15 (FY2009–11)

The fiscal disparity in aid-giving between the EU donors and the USA was further widened in IDA-15.[59] EU Member States in May 2005 pledged to increase ODA to 0.7 per cent of Gross National Income (GNI) by 2015, with an interim target of 0.56 per cent ODA/GNI by 2010, which would result in an additional annual €20 billion ODA.[60] By contrast, the Bush Administration was mired in the 'War on Terror', with spiralling costs. Its financial strength was further vitiated by dollar

themselves. Aid dependence is measured as aid a percentage of GDP and of total
government expenditure. See ActionAid (2011).
[59]  IDA-15 covered FY2009–11, negotiated between March 2007
and December 2007.
[60]  Council of the European Union (2005: para. 4).

depreciation. Accordingly, should better-off European donors support a larger target total regardless of the US dollar contribution, the US share would probably drop again, at the cost of losing its top donor position.

The key decision faced by other donors, especially the UK, was whether they would continue to insist that the USA should/must be the largest donor, driven by their fairness concerns and/or their fear of a US exit.

In IDA-14 the UK had avoided surpassing the United States as the largest donors by deliberately setting aside a special fund of GBP250 million outside the ordinary IDA burden-sharing system. This decision was made due to the political concern that the United States would lose any stake in IDA once it slipped into second place.[61]

The dilemma was that if the UK did not move to the top position, IDA-15 would be much smaller than it would otherwise be. Should other donors persist in positioning the United States as the No. 1 donor, this would compel the UK to cut its planned contribution to keep its share below that of the United States. The UK basic share had almost reached parity with that of the United States in IDA-14, at the narrow margin of less than 1 per cent. And if the UK did not move into the top position, most other European donors would probably cut back on their contributions.

To devise a way out of the predicament, Bank Management proactively persuaded other donors to reassess the pros and cons of preserving the United States' 'largest donor' position for the sake of a larger IDA-15.

Bank Management acted as a 'quasi-donor' in IDA-15, mobilising internal resources in an effort to alleviate other donors' fairness concerns, thus boosting overall donor contributions. Most donors were used to setting their contributions primarily with reference to the USA. But, as its share dropped to a level of about 13 per cent in IDA-14, the US contribution was reduced to one of several possible benchmarks. A revealing insight from in-depth case studies was that the 'World Bank contribution' served as one of these benchmarks, because donors maintained that 'a critical component' of their support for an 'ambitious' IDA-15 was 'the continued ability of IBRD and IFC to contribute financial resources to IDA'.[62] Accordingly, the Bank

[61] Interview with the former UK IDA-15 Deputy, 31 October 2012, London.
[62] World Bank (2007b).

President, Robert Zoellick, played an active role in persuading the Board to support a record $3.5 billion from its own income as a contribution to IDA.[63] As he proudly highlighted, 'I am pleased to say the board helped us put our money where our mouth is ... This should help us gain momentum as we urge donor countries to increase their commitment'.[64] Such a generous World Bank Group internal income transfer accounted for more than 10 per cent of the total financing package, which helped mitigate other donors' preoccupation with the 'unfair' US share cut.

What about other donors' fear of a US exit? Although the USA acknowledged the potentially growing irrelevance of the World Bank 'as more countries gain market access and no longer need to rely on the Bank to finance development needs',[65] it called upon the World Bank to adapt to the changing landscape of development finance. Moreover, the United States explicitly supported 'a successful replenishment of IDA'.[66] Bank Management actively kept the United States engaged to assure other donors of constructive US participation. Accordingly, it did not display any disturbing sign of a severe cut or an outright withdrawal. Thus, the UK and other donors breathed a sigh of relief, because the fear of a US exit was not as acute as before.

Subsequently, it was up to the UK to decide whether it was willing to overtake the USA as the largest donor.

On the one hand, the UK was hesitant to surpass the United States because it did not want to be viewed as engaging in a 'global power play' to challenge US supremacy.[67] From the standpoint of the UK, being the largest IDA contributor was not its main policy objective. Rather, it was a means of achieving its primary goal of leveraging its aid to augment total donor contributions to IDA.

On the other hand, the UK found a more compelling reason for outstripping the United States: it could put pressure on the USA to

---

[63] For the first time, International Finance Corporation (IFC) made income transfers to IDA.

[64] Dunphy (2007).

[65] Statement by the US Alternate Governor, Clay Lowery, from World Bank, *2006 Annual Meetings of the Boards of Governors: Summary Proceedings* (Washington, DC, September 18, 2006), 182.

[66] Statement by the US Governor, Henry M. Paulson, World Bank, *2007 Annual Meetings of the Boards of Governors: Summary Proceedings* (Washington, DC, 21 October 2007), 165.

[67] Interview with the former UK IDA-15 Deputy, 31 October 2012, London.

catch up with the UK next time. Therefore, the UK decided to move away from its previously cautious approach to a 'risk-taking' one.[68] It turned out that the UK strategy paid off, since the United States increased its dollar contribution by 30 per cent in IDA-15 and became the largest donor again in IDA-16.[69]

Eventually, the UK decided to contribute to IDA based on its own ability and willingness regardless of the US contribution, even though this approach meant it would overtake the United States.

In summary, Bank Management proactively mitigated other donors' fairness concerns as well as their fear of a US exit. This helped to persuade other donors, especially the UK, to accept a further US share cut for the sake of a larger total size of IDA-15. Accordingly, the UK surpassed the United States as the largest donor in IDA.

## 7.3 Leadership in Transition? An Assessment of US and UK Influence

The new millennium saw the UK replacing the USA as the top donor for the first time. What implications would this burden-shifting have for leadership and influence in the World Bank? Did it herald leadership in transition from the US to the UK?

A preliminary assessment shows that the USA still remained capable of achieving most of its negotiating objectives despite a slump in its share in IDA-14 (FY2006–08, negotiated between February 2004 and February 2005).

In IDA-14, the United States successfully secured a number of policy changes including: (a) the improvement of IDA's results measurement system; (b) a projected increase in grant share from 18–22 per cent to a projected 30 per cent; (c) promotion of private sector development; and (d) expanded transparency (full disclosure of the numerical ratings of IDA recipients' policy performance, known as the CPIA – 'Country Policy and Institutional Assessment').[70]

---

[68] Ibid.

[69] Since IDA-14, each donor contribution has included several additional categories (such as HIPC costs, grant compensations) in conjunction with basic contributions. While the US basic contribution was still below that of the UK in IDA-16, its overall share overtook the UK.

[70] US Department of the Treasury, *Treasury International Programmes: Justification for Appropriations: FY2006 Budget Request*, 2006, 45.

In IDA-15, the United States supported further policy reforms, including: (a) an expanded results measurement system; (b) improvements to the operational framework in fragile states; (c) measures to enhance debt sustainability; and (d) progress towards greater transparency.[71]

Yet the above evidence alone does not suffice to serve as a robust test of whether the US influence has endured or even strengthened over time, because a real test needs to factor in how difficult it was to achieve the US objectives. A closer examination finds that the United States had shifted from accomplishing dramatic policy initiatives to fine-tuning incremental changes. Thus, rather than pushing through ground-breaking reforms (such as the grant proposal in IDA-13), the United States came to focus on consolidating its gained influence in cases where there was not much controversy (i.e., there was no substantial division regarding donor preferences).

First-hand interviews with US policy-makers reveal that the United States had increasingly realised the limitations of relying on financial leverage alone to seek influence and the importance of rallying most donors behind its initiatives. As a former US IDA Deputy reflected:

[T]he decision in IDA policy discussions is based on consensus: "one donor, one microphone." So the sense of the meeting is very important to see where consensus goes. Even if you are the biggest donor, you will be isolated if your proposal cannot be accepted by the majority. If you are a small donor, you can build up your constituency and persuade others to accept your proposal. In that sense, small donors can have a disproportionate influence compared with their contribution in IDA replenishment negotiations.[72]

The reason why the United States increasingly paid attention to the power of persuasion might be associated with the substantial reduction in its financial weight. For one thing, the US share dropped to such a mediocre level that it no longer occupied an unassailable place. For

---

At the urging of the US Bush Administration, the Board of Executive Directors approved the disclosure of the numerical CPIA scores for IDA recipients in September 2004.

See World Bank, 'Country Policy and Institutional Assessment: Frequently Asked Questions', 9, www.worldbank.org/ida/IRAI/2011/webFAQ11.pdf (accessed 26 November 2014).

[71] US Department of the Treasury, *Treasury International Programmes: Justification for Appropriations: FY2009 Budget Request*, 2009, 33.

[72] Interview with the former US IDA-16 Deputy, 9 August 2012, Washington, DC.

another, and more importantly, the USA no longer served as the most important reference donor against which other donors set their contribution levels. No longer could the US cash contribution dictate the total size of IDA replenishment, as other donors had dropped their rigid direct pegging burden-sharing system in IDA-14.

Yet the weakened US financial weight did not necessarily result in a loss in its policy influence, since factors other than financial leverage determined the degree of success in achieving its goals. Firstly, the USA still possessed high research capacity that generated innovative ideas and convincing arguments. Secondly, it was committed to achieving prioritised policy reforms by articulating its positions forcefully. Last but not least, it built coalitions with other major donors through G8 and G20 processes.

The following section analyses the UK influence in IDA replenishment negotiations.

To conduct a tough test of the UK influence, it would be useful to focus on its new policy initiatives that might meet potential objections from other donors, especially the United States and Bank Management.

The UK-DFID had developed a systematic approach to influencing the agenda of the World Bank through the production of an *Institutional Strategy Paper*, normally every three years, which set out UK objectives and an action plan. Progress was reviewed on an annual basis. In IDA-14, the UK had published a statement of its objectives before replenishment negotiations got started to help to identify common ground between its own objectives and those of other donors.[73]

One successful UK initiative was to reform the World Bank's conditionality policy. Conventionally, donors frequently attached conditions to their aid in order to 'buy' particular policy changes in recipient countries. Empirical evidence has shown that such kinds of donor-driven conditionality approaches were neither effective nor desirable without the buy-in of recipient countries. To address these flaws, the UK took the lead in adopting a new approach in its bilateral conditionality policy based on 'an open dialogue, with rights and responsibilities on both donor and developing countries'.[74] It explicitly stated that 'DFID does not use conditions to impose economic policy choices on partner countries, but ... will only consider

---

[73] DFID (2004:12).     [74] DFID (2005: para. 1.3).

suspending or reducing aid where a partner government has seriously breached its commitment to poverty reduction, human rights or sound financial management'.[75]

Subsequently, the UK regarded IDA-14 negotiations as a key opportunity to reform the World Bank's conditionality policy. From the UK's perspective, countries should lead their own development, and conditions linked to aid should not be used to impose policies on governments; hence, 'World Bank diktat is no substitute for thorough debate and engagement of stakeholders' by the borrower country government.[76] Many UK-based NGOs had vocally criticised the World Bank for pushing 'fundamental and often highly controversial changes in economic policy' (known as 'Washington Consensus').[77]

To advance its influence, the UK pledged to provide an additional 'incentive contribution' of £100 million whose release would partly hinge on the World Bank improving its practice on conditionality. First, the UK pressed for a thorough review of the Bank's policy and practice on conditionality. In response, the Bank carried out such a review and proposed five 'Good Practice Principles',[78] aimed at reducing the overall number of conditions and ensuring country ownership. The findings and recommendations of the review were discussed at the Bank's Board in September 2005, and the proposed principles were then endorsed by governors at the annual meetings. Accordingly, the UK released the first £50 million.[79] Then, to further enhance its influence, the UK publicly stated in September 2006 that it would only release its second contribution of £50 million once it saw clear evidence that the principles were being applied.[80] In December 2006, the Bank made a progress report[81] that provided evidence that real progress had been made. The report also reiterated Bank Management's strong commitment to making further improvements in its use of

---

[75]  DFID (2007: 122).
[76]  UK Parliamentary International Development Committee (2008: 3).
[77]  Bretton Woods Project (2004).      [78]  World Bank (2005a).
[79]  UK Parliament (2006).
[80]  *Ministerial Statement to the Development Committee by the Rt Hon Hilary Benn MP, Secretary of State for International Development and the Rt Hon Gordon Brown MP, Chancellor of the Exchequer*, The Annual Meetings of the IMF and World Bank, Singapore, 18 September 2006, www.publications .parliament.uk/pa/cm200506/cmselect/cmintdev/1622/1622we02.htm#a2 (accessed 16 March 2014).
[81]  World Bank (2006).

conditionality, including 'avoiding the use of sensitive economic policy conditions such as privatisation'. The UK therefore released the second £50 million contribution.[82]

Another key UK-led initiative was the establishment of a permanent 'Crisis Response Window' (CRW) in IDA-16 (FY2012–14, negotiated between March and December 2010).[83] The UK realised that 'the 2008 global financial crisis revealed a fundamental weakness in IDA architecture, namely: IDA's fixed capital prevented it from responding flexibly and promptly to help poor countries affected by the global financial crisis'. Hence, the UK collaborated with Bank Management in setting up a crisis response facility on a pilot basis in November 2009. The World Bank allocated $1.6 billion (£1 billion) of resources for this purpose, including £100 million from the UK. This pioneering experiment proved useful in dealing with urgent crises such as the Bank's emergency response to the Haiti earthquake. As IDA-16 was approaching, the UK played 'a pivotal role' in encouraging Bank Management to consider the feasibility of establishing a permanent crisis response facility.[84]

Yet the proposed CRW could potentially encounter opposition from the United States, since it was an 'exception' to the well-established PBA system it greatly valued. Initially, the United States stood firm on its principle that aid allocations give priority to 'performance' over 'need' because it firmly believed that 'aid should be allocated to countries where funds can be used most effectively'.

Later, however, the pilot facility persuaded the United States that the current PBA system could not accommodate other compelling needs (such as fragile states, regional projects, and crisis response). Hence, even though it did not initiate this exception, the US did not make a principled rejection.

But the United States did have strong reservations regarding the exact shape of this proposed window. From the its perspective, the original Bank's proposal suffered from two flaws: first, there were no clear allocation criteria, which ran the risk of allocating funds to 'poor performers' identified by the PBA system; second, it might entail 'contingent donor contributions' – if the initial ring-fenced funds

---

[82] DFID (2007: 142).
[83] IDA-16 covered FY2012–14, negotiated between March and December 2010.
[84] UK Parliamentary International Development Committee (2011).

were used up, donors were obligated to offer additional funds. The United States attributed these drawbacks to Bank Management's 'business-like' approach to fund-raising – maximising IDA-core with maximum flexibility in allocating funds.[85] Ultimately, due to strong US urging, the final proposal was 'improved' with a clear allocation criterion and no contingent donor contributions.[86]

To sum up, the above two cases provide evidence that the UK had enhanced its influence in initiating new policy changes and initiatives in the World Bank. Traditionally, major policy and institutional reforms mainly came from the United States, such as the establishment of the Inspection Panel, the overhaul of the disclosure policy, the transparent and formula-based aid allocation system, and the introduction of grants. Equipped with a strong research base and a vibrant development community, the UK was increasingly in a strong position to influence changes in the Bank's development policies and practices.

The comparison of the two cases illustrates that the UK began to rely more on persuasion than direct financial leverage to gain its desired policy influence. In the first case on aid conditionality, the UK directly tied its contribution to the Bank's fulfilment of certain agreed sets of actions, whereas in the second case, on the crisis response window, the UK relied more on the effect of demonstration and persuasion through a bottom-up pilot project which was then mainstreamed into IDA's operations.

Why did the UK seem to have forgone the 'incentive contribution' that it once used in IDA-14 to produce swift policy changes? While the UK parliament and domestic NGOs (e.g., the Bretton Woods Project) explicitly urged DFID to condition its contribution upon the Bank making substantial policy reforms in IDA-16, Andrew Mitchell, the Secretary of State for International Development, resisted this temptation because he believed that 'waving such a big stick' was not 'the right way' to achieve policy influence in the long run. The rationale behind the abandonment of 'incentive contributions' was that this unilateral action would result in the adverse consequence that IDA donors would seek to attach their own separate conditions to IDA. Hence, a DFID official concluded that 'there would be absolutely no certainty, no predictability and no ability for countries to know how much money

---

[85]  Interview with the former US IDA-16 Deputy, 9 August 2012, Washington DC.
[86]  Ibid.

they were going to get, and the whole thing would collapse'.[87] As a result, the 'incentive contribution' option was dropped by all donors in IDA-16.

In a nutshell, the profound impact of *'Accelerated Burden-Shifting'* upon World Bank governance was less of a leadership transition from the United States to the UK, and more of a nuanced shift from a coercion-anchored power relationship to a persuasion-oriented one. The absence of a predominant donor rendered less effective the exercise of power primarily based on material capabilities. Increasingly, the power of persuasion gained importance in seeking influence among roughly equal-size donors.

## 7.4 Conclusion

To what extent does a close process-tracing of replenishment negotiations help to solve the intriguing puzzle of the substantial shift in IDA's burden-sharing of a falling United States and a rising UK?

An immediate cause of the precipitous decline in the US share was its inability and unwillingness to sustain its financial support for IDA. First, the US fiscal capacity was aggravated by budgetary austerity and dollar depreciation, so it was unable to maintain its traditional share of an increased total size of IDA replenishment preferred by most donors. Second, the resurgence of unilateralism in US foreign policy generated a declining hegemonic interest in multilateral development cooperation as the order of the day. As the Bush Administration reignited the US 'imperial ambition', it dramatically shifted aid money away from multilateral channels to bilateral initiatives, since it favoured unilateral and bilateral means over multilateral solutions.

By contrast, the UK and other European donors stepped up their aid efforts and valued IDA as an effective multilateral aid organisation. This led to an ever-widening fiscal gap between the USA and European donors. In other words, IDA's traditional burden-sharing arrangement no longer reflected the new balance of donors' fiscal ability and political willingness to contribute to IDA. Whether IDA burden-sharing patterns swiftly reflected the underlying shift in fiscal capacities between the USA and other donors depended upon whether there

---

[87] UK Parliamentary International Development Committee (2011).

was a driving force to expand IDA, temporarily overriding other donors' fairness concern.

A crucial factor in breaking the traditional equilibrium of the direct pegging burden-sharing system was the UK drive for IDA expansion. Historically, secondary states usually proportionately cut back on their cash contributions in order to keep a fixed traditional US 'fair' share in the absence of a drive for a larger IDA, as happened in IDA-11/-12. By contrast, other donors accepted successive US share cuts in IDA-9/-10 because North–South power struggles necessitated accomplishing a sufficient size of total IDA donor contributions. As the North–South power struggles faded away, the UK played a leading role in driving for an IDA expansion in IDA-14. What motivated the UK to become a lead donor was its overarching strategy of using its buoyant aid budget to leverage as much aid as possible from relatively 'less effective' bilateral donors to the 'more effective' IDA (in the eyes of the UK) in an effort to improve the overall efficiency of global aid spending. Moreover, the UK aimed to enhance its policy influence in the World Bank to shape the direction of the entire development community.

A closer examination further reveals that the root cause of why other donors supported the high UK-proposed target total and thus accepted a substantial US share reduction was that secondary states accelerated their 'voice' option to redress the imbalance between contribution and influence. Voice opportunities helped mitigate other donors' previous preoccupation with fairness concerns, hence lowering their expectations of the minimum US 'fair' share.

The early signs of loss in US influence were the deep mistrust of other donors of the US motives in the 'Grants vs. Loans' debate in IDA-13, which hampered the US ability to achieve its announced goal. Further evidence of fading US influence was the fiasco of the US attempt to initiate a change in the IDA replenishment procedure in IDA-14 (i.e., replacing senior Bank Management with external candidates as IDA replenishment chairpersons).

The acceleration in the 'voice' option taken by other donors was mainly driven by their fairness concern, exacerbated by the US salient unilateral influence attempt (via the 'incentive contribution' route) and its failure to honour its commitments in IDA-13. Such acceleration was also facilitated by the lessening of their structural dependence upon the hegemon.

Finally, what implications did the watershed in IDA burden-sharing have for leadership and influence in World Bank governance?

Despite a slump in its share, the United States still managed to obtain most of its negotiating objectives, because it consciously sought incremental policy changes with broad donor support rather than initiating controversial ground-breaking reforms. But a robust test of US influence requires a case where preferences of key stakeholders diverged from those of the USA.

Yet it was clear that the US financial weight was weakening, since other donors no longer rigidly tied their cash contributions to that of the United States. This in turn encouraged the United States to rely more on the power of persuasion than on financial clout to advance its policy influence.

What about the UK influence? As the principal donor, the UK had successfully achieved new policy changes and initiatives in the World Bank. Initially, it deployed unilateral incentive contribution to push through swift policy reforms. It then realised the risk of unilateral influence contests among donors and thus forwent the option of 'incentive contribution' contingent upon specific Bank performance (despite the strong pressure from its Parliament and NGOs to continue such conditional contributions). Later, the UK relied more on the power of persuasion by using bottom-up pilot projects (financed by the trust fund route) to demonstrate the virtue of its proposed policy reforms.

To conclude, the nuanced change in donor influence was less to do with a leadership transition from the US to the UK, but, rather, a shift from a coercion-anchored power relationship to a persuasion-oriented process.

The next chapter will explore why China decided to become a new donor to IDA in 2007. Did it herald that a rising China was taking more international responsibility as it grew richer? First-hand information on China's decision-making processes will uncover the driving forces behind this emerging power's milestone decision.

# 8 | *China's Ascendancy: Influence from Within and Impact from Outside*

China's rise as a development financer has sparked a heated debate about its implications for the international development system. On the one hand, some contend that China has undermined norms and rules established by traditional donors and should be socialised into the existing international aid regime.[1] On the other hand, others maintain that China has presented a 'golden opportunity' for Africa, providing a 'win–win' alternative through trade and investment to break the vicious circle of aid dependency.[2]

The debate on China's ascendancy as a development financer is gaining much more salience, as ascending China is unprecedentedly establishing new multilateral financing institutions, alongside its mighty bilateral financing arms, outside the US-centred international economic order. This brings about a set of compelling questions: What motivates China to set up a new set of multilateral development institutions without the US participation? Will the World Bank lose its relevance, falling into oblivion? Or, will the World Bank re-invent itself to accommodate China's concepts and aspirations so as to harness the Chinese financial power as a force for good?

Against the above grand debate, China's decision to become a new donor to IDA in 2007 represents a crucial case in exploring what motivated China to contribute to IDA and the implications for China's influence in the World Bank.

This chapter proceeds as follows: firstly, it presents the empirical puzzle; secondly, it examines alternative hypotheses in explaining China's decision to become a new donor in IDA-15 (FY2009–11); thirdly, it explains why China bolstered its support in the subsequent IDA-16 (FY2012–14); fourthly, it evaluates China's influence in the World Bank after becoming a new IDA donor; finally, it concludes with the main arguments and implications.

---

[1] Paulo and Reisen (2010).    [2] Moyo (2009).

228

## 8.1 An Empirical Puzzle

China became a new donor in IDA-15 in 2007. This decision was a milestone in China's relationship with the World Bank, symbolising a shift in its status from a former recipient to a new donor.[3]

It poses an intriguing puzzle because compelling rationales lead us to expect that China should have *not* contributed to IDA.

First, the old Western-dominated governance structure was so deeply entrenched that China's voting rights in the IBRD were much lower than its ascending economic status would have warranted. China merely ranked sixth in the IBRD shareholding, although it was the third largest world economy in 2007.

Second, China had viable alternatives for growing bilateral assistance over which it had full control. The Department of Aid to Foreign Countries in the Ministry of Commerce (MOFCOM) was mainly responsible for China's bilateral aid. China's Ex-Im Bank was a key player in providing concessional loans.[4]

Third, a premature acceptance of an international donor status would contradict China's self-proclaimed identity as a developing country, potentially undercutting its advantages in the WTO, climate change negotiations, etc. Meanwhile, China remained a recipient country of foreign aid in 2007; a noticeable assumption of IDA donorship might offer rich countries excuses to wean China off foreign assistance.

Finally, joining the IDA donor club might undermine China's solidarity with recipient countries, because they lamented the trend of socialising China into the Western aid group, thus depriving them of alternative financing options and stifling their policy space.

As seen in the case studies that follow, the above counterarguments are not simply logical reasoning, but actual concerns expressed by high-level governmental officials in China. Then how did China, in the face of these countervailing facts and arguments, eventually make up its mind to embark on its IDA donorship?

---

[3] The People's Republic of China replaced Taiwan and became a member in the IMF and the World Bank in 1980. See Jacobson and Oksenberg (1990: 77–81).
   Since 1980, China had been eligible for IDA's development assistance until it graduated in 1999.

[4] PRC (2011).

## 8.2 Explaining Why China Became a New IDA Donor in IDA-15 (FY2009–11)

This section first examines the extent to which conventional explanations – capacity-to-pay and country-specific interests – help to explain why China decided to become a new donor to IDA, then assesses the plausibility of alternative explanations drawn from history and theories, and finally conducts in-depth process-tracing to discover the driving force behind China's decision to start contributing to IDA.

### 8.2.1  Conventional Explanations: Capacity or Interests?

The baseline 'capacity-to-pay' principle expects that as countries get richer, they would be positioned to assist poor countries.

At first glance, this argument sounds plausible, since China's spectacular economic growth had enabled it to become the world's third largest economy in 2007, second to the United States and Japan.

Yet this aggregate GNP data is misleading. With a population of 1.3 billion, China was still a lower-middle-income country faced with the daunting development challenge of lifting over 200 million people – accounting for nearly one-sixth of poverty-stricken people worldwide – out of extreme poverty.[5] Hence, China represents a unique case of rising powers: despite its economic miracle China remained far from rich on a per capita basis.

China's economic miracle did raise international expectations that China should shoulder more international responsibility. As seen in the previous chapters, ascending/emerging powers took the heat to contribute to IDA, as with Germany and Japan who enjoyed economic miracles in the 1960s/70s, and oil-producing countries with their windfall wealth in the mid-1970s. But history shows that international pressures alone were not sufficient to persuade rising stars to donate more to IDA.

A second conventional explanation is that China started contributing in order to harvest IDA country-specific interests.

One tangible country-specific interest is procurement benefits. On the surface, China did well in its procurement performance. For example, in 2006 China won over 13 per cent ($400 million) of the total

---

[5] See WDI.

value of IDA-financed contracts, surpassing the record of the top five traditional donors combined. Yet China's eligibility for procurement bidding did not hinge on its IDA donorship, because the World Bank adhered to the guideline that 'suppliers and consultants from *any* country are eligible to participate in Bank-financed procurement for *all* loans or credits' (emphasis added).[6]

But it would be hasty to conclude that procurement benefits played no role in China's decision to become a new donor. History shows that the UK had high stakes in striving for an enlarged IDA as the principal beneficiary of IDA procurement. It might thus be plausible to expect that domestic business firms lobbied the Chinese government to become an IDA donor in order to encourage traditional donors to do more for an ambitious IDA replenishment. An in-depth case study is needed to discover whether commercial interests played any significant role in China's decision to become a new donor as presented below.

Another intangible country-specific factor is reputation, since IDA burden share symbolised donor commitment to multilateralism and international responsibility.

IDA burden shares are not simply arithmetic calculations, but also carry symbolic meaning. As seen in the previous chapters, many donors strived to honour their traditional shares even in the face of domestic budgetary difficulties because they wanted to avoid sending negative signals to an international audience about their willingness to shoulder international responsibility.

So it is reasonable to assume that China could employ 'multilateral diplomacy' to 'facilitate foreign recognition of China as a responsible great power'.[7] Preliminary evidence seems to confirm the plausibility of this hypothesis. Upon China's announcement of joining the IDA donor group, Chinese media commented that this landmark move to become a new IDA donor 'symbolised' China's dedication to being 'a responsible great nation'.[8] Yet the public stance might mask under-lying motives in China's position, to be discovered in case studies later in the chapter.

---

[6] This new guideline became effective in May 2004. Previously, only Bank members were eligible. This change in policy actually made little difference, since over 180 countries had membership of the World Bank. World Bank, *Eligibility for the Provision of Goods, Works and Services in Projects Financed by the World Bank*, http://go.worldbank.org/ZGK0D5OHE0 (accessed 12 March 2014).
[7] Deng (2008: 235).      [8] China Online (2007).

In summary, a preliminary analysis suggests that conventional explanations are insufficient to answer the question of what motivated China to become a new IDA donor. Yet they do help to guide us to find out more about how China coped with heightening international pressures and what China really wanted: commercial interests, international image, or something else.

## 8.2.2  Other Alternative Explanations

This section draws hypotheses from the history and theories of IDA replenishment to seek explanations for China's decision to become a new IDA donor. First, we explore whether China was coerced by the United States to start contributing to IDA. Second, we examine whether China became a new donor in order to signal its compliance with the principles and practices of the existing international aid architecture.

### Hegemonic Coercion

As seen in the previous chapters, ascending powers (Japan and Germany) were coerced to step up their financial support for IDA in the 1970s. This generates a hypothesis that China, as a contemporary emerging power, became a new IDA donor under hegemonic coercion.

Below is an analysis of whether the United States had the interest and ability to co-opt China to assume its IDA donorship.

Regarding the US readiness to exert hegemonic coercion, the previous chapter shows that US interest in IDA was waning as the Bush Administration made a unilateralist turn in foreign policy. Thus, it seems overstretched to argue that the hegemon bothered coercing China to donate aid to IDA in which the United States felt no vital stake.

Even assuming that the hegemon did have incentive to do so, its ability to coerce was in serious doubt. Unlike past ascending powers, China did *not* depend upon the United States for military protection. Rather, the United States relied on China's abundant foreign reserves to service its debt, whereas China counted on US consumption to sustain its export-oriented growth. Thus, the US–China relationship was characterised more by complex interdependence than by asymmetrical dependence.

On balance, the coercion thesis hardly holds water.

Yet, it is worth noting that the United States did exert diplomatic pressure to urge China to become a 'responsible stakeholder'.[9] More analysis needs to be done to examine the extent to which China's decision was a passive response to external pressures or a proactive action to seek its strategic goals.

### A Compliance Process at Work: Socialising China as a 'Normal' Donor?

A theoretically potent hypothesis is that China's decision to become a new IDA donor signified its willingness to comply with international best practice of aid-giving due to the successful Western 'engagement' strategy.[10] Evidence shows that China had been a learner of playing by the rules rather than a spoiler of overturning the established norms – a rule-taker rather than a rule-breaker – in key international economic organisations.[11]

Using the traditional donors' standards as the benchmark,[12] it was often remarked that China had fallen well short of the mainstream proper rules of conduct. The OECD's Development Assistance Committee (DAC) is the institutional forum where traditional donors agree upon 'best practices' and induce compliance via regular peer reviews.

First, traditional donors viewed China's aid with 'no strings attached' as a challenge to Western-style good governance, with its emphasis on the protection of human rights and advancing democracy, because it negated their financial leverage in 'rogue states'.[13]

Second, China seemed not to enforce social and environment safeguards as stringently as traditional donors, at the risk of degenerating the environment and exacerbating social inequality on the ground.[14]

---

[9] Zoellick (2005).      [10] Pearson (1999: 211).

[11] Jacobson and Oksenberg (1990: 1).

[12] Yet it is worth noting that the bulk of China's development finance goes well beyond traditional ODA such as export credits and investments with implicit state guarantees. Thus, Deborah Bräutigam (2011) points out that DAC's foreign aid regime may not be the right one to govern the Chinese growing development finance.

[13] Naím (2007).

[14] For instance, in October 2006 World Bank President Paul Wolfowitz maintained that Chinese banks 'do not respect' environmental standards when lending in Africa. 'World Bank President Criticizes China's Banks over Africa Lending', *The Associated Press*, 24 October 2006.

Last but not least, China's 'state capitalism' risked undermining the liberalisation agenda and breeding crony capitalism.[15] Here the question was whether the 'China model' offered a viable alternative to liberal democracy and the free market.

Given the Western perception of China's divergent and potentially pernicious development assistance, traditional donors stepped up their efforts to socialise China to embrace their 'best' practices by adopting an *Outreach Strategy* in 2005 to 'bring partners closer to the OECD ... through the adoption of OECD practices, policies, guidelines or instruments'.[16]

The compliance thesis, however, does not stand up to empirical scrutiny.

For one thing, China took an even more proactive stance to articulating its foreign aid principles, as anchored in South–South Development Cooperation after it became a new IDA donor in 2007. In April 2011, the Chinese government published its first white paper on foreign aid, where it reaffirmed its basic principles, including 'helping recipient countries build up their self-development capacity', 'imposing no political conditions', and 'adhering to equality, mutual benefit and common development'.[17] Thus, China has consciously distanced itself from the North–South aid relationship.

For another thing, after its initial failure to 'normalise' emerging powers, the DAC was compelled to give up the self-claimed moral high ground and adjust its own strategy to recognise diversity and mutual learning. In November 2011, the DAC agreed on a 'Global Relations Strategy' aimed to 'forge new relationships with these new partners through open dialogue *without preconditions*' (emphasis added).[18]

When it comes to China's relationship with the World Bank, the empirical evidence turns the compliance thesis on its head.

One notable effort made by the World Bank to exert compliance pressure on China was its policy framework on debt sustainability. Beginning around 2000, China's infrastructure financing, notably for power and transportation, has risen with extraordinary rapidity in poor countries. While China maintained that large-scale investments could advance economic take-off, thus ending aid dependence, the

---

[15] Halper (2010).   [16] OECD (2008).   [17] PRC (2011: 5–6).
[18] DAC (2011).

World Bank President Paul Wolfowitz criticised China as a 'free-rider' because China's large-scale development finance backed by implicit state guarantees risked throwing poor countries back into a vicious indebting-and-forgiving cycle after the large-scale Western debt relief efforts.[19] To avoid debt re-accumulation, the World Bank put in place a Non-Concessional Borrowing Policy (NCBP) in 2006, implemented by fostering creditor coordination on the one hand and using IDA's financial leverage to deter imprudent borrowing and build debt management capacity in recipient countries on the other hand.[20]

Yet it turns out that it was the World Bank rather than China that adjusted its policy on the issue of debt sustainability. In 2010 the NCBP introduced more flexibility by moving away from its previous one-size-fits-all approach to a more differentiated approach in setting debt limits.[21] Since this policy change occurred after China acquired donor status, it might be reasonable to assume that China used its financial leverage as an IDA donor to push through its desired policy change. Section 8.4 below will investigate this thesis.

To sum up, the compliance thesis is of little help in explaining China's decision to become a new IDA donor.

### 8.2.3 Aspirations for Influence: China's Stakeholder Strategy for Redressing the Contribution-to-Influence Disparity

This section traces the process of China's decision-making to explore an alternative hypothesis, namely whether China was motivated to vie for influence by becoming an IDA donor. First-hand data was collected from elite interviews with senior Chinese decision-makers, Bank Management, and traditional donors.

As we learn from the third layer of power play about the informal donor influence upon Bank Management, the notion of equity and fairness played a pivotal role in shaping IDA burden-sharing dynamics. As a member of the World Bank, China felt keenly that the equity line between influence and contribution was skewed to breaking point, and so decided to work proactively to win 'voice opportunities'.

---

[19] 'World Bank President Criticizes China's Banks over Africa Lending', *The Associated Press*, 24 October 2006.
[20] IDA (2006).    [21] IDA (2010).

As a former IDA recipient, China was full of indignation that the IDA donor forum (the 'IDA Deputies' – representatives from donor governments at IDA replenishment negotiations) had grasped the de facto decision-making power, surpassing the Executive Board in the formal governance procedures of the World Bank. Consequently, recipient countries had little voice at the IDA replenishment negotiation table where priorities and policies were set, but had to bear direct consequences of donor-driven policy orientations (even if they were not the right recipes for how to cope with development challenges). Moreover, such donor-driven policy prescriptions were extended to the whole World Bank operations. Hence, IBRD borrowers (such as China) had to comply with policy conditionality set by IDA Deputies, even though these middle-income IBRD countries did not receive a single IDA penny from rich donor countries.

First, the 'basic needs' approach had narrowly focused on direct poverty reduction (with 'visible' achievements that could easily garner support from domestic constituency in donor countries), downplaying the importance of economic growth that served as the engine for sustainable large-scale poverty alleviation. Such an emphasis upon social sectors was accompanied by shrinking infrastructure financing; the assumption that the free market would automatically channel capital where it was needed turned out to be a false hope. The reality was that capital markets were riddled with an excessive focus on short-term performance and could not alone overcome high risks to provide long-term finance. Consequently, developing countries faced a daunting infrastructure gap that severely constrained their potential for economic transformation.[22]

China's critique of the mainstream 'basic needs' development paradigm was based on its own recent development experience that economic success was the underlying driving force for lifting more than 600 million people out of extreme poverty. While it recognised that economic growth alone did not automatically lead to welfare-improvement for all,[23] it maintained that economic growth was

---

[22]  Zou and Mo (2002: 39).
[23]  The Chinese government had established a nationwide administrative system, headed by a State Council Leading Group, especially designed for poverty reduction as its economic growth had widened the income gap between the rich and the poor.

a necessary, albeit insufficient, condition for large-scale and self-sustaining poverty reduction.[24]

While China realised that the prevailing basic needs approach was an antidote to economic structural adjustments without a human face in the 1980s,[25] it felt that the pendulum had swung back too far, shying away from fundamental challenges of improving productivity, diversifying industrial structures, and moving up the global value chain.[26]

Second, unduly stringent environmental and social safeguards risked putting poor countries at a competitive disadvantage in their catching-up integration into the global economy. In an ideal world without difficult trade-offs, developing countries recognised the importance of striking a balance between economic growth, human rights, and environmental protection. But, in the real world, China shared the concerns of many other developing countries: that prematurely adopting demanding standards would hamper economic development and trap poor countries in a vicious cycle of economic stagnation, conflict, and destitution. While China recognised that lop-sided emphasis on economic growth could incur irreversible environmental damage and entrench social inequality, it maintained that environmental and governance problems were symptoms of underdevelopment rather than root causes. Hence, these problems had to be incrementally improved in a dynamic development process.[27] Moreover, it was unfair if donor countries leveraged their financial clout to compel poor countries with electricity deficits to use high-cost renewable energy with no additional financial and technical support when rich countries still relied on coal-fired plants for energy supply.[28]

Furthermore, China was informed by its own experience as a former IDA recipient that the demand for 'zero tolerance' in environmental and social safeguards could sometimes run the risk of 'politicising' the World Bank.[29] While it recognised that well-intentioned NGOs had not only helped to reform the World Bank to put necessary safeguards in place, but also hold it accountable, it found that a small group of

---

[24] Ibid.    [25] Cornia, Jolly, and Stewart (1987).
[26] Similar reflections were also made by development economists (Chang 2011).
[27] Interview with a former Chinese Executive Director at the World Bank, 15 December 2011, Beijing.
[28] Interview with a former Chinese Executive Director at the World Bank, 13 December 2011, Beijing.
[29] Ibid.

vocal Western NGOs with privileged access to international agenda-
setting might compromise Bank Management's professional judge-
ments to the detriment of the welfare of local people.

The Western Poverty Reduction Project in Qinghai – a remote western province of China – was a case in point in illustrating how
accountability mechanisms could be abused. The World Bank started
to prepare this small, routine irrigation and voluntary resettlement
project in 1997, since the Chinese government had done similar and
bigger projects elsewhere in western China that offered hope to people
trapped in harsh natural environments in abject poverty by resettling
them to a new place.[30] But shortly before the Board's decision for
project approval, Western pro-Tibet NGOs seized the project approval
process as a campaign vehicle to wage 'the biggest campaign' against
the World Bank under the slogan 'World Bank Approves China's
Genocide in Tibet'.[31] This campaign was hugely magnified by the
Western media. Under this global spotlight, in June 1999 the Board
decided to authorise the Bank's Inspection Panel to undertake a first-
ever full-scale investigation. The inspection delayed the project by more
than a year, producing a report with 'a selective exposition of facts' to
support the campaigners' claims that the Bank had failed to comply
with its own environmental and social directives in preparing the
project,[32] since the Panel's 'image of success is to find projects out of
compliance'.[33] Eventually, in July 2000, the Board discussion reached
a stalemate split between the representatives of developing countries
and developed countries. At this critical juncture, China decided to
withdraw the project from the Bank but proceeded with alternative
sources of finance.[34] NGOs declared a great victory.

The above case illustrates how accountability could go wrong, opening up 'the risk that minor "legal" infractions can be used as a weapon
for much larger political purposes'.[35] In hindsight, Robert Wade, one
of the expert consultants who advised the Inspection Panel in this case,
reflected that the primary leverage of these NGOs came from the
US Congressional threat to cut IDA contributions.[36] He further points
out that this creates a 'moral hazard' problem because rule-makers (the
US Congress and transnational NGOs) are 'not affected by the costs of

---

[30] Wade (2009: 30).    [31] Ibid.    [32] Ibid., 38.    [33] Wade (2000).
[34] Wade (2009: 25).    [35] Woods (2001: 94).    [36] Wade (2009: 28).

the policies they demand that others adopt'.[37] Thus, he warned that that the outcome of China withdrawing the project was 'another victory for US unilateralism and another step towards the Bank's irrelevance', as alternative sources of finance were growing for all except the poorest borrowing countries.[38]

It is worth noting that the tendency towards zero tolerance of risks is not confined to this single Bank project in China. Under intense scrutiny from NGOs, the Bank staff tended to foster a risk-averse culture that discouraged them from contemplating potentially risky projects. Of course, this critique of excessive precaution is by no means an excuse to exempt Bank Management from diligently implementing their safeguard policies in such contexts. But what concerned observers was that some advocacy NGOs skew information and take principled stands against any project with potential environmental or social risks 'without giving attention to developmental alternatives' or weighing up trade-offs to seek a better solution.[39]

Last but not least, China took the view that externally imposed policy conditionality (i.e., using financial leverage to coerce recipients into making policy change) did not work, because it at best induced mock compliance in aid-dependent countries and at worst triggered political backlash against the World Bank, tarnishing its reputation as a neutral and apolitical development institution.[40]

China's above critiques do not mean that it denied the role of the World Bank in helping developing countries to improve policies and institutions. On the contrary, China's own development cooperation with the Bank recognised the pivotal role of the Bank in fostering frontier institutional innovations ranging from modern project management to managed trade liberalisation.[41] But such kinds of policy change depended less on conditionality than persuasion. Most importantly, government leadership played a crucial role in piloting innovations, fostering bottom-up learning-by-doing experiments, and then introducing nationwide policy change in a gradual and pragmatic manner.[42]

One might argue that China's critique of coercive policy conditionality might be irrelevant since the World Bank had already learnt lessons from the past and redressed undue conditionality. At strong

---

[37] Ibid., 27.     [38] Ibid., 45.     [39] Ibid., 27.     [40] Zou and Mo (2002: 39).
[41] World Bank (2007a).     [42] Operation Evaluation Department (2005: 9).

UK urging in IDA-14, the World Bank had instigated 'good practice principles' of policy conditionality. Indeed, World Bank President James Wolfensohn publicly acknowledged that 'The Washington Consensus has been dead for years' at the Shanghai Conference on Scaling Up Poverty Reduction, hosted by China in 2004 and aimed at fostering a global learning process on how to accelerate growth and progress in poverty reduction.[43] (Despite President Wolfensohn's public denial of any Washington Consensus, the World Bank was still significantly imprinted with free-market ideology, as will be shown next.)

Despite the substantial reduction in the Bank's explicit conditionality, however, China considered that the Bank had implicitly implanted one-size-fits-all policy prescriptions in its aid allocation criteria. In order to 'earn' more aid, aid-dependent recipients had to make policy changes in advance in line with the yardsticks prescribed by donors (known as the 'Country Policy and Institutional Assessment' [CPIA]). Yet based on its own catching-up experiences, China felt that the CPIA had a built-in bias in favour of liberalisation and deregulation that could shrink the development space of late-comers in achieving structural economic transformation.[44]

China's concern over the Bank's implicit conditionality has been echoed by critiques from external stakeholders. Professor Ravi Kanbur warned in 2005 that the CPIA was imposing a common development model – a universal prescription not backed up by rigorous scientific evidence in supporting growth and development outcomes.[45] This critique was sharpened by a European scholar who made a thorough assessment of the CPIA and concluded that 'CPIA-steered selectivity ... seeks to promote further the adoption of the WB [World Bank]'s traditional (neo-liberal) reform agenda and precludes strategic state interventions deployed by the East Asian tiger economies'.[46] Think-tank reports have echoed the point that as a prescriptive tool the CPIA 'penalizes' poor countries for adopting alternative

---

[43]  James D. Wolfensohn, 'Opening Remarks at the Shanghai Conference on Scaling Up Poverty Reduction', 26 May 2004, http://go.worldbank.org/1XM NPFRIl0 (accessed 29 March 2014).

[44]  Interview with a former Chinese Executive Director at the World Bank, 13 December 2011, Beijing.
     This concern was also shared by development economists (Wade 2004: xliv).

[45]  Kanbur (2005: 130, 135).     [46]  Van Waeyenberge (2009: 802, 806).

development strategies such as the implementation of prudent industrial policies. Indeed, the importance of these alternative strategies had
been recognised by the eminent Commission on Growth and
Development chaired by Nobel Laureate Michael Spence.[47] NGOs
also harshly criticised the CPIA for imposing a policy straightjacket
upon aid-dependent recipient countries.

In response to these critiques, the Bank's Independent Evaluation
Group made a thorough assessment of the CPIA in 2009. Its central
conclusion was that empirical analysis failed to support the preponderant weight granted to 'governance indicators'. Such a bias might be
'driven much more by fiduciary and possibly other concerns of donors
than by the objectives of achieving sustained growth and poverty
reduction'.[48]

Tensions escalated as the Bank President Paul Wolfowitz adopted
'heavy-handed' methods for pushing the governance and anticorruption agenda. President Wolfowitz took the helm in May 2005, in
succession to James Wolfensohn (after his ten-year presidency), and
espoused his commitment to fighting corruption in developing countries after his famous 'cancer of corruption' speech in Indonesia
in April 2006. Recipient countries resisted governance-based conditionality as 'an intrusion on their sovereignty'. The objection also came
from a core group of European donors who maintained that the arbitrary choice of loan cancellations or suspensions was 'suspiciously
aligned with US geopolitical objectives and selectively applied without
due process'. China, backed by other borrowers, threatened to suspend
future borrowing if Wolfowitz did not rein in his 'punitive and arbitrary' anticorruption investigations into the Bank's portfolio. President
Wolfowitz had to resign in 2007 because of perceived conflict of interests in his management of the Bank. This led a commentator to call
Wolfowitz 'a perpetuator of cronyism'. This was a severe blow to the
Bank's anticorruption agenda, since its top leader 'failed to practice
what he so ardently preached'.[49] Consequently, China's sense of
unfairness was on the verge of eruption, compelling immediate action
to redress the contribution-influence disparity in World Bank
governance.

---

[47] Commission on Growth and Development (2008).    [48] IEG (2009: x).
[49] For citations throughout this paragraph, see Weaver (2008: 92–110).

It is worth noting that China's critiques outlined above on development policies and practices were not simply confined to IDA, because donors had mainstreamed IDA priorities and policies into the whole World Bank Group's strategy and operations, so the Board of Executive Directors (where IBRD borrowers and IDA recipients had formal representation) had been substantially marginalised. One researcher of the World Bank who has penetrated the functioning of its governance system had previously summed up this situation: 'the US has used threats to reduce or withhold contributions to the IDA in order to demand changes in policy, not just in the IDA but in the World Bank as a whole' (i.e., the 'tail' that wags the 'dog').[50] Accordingly, China bore the direct consequence of the donor-driven policy framework as a major client country in the IBRD, even though it had graduated from IDA in 1999.

Furthermore, the IDA Deputies' assumption of policy-making powers had been consolidated over time. From IDA-1 to IDA-6 (from the early 1960s and the late 1970s), the replenishment agreements endorsed by Deputies were confined to financial issues alone. From IDA-7 to IDA-8 (during the 1980s), Deputies' decisions on terms, eligibility, and allocations of IDA credits became an integral part of IDA Replenishment Agreements. But Deputies still normatively professed that the actual determination of these policies should 'remain a matter for final decision' by Executive Directors.[51] Yet, after the end of the Cold War (since IDA-9), the scope and depth of policy influence by IDA Deputies had expanded and deepened. Moreover, IDA Replenishment Agreements were replete with what Deputies 'propose' and 'recommend' that Executive Directors 'should' do. While the drafts were presented by Management to IDA Executive Directors for their review, discussion, and approval, experience indicated that 'there have been no changes made to the Deputies' report [IDA Replenishment Agreement] by the Board before it is sent to the Board of Governors for approval'.[52] From the legal perspective, Ibrahim Shihata, the World Bank former General Counsel, had maintained that IDA Deputies had no legal status in decision-making and should not attach policy conditions to IDA replenishment. He had further proposed that the

[50]  Woods (2006: 28).    [51]  IDA-7 Replenishment Agreement, para. 3.3.
[52]  Development Committee Communiqué, DC 2007–0024, 11 October 2007, para. 35.

Executive Directors' approval ought to result from their 'free deliberation', rather than 'a pro forma agreement to a document they had no role in preparing'.[53] In sum, since IDA Deputies had firmly usurped the power of decision-making in the World Bank Group, China deemed it impossible in practice to shake the prevailing norm by restoring the authority of the Board.

In summary, China came to the view that the World Bank's decision-making was dominated by donor countries, especially the United States, so that client countries lacked voice in policy-making but bore the direct effect of Bank policies on their economic and social development.

Apart from its lack of influence in decision-making, what further exacerbated China's sense of unfairness was that China and other IBRD borrowers were co-opted into being 'quasi-IDA donors' by transferring IBRD net income to IDA.

Transferring IBRD net income to IDA boiled down to a distributional issue with fault lines running between IDA donors (HICs) and IBRD borrowers (MICs) on how to allocate the IBRD's revenues stemming from loan charges paid by IBRD borrowers. The debate traced back to the early Board deliberations in the 1960s on whether profits from 'hard loan' windows (IBRD) should be used to supplement donor contributions to 'soft loan' windows (IDA). During initial deliberations, members emphasised that transferring IBRD net income to IDA could be seen as 'an income transfer from IBRD [MICs] to IDA borrowers [LICs]',[54] since these revenues could be used to reduce borrowing costs of IBRD borrowers should they not be transferred IDA. This led to a contentious burden-sharing issue regarding who should bear the burden of assisting poor countries: rich industrialised countries (often former colonial powers), or middle-income countries (including some graduating from LIC status after decolonisation). Eventually, at the strong urging of the United States and other G-7 countries, the Board decided to start to transfer some IBRD net incomes to IDA from FY1964.[55] This was a compromise between HICs and

---

[53] Shihata (2000: 567–68).
[54] World Bank, *History of Bank Policy Relating to Transfer of IBRD Net Income to IDA*, from the UK National Archives, IDA: Its Future Direction and the Eighth Replenishment (1985–87).
[55] United States Code Congressional and Administrative News: Legislative History, 92nd Congress, 2nd Session, 1972, 2015. In early years up to FY1963,

MICs based on the tacit agreement that such transfers should *supplement* rather than *substitute* fresh donor contributions. Thereafter, IBRD income transfers to IDA had become a routine. Even though procedurally the Board of Governors annually approved how to ration profits, Bank Management had already promised three-year planning contributions at the time of IDA replenishment negotiations in order to secure more donor contributions.[56] Hence, IBRD borrowers argued that the transfers had been decided in a 'non-transparent' way for the rich economies to 'minimize their direct contributions to IDA'.[57]

The tensions on the welfare transfer from MICs to LICs had heightened since the mid-1980s, as donor contributions to IDA had been stagnant or even shrinking whereas IBRD net income transfers to IDA had steadily grown. Because major shareholders (who were, also, big donors) enjoyed a lion's share of voting rights on the Board, they could successfully demand that IDA be a priority call on net income. Moreover, in the first decade of the new century, IDA donors shifted some of their bilateral obligations of debt relief (known as the Highly Indebted Poor Countries Initiative [HIPC]) to IBRD borrowers, since this debt initiative represented 'another new and significant claim' on net income.[58] Devesh Kapur, a co-author of the World Bank's history, had pointed out in 2002 that big shareholders had been using their 'control rights', locked in to the historical institutional design, to press for private interests in the guise of global public goods.[59] Consequently, a perceptible shift in burden-sharing silently occurred – fresh donor contributions as a percentage of IDA's total financing package dropped to about half in IDA-14,[60] with the balance essentially funded by IDA reflows and IBRD net income transfers.

But IDA donors contended that MICs should directly contribute more to IDA as they prospered. Given the voluntary nature of IDA

all these profits had been automatically allocated to the Bank's reserves to ensure the market confidence of its prudential financial management.

[56] Bank Management proactively used IBRD income transfer to IDA to leverage more donor contributions, thus acting like a quasi-donor. This point was mentioned in Chapter 7 on IDA-15 and Chapter 3 on the independent role of Bank Management.

[57] By comparison, at the Inter-American Development Bank, Brazil and other developing country members have had the votes to avoid transferring net income from its regular income-earning loan facilities to its concessional facility (Birdsall 2012).

[58] Kapur (2002: 345).     [59] Ibid., 349, 351.     [60] World Bank (2005b).

contributions, they viewed IBRD net income transfers as 'an imperfect alternative' to gain donations from MICs. Moreover, they contended that IBRD borrowers did not deserve all the credit of the Bank's revenues, since the reason why the World Bank could borrow on world credit markets at relatively low interest rates was largely the guarantees of the major AAA-shareholders (i.e., rich HICs).[61] Yet a counter-argument could be that the low cost of IBRD borrowings also stemmed from the much lower default rates of IBRD loans (especially as the Bank built up its creditworthiness in the later years, which almost precluded the possibility of callable capital ever being needed).[62] Consequently, the above fissure tended to generate polarising views between developed countries and developing countries.

As a result, China, together with IBRD borrowers, lamented the widening disparity between influence and contribution. On the one hand, they complained that IDA donors used IDA replenishments as a back-door means of amplifying donor influence across the whole World Bank Group. On the other hand, they came to view that their forgone welfare via the income transfers had resulted in an erosion of direct donor funding for IDA. Therefore, China resented the status quo of being 'quasi-donors without rights'.[63]

How, then, did Chinese decision-makers respond to the deepening discrepancy between influence and contribution?

The leading Ministry of Finance (MOF) decided that it was high time to become an IDA donor as an investment to win a 'voice opportunity' on how to govern the World Bank. The MOF was responsible for China's participation in the World Bank, which managed the Bank's lending to China and nominated Executive Directors to the Board where China had an independent seat. The then Chinese Executive Director urgently felt that inaction would not be a viable option going forward, because a business-as-usual scenario would see China's influence being further marginalised should it be neither a big borrower nor a big donor.[64] Since 1993, China had been one of the biggest borrowing member countries with 'one of the best project implementation records'.[65] Because the Bank relied on its major client

---

[61] Interview with the former IDA Deputy, 31 October 2012, London.
[62] Kapur (2002: 350).
[63] Interview with the former Chinese Executive Director at the World Bank, 13 December 2011, Beijing.
[64] Ibid.    [65] Lichtenstein (1996: 397).

countries to generate its income, big borrowers had some leverage over how to run the Bank. Yet it was anticipated that China would graduate from IBRD in the medium term, as its economy continued to grow. Hence, the MOF came to believe that becoming an IDA donor was a crucial step towards the strategic transition from 'a big borrower' to 'a big donor' in order to enhance China's influence in the World Bank.

However, the conventional presumption that China was a unified actor was far from reality: the MOF had to persuade other relevant domestic agencies to endorse its proposal before gaining the final approval of the State Council. This involved some major strategic questions.

The first strategic question was whether international development matters. A prevailing inward-looking mindset was that 'For China, the most populous country, to run itself well is the most important fulfilment of its international responsibility'.[66] This was justified by historical precedent – that the US had not assumed full leadership until the end of World War II even though it surpassed the UK as the No. 1 economy as early as the late nineteenth century. Such a cautious strategy stemmed from a grave concern that a premature fulfilment of international obligations would overburden China, thus hampering its development. Along this line of thinking, joining the IDA donor club would trigger a hasty shift away from China's developing country status, with unforeseen repercussions in WTO and climate change negotiations and even a termination of China's borrower status in multilateral development banks. Hence, the Ministry of Foreign Affairs (MOFA) insisted on the need to avoid prematurely assuming undue aid burdens. However, as China's economic links with developing countries deepened, it had high stakes in a stable and peaceful international environment. Accordingly, there was a growing consensus in China's high-level strategic thinking that China's national interests were intrinsically linked with the existing international system so that China should focus on how to better manage and improve the existing institutions as a beneficiary and a stakeholder rather than calling for 'building a new international economic order'.[67]

---

[66] This view is currently reflected in China's official document. See P.R. China, 'White Paper on China's Peaceful Development', 6 September 2011.

[67] Interview with the former Chinese Executive Director at the World Bank, Washington, DC, 6 September 2012.

This shift towards a stakeholder strategy convinced MOFA of the merits of contributing to IDA – mitigating suspicion and fears that China would overturn the existing system as it ascended. Meanwhile, MOF downplayed MOFA's concern about a potential change in China's international identity as a developing nation by highlighting that several other MICs (such as Brazil) had already contributed to IDA but kept their identity intact. The World Bank also played an active role in assuring its continued support for China's domestic development through both financial lending and knowledge sharing.

The next strategic question was why use multilateral aid channels. While international development rose up China's agenda, buttressed by burgeoning aid budgets, there was little consensus on how to strike a balance between bilateral and multilateral channels. MOFCOM had the main responsibility in disbursing China's bilateral aid, whereas contributions to multilateral institutions were not within the turf of one ministry.[68] MOFCOM was against multilateral aid because China had full control over bilateral aid whereas China would have little say in how to allocate IDA's resources in a World Bank predominantly influenced by big Western shareholders. To soften MOFCOM's opposition, MOF emphasised the danger of isolating China from multilateral institutions where rules were made. First, China's bilateral development assistance carried no voice in rule-making and norm-setting. Second, bilateral aid was good at establishing good relationships with specific developing countries, but it was so dispersed that it could not signal China's support for international development. In fact, China's opposition to the IBRD net income transfers to IDA had undermined its 'solidarity' with low-income developing countries. Hence, rather than continuing to make indirect welfare transfers without any rights or recognition, China should make direct contributions to IDA to participate in rule-making and gain broad support from LICs. Eventually, MOFCOM budged, but insisted upon a modest contribution level.[69]

The final question was why to invest in IDA. Given China's stake in an effective multilateral development, two options were debated

---

[68] MOF is responsible for China's participation in the World Bank, AsDB, IFAD, and GEF; the People's Bank of China is in charge of China's engagement with IDB and AfDB.

[69] Interview with the former Chinese Executive Director at the World Bank, 13 December 2011, Beijing.

among policy-makers regarding how to achieve this goal – reforming the existing institutions or creating new ones. This was not necessarily an either/or choice. Establishing new institutions could put pressures on the traditional ones to speed up the reform process. Yet given high set-up costs, MOF viewed an initial attempt to reform the World Bank as a dominant strategy, because it could leverage in-house expertise and global footprints.[70]

Eventually, MOF played a pivotal role in convincing domestic stakeholders of the merits of investing in IDA to obtain 'voice opportunity' on how to influence the World Bank and beyond.

The issue then became how much to contribute. While MOF initially proposed no less than $50 million, it made a concession to MOFCOM by reducing the level to $30 million, equal to China's initial contribution to the AsDF in 2004. This compromise was made in light of unfavourable public opinion towards foreign aid spending given the compelling challenge of eradicating abject poverty at home. Hence, it was hard for policy-makers to justify decisions to give generous donations abroad, especially as transparency had made the national budget accessible online.[71]

In the end, China's decision to become a new donor in IDA-15 gained positive feedback from the international community. The World Bank President Zoellick saw it as 'a significant breakthrough to have China become a contributor', for it 'signals China's intention to help shape the international aid architecture through multinational channels'.[72]

In summary, China was not only frustrated by donor-driven policy prescriptions in IDA, it also was resentful of the marginalisation of its voice in the whole World Bank operations where the decision-making power of the Board had been usurped by an informal IDA donor forum (the IDA Deputies). China's indignation was further aggravated by its indirect contribution via IBRD net income transfers. In response to the widening disparity between influence and contribution, China decided, after intense domestic deliberation, to become a new IDA donor to gain a 'voice' opportunity. Apart from the above primary motivation, China's decision was also motivated by its pursuit of country-specific interests such as reputation concerns.

---

[70] Ibid.
[71] Interview with the Senior Advisor to the Chinese Executive Director, 14 June 2012, Washington, DC.
[72] Xinhua News Agency (2007).

## 8.3 Explaining China's Increased Financial Contribution to IDA-16 (FY2012–14):[73] Bank Management as Policy Entrepreneurs

China's contribution level became pivotal to the success of IDA-16 because traditional donors maintained that they would shirk their responsibilities should China not play its fair part. While developed countries celebrated China becoming a new donor in IDA-15, they generally viewed its initial contribution as too modest.[74] Hence, they set high expectations for China, which were further raised after the far-reaching global financial crisis broke out in 2008. Since fiscal austerity put tremendous budgetary constraints on traditional donors, they counted on China to shoulder a greater burden. From the standpoint of major traditional donors, China became the 'reference donor' – their contribution levels hinged on how much China was willing to put on the table; they believed that China enjoyed enhanced economic status and was bound to gain a substantial increase in its IBRD voting rights as agreed in the G-20 Pittsburgh Summit.[75] For instance, in establishing its contribution range during its consultation with Congress, the US Treasury explicitly brought into account China's contribution as a key determinant for its own contribution level.[76]

But China was reluctant to increase its contribution because it was concerned that traditional donors would shirk their burdens. China insisted that voluntary contributions from developing countries should not substitute for international obligations by developed countries. Moreover, it contended that its enhanced economic status entitled it to gain more IBRD voting rights. Indeed, the breakthrough in its uphill struggle for voting rights was largely because developed countries realised that they had to rely on emerging powers to tackle the

---

[73] IDA-16 covered FY2012–14, negotiated between March and December 2010.

[74] Interview with the former Chinese Executive Director at the World Bank, 13 December 2011, Beijing.

[75] 'We stressed the importance of adopting a dynamic formula at the World Bank ... that generates an increase of at least 3% of voting power for developing and transition countries, to the benefit of under-represented countries'. G20 Leaders' Statement: The Pittsburgh Summit, 24–25 September 2009, para. 21, www.g20.utoronto.ca/2009/2009communique0925.html (accessed 26 October 2012).

[76] Interview with the former Assistant Secretary of the US Treasury, 9 August 2012, Washington DC.

devastating financial crisis. Hence, China did not need to resort to IDA contributions to gain more IBRD voting rights.

Given a potential gridlock on the horizon, the challenge for Bank Management was how to provide incentives to China to mobilise substantial fresh money so as to put pressure on traditional donors in an effort to accomplish a successful IDA-16. Normally, donors gave grants to IDA from their budgets. But this traditional approach had a limited role in mobilising additional fresh contributions from China, not only because a dramatic increase in its IDA contribution would not be acceptable to China due to its fairness concern and domestic political pressure, but also because it would not satisfy the high expectations of traditional donors even if China doubled or tripled its contribution from a very low base.

To think out of the box, senior Bank Management proactively proposed an innovative contribution scheme involving accelerating repayments of past IDA loans. Given China's abundant foreign reserves, this innovative approach would be feasible.[77]

In order to win China's support, Bank Management conducted intensive bilateral consultations with China. On the one hand, it tried to convince China of the benefits of accelerated repayments (such as IDA voting rights and discounted rates to reduce obligations). On the other hand, it attempted to put pressure on Chinese counterparts via high-level engagements. The Bank President Zoellick visited Beijing and met with the MOF to make the case. The IDA Replenishment Chairperson also constantly reminded China that 'if China does not step up its contributions to IDA, it would drag down the whole IDA-16'.[78]

In response to these extremely high international expectations, China was prepared to accept the Bank's proposal of accelerating its IDA repayments conditional upon traditional donors not shirking their obligations.[79] Meanwhile, traditional donors signalled that they would do their utmost if China played its fair part. Consequently, neither side wanted to commit itself first.

---

[77] Interview with the former Vice President for concessional finance in the World Bank, 26 July 2012, Washington DC.

[78] Interview with former senior staff in IDA Resource Mobilisation Department, 24 July 2012, Washington DC.

[79] Interview with the advisor to China's Executive Director, 14 September 2012, Washington DC.

To break the stand-off, Bank Management innovatively proposed a 'two-stage' pledging tactic. Bank Management knew that other donors had 'two pledging numbers' in mind: a higher case if China significantly increased its contribution, and a lower case if China did not increase its contribution as expected. So Bank Management encouraged China to make a positive pledge, first by indicating that it would choose an approach to accelerate its repayment (hinting at huge fresh money upfront) *without* indicating the exact amount. This helped build a positive momentum at the pledging meeting. After China took the lead, the United States and Japan not only pledged to maintain their traditional basic shares, but also promised to make a modest increase. After gaining assurance from the two major donors, China made its pledge for the second time that it would not only speed its repayments with one-off accelerated repayments of $1 billion, but also make a basic contribution of $50 million.[80]

In hindsight, the proactive initiative of Bank Management was pivotal to a record-high IDA-16 because it boosted China's contribution, symbolising a more equitable burden-sharing within an expanded global coalition.[81] This underlines the independent role that IOs can play in offering selective incentives to member states to achieve their primary objective of maximising total financial resources.

To conclude, enhanced Chinese financial support for IDA-16 was primarily attributable to the proactive role of Bank Management in proposing an innovative contribution scheme to overcome the gridlock (generated by the fairness concern) in burden-sharing negotiations between traditional donors and China.

## 8.4 China's Influence as Both an Insider and an Outsider

This section provides a preliminary assessment of China's influence in IDA replenishment negotiations and beyond. It is preliminary in a sense that China had a realistic expectation in the first place that its modest contribution would not change policy directions within a short

---

[80] Ministry of Foreign Affairs, P.R. China, 'International Development Association', www.fmprc.gov.cn/mfa_chn/wjb_602314/zzjg_602420/gjjj s_612534/gjzzyhygk_613182/gjkf_613366/ (accessed 25 December 2013).

[81] Interview with the former Vice President for Concessional Finance and Global Partnership, 1 October 2012, Washington DC.

timeframe.[82] Hence, it may be too early to make a conclusive judgement on both the scale and nature of China's influence.

A tentative appraisal reveals that China's direct policy influence through its participation in IDA replenishment negotiations was limited. Although the fundamental motivation behind China's decision to become a new IDA donor was its aspirations to restore the disparity between contribution and influence, Chinese negotiators were very reserved and seldom proactively engaged in policy debates, let alone made their own proposals.

How, then, to account for the lag between a boost in China's contribution and an increase in its influence? One major reason is that China's research capacity in international development is still in its infancy, albeit burgeoning. By contrast, traditional donors (especially, the United States, the UK, Germany, and France) enjoyed unrivalled expertise that could frame and guide policy discussions. While China's recent economic transformation and daunting future development challenges represent an exciting laboratory for piloting solutions and fostering innovations, it takes time to build up the human resources necessary for distilling the lessons of its own development and shaping dialogue with the international development community. In addition, language barriers and cultural factors also contribute to the fact that China has not articulated its distinctive policy proposals. Yet this might be changing in the near future, as China has increasingly gained senior-level positions in the World Bank Group as a means of building direct policy influence.[83]

Despite its limited direct policy influence, however, China has been a driver of policy change because, as a rising development financer, it has created and deployed outside options to exert competition pressure on the World Bank to adjust its development policies.[84]

The first example is change in the Bank's debt sustainability policy – the Non-Concessional Borrowing Policy (NCBP). The NCBP was put into place in 2006 after the introduction of the IDA grants and the Multilateral Debt Relief Initiative (MDRI). It was initially phrased as an anti-free-riding policy framework that coincided with the media

---

[82] Interview with the former Chinese Executive Director at the World Bank, 13 December 2011, Beijing.

[83] Vestergaard and Wade (2013: 153–64).

[84] Researchers have also pinpointed similar Chinese impacts on the international aid regime (Woods 2008).

reports on the IMF and the World Bank's critiques of China as a 'free-rider' in its economic cooperation with Africa.[85] As a result, China perceived the NCBP as a tool used by G7-led IFIs to criticise emerging economies' economic and development cooperation with LICs.[86] China maintained that while there was legitimate concern about debt re-accumulation after debt-relief initiatives, debt relief does not generate fresh cash flows, and grants can only dilute debt burden; thus, debt relief alone cannot achieve economic transformation for self-reliant development.[87] Originally the Bank stipulated an across-the-board debt limit (with a fixed concessionality of 35 per cent to distinguish potentially risky 'non-concessional finance' from safe 'concessional finance'). Any 'breach' of this rule (i.e., borrowing on expensive terms) would be punished by a cut in IDA credits or hardening of IDA terms.[88] However, as development finance from emerging economies (especially China) surged into LICs, compliance with this policy framework was rendered hard to enforce. Many African countries were prepared to accept any 'punishment' by IDA (given its small volume) rather than complying with the NCBP to reject alternative sources of financing. Indeed, China's presence had diluted the World Bank's leverage upon recipient countries. Hence, the World Bank ran 'a reputational risk' in retaining an ineffective policy because its limited financial leverage could not achieve the desired objective of inducing changes in borrowing behaviours of LICs.[89]

Eventually, at the strong urgings of African countries,[90] the NCBP rule was modified in April 2010 to take a more differentiated approach to setting debt limits (based on a country's macroeconomic and public financial management capacity and debt vulnerability).[91] This change was made *before* the substantial policy discussion started in IDA-16.

---

[85]  For instance, Gobind Nankani, the World Bank's Vice President for Africa, told the Associated Press his organisation was concerned that Chinese loans were not lent at concessional rates or were used for projects that would not boost development (Lee 2006).

[86]  Li (2007).      [87]  Ibid.      [88]  IDA (2006).

[89]  Interview with the former Vice President for concessional finance in the World Bank, 26 July 2012, Washington DC.

[90]  African leaders rallied together in 2008 to urge the Bretton Woods Institutions to introduce more flexibility in the application of the concessionality thresholds to reflect their development financing needs. The African Caucus of the IMF and the World Bank (2008).

[91]  IDA (2010).

So, it is reasonable to infer that China did not proactively bring this issue to the IDA donor forum. Hence, this policy change was more to do with the sheer scale of Chinese development finance on the ground vitiating the financial leverage of the Bank's conventional 'money-for-policy-change' approach.

A second example is a potential trend towards the streamlining of social and environmental safeguards. Development finance from emerging economies tends to have a greater risk appetite, exerting competitive pressures on the World Bank on the ground. This pressure had been especially strong from China, due to both its sheer financial might and speedy project execution. For instance, China's big national development finance institutions (China Development Bank and China's Ex-Im Bank) had surpassed the Bank's lending capacity.[92] In response, the World Bank commissioned a report to gather ideas from leaders around the world on how to modernise the World Bank governance. The report in 2009 highlighted the necessity to make its safeguards policy less cumbersome: 'MICs reduced their demand for IBRD loans in part because of the relatively high financial and non-financial costs of these loans (the "hassle factor"). If the Bank seeks to lend more to MICs in the future, these costs will have to be contained and reduced.'[93] To maintain its relevance, the new World Bank President Jim Yong Kim called for a 'Solutions Bank' to meet global challenges. One priority action was to streamline procedures, simplify processes, and cut down project preparation time from existing preparation periods as long as two years.[94] In October 2012 the World Bank began a two-year process to review and update its environmental and social safeguard policies.[95] Two forces were at work: on the one hand, some urged further strengthening of safeguards across the whole World Bank Group; on the other hand, others underlined the need to 'balance safeguards (do not harm) and performance standard management (management of risks)' and cautioned against unified safeguard standards.[96]

While it is still too soon to tell the actual effect of China on the safeguard standards, the World Bank has tended to have greater risk

[92]  Financial Times Research, see Dyer, Anderlini, and Sender (2011).
[93]  The High-Level Commission on Modernization of World Bank Group Governance (2009: 10–11).
[94]  World Bank (2012b).    [95]  World Bank (2012a).
[96]  Committee on Development Effectiveness (2010).

appetite than before. During 1999–2010, the proportion of category A (very high impact) had increased from 5 to 11 per cent, with the increase in the volume and scale of infrastructure lending.[97] The World Bank's publications also tend to take a benign view about China's development finance in filling the infrastructure financing gap. In contrast with the previous Bank President Wolfowitz's harsh criticism, the Bank's most recent report on development financing says that 'New development partners are breaking out of the mold of traditional ODA financing . . . partially meeting needs not addressed by traditional donors. This flexibility is often made possible by different transparency and safeguard standards than those governing traditional donors.'[98]

Looking forward, China's influence via outside options is likely to grow as it strategically creates and deploys alternative channels. Recently, China proactively adopted a 'two-leg' strategy – reforming the existing institutions and establishing new multilateral institutions owned by developing nations – in an effort to better improve global economic governance.[99] China's entrepreneurial strategy of launching new initiatives was largely due to the slow pace of change in existing institutions and the eroding US credibility in ceding influence. While the US Administration promised a greater voice for emerging economies in the IMF under the G-20 framework in December 2010 after the financial crisis, Congress refused to ratify it despite intense lobbying by the Treasury and the White House after a delay of four years.[100] The US veto power rendered the reform efforts futile. The slim possibility of achieving shared leadership in the US-centred institutions rallied China and emerging powers together to initiate regional alternatives that excluded the hegemon. Hence, China has proposed or facilitated the establishment of 'three new banks and two institutes': the AIIB,[101] the BRICS New Development Bank,[102] and the Shanghai Cooperation

---

[97] IEG (2010: 11).     [98] World Bank (2013a: 19).     [99] Shi (2014).
[100] Harding (2014).
[101] China announced the creation of the AIIB with start-up capital of $50 billion in October 2013 before the annual meeting of the Asia-Pacific Economic Co-operation (APEC) forum. See Xinhua, 'China proposes an Asian infrastructure investment bank', 3 October 2013, www.chinadaily.com.cn/china/2013-10/03/content_17007977.htm (accessed 18 June 2014).
[102] The BRICS Summit agreed to establish a New Development Bank in March 2013. See 'Statement by BRICS Leaders on the Establishment of the BRICS-Led Development Bank', Durban, South Africa, 27 March 2013, www

Organisation (SCO) Development Bank,[103] as well as the Central Asia Institute[104] and the Asian-Pacific Finance and Development Institute.[105] Recently, a $40 billion Silk Road Fund was initiated by President Xi Jinping in November 2014 to 'break the bottleneck in Asian connectivity by building a financing platform'.[106] According to the US Executive Director at the AsDB, Ambassador Robert Orr, the AIIB could be seen as a response to China's inability to increase its influence in leading global and regional multilaterals, as well as a 'political tool' to challenge the ADB.[107] These ventures are aimed at providing both financing and ideas to bridge the huge infrastructure financing gaps and to remedy the poverty of alternative development thinking.

Apart from creating new institutions, China has also actively collaborated with existing multilateral development banks via alternative co-financing mechanisms. The People's Bank of China (PBOC) provided a $2 billion co-financing fund for the IDB to promote sustainable economic growth in March 2013.[108] The PBOC pledged $3 billion for joint investments with the World Bank Group's International Finance Cooperation (IFC) to assist the launch of a new IFC syndications programme in September 2013 that enabled investors to co-invest with IFC in a portfolio of future emerging market loans.[109] The PBOC injected $2 billion into the African Development Bank to establish

.brics.utoronto.ca/docs/130327-brics-bank.html (accessed 18 June 2013). The Bank will be located in Shanghai.

[103] This bank was proposed by China and Russia at the SCO summit in June 2012 and then endorsed by members in November 2013. See TCA, 'SCO Member States Sign Joint Communique on the 12th Council Meeting Results', *The Times of Central Asia*, 2 December 2013, www.timesca.com/index.php/news/5698-joint-communique-of-the-results-of-the-12th-meeting-of-the-council-of-heads-of-government-prime-ministers-of-the-shanghai-cooperation-organisation-member-states (accessed 15 December 2013).

[104] This Institute is located in Urumqi, Xinjiang Province of China, under Central Asia Regional Economic Cooperation, www.adb.org/countries/subregional-programs/carec (accessed 18 June 2014).

[105] This Institute will be upgraded from the current Chinese initiative – the Asian-Pacific Finance and Development Centre. See www.afdc.org.cn/default.aspx?l=english (accessed 18 June 2014).

[106] Xinhua (2014).    [107] Bretton Woods Observer (2014).    [108] IDB (2013).

[109] 'China Pledges $3 Billion to IFC for Joint Investments in Emerging Markets', http://ifcext.ifc.org/IFCExt/pressroom/IFCPressRoom.nsf/0/54E947DE6E6C5BF085257BEA002E65A6 (accessed 18 June 2014).

an 'Africa Growing Together Fund' in May 2014.[110] These initiatives outside the traditional arrangements are propelled by the objective of diversifying China's assets accumulated in a US-dominated international monetary system.[111] Astoundingly, China has accumulated nearly one-third of the world's foreign reserves, carrying the risk of dramatic depreciation if the United States continues to exploit its privilege as the major international reserve currency country to fill a domestic savings shortfall with little regard for the repercussions of this unilateral position upon global economic and financial stability.[112] Therefore, it is imperative for China to invest its large foreign exchange reserves in real assets that generate a reliable flow of returns over the coming decades.

To sum up, the above initiatives reveal that China is not undercutting the existing institutions, but, rather, innovating cooperative mechanisms to meet its strategic needs and the needs of global development financing.

## 8.5 Conclusion

Going back to the core questions, this chapter has explored what motivated China to become a new IDA donor and then further step up its financial support, and what the implications are for China's influence in the World Bank.

First, China's primary motivation to become a new IDA donor was to redress the balance between influence and contribution in the World Bank. This disparity stems from two major factors. On the one hand, the IDA donor forum captured a de facto decision-making power that further marginalised the voice of recipient countries; moreover, donors extended their policy influence well beyond IDA, shaping the whole World Bank Group. On the other hand, China and other IBRD borrowers have increasingly made indirect welfare transfers to IDA via IBRD net income transfers, because they do not have enough voting rights on the Board to counterbalance the G-7 countries' influence on revenue

---

[110] AfDB announces US$2 billion fund with China, 22 May 2014, www.afdb.org /en/news-and-events/article/afdb-announces-us-2-billion-fund-with-china-13165/ (accessed 18 June 2014).
[111] McKinnon (2013).    [112] Zhou (2009).

allocations. Thus, China aspired to seek 'influence from within' by winning a 'voice' opportunity at the IDA's decision-making table.

Second, China's subsequent decision to increase its IDA contribution was largely driven by its desire to meet international expectations in order to signal its commitment to international development. Especially after the financial crisis, China's growing relative capacity did heighten international pressures. Meanwhile, Bank Management played a proactive role in innovating the contribution scheme to make a substantial increase in China's contribution possible.

What about China's influence in the World Bank after it became a new IDA donor?

First, China's direct policy influence in the IDA donor forum was limited. China's initial aspiration to seek policy influence stood in sharp contrast with its subsequent passive stance towards policy discussions during IDA replenishment negotiations. Such a time lag between increasing financial contribution and gaining policy influence largely reflected its limited, albeit rapidly developing, human research capacity.

Second, China's indirect influence via outside options was much more profound in World Bank governance. China has proactively adopted a two-track ('two-leg') strategy by establishing new multilateral financing arrangements to speed reform in existing IFIs after its initial failure in gaining influence from within. Although China is not fully ready to play a proactive role in shaping the Bank's decision-making, the World Bank has made some adjustments in its development ideas and policies in response to competitive pressures from China's rise as a development financer. Such policy changes are more to do with China's leverage, derived from newly created multilateral arrangements as an outsider, than its direct and proactive influence efforts as an insider.

Looking ahead, a fundamental challenge in the international development system is how to intermediate China's abundant foreign reserves into productive development investments. While Bank Management proactively innovated the contribution scheme to make possible a substantial boost in China's contribution in IDA-16, it was a one-off measure since China could only repay its loans as a former IDA recipient once and for all. It remains to be seen how newly created financing institutions and arrangements sponsored or initiated by China can help China meet this core strategic interest in diversifying its international financial assets and what kinds of impact they will have upon the existing multi-lateral development financing system.

# Conclusion

Contributing to the understanding of the implications of power transitions for a US-led hegemonic international system has motivated the exploration in this book of the international diplomacy behind donor financing of the World Bank-IDA over the past five decades. Focusing on the crucial case of the World Bank helps us to reveal the political dynamics which have shaped the burden-sharing outcomes across the sixteen IDA replenishments between 1962 and 2010. The official World Bank version of the burden-sharing dynamics holds that the cost of financing IOs will be redistributed in line with changing relative economic fortunes. We have shown, for the first time, how the realities in the form of different layers of intricate power plays have generated major departures from the capacity-to-contribution and contribution-to-influence equity lines implicit in this official account of the burden-sharing principles of IDA.

Conventional explanations in the existing literature – ability-to-pay and country-specific interests – have offered a useful starting point in analysing donors' ability and willingness to contribute to IDA. Yet they fall short of explaining why the hegemon maintained its burden share despite a decline in its relative economic capabilities, why the hegemon preserved and even amplified its policy influence in the World Bank in spite of its flagging financial contributions, and why erosion in hegemonic influence began to set in after the new millennium as the legitimacy of the US power exercise was contested by other donors.

Deciphering the politics of IDA replenishments has entailed exploring the central features of three key power plays, namely:

1. The US-led donor group versus external threats: *the hegemon was more likely to maintain its burden share, as the hegemon-centred Western world order faced looming external threats from the East and the South;*

2. The internal donor struggle over voting rights between ascending powers and the hegemon/waning powers: *if the hegemon and waning powers desired to expand total IDA resources, they were likely to cede voting rights to ascending powers in exchange for financial support*;
3. The informal donor influence upon Bank Management: *if the hegemon violated the 'fairness' principle by shirking obligations but pursuing undue influence, secondary states were likely to take 'exit/voice' measures to restore the implicit contribution-to-influence equity line; secondary states would postpone their 'exit/voice' measures, if they were structurally dependent upon the hegemon and/or lack viable outside options.*

This chapter first synthesises the overall trends in the power dynamics of IDA replenishment history in times of power transitions, then explores how the crucial case of the World Bank-IDA helps to grasp the nature of the contemporary hegemonic transition from the United States to China, and finally draws lessons from history in order to look ahead.

## C.1 A Synthesis of Power Dynamics in IDA Replenishment History

Changing power dynamics in East–West and North–South struggles have consistently reshaped the US strategies on *what IDA was for* and *how best to achieve its goals*. According to the US objectives, IDA replenishment history can be broadly divided into three stages with distinctive power dynamics:

At the first stage in the 1960s and 1970s, the primary US goal was to expand total IDA resources in order to counter looming external threats from the Soviet Union and the united Third World.

Thus, whenever external threats loomed large (e.g., the Soviet-led Warsaw Pact invasion of Czechoslovakia in the late 1960s and the Third World's demand for a New International Economic Order in the mid-1970s), the USA tactically honoured its traditional burden share in order to foster internal Western donor solidity to achieve an ambitious total size of IDA replenishments. In these scenarios, what mattered for the USA was the total target of IDA replenishment, since a large total could not only sharpen its competitive edge in aid-giving competition with the Soviet-led communist bloc, but also could dissuade developing countries from overhauling a US-dominated international economic order. In retrospect, the USA achieved great success in its goal of IDA expansion: IDA enjoyed an average growth rate of 24 per cent per replenishment in real terms during the first two decades of its history. Moreover, to exercise hegemonic leadership, the USA largely refrained from claiming undue political influence in World Bank governance. Hence, the fairness concern at the third layer of power play was not salient in this period.

By contrast, when external threats from both the East and the South subdued, as in the early and late 1970s, US Administrations shifted priority from aspirations for IDA expansion to a desire for cuts in the US burden share. Such claims for share cuts were mainly driven by the desire of the Executive Branch to accommodate the demand of the Legislative Branch for minimising the fiscal cost of US participation in IDA. In stark contrast with the initial Congressional leadership in founding IDA, deteriorating balance-of-payments accounts fostered growing Congressional hostility towards IDA (despite the moderate budgetary cost of financial contributions to IDA compared with the huge US military expenditure). Meanwhile, the US Administration strategically used Congressional threats of steep share cuts to seek short-term foreign policy interests (such as skewing resource allocations in both IBRD and IDA to repair the damage in Indo-China associated with the Vietnam War in IDA-4 in the early 1970s). Other donors accommodated such undue US policy demands in order to encourage the United States to make a milder share cut. Eventually, the United States successfully made substantial share cuts, largely compensated for by share increases from Japan and Germany in IDA-4/-6, negotiated in the early and late 1970s. A primary reason why other donors ceded ground to accommodate short-term US interests and compensated for its share cuts in spite of their acute sense of unfairness was that they were so structurally dependent upon the United States for military protection and market access that they tolerated a preponderant US influence in the World Bank. Meanwhile, few outside options of aid-giving were available during this period, so other donors seldom diverted their resources elsewhere.

At the second stage in the 1980s and 1990s, the main US objective was to control Bank Management to enforce policy conditionalities upon developing countries. In the 1980s, the Reagan Administration aimed to spread its economic ideology of free markets across the globe and used the World Bank's structural adjustment loans to compel developing countries to liberalise and privatise their economies. In the 1990s, lobbied by international NGOs in Congress, the USA was at the forefront of pushing through sweeping institutional and policy reforms to make the World Bank more 'transparent and accountable' and to enforce social and environmental safeguards in development projects in developing countries.

During this period, the power play between the US-led donor group and external threats faded away. The USA was almost indifferent to the total size of IDA replenishment, since it believed that aid-dependent developing countries had no option but to adopt policy changes promoted by the financially powerful World Bank. In the first term of the Reagan Administration in the early 1980s, the USA even sought to amputate total IDA resources in IDA-7, for it believed that such North–South welfare transfers hindered free markets from flourishing. As a result, IDA suffered from almost stagnant growth in its total resources throughout the two decades, with even a precipitous fall of 25 per cent in nominal terms in IDA-7 (FY1985–87).

An intriguing pattern during this period was that the United States managed to strengthen its policy influence in the World Bank despite being a laggard in its financial contributions to IDA. The flagging US financial support largely resulted from mounting Congressional hostility towards IDA. This was not only because the US budgetary deficits were rocketing, but also because the reputation of the World Bank as an effective development institution was severely questioned by NGOs. Hence, Congressmen, especially Republicans, saw little rationale in donating taxpayers' money amid severe budget austerity to an IDA held by NGOs to exacerbate social inequality, economic stagnation, and environmental degradation. Such Congressional difficulties were manifested in two ways: first, overdue US obligations accumulated to an unsustainable level, creating funding crises for IDA in FY84 and FY97, since the United States decided to clear its arrears first before entering a new round of IDA replenishment; and, second, there was no single stand-alone bill for authorising US contributions to IDA, so that the US Administration had to tie IDA with other 'must-pass' bills to save the day.

Despite the waning US financial support for IDA, however, the United States succeeded in achieving profound policy influence in the

World Bank in the 1980s and 1990s. This runs contrary to the conventional wisdom that, as a donor cuts its financial contributions to IOs, it would suffer from withering policy influence. Why?

A traditional factor was still at work, especially in the early 1980s – other donors still depended upon the United States for military protection in the face of a Soviet threat and for export markets during economic recession amid debt crises in developing countries. Consequently, due to their structural dependence upon the hegemon in other international arenas, other donors had to recognise US leadership in the World Bank although they regretted a steep fall in the US contribution in IDA-7.

Another counterintuitive factor is that the rigid pursuit of the fairness principle by other donors became a boost for, rather than a constraint on, US policy influence in the Bank from the mid-1980s throughout the 1990s. Other donors resented the USA unilaterally using Congressional threats to push through sweeping policy changes in the World Bank but failing to honour its financial commitments to IDA. Starting from IDA-8 in 1986, this acute sense of unfairness incentivised other donors to proportionately cut back on their cash contributions in order to avoid legitimising any further US share cut (even at the expense of a larger size of total IDA replenishment). In effect, this multiplied the financial leverage of the USA in deciding how large total IDA resources could be. For every \$1 cut by the USA, the Bank would lose \$5 (given a US burden share of about 20 per cent). Take IDA-11 (negotiated in the mid-1990s), for example: Congressional hostility resulted in a substantial cut in the US annual dollar contribution from \$1,250 million in IDA-10 (FY1994–96) to \$800 million in IDA-11 (FY1998–99), which led to a precipitous fall of more than 40 per cent even in nominal terms in the total size of the IDA replenishment. Given this preponderant and systematic financial leverage (far greater than the US contribution would have indicated), Bank Management had a strong incentive to accommodate US demands for policy changes.

The widening disparity between the US financial contribution and its policy influence exacerbated an acute sense of unfairness among other donors, so they deployed the 'exit' option by diverting resources away from the established IDA window. Initially in the 1980s, other donors topped up their basic contributions to IDA with supplementary contributions or special funds administered by Bank Management but separate from their contributions to IDA replenishments so as to avoid any further US share cut. For instance, when the Reagan Administration put a cap on its cash contribution in IDA-7, resulting in a much smaller total size in the mid-1980s, other donors decided to set up a *Special Facility for Africa* outside the traditional burden-sharing scheme to disburse their 'surplus' aid money. Later, in the 1990s, other donors more forcefully diverted their resources to Bank-administered trust funds or elsewhere. This trend of diverting aid away from the established IDA window was facilitated by two factors: first, the collapse of the Soviet Union reduced other donors' dependence upon the USA; and, second, multilateral aid channels began to proliferate from the early 1990s. As a result, core donor contributions to IDA as a percentage of total donor contributions to multilateral aid organisations dropped from an annual average of one-third in the 1980s to one-fourth in the 1990s.

In short, despite its flagging financial support for IDA, the USA achieved significant policy influence in the World Bank, hence enforcing policy conditionalities upon developing countries in the 1980s and 1990s. Other donors began to divert their resources away from core contributions to IDA, leading to an expansion of the Bank-administered trust funds which has been ongoing since the early 1990s.

At the third stage, in the 2000s, the significance of IDA was diminishing in the eyes of the anti-multilateralist Bush Administration, though the USA continued to push for policy reforms in the World Bank. The hegemonic legitimacy began to be contested in the Bank.

In the aftermath of salient US violations of the 'fairness' principle, the legitimacy of the exercise of US power in the World Bank was severely contested by other donors from the beginning of the new millennium. In IDA-13, negotiated in the early 2000s, other donors started to oppose US initiatives more forcefully. They openly challenged the Bush Administration's proposal to provide half of IDA resources as grants (as opposed to traditional loans) to LICs, suspecting its motivation was to reduce the future financial autonomy of IDA. Further opposition to US initiatives was aroused when the USA unilaterally attached policy strings to its financial contributions but failed to honour its commitments despite Bank Management's compliance with this conditionality. In IDA-14, negotiated in the mid-2000s, other donors unanimously vetoed the US proposal that an external candidate be selected to chair IDA replenishment to break the traditional practice of using high-level Bank officials as chairpersons.

Furthermore, other donors eventually got rid of the previously rigid practice of pegging their own cash contributions to those of the USA in order to hold the US burden share constant to preserve their fairness concern in IDA-14 (negotiated in the mid-2000s). Previously, when supporting a greater target total entailed a significant fall in the US burden share (due to the US budgetary and Congressional constraints), other donors usually accepted a smaller target total of IDA replenishment to avoid any further US share cut. However, in IDA-14, under the UK leadership for augmenting total IDA resources, small-/medium-sized donors agreed to maintain or even increase their burden shares of a much greater total size of IDA replenishment, even when the Bush Administration placed a cap on its dollar contributions that could result in a precipitous fall in the US burden share. In IDA-15, negotiated in 2007, the UK even took a step further, replacing the United States as the largest donor in IDA. As a result, IDA benefited from the breakdown of the rigid pegging scheme that had lasted for over a decade. IDA-14 achieved a record total of \$33 billion, representing an increase of 25 per cent over the previous replenishment and reversing a two-decade flat (or even negative) growth in total IDA resources in the 1980s and 1990s. This substantially weakened the US financial leverage in IDA replenishment negotiations, for other donors reduced their reliance on the US position in deciding their own contribution levels.

Looking ahead, the World Bank is heading towards a turning point where financing and governing the World Bank-IDA no longer requires full US participation.

## C.2 An Entrepreneurial China as a Reform-Minded Stakeholder

Going back to the grand debate about the nature of hegemonic transition from the United States to China, IDA replenishment history reveals that conventional labels (such as 'spoiler', 'supporter', and 'shirker')[1] fail to capture the nuanced yet significant implications of China's

---

[1] Schweller and Pu (2011).

ascendancy as a development financer for the international development financing system – China is a reform-minded stakeholder, transforming the landscape of international development financing *within* the order.

China is not a revolutionary 'spoiler' seeking to destroy the existing order and replace it with something entirely different. Its initiatives to create an AIIB, host the BRICS New Development Bank, set up a Silk Road Fund, and press ahead with the project for a Shanghai Co-operation Organisation Development Bank have certainly shaken up the world of multilateral finance and drawn the ire of the United States, precisely because of the explicit challenge to its hegemony. But this set of initiatives is not being pushed forward as a competing view of how a new international development financing architecture should be structured – at least not yet, and it is unlikely. China has adopted a stakeholder strategy for actively engaging with existing multilateral development financing institutions to advance its strategy. In China's account of the outcome of the summit meeting of Presidents Xi and Obama in September 2015,[2] China has undertaken to ensure that any new development finance institutions it sponsors will be structured and managed professionally and will have continuously improving governance, environmental, and transparency standards in line with the traditional development banks. Suspicions that China's commitment to work with the existing system is mere rhetoric disguising a longer term Chinese insurgency have to encounter the fact that China's rise as a development financer has reached the point where it now has basic interests and responsibilities in the systemic functioning of global development financing, as it is intimately integrated with the international economic system that incubates its ascendancy.[3] Indeed, China pragmatically views the existing MDBs as a useful instrument for advancing its Belt and Road Initiative. For example, China's application to join the European Bank for Reconstruction and Development (EBRD) in December 2015 was partly motivated by its desire to co-invest with the EBRD in order to obtain local knowledge – and potentially even protection of its overseas investment – as it navigates new markets.[4] Furthermore, the AIIB signed a co-financing framework agreement with the World Bank and AsDB in April 2016 to work together to fill the infrastructure gap in Asia, with the first group

[2] Xu and Carey (2015c).    [3] Xu and Carey (2015a).    [4] Berglöf (2015).

of co-financed projects to be jointly approved in June 2016.[5] In short, far from sabotaging existing MDBs, China views itself as a beneficiary of the current world order and utilises long-standing institutions to advance its goals abroad.

What has changed is that China is now proactively seeking leadership both institutionally and intellectually in the international development financing system. Where China's top political leaders such as Deng Xiaoping used to emphasise the importance of keeping a low profile on the international arena, now there are concrete initiatives clearly showing that China aspires to take a leadership role in the field of international development. As clearly demonstrated in the case of IDA, China became disenchanted with being 'a quasi-donor without rights or influence'.

China's proactive attempts to seek leadership may have profound transformational impacts upon the US-centred international development architecture:

On the institutional front, the underlying programmatic objectives are spearheading a leaner and faster approach to development financing in an effort to fill vast infrastructure investment gaps and mitigating the problem of industrial overcapacity domestically. The establishment of the AIIB, with fifty-seven prospective founding members, which vows to be 'lean, clean and green', has been one of the most significant initiatives of recent decades in the multilateral development financing system. And on China's initiative, a High-Level Roundtable on South–South Cooperation was convened at the UN in September 2015. At this event, China announced the establishment of the Institute of South–South Cooperation and Development (ISSCAD) to foster mutual learning among mid-career professionals from China and other developing countries on how to catch up with advanced economies.[6] Further initiatives include significant special funds for Regional Development Banks.

On the intellectual front, China is bringing a fresh perspective to the development effectiveness agenda, learning from its recent rapid economic transformation of the past thirty years, wherein the state has played a vital facilitating role in creating a dynamic market economy, integrating with and moving up global value chains. Justin Yifu Lin, the

---

[5] 'Xinhua, AIIB, WB&ADB to jointly approve first batch of projects in June', www
.chinadailyasia.com/business/2016-04/14/content_15416060.html,
14 April 2016 (accessed 20 April 2016).
[6] MOFCOM (2016).

former Chief Economist at the World Bank and also the first intellectual from a developing country to take this idea-shaping position, has studied China's economic transition and transformation over the past thirty years and proposed and championed a new school of thinking – New Structural Economics (NSE)–with a special emphasis on the synergies between an effective market and a facilitating government to foster industrial upgrading and economic transformation. The NSE maintains that developing countries should focus on 'what they have' (factor endowment) to identify 'what they can potentially do well' (latent comparative advantage). This stands in sharp contrast with the mainstream development thinking that often uses developed countries as the benchmark to emphasise 'what developing countries lack' (capital-intensive industries) and 'what they do badly' (bad governance). In order to achieve quick wins of job creation and export promotion on the ground, the NSE proposes the Growth Identification and Facilitation Framework (GIFF), which is designed to help policy-makers in catching-up developing countries to develop feasible and sharply focused policies in an effort to identify and unlock their latent comparative advantages to achieve economic structural transformation.[7]

Accurately depicting the role of China is crucial to predicting the nature of the future world order. If China develops its role as a reform-minded stakeholder, how might the future international development system look?

A clear trend is that China is advancing an agenda of going beyond aid by igniting the renaissance of market-based official development finance, as exemplified in the China Development Bank (CDB) and China's Ex-Im Bank. Like MDBs, the CDB and Ex-Im Bank rely on sovereign creditworthiness to raise funds from capital markets.

Scale matters. CDB is the largest development bank worldwide. After an average five-year (2009–13) growth rate of 16 per cent, total assets of CDB reached RMB10 trillion (US$1.6 trillion) as of the end of 2014 – more than four times the assets of the World Bank Group's International Bank for Reconstruction and Development at US$359 billion. CDB's gross loans outstanding totalled RMB7.15 trillion (US$1.18 trillion) at the end of 2013, with 16 per cent of this lending outside mainland China.[8]

---

[7] Lin (2012a; 2012b).    [8] CDB (2015); World Bank (2014: 4).

What matters more is the spirit of 'public entrepreneurship' embedded in the Chinese approach to development finance. Public entrepreneurship is the capacity to organise, scale up, and sustain long-term finance. Three interactive dimensions are involved here: (a) a comprehensive long-term vision; (b) acting on a decisive scale in the presence of uncertainty and risk; and (c) the creation of learning-by-doing societies via spreading innovation.[9] The Chinese policy banks are a central part of the 'public entrepreneurship' that has enabled China to overcome the first-mover problem long identified by development economists, whereby the development process must be co-created by the public sector and the private sector in close interaction.[10] For these private companies, the loan terms for Ex-Im Bank and CDB credit lines are not necessarily concessional, but they provide the confidence to work with long-term horizons and to scale up. They also crowd in financing from other financial institutions, both Chinese and international.[11]

In response to this burgeoning official finance from emerging economies – especially China, once on the margins or outside of these established systems – potentially seismic shifts are occurring in three central governance systems of development finance: the reporting systems for ODA in the OECD Development Assistance Committee, OECD export credit disciplines, and debt sustainability in the Bretton Woods Institutions (as elaborated in the Chapter 8).

China's rise as a development financer has sparked a process of 'creative destruction' in the established governance frameworks. On the one hand, surges in official development finance from emerging economies, once at the margins or outside the existing governance frameworks, challenge the effectiveness of traditional disciplines and surveillance frameworks running the risk of further rounds of financial arms races and debt crises. On the other hand, rapid expansion of officially support market-based finance from emerging economies, which are largely outside the established governance framework, might bring about potentially seismic shifts in the old development finance industry, creating scope for public entrepreneurship to flourish.[12]

---

[9]  Xu and Carey (2015b: 859).      [10]  Klein et al. (2010); Xu and Carey (2015b).
[11]  Sanderson and Forsythe (2013).      [12]  Xu and Carey (2015b).

In a nutshell, rather than containing or assimilating China when it is depicted as the 'spoiler' or 'shirker', the world needs to learn how to work together with China – a gigantic reform-minded stakeholder – to harness its growing financial strength as a force for good.

## C.3 IDA as History and Looking Ahead

Looking ahead, what insights can we draw from the history of IDA replenishments?

First, during the Cold War, the hegemonic leadership fostered internal Western donor solidarity to expand IDA in order to counter the Soviet threat. Yet, as this bipolar rivalry faded away over more than two decades, the geopolitical shift has undercut the shared vision, leading to two consequences. First, IDA burden-sharing has evolved from a *quasi-obligatory* framework (where donors should maintain their traditional shares unless their claims for share cuts were justified by a prolonged economic decline) to a *voluntary* scheme (where donors readily cut their shares if their ability or willingness deteriorated). Consequently, IDA has fallen prey to exogenous adversities such as budgetary austerity, currency depreciations, erosion in donor interests, and swings between multilateralism and unilateralism/ bilateralism. Second, IDA began to be overtaken by 'earmarked' trust funds where the Bank has been hired as 'a service provider' to implement programmes in areas of specific donor interest. These trust funds have been set up outside the traditional IDA burden-sharing framework to advance specific donor interests and values.

Looking forward, a shared vision seems to fall apart, portending a shrinking IDA and much debate. A business-as-usual scenario foresees that IDA's client base will be rapidly shrinking because more than half of currently IDA-eligible recipient countries will grow into the MIC status, hence graduating from IDA by 2025.[13] Donors could justifiably declare 'success' and amputate IDA, since the remaining needs of small conflict-ridden African countries would be much smaller after the 'mega-exits' of India and other big borrowers.

But others contend that narrowly focusing on 'poor countries' would disengage IDA from the bulk of the world's poor, since a new geography of poverty shows that three-quarters of poor people now live in

[13]  The Future of IDA Working Group (2012: 5).

MICs, as compared with 90 per cent in LICs two decades ago. Thus, IDA should overhaul its graduation policy in order to target 'poor people' in MICs.[14] Yet this raises a fundamentally moral and politically controversial issue of whether nation states should take full responsibility for poverty reduction themselves when they cease to be poor countries.

Setting aside the divisive debate on 'poor countries vs. poor people', another fault line is whether IDA should go beyond poverty alleviation to provide 'global public goods' (GPGs).[15] Yet no consensus exists on what count as GPGs. Climate change financing has emerged as a frontier, with the World Bank as one provider, but together with other major international agency suppliers, including the United Nations Environment Programme (UNEP) and the new Green Climate Fund as a central part of political bargaining in the UN climate change negotiating framework.

In summary, IDA is standing at a crossroads, demanding leadership for forging a consensus on 'what and whom IDA is for'. Yet it is not on the horizon, with huge confusion prevailing at this point, both inside and outside the Bank.

Second, although a grand bargain is hard to come by, silent revolutions are underway. Institutional bargaining between the hegemon and emerging powers is a much harder challenge now than before.[16] Unlike the past ascending powers that rarely challenged the US primacy, the United States now fears that China is advancing a rival development model, undercutting its decades-long endeavour to foster free markets and liberal democracy. This might discourage the United States from advancing shared leadership with a rising China. The strong resistance to China's initiative to establish the AIIB is a case in point. The slow progress in gaining voice in the World Bank has motivated China to host the BRICS New Development Bank and to pursue other initiatives outside the US-led international institutions. This may in turn speed up reforms in the existing Bretton Woods Institutions.

New regional and bilateral initiatives are flourishing, heralding silent revolutions in global development governance.[17] The pre-eminence of the World Bank is in rapid decline, outpaced by burgeoning outside

---

[14]  Kanbur (2014).      [15]   The Future of IDA Working Group (2012: 11).
[16]  Khong (2001).
[17]  It accords with a theoretical insight that 'declining hegemony' accompanies
    revival of regional arrangements (Hurrell 1995: 52).

options. What ramifications may emerge from the multiplying sources and modalities of development finance remain to be seen. Pessimists warn against regional blocs competing for spheres of influence and are concerned that fragmentation comes at the expense of efficiency. Optimists contend that healthy competition helps to break the traditional hegemony of the World Bank in shaping development thinking and practices. So developing countries will not suffer from a poverty of alternatives.

Finally, going back to the grand debates on power transitions and the international system, IDA history calls for greater attention to the understudied links between *order* and *justice*,[18] as evidenced in the indispensable role of the fairness concern in shaping IDA governance. Most discussions so far have focused on great power politics and the implications for world order. From this perspective, power transitions are often cast as harbingers of chaos, violence, and war. Yet from a fresh angle of global justice, a multi-polar order may be viewed as 'a morally better system than one in which power is heavily concentrated'.[19] IDA history reveals that the ascendancy of emerging powers, once on the margins of the US-dominated hegemonic system, offers alternative sources of development financing and thinking, thus mitigating the inherent inequality between donors and recipients. Yet, it remains to be seen how this phenomenon can be harnessed as a force for good in the future.

The question becomes how to manage a pluralistic world with multiplying actors having the capacity to make their voices heard. The history of IDA reveals that it is 'unhelpful' to frame the issue in binary terms – as a 'rising rest' challenging the 'liberal' order from outside.[20] Firstly, it is historically inaccurate, because the existing order is far from 'liberal' when it comes to the hegemon's relations with developing countries[21] – the voices of both IDA recipients and IBRD borrowers had been marginalised in World Bank governance, but they bore direct consequences of donor-driven policy agendas. Secondly, politically it fosters mistrust and polarisation, because allowing particular development pathways to claim moral high ground puts alternative thinking and practices in a defensive position. This stifles mutual trust and learning at the heart of any successful pursuit of

---

[18] For academic efforts to link order with justice, see Hurrell (2007).
[19] Hurrell (2013b: 196).    [20] Ibid., 203.    [21] Hurrell (2005: 45–46).

solving common problems. Perhaps a useful starting point for co-existence is to recognise and respect diversity to work out 'how divergent historic experiences and values can be shaped into a common order'.[22]

Navigating this new world demands entrepreneurship to bridge differences and harness the energy of the new power politics. We look ahead with guarded optimism.

---

[22] Kissinger (2014).

# Bibliography

## Archives

Below are the main categories of cited archival materials.

### World Bank Archives

IDA Deputies' Meetings Memos.
IDA Replenishment Agreements, from IDA-1 to IDA-16.
IDA Replenishment Discussion Papers, from IDA-1 to IDA-16.
IDA Replenishment Negotiations – Board Memos.
Annual Meetings of the Boards of Governors: Summary Proceedings, various years.
Major Donors: IDA Negotiation and Country Allocation.
Presidential Chronological Correspondence of IDA Replenishment Chairpersons.
World Bank Oral History Programme.
World Bank's Annual Reports, various years.
World Bank's Selective Capital Increases resolutions and official memorandums.

### The UK National Archives

Foreign and Commonwealth Office, IBRD/IDA & Oil-Producing Countries, FCO59/123.
Foreign and Commonwealth Office, IDA Credit Allocations: India's Share, 1968–69, FCO37/412.
Foreign and Commonwealth Office, IDA Fourth Replenishment, FCO59/1032.
Ministry of Overseas Development, Current and Future Aid Framework Provision for the World Bank Group/IMF, 1976–78, OD36/382.
Ministry of Overseas Development, IDA Fifth Replenishment, 1976–78, OD20/519, OD36/250, OD36/251, OD36/252, OD36/253, OD36/254, OD36/348.

Ministry of Overseas Development, IDA Fourth Replenishment, 1973–75, OD33/198, OD33/199, OD33/200, OD33/202.

Ministry of Overseas Development, IDA Second Replenishment, OD9/202, OD9/254, OD9/255, OD9/256, OD9/257.

Ministry of Overseas Development, IDA Third Replenishment, OD9/269, OD9/270, OD9/272, OD9/273.

Ministry of Overseas Development, Multilateral Untying, 1976–78, OD36/386.

Ministry of Overseas Development, Regional Development Bank Replenishments, 1979–81, OD36/453.

Ministry of Overseas Development, Regional Development Banks Relations with IBRD and IDA, 1970–72, OD9/371.

Overseas Development Administration, IDA: Future Directions of Eighth Replenishment, 1985–87, OD57/14, OD57/15, OD57/16, OD57/17, OD57/18, OD57/20.

Overseas Development Administration, IDA Seventh Replenishment, 1985–87, OD57/24, OD57/25, OD108/27, OD108/28.

The Department for International Department's Reports on IDA.

The UK Parliamentary Reports on the World Bank-IDA.

Treasury, IBRD/IDA: Information Relating to Procurement under IBRD Loans and IDA Credits, 1964–75, T317/2274.

Treasury, Negotiations for the Fourth Replenishment of the International Development Association, 1973, 317–1669, T317-1833, T317/1834.

## The US National Archives

Foreign Assistance, International Development, Trade Policies, 1969–72, Volume IV, Foreign Relations of the United States.

Foreign Economic Policy, 1969–76, Volume VIII, Foreign Relations of the United States.

Foreign Economic Policy, 1973–76, Volume XXXI, Foreign Relations of the United States.

Foreign Economic Policy; International Monetary Policy, 1969–72, Volume III, Foreign Relations of the United States.

General Records of the Department of the Treasury, Chronological files, 1973–75, Record Group 56, Entry A1-780, Boxes 1–4.

## Other US Official Documents

Department of the Treasury, Treasury International Programmes: Justification for Appropriations: Budget Request, various fiscal years.

Messages from the President of the US to the Congress.

National Advisory Council on International Monetary and Financial Policies, Special Report to the President and to the Congress of the Proposed Replenishment of the Resources of the International Development Association, various years.

Presidential Documents, various years.

The US Congress. *Congressional Quarterly Almanac.* Washington, D.C: Congressional Quarterly Inc., various years.

The US Congressional Hearings on IDA Replenishments.

The US Congressional Reports on IDA Replenishments.

# References

Abbott, G.C. 'United States: Who Pays the Piper?' In *The Recalcitrant Rich: A Comparative Analysis of the Northern Responses to the Demands for a New International Economic Order*, edited by Helge Ole Bergesen, Hans Henrik Holm, and Robert D. McKinlay. London: Pinter, 1982.

ActionAid. *Real Aid: Ending Aid Dependency*, 2011. www.actionaid.org.uk /sites/default/files/doc_lib/real_aid_3.pdf.

Addison, Tony, Mark McGillivray, and Matthew Odedokun. 'Donor Funding of Multilateral Aid Agencies: Determining Factors and Revealed Burden Sharing'. *The World Economy* 27, No. 2 (2004): 173–91.

AfDB. 2014. 'AfDB announces US $2 billion fund with China'. 22 May. www .afdb.org/en/news-and-events/article/afdb-announces-us-2-billion-fund-with-china-13165/, accessed 18 June 2014.

'Aid Fatigue'. *The Washington Post*, 19 April 1983.

Alacevich, Michele. *The Political Economy of the World Bank: The Early Years*. Stanford: Stanford Economics and Finance, 2009.

Albin, Cecilia. *Justice and Fairness in International Negotiation*. Cambridge: Cambridge University Press, 2001.

Alesina, Alberto, and David Dollar. 'Who Gives Foreign Aid to Whom and Why?' *Journal of Economic Growth* 5, No. 1 (2000): 33–63.

Ali, S. Mahmud. *US-China Cold War Collaboration, 1971–1989*. New York: Routledge, 2005.

Amin, Samir. 'After the New International Economic Order: The Future of International Economic Relations'. In *New International Economic Order: A Third World Perspective*, edited by Pradip K. Ghosh, 297–312. Westport; London: Greenwood Press, 1984.

Andersen, Thomas Barnebeck, Henrik Hansen, and Thomas Markussen. 'US Politics and World Bank IDA-Lending'. *Journal of Development Studies* 42, No. 5 (2006): 772–94.

Arase, David. *Buying Power: The Political Economy of Japan's Foreign Aid.* Boulder; London: Lynne Rienner, 1995.

Auer, James E. 'Defence Burden-Sharing and the US-Japanese Alliance'. In *Japan and the United States: Troubled Partners in a Changing World*, edited by Mike Mochizuki, James E. Auer, Noboru Yamaguchi, Tsuyoshi Hasegawa, Reizo Utagawa, John Curtis Perry, and Jacquelyn K. Davis. Washington; London: Brassey's US, 1991.

Bachrach, Peter, and Morton S. Baratz. 'Two Faces of Power'. *American Political Science Review* 56, No. 04 (1962): 947–52.

Baldwin, David A. 'The International Development Association: Theory and Practice'. *Economic Development and Cultural Change* 10, No. 1 (1961): 86–96.

'Interdependence and Power: A Conceptual Analysis'. *International Organization* 34, No. 04 (1980): 471–506.

*Economic Statecraft.* Princeton: Princeton University Press, 1985.

Barnett, Michael, and Raymond Duvall. 'Power in Global Governance'. In *Power in Global Governance*, edited by Michael N. Barnett and Raymond Duvall, 98: 1–32. New York: Cambridge University Press, 2005.

Barnett, Michael, and Martha Finnemore. *Rules for the World: International Organizations in Global Politics.* Ithaca: Cornell University Press, 2004.

Beattie, Alan. 'Deadlock in Dispute over Money for Poor Nations: World Bank Contributions'. *Financial Times*, 15 January 2002.

Becker, Abraham S. 'The Soviet Union and the Third World: The Economic Dimension'. In *The Soviet Union and the Third World: The Last Three Decades*, edited by Andrzej Korbonski and Francis Fukuyama, 67–93. Ithaca; London: Cornell University Press, 1987.

Bennett, Andrew, Joseph Lepgold, and Danny Unger. 'Burden-Sharing in the Persian Gulf War'. *International Organization* 48, No. 1 (1994): 39–75.

Berglöf, Erik. 2015. China's Multilateral Financial Mobilization. At www.project-syndicate.org/commentary/increased-engagement-likely-to-change-china-by-erik-berglof-2015-11?barrier=true, accessed 28 November 2015.

Bergsten, C. Fred. *The International Economic Policy of the United States: Selected Papers of C. Fred Bergsten, 1977–1979.* Lexington; Toronto: Lexington Books, 1980.

Berthélemy, Jean-Claude. 'Bilateral Donors' Interest vs. Recipients' Development Motives in Aid Allocation: Do All Donors Behave the Same?' *Review of Development Economics* 10, No. 2 (1 May 2006): 179–94.

Bird, Graham. 'The Informal Link between SDR Allocation and Aid: A Note'. *Journal of Development Studies* 12, No. 3 (1976): 268–73.

Birdsall, Nancy. 'Three Questions to Ask the Three Candidates to Lead the World Bank', 25 March 2012. www.cgdev.org/blog/three-questions-ask-three-candidates-lead-world-bank.

Bräutigam, Deborah. 'Aid 'With Chinese Characteristics': Chinese Foreign Aid and Development Finance Meet the OECD-DAC Aid Regime'. *Journal of International Development* 23, No. 5 (2011): 752–64.

Bretton Woods Observer. 'The Rise of the Infrastructure Giants: Bank's Infrastructure Hegemony Challenged in Asia', Summer 2014, http://www.brettonwoodsproject.org/wp-content/uploads/2014/06/Observer_june_2014_FINAL1.pdf, accessed 10 September 2014.

Bretton Woods Project. 'Ties That Bind: Possible Shifts on Conditionality?', 28 May 2004. www.brettonwoodsproject.org/2004/05/art-51274/.

Brooks, Stephen G., and William C. Wohlforth. *World out of Balance: International Relations and the Challenge of American Primacy.* Princeton; Oxford: Princeton University Press, 2008.

Brown, Bartram Stewart. *The United States and the Politicization of the World Bank: Issues of International Law and Policy.* London: Kegan Paul International, 1992.

Busby, Joshua William. 'Bono Made Jesse Helms Cry: Jubilee 2000, Debt Relief, and Moral Action in International Politics'. *International Studies Quarterly* 51, No. 2 (2007): 247–75.

Buzan, Barry. 'China in International Society: Is 'Peaceful Rise' Possible?', *Chinese Journal of International Politics*, 2010, Vol. 3, No. 1: 5–36.

Carr, Edward Hallett. *The Twenty Years' Crisis, 1919–1939: An Introduction to the Study of International Relations.* 2nd edn. London: Macmillan, 1946.

Caufield, Catherine. *Masters of Illusion: The World Bank and the Poverty of Nations.* London: Macmillan, 1997.

Chang, H. J. 'Hamlet without the Prince of Denmark: How Development Has Disappeared from Today's 'Development'Discourse'. In *Towards New Developmentalism: Markets as Means rather than Master*, edited by Shahrukh Rafi Khan and Jens Christiansen. London: Routledge, 2011.

Chhotray, Vasudha, and David Hulme. 'Contrasting Visions for Aid and Governance in the 21st Century: The White House Millennium Challenge Account and DFID's Drivers of Change'. *World Development* 37, No. 1 (2009): 36–49.

China Development Bank (CDB). 2015. Annual Report.

China Online, 'China Became an IDA Donor for the First Time' (in Chinese), 28 December 2007, http://gb.cri.cn/18824/2007/12/28/2185@1893561.htm, accessed 22 May 2012.

Ciro, Tony. *The Global Financial Crisis: Triggers, Responses and Aftermath*. Farnham; Burlington: Ashgate, 2012.

Clark, Ian. *Legitimacy in International Society*. Oxford: Oxford University Press, 2005.

Clark, William. 'Robert McNamara at the World Bank'. *Foreign Affairs* (1981): 167–84.

'Clausen: World Economic Situation "Grim"', *The Washington Post*, 7 September 1982.

Clegg, Liam. *Controlling the World Bank and IMF: Shareholders, Stakeholders, and the Politics of Concessional Lending*. New York: Palgrave Macmillan, 2013.

Clegg, Liam. 'The Governance of the World Bank', from *Handbook of the International Political Economy of Governance*, edited by Anthony Payne and Nicola Phillips, 259–74. Cheltenham and Northampton: Edward Elgar, 2014.

Cohen, Benjamin J. 'An Explosion in the Kitchen? Economic Relations with Other Advanced Industrial States'. In *Eagle Resurgent?: The Reagan Era in American Foreign Policy*, edited by Kenneth A. Oye, Robert J. Lieber, and Donald S. Rothchild, 115–43. Boston: Little, Brown, 1987.

Commission on Growth and Development. *The Growth Report: Strategies for Sustained Growth and Inclusive Development*, 2008.

Committee on Development Effectiveness. *Chairperson's Summary on the Independent Evaluation Group's Report on Safeguards and Sustainability Policies in a Changing World*, 28 July 2010.

Congressional Quarterly. *US Foreign Policy: The Reagan Imprint*. Washington, DC: Congressional Quarterly, 1986.

Cornia, Giovanni Andrea, Richard Jolly, and Frances Stewart, eds. *Adjustment with a Human Face*. Oxford: Clarendon Press, 1987.

Cornes, Richard, and Todd Sandler, 'The Theory of Public Goods: Non-Nash Behaviour', *Journal of Public Economics* 23, No. 3 (April 1984): 367–79.

Council of the European Union. *On Accelerating Progress towards Attaining the Millennium Development Goals*, 24 May 2005. http://aei.pitt.edu/37776/1/COM_(2005)_133_final.pdf.

Cox, Robert W., and Harold K. Jacobson. 'The Framework for Inquiry'. In *The Anatomy of Influence: Decision Making in International Organization*, edited by Robert W. Cox and Harold K. Jacobson, 1–36. New Haven; London: Yale University Press, 1974.

Cronin, Bruce. 'The Paradox of Hegemony: America's Ambiguous Relationship with the United Nations'. *European Journal of International Relations* 7, No. 1 (2001): 103–30.

DAC. *United Kingdom: Development Assistance Committee (DAC) Peer Review*, 2001.

    *United Kingdom: Development Assistance Committee (DAC) Peer Review*, 2006.

    *Welcome New Partnerships in Development Co-Operation*, 2011.

Dahl, Robert A. 'The Concept of Power'. *Behavioural Science* 2, No. 3 (1957 July): 201–15.

Darst, Guy. 'Environmentalists Lobby World Bank for Increased Safeguards'. *The Associated Press*, 28 September 1987.

Deng, Yong. *China's Struggle for Status: The Realignment of International Relations*. New York; Cambridge: Cambridge University Press, 2008.

Department for International Development (DFID). *Loans or Grants: IDA's Concessional Lending Role*. UK National Archives, 2002. http://webarc hive.nationalarchives.gov.uk/+/http:/www.dfid.gov.uk/news/News/file s/bg_ida_grants.htm.

    *Working with the World Bank to Become More Effective Partners*. World Bank Institutional Strategy, September 2004.

    'Partnerships for Poverty Reduction: Rethinking Conditionality'. A UK Policy Paper, March 2005. www2.ohchr.org/english/issues/develop ment/docs/conditionality.pdf.

    *Development on the Record*. DFID Annual Report 2007, May 2007. https://www.gov.uk/government/uploads/system/uploads/attach ment_data/file/231305/0514.pdf.

Development Assistance Committee (DAC). *Recommendation on Untying ODA to the Least Developed Countries*, April 2001.

Dunphy, Harry. 'Record World Bank Contribution to International Development Agency Designed to Lure Donors'. *Associated Press International*, 27 September 2007.

Dyer, Geoff, Jamil Anderlini, and Henny Sender, 'China's lending hits new heights', *Financial Times*, 17 January 2011, www.ft.com/cms/s/ 0/488c60f4-2281-11e0-b6a2-00144feab49a.html#axzz3LIaMGX1 a, accessed 26 March 2012.

European Union. *The European Consensus on Development*, 2005. http://ec .europa.eu/development/icenter/repository/european_consensu s_2005_en.pdf.

Fang, Songying, and Kristopher W. Ramsay. 'Outside Options and Burden Sharing in Nonbinding Alliances'. *Political Research Quarterly* 63, No. 1 (2010): 188–202.

Fearon, James D. 'Counterfactuals and Hypothesis Testing in Political Science'. *World Politics* 43, No. 02 (1991): 169–95.

Feinberg, Richard E. 'American Power and Third World Economies'. In *Eagle Resurgent?: The Reagan Era in American Foreign Policy*, edited by Kenneth A. Oye, Robert J. Lieber, and Donald S. Rothchild, 145–65. Boston: Little, Brown, 1987.

Feldstein, Martin. 'EMU and International Conflict'. *Foreign Affairs* (1997): 60–73.

Fiorina, Morris P. *Divided Government*. 2nd edn. Boston: Allyn and Bacon, 1996.

Fleck, Robert K., and Christopher Kilby. 'World Bank Independence: A Model and Statistical Analysis of US Influence'. *Review of Development Economics* 10, No. 2 (2006): 224–40.

Franck, Thomas M. *The Power of Legitimacy among Nations*. New York; Oxford: Oxford University Press, 1990.

Friedberg, Aaron L. 'The Future of US-China Relations: Is Conflict Inevitable?' *International Security* 30, No. 2 (2005): 7–45.

Friedland, Jonathan. 'Environment: World Bank Programmes under Renewed Attack'. *IPS-Inter Press Service*, 17 March 1987.

G7 Summit Communiqué. *Economic Declaration: Working Together for Growth and a Safer World*. Munich, Germany, 6 July 1992. www.g8.utoronto.ca/summit/1992munich/index.html.

G24. *The Group of Twenty-Four Ministerial Declaration*, 1989.

Garthoff, Raymond L. *Détente and Confrontation: American-Soviet Relations from Nixon to Reagan*. Revised (2nd) edn. Washington, DC: Brookings Institution, 1994.

Gilpin, Robert. *War and Change in World Politics*. Cambridge: Cambridge University Press, 1981.

Goldstein, Judith, and Robert O. Keohane, eds. *Ideas and Foreign Policy: Beliefs, Institutions, and Political Change*. Ithaca; London: Cornell University Press, 1993.

Gosovic, Branislav, and John Gerard Ruggie. 'On the Creation of a New International Economic Order: Issue Linkage and the Seventh Special Session of the UN General Assembly'. *International Organization* 30, No. 2 (1976): 309–45.

Gowa, Joanne. *Closing the Gold Window: Domestic Politics and the End of Bretton Woods*. Ithaca; London: Cornell University Press, 1983.

  'Bipolarity, Multipolarity, and Free Trade'. *The American Political Science Review* (1989): 1245–56.

Gruber, Lloyd. *Ruling the World: Power Politics and the Rise of Supranational Institutions*. Princeton: Princeton University Press, 2000.

Gyohten, Toyoo. 'Japan and the World Bank'. In *The World Bank: Its First Half Century*, edited by Devesh Kapur, John P. Lewis, and Richard Webb, 2: 275–316. Washington, DC: Brookings Institution, 1997.

Halper, Stefan A. *The Beijing Consensus: How China's Authoritarian Model Will Dominate the Twenty-First Century*. New York: Basic Books, 2010.

Hanrieder, Wolfram F. 'The FRG and NATO: Between Security Dependence and Security Partnership'. In *The Federal Republic of Germany and NATO: 40 Years After*, edited by Emil Joseph Kirchner and James Sperling, 194–220. Basingstoke: Macmillan, 1992.

Harding, Robin. 'US Fails to Approve IMF Reforms', *Financial Times*, 14 January 2014.

Hart, Jeffrey. 'Three Approaches to the Measurement of Power in International Relations'. *International Organization* 30, No. 2 (1976): 289–305.

Hawkins, Darren G., David A. Lake, Daniel L. Nielson, and Michael J. Tierney, eds. *Delegation and Agency in International Organizations*. Cambridge: Cambridge University Press, 2006a.

'Delegation under Anarchy: States, International Organizations, and Principal-Agent Theory'. *Delegation and Agency in International Organizations*, 2006b, 3–38.

Hayter, Teresa. *French Aid*. London: Overseas Development Institute, 1966.

Hearing of the Foreign Operations Subcommittee of The Senate Appropriations Committee. *Multilateral Funding and Policy Issues*, 27 April 1993.

Hirschman, Albert O. '"Exit, Voice, and Loyalty": Further Reflections and a Survey of Recent Contributions'. *Social Science Information* 13, No. 1 (1974): 7–26.

*Exit, Voice, and Loyalty: Responses to Decline in Firms, Organizations, and States*. Cambridge, Mass.: Harvard University Press, 1970.

Hurd, Ian. 'Legitimacy and Authority in International Politics'. *International Organization* 53, No. 02 (1999): 379–408.

Hurrell, Andrew. 'Regionalism in Theoretical Perspective'. In *Regionalism in World Politics: Regional Organization and International Order*, edited by Louise Fawcett and Andrew Hurrell, 37–73. Oxford: Oxford University Press, 1995.

'Power, Institutions, and the Production of Inequality'. In *Power in Global Governance*, edited by Michael N. Barnett and Raymond Duvall, 33–58. Cambridge: Cambridge University Press, 2005.

*On Global Order: Power, Values, and the Constitution of International Society*, Oxford: Oxford University Press, 2007.

'Effective Multilateralism and Global Order'. In *Effective Multilateralism: Through the Looking Glass of East Asia*, edited by Jochen Prantl, 21–42. Houndmills; New York: Palgrave Macmillan, 2013a.

'Power Transitions, Global Justice, and the Virtues of Pluralism'. *Ethics and International Affairs* 27, No. 02 (2013b): 189–205.

IDA. *IDA-9 Burden Sharing*. IDA-9 Discussion Paper, June 1989.

*The IDA Deputies: An Historical Perspective*, November 2001.

*IDA Countries and Non-Concessional Debt: Dealing with the 'Free Rider' Problem in IDA-14 Grant-Recipient and Post-MDRI Countries*, 19 June 2006.

*IDA's Non-Concessional Borrowing Policy: Progress Update*, April 2010.

IDB. 2013. 'China to Provide $2 Billion for Latin America and the Caribbean Co-financing Fund'. 16 March. www.iadb.org/en/news/news-releases/2013-03-16/china-co-financing-fund,10375.html, accessed 18 June 2013.

Ikenberry, G. John. *After Victory: Institutions, Strategic Restraint, and the Rebuilding of Order after Major Wars*. Princeton and Oxford: Princeton University Press, 2001.

'America's Imperial Ambition'. *Foreign Affairs* 2002a, 44–60.

'Multilateralism and US Grand Strategy'. In *Multilateralism and U.S. Foreign Policy: Ambivalent Engagement*, edited by Stewart Patrick and Shepard Forman, 121–40. Boulder; London: Lynne Rienner, 2002b.

Independent Evaluation Group (IEG). *The World Bank's Country Policy and Institutional Assessment: An Evaluation*, 30 June 2009.

*Safeguards and Sustainability Policies in a Changing World: An Independent Evaluation of World Bank Group Experience*. Washington, DC: World Bank, 2010.

*An Evaluation of the World Bank's Trust Fund Portfolio: Trust Fund Support for Development*. Washington, DC: World Bank, 2011a.

*Liberal Leviathan: The Origins, Crisis, and Transformation of the American World Order*. Princeton; Oxford: Princeton University Press, 2011b.

International Development Committee. *DFID and the World Bank*, 5 March 2008.

International Monetary Fund (IMF). *Government Finance Statistics*, n.d. http://elibrary-data.imf.org/FindDataReports.aspx?d=33061&e=170809.

Jacobson, Harold Karan, and Michel Oksenberg. *China's Participation in the IMF, the World Bank, and GATT: Toward a Global Economic Order*. Ann Arbor: University of Michigan Press, 1990.

Jervis, Robert. *Perception and Misperception in International Politics*. Princeton: Princeton University Press, 1976.

Joint Communiqué of the results of the 12th meeting of the Council of Heads of Government (Prime Ministers) of the Shanghai Cooperation Organisation Member States, 29 November 2013, www.sectsco.org/E N123/show.asp?id=483, accessed 18 June 2014.

Kanbur, Ravi. 'Reforming the Formula: A Modest Proposal for Introducing Development Outcomes into IDA Allocation Procedures'. In *Development Aid: Why and How? Towards Strategies for Effectiveness*, 115–37. Proceedings of the AFD-EUDN Conference in 2004, African Development Bank, 2005.

   'Resetting IDA's Graduation Policy'. In *The Donors' Dilemma: Emergence, Convergence and the Future of Foreign Aid*, edited by Andy Sumner and Tom Kirk (e-book, available at www.globalpolicyjournal.com/projects/ gp-e-books/donors%E2%80%99-dilemma-emergence-convergence-and -future-foreign-aid). *Global Policy Journal*, 2014.

Kapstein, Ethan B. 'Power, Fairness, and the Global Economy'. In *Power in Global Governance*, edited by Michael N. Barnett and Raymond Duvall, 80–101. Cambridge: Cambridge University Press, 2005.

Kapur, Devesh. 'The Common Pool Dilemma of Global Public Goods: Lessons from the World Bank's Net Income and Reserves'. *World Development* 30, No. 3 (2002): 337–54.

Kapur, Devesh, John P. Lewis, and Richard Webb. 'IDA: The Bank as a Dispenser of Concessional Aid'. In *The World Bank: Its First Half Century*, Vol. 1. Washington, DC: Brookings Institution, 1997a.

   *The World Bank: Its First Half Century*. Vol. 1. Washington, DC: Brookings Institution, 1997b.

Kegley, Charles W., and Eugene R. Wittkopf. *American Foreign Policy: Pattern and Process*. 5th edn. New York: StMartin's Press, 1996.

Kennedy, Paul M. *The Rise and Fall of the Great Powers: Economic Change and Military Conflict from 1500 to 2000*. London: Unwin Hyman, 1988.

Keohane, Robert O. 'Closing the Fairness-Practice Gap'. *Ethics and International Affairs* 3 (1989a): 101–16.

   *Power and Interdependence*. 2nd edn. New York; Harlow: Longman, 1989b.

Khong, Yuen Foong. 'Structural Constraints and Decision-Making: The Case of Britain in the 1930s'. In *Ideas and Ideals: Essays on Politics in Honuor of Stanley Hoffmann*, edited by Linda B. Miller and Michael J. Smith, 296–312. Boulder; Oxford: Westview, 1993.

   'Negotiating 'Order' During Power Transitions'. In *Power in Transition: The Peaceful Change of International Order*, edited by Charles Kupchan, Emanuel Adler, Jean-Marc Coicaud, and Yuen

Foong Khong, 34–67. Tokyo; New York: United Nations University Press, 2001.

Kilby, Christopher. 'An Empirical Assessment of Informal Influence in the World Bank'. *Economic Development and Cultural Change* 61, No. 2 (2013): 431–64.

Kissinger, Henry. *Diplomacy*. London: Simon & Schuster, 1994.

  *World Order: Reflections on the Character of Nations and the Course of History*. London: Penguin Press, 2014.

Klein, Peter G., Joseph T. Mahoney, Anita M. McGahan, and Christos N. Pitelis. 2010. 'Toward a Theory of Public Entrepreneurship'. *European Management Review* 7 (1): 1–15.

Knorr, Klaus. *The Power of Nations: The Political Economy of International Relations*. New York: Basic Books, 1975.

Krasner, Stephen D. 'Power Structures and Regional Development Banks'. *International Organization* 35, No. 02 (1981): 303–28.

Kratochwil, Friedrich, and John Gerard Ruggie. 'International Organization: A State of the Art on an Art of the State'. *International Organization* 40, No. 04 (1986): 753–75.

Krauthammer, Charles. 'The Unipolar Moment'. *Foreign Affairs* (1990): 23–33.

Kupchan, Charles. *No One's World: The West, the Rising Rest, and the Coming Global Turn*. New York: Oxford University Press, 2013.

Lake, David A. *Hierarchy in International Relations*. Ithaca; London: Cornell University Press, 2009.

  'John Ikenberry's Liberal Leviathan'. *Global Governance: A Review of Multilateralism and International Organizations* 18, No. 2 (2012): 249–52.

Lancaster, Carol. *Foreign Aid: Diplomacy, Development, Domestic Politics*. Chicago; London: University of Chicago Press, 2007.

Lanteigne, Marc. *China and International Institutions: Alternate Paths to Global Power*. London: Routledge, 2005.

Lavelle, Kathryn C. *Legislating International Organization: The US Congress, the IMF, and the World Bank*. Oxford: Oxford University Press, 2011.

Lebow, Richard Ned. *Forbidden Fruit: Counterfactuals and International Relations*. Princeton: Princeton University Press, 2010.

Lee, Bryan. 'Slow financial aid prompts Africa to Turn to China for Loans; World Bank and IMF Funds Come too Slowly and with Too Many Conditions Attached: Finance Ministers'. *The Straits Times*, 18 September 2006.

Leighty, John. 'Activists Launch Campaign against World Bank'. *United Press International*, 5 February 1989.

Li, Ruogu (former President of China's Ex-Im Bank), 'A Proper Understanding of Debt Sustainability Issue in Developing Countries', *World Economics and Politics*, Vol. 4, 2007.

Libby, Ronald T. 'International Development Association: A Legal Fiction Designed to Secure an LDC Constituency'. *International Organization* 29, No. 04 (1975): 1065–72.

Liechtenstein, Natalie. 'China and the World Bank', in Proceedings of the 90th Annual Meeting, *The American Society of International Law* 90 (1996): 397–401.

Lin, Justin Yifu. 2012a. *New Structural Economics: A Framework for Rethinking Development and Policy*. Washington, DC: The World Bank.

2012b. *The Quest for Prosperity: How Developing Economies Can Take Off*. Princeton and Oxford: Princeton University Press.

Litwak, Robert S. *Détente and the Nixon Doctrine: American Foreign Policy and the Pursuit of Stability, 1969–1976*. Cambridge; New York: Cambridge University Press, 1984.

Luck, Edward C. 'The United States, International Organisations, and the Quest for Legitimacy'. In *Multilateralism and US Foreign Policy: Ambivalent Engagement*, edited by Stewart Patrick and Shepard Forman, 47–74. Boulder; London: Lynne Rienner, 2002.

Lukes, Steven. *Power: A Radical View*. London: Macmillan, 1974.

Lumsdaine, David H. *Moral Vision in International Politics: The Foreign Aid Regime; 1949–1989*. Princeton: Princeton University Press, 1993.

Lunn, Simon. *Burden-Sharing in NATO*. London; Boston: Routledge and Kegan Paul, 1983.

Machowski, Heinrich, and Siegfried Schultz. 'Soviet Economic Policy in the Third World'. In *The Soviet Union, Eastern Europe and the Third World*, edited by Roger E. Kanet and American Association for the Advancement of Slavic Studies, 117–40. Cambridge: Cambridge University Press, 1987.

Malone, David M., and Yuen Foong Khong. 'Resisting the Unilateral Impulse: Multilateral Engagement and the Future of US Leadership'. In *Unilateralism and US Foreign Policy: International Perspectives*, edited by David M. Malone and Yuen Foong Khong, 421–29. Boulder; London: Lynne Rienner Publishers, 2003.

Manning, Richard. *The Multilateral Aid System: An Assessment Following the Major Replenishments of 2013*. World Institute for Development Economics Research Working Paper 2014/110, September 2014.

Martin, Lisa L. 'Interests, Power, and Multilateralism'. *International Organization* 46, No. 04 (1992): 765–92.

Mascarenhas, Raechelle, and Todd Sandler. 'Do Donors Cooperatively Fund Foreign Aid?' *The Review of International Organizations* 1, No. 4 (2006): 337–57.

Mason, Edward S., and Robert E. Asher. *The World Bank since Bretton Woods*. Washington, DC: Brookings Institution, 1973.

McKinnon, Ronald I. *The Unloved Dollar Standard: From Bretton Woods to the Rise of China*. Oxford: Oxford University Press, 2013.

Mearsheimer, John J. 'Structural Realism'. In *International Relations Theories: Discipline and Diversity*, edited by Timothy Dunne, Milja Kurki, and Steve Smith, 3rd edn, 77–93. Oxford: Oxford University Press, 2013.

*Ministerial Statement to the Development Committee by the Rt Hon Hilary Benn MP, Secretary of State for International Development and the Rt Hon Gordon Brown MP, Chancellor of the Exchequer.* The Annual Meetings of the IMF and World Bank. Singapore, September 18, 2006. www.publications.parliament.uk/pa/cm200506/cmselect/cmintdev/16 22/1622we02.htm#a2.

Ministry of Foreign Affairs, P.R. China, 'International Development Association', www.fmprc.gov.cn/mfa_chn/wjb_602314/zzjg_602420/gjjj s_612534/gjzzyhygk_613182/gjkf_613366/, accessed 25 December 2013.

2015. Xi Jinping Delivers Speech at High-level Roundtable on South-South Cooperation, Expounding on Cooperation Initiatives on South-South Cooperation in the New Era and Stressing to Uplift South-South Cooperation Cause to a New High. www.fmprc.gov.cn/mfa_eng /zxxx_662805/t1302399.shtml, accessed 1 October 2015.

MOFCOM, 'Institute of South-South Cooperation and Development (ISSCAD) Established in Peking University', 2 May 2016, http://english .mofcom.gov.cn/article/newsrelease/significantnews/201605/20160501 314609.shtml, accessed 5 May 2016.

Morgenthau, Hans. 'A Political Theory of Foreign Aid'. *American Political Science Review* 56, No. 02 (1962): 301–9.

Mosley, Paul, Jane Harrigan, and J. F. J. Toye. *Aid and Power: The World Bank and Policy-Based Lending*. London: Routledge, 1991.

Moyo, Dambisa. *Dead Aid: Why Aid Is Not Working and How There Is a Better Way for Africa*. New York: Macmillan, 2009.

Mueller, Dennis C. *Public Choice*. Cambridge: Cambridge University Press, 1979.

Murdoch, James C., and Todd Sandler. 'Complementarity, Free Riding, and the Military Expenditures of NATO Allies'. *Journal of Public Economics* 25, No. 1 (1984): 83–101.

Naím, Moisés. 'Rogue Aid'. *Foreign Policy* 159 (2007): 95–96.

National Intelligence Council. *Global Trends 2030: Alternative Worlds*. Washington, DC: Central Intelligence Agency, 2013.

Neumayer, Eric. 'Arab-Related Bilateral and Multilateral Sources of Development Finance: Issues, Trends, and the Way Forward'. World Institute for Development Economics Research Discussion Paper No. 2002/96, October 2002.

'The Determinants of Aid Allocation by Regional Multilateral Development Banks and United Nations Agencies'. *International Studies Quarterly* 47, No. 1 (2003): 101–22.

Nye, Joseph S. *The Future of Power*. New York: Public Affairs, 2011.

OECD. *The DAC in Dates: The History of OECD's Development Assistance Committee*, 2006.

*DAC Outreach Strategy*. Paris: OECD/DAC, 2008.

*The 0.7% ODA/GNI Target – a History*. www.oecd.org/investment/stats/the07odagnitarget-ahistory.htm, accessed 22 June 2010.

*Net Official Development Assistance from DAC and Other OECD Members in 2011*, 2012. www.oecd.org/investment/stats/50060310.pdf.

Ogata, Sadako. 'Shifting Power Relations in Multilateral Development Banks', *Journal of International Studies*, No. 22 (1989): 1–25.

Olson, Mancur. *The Logic of Collective Action: Public Goods and the Theory of Groups*. 2nd edn. Cambridge, Mass: Harvard University Press, 1965.

'Increasing the Incentives for International Cooperation'. *International Organization* 25, No. 04 (1971): 866–74.

Olson, Mancur, and Richard Zeckhauser. 'An Economic Theory of Alliances'. *The Review of Economics and Statistics* 48, No. 3 (1966): 266–79.

Oneal, John R. 'Testing the Theory of Collective Action NATO Defence Burdens, 1950–1984'. *Journal of Conflict Resolution* 34, No. 3 (1990a): 426–48.

'The Theory of Collective Action and Burden Sharing in NATO'. *International Organization* (1990b): 379–402.

Oneal, John R., and Mark A. Elrod. 'NATO Burden Sharing and the Forces of Change'. *International Studies Quarterly* (1989): 435–56.

Operation Evaluation Department (OED). *Review of the Performance-Based Allocation System, IDA10-12*, 14 February 2001, 2005.

*China: An Evaluation of World Bank Assistance*. Washington, DC: World Bank

Orr, Robert M. *The Emergence of Japan's Foreign Aid Power*. New York: Columbia University Press, 1990.

Pallas, Christopher. *Transnational Civil Society and the World Bank: Investigating Civil Society's Potential to Democratize Global Governance.* Basingstoke: Palgrave Macmillan, 2013.

Patrick, Stewart. 'Multilateralism and Its Discontents: The Causes and Consequences of US Ambivalence'. In *Multilateralism and U.S. Foreign Policy: Ambivalent Engagement,* edited by Stewart Patrick and Shepard Forman, 1–44. Boulder; London: Lynne Rienner, 2002.

Paulo, Sebastian, and Helmut Reisen. 'Eastern Donors and Western Soft Law: Towards a DAC Donor Peer Review of China and India?' *Development Policy Review* 28, No. 5 (2010): 535–52.

Pearson, Margaret M. 'The Major Multilateral Economic Institutions Engage China'. In *Engaging China: The Management of an Emerging Power,* edited by Alastair I. Johnston and Robert S. Ross, 207–34. London: Routledge, 1999.

Pearson Commission on International Development. *Partners in Development: Report of the Commission on International Development.* London: Pall Mall Press, 1969.

Pfeffer, Jeffrey. *The External Control of Organizations: A Resource Dependence Perspective.* New York: Harper & Row, 1978.

Pierson, Paul. *Politics in Time: History, Institutions, and Social Analysis.* Princeton; Oxford: Princeton University Press, 2004.

Raj, Christopher S. *American Military in Europe: Controversy over NATO Burden Sharing.* New Delhi: ABC PubHouse, 1983.

Rapkin, David P., Joseph U. Elston, and Jonathan R. Strand, 'Institutional Adjustment to Changed Power Distributions: Japan and the United States in the IMF', *Global Governance* 3, No. 2 (May–August 1997): 171–95.

Reisinger, William M. 'East European Military Expenditures in the 1970s: Collective Good or Bargaining Offer?' *International Organization* 37, No. 01 (1983): 143–55.

Renninger, John P. 'After the Seventh Special General Assembly Session: Africa and the New Emerging World Order'. *African Studies Review* 19, No. 2 (1976): 35–48.

Reus-Smit, Christian. *American Power and World Order.* Cambridge: Polity Press, 2004.

Rix, Alan. *Japan's Aid Program: Quantity versus Quality: Trends and Issues in the Japanese Aid Program.* Canberra: Australian Government Publishing Service, 1987.

Rodrik, Dani. *Why Is There Multilateral Lending?.* National Bureau of Economic Research Working Paper No. 5160. NBER, 1995.

Roper, Steven D., and Lilian A. Barria. 'Burden Sharing in the Funding of the UNHCR: Refugee Protection as an Impure Public Good'. *Journal of Conflict Resolution* 54, No. 4 (August 2010): 616–37.

Rosecrance, Richard, and Jennifer Taw. 'Japan and the Theory of International Leadership'. *World Politics* 42, No. 02 (1990): 184–209.

Ross, Robert S. and Zhu Feng, eds. *China's Ascent: Power, Security, and the Future of International Politics*. Ithaca: Cornell University Press, 2008.

Rothchild, Donald, and John Raven. 'Subordinating African Issues to Global Logic: Reagan Confronts Political Complexity'. In *Eagle Resurgent?: The Reagan Era in American Foreign Policy*, 393–429. Boston: Little, Brown, 1987.

Rowen, Hobart. 'U.S. May End Aid to IDA, Sprinkel Hints'. *The Washington Post*, 24 September 1981.

Russett, Bruce M. *What Price Vigilance?: The Burdens of National Defense*. New Haven: Yale University Press, 1970.

Ruttan, Vernon W. *United States Development Assistance Policy: The Domestic Politics of Foreign Economic Aid*. Baltimore; London: Johns Hopkins University Press, 1996.

Salazar, V. C. 'Taken for Granted? US Proposals to Reform the World Bank's IDA Examined'. Bretton Woods Project. March 2002. Available at: www.brettonwoodsproject.org/2002/03/art-16169/, accessed 18 March 2012.

Sanderson, Henry, and Michael Forsythe. 2013. *China's Superbank: Debt, Oil and Influence – How China Development Bank Is Rewriting the Rules of Finance*. Wiley: Bloomberg Press.

Sandler, Todd. 'Impurity of Defence: An Application to the Economics of Alliances'. *Kyklos* 30, No. 3 (1977): 443–60.

'The Economic Theory of Alliances: A Survey'. *Journal of Conflict Resolution* 37, No. 3 (1993): 446–83.

Sandler, Todd, and Jon Cauley. 'On the Economic Theory of Alliances'. *Journal of Conflict Resolution* 19, No. 2 (1975): 330–48.

Sandler, Todd, and John F. Forbes. 'Burden Sharing, Strategy, and the Design of NATO'. *Economic Inquiry* 18, No. 3 (1980): 425–44.

Sandler, Todd, and Keith Hartley. 'Economics of Alliances: The Lessons for Collective Action'. *Journal of Economic Literature* (2001): 869–96.

Sanford, Jonathan E. *US Foreign Policy and Multilateral Development Banks*. Boulder, Colorado: Westview Press, 1982.

Sanford, Jonathan E. 'World Bank: IDA Loans or IDA Grants?' *World Development* 30, No. 5 (May 2002): 741–62.

Schelling, Thomas C. *The Strategy of Conflict*. Cambridge, Mass: Harvard University Press, 1960.

Schweller, Randall L., and Xiaoyu Pu. 2011. 'After Unipolarity: China's Visions of International Order in an Era of U.S. Decline'. *International Security* 36 (1): 41–72.

Schweitzer, Carl-Christoph. 'American Threat Analyses in the 1950s'. In *The Changing Western Analysis of the Soviet Threat*, edited by Carl-Christoph Schweitzer, 57–81. London: Pinter in association with Nomos Verlagsgesellschaft, 1990a.

'The Federal Republic of Germany in the 1980s'. In *The Changing Western Analysis of the Soviet Threat*, edited by Carl-Christoph Schweitzer, 244–63. London: Pinter in association with Nomos Verlagsgesellschaft, 1990b.

Schweller, Randall L. 'Managing the Rise of Great Powers: History and Theory'. In *Engaging China: The Management of an Emerging Power*, edited by Alastair I. Johnston and Robert S. Ross, 1–31. London: Routledge, 1999.

Shaw, D. John. 'Turning Point in the Evolution of Soft Financing: The United Nations and the World Bank'. *Canadian Journal of Development Studies* 26, No. 1 (2005): 43–61.

Shi, Yaobin. 'Re-orient Strategies, Promote Innovations, and Initiate New Cooperation with International Financial Institutions', Key Speech by the Deputy Minister of Ministry of Finance, 2 April 2014, www.mof.gov.cn/buzhangzhichuang/syb/zywg/201404/t2014 0402_1062857.html, accessed 16 June 2014.

Shihata, Ibrahim. 'Issues Related to the International Development Association'. In *The World Bank Legal Papers*, 553–90. The Hague, Boston, London: Martinus Nijhoff Publishers, 2000a.

*The World Bank Inspection Panel: In Practice*. 2nd edn. New York: Oxford University Press, 2000b.

Shihata, Ibrahim, and Robert Mabro. *The OPEC Aid Record*. 2nd edn. Vienna: The OPEC Special Fund, 1978.

Silk, Leonard. 'McNamara Warns US of Perils in Reducing Aid to World's Poor', *The New York Times*, 21 June 1981.

Snyder, Glenn H. 'The Security Dilemma in Alliance Politics'. *World Politics* 36, No. 4 (1984): 461–95.

Solomon, Hyman. 'US Policy Blocks World Lending Program'. *The Financial Post*, 2 October 1989.

Spencer, Robert. 'Alliance Perceptions of the Soviet Threat, 1950–1988'. In *The Changing Western Analysis of the Soviet Threat*, edited by Carl-Christoph Schweitzer, 9–48. London: Pinter in association with Nomos Verlagsgesellschaft, 1990.

Sperling, James. 'America, NATO, and West German Foreign Economic Policies, 1949–89'. In *The Federal Republic of Germany and NATO:*

*40 Years after*, edited by Emil Joseph Kirchner and James Sperling, 157–93. Basingstoke: Macmillan, 1992.

'Statement by BRICS Leaders on the Establishment of the BRICS-Led Development Bank', Durban, South Africa, 27 March 2013, www.brics .utoronto.ca/docs/130327-brics-bank.html, accessed 18 June 2013.

Stern, Ernest. 'Mobilizing Resources for IDA: The Ninth Replenishment'. *Finance and Development* 27, No. 2 (1990): 20–23.

Stone, Randall W. *Controlling Institutions: International Organizations and the Global Economy*. Cambridge: Cambridge University Press, 2011.

'Informal Governance in International Organizations: Introduction to the Special Issue'. *The Review of International Organizations* 8, No. 2 (2013): 121–36.

Swearingen, Rodger. *The Soviet Union and Postwar Japan: Escalating Challenge and Response*. Stanford: Hoover Institution Press, 1978.

Tammen, Melanie S. *World Bank Snookers US Congress, Again*. Heritage Foundation Reports, 1988.

Telephone interview with the former director of IDA Resource Mobilisation Department, 15 September 2012.

The African Caucus of the IMF and the World Bank. *Nouakchott Declaration on Financing for Development in Africa: The Role of Nontraditional Donors*, 1 August 2008. https://www.imf.org/external/ np/sec/pr/2008/pdf/nouakdecl.pdf.

The Future of IDA Working Group. *Soft Lending without Poor Countries: Recommendations for a New IDA*. Centre for Global Development, October 2012.

The High-Level Commission on Modernization of World Bank Group Governance. *Repowering the World Bank for the 21st Century Report (The Zedillo Commission Report)*, October 2009. http://siteresources .worldbank.org/NEWS/Resources/WBGovernanceCOMMISSIONREP ORT.pdf.

'The Maddison Project Database', n.d. www.ggdc.net/maddison/maddison-project/data.htm.

The People's Republic of China. *China's Foreign Aid*. Beijing: Information Office of the State Council, April 2011.

The US Congress. *Congressional Quarterly Almanac*. Washington, DC: Congressional Quarterly Inc., various years.

Thielemann, Eiko R. 'Between Interests and Norms: Explaining Burden-Sharing in the European Union'. *Journal of Refugee Studies* 16, No. 3 (2003a): 253–73.

'Editorial Introduction'. *Journal of Refugee Studies* 16, No. 3 (2003b): 225–35.

Tōgō, Kazuhiko. *Japan's Foreign Policy, 1945–2003: The Quest for a Proactive Policy*. Leiden: Brill, 2005.

Treisman, Daniel. 'Rational Appeasement'. *International Organization 58*, No. 2 (1 April 2004): 345–73.

UK House of Commons. *Written Answers to Questions: International Development Association*. Foreign and Commonwealth Affairs, 23 July 2002. www.publications.parliament.uk/pa/cm200102/cmhans rd/vo020723/text/20723w06.htm.

UK International Development Committee. *The World Bank: Fourth Report*. 15 February 2011. www.publications.parliament.uk/pa/cm201011/cmse lect/cmintdev/606/60602.htm, accessed 27 March 2014.

UK Parliament. *Written Answers Responding to Questions from the International Development Committee on DFID's Annual Report 2005*, 20 March 2006. www.publications.parliament.uk/pa/c m200506/cmselect/cmintdev/998/99802.htm.

United Nations. *Monterrey Consensus on Financing for Development*. International Conference on Financing for Development, 18–22 March 2002, Monterrey, Mexico, 2003. www.un.org/esa/ffd/monter rey/MonterreyConsensus.pdf.

*Agenda 21: United Nations Conference on Environment & Development, Rio de Janerio, Brazil, 3 to 14 June 1992*. http://sustainabledevelop ment.un.org/content/documents/Agenda21.pdf, accessed 24 February 2014.

Urpelainen, Johannes. 'Unilateral Influence on International Bureaucrats: An International Delegation Problem'. *Journal of Conflict Resolution 56*, No. 4 (2012): 704–35.

US Congress. *Authorisation for Multilateral Development Banks*. Hearing before the House Committee on Banking and Financial Services (Serial No. 105–8), 13 March 1997.

US Department of the Treasury. *International Programs: Justification for Appropriations, FY1997*, n.d.

*International Programs: Justification for Appropriations, FY1998*, n.d.

*United States Participation in the Multilateral Development Banks in the 1980s*. Washington, DC: Department of the Treasury, 1982.

*Treasury International Programmes: Justification for Appropriations: FY2006 Budget Request*, 2006.

*Treasury International Programmes: Justification for Appropriations: FY2009 Budget Request*, 2009.

US Task Force on International Development. *US Foreign Assistance in the 1970s: A New Approach*. Washington, DC: Government Printing Office, 1970.

Valkenier, Elizabeth Kridl. *The Soviet Union and the Third World: An Economic Bind.* New York: Praeger, 1983.

Van Waeyenberge, Elisa. 'Selectivity at Work: Country Policy and Institutional Assessments at the World Bank'. *European Journal of Development Research* 21, No. 5 (2009): 792–810.

Vestergaard, Jakob, and Robert H. Wade. 'Protecting Power: How Western States Retain the Dominant Voice in the World Bank's Governance'. *World Development* 46 (2013): 153–64.

'Views Clash on World Bank Agency', *The New York Times*, 8 September 1982.

Voeten, Erik. 'Outside Options and the Logic of Security Council Action'. *American Political Science Review* 95, No. 4 (2001): 845–58.

Vreeland, James Raymond. *The Political Economy of the United Nations Security Council: Money and Influence.* New York: Cambridge University Press, 2014.

Wade, Robert. 'Japan, the World Bank, and the Art of Paradigm Maintenance: The East Asian Miracle in Political Perspective'. *New Left Review* 217 (1996): 3–36.

'A Defeat for Development and Multilateralism: The World Bank Has Been Unfairly Criticised over the Qinghai Resettlement Project', *Financial Times*, 4 July 2000.

'US Hegemony and the World Bank: The Fight over People and Ideas'. *Review of International Political Economy* 9, No. 2 (2002): 215–43.

*Governing the Market: Economic Theory and the Role of Government in East Asian Industrialization.* Princeton; Oxford: Princeton University Press, 2004.

'Accountability Gone Wrong: The World Bank, Non-Governmental Organisations and the US Government in a Fight over China'. *New Political Economy* 14, No. 1 (2009): 25–48.

Wallace, William. 'US Unilateralism: A European Perspective'. In *Multilateralism and US Foreign Policy: Ambivalent Engagement,* edited by Stewart Patrick and Shepard Forman, 141–64. Boulder; London: Lynne Rienner, 2002.

Walt, Stephen M. *The Origins of Alliances.* Ithaca; London: Cornell University Press, 1987.

'The Enduring Relevance of the Realist Tradition'. In *Political Science: The State of the Discipline,* edited by Ira Katznelson and Helen V. Milner, 3rd edn. New York; London: Norton; Washington, DC, 2002.

*Taming American Power: The Global Response to US Primacy.* New York: Norton, 2005.

Waltz, Kenneth N. *Theory of International Politics*. Reading, Mass.: Addison-Wesley, 1979.

Weaver, Catherine. *Hypocrisy Trap: The World Bank and the Poverty of Reform*. Princeton; Oxford: Princeton University Press, 2008.

Weaver, James H. *The International Development Association: A New Approach to Foreign Aid*. New York: Praeger, 1965.

White, John. *Regional Development Banks: The Asian, African, and Inter-American Development Banks*. New York; London: Praeger, 1972.

Wickes, R. J. 'The New International Economic Order: Progress and Prospects'. In *New International Economic Order: A Third World Perspective*, edited by Pradip K. Ghosh, 66–99. Westport; London: Greenwood Press, 1984.

Wolfensohn, James D. 'Opening Remarks at the Shanghai Conference on Scaling Up Poverty Reduction'. *President, The World Bank Group*, 26 May 2004. http://go.worldbank.org/1XMNPFRII0.

Woods, Ngaire. 'Making the IMF and the World Bank More Accountable'. *International Affairs* 77, No. 1 (January 2001): 83–100.

'The United States and the International Financial Institutions: Power and Influence within the World Bank and the IMF'. In *US Hegemony and International Organizations*, edited by Rosemary Foot, S. Neil McFarlane, and Michael Mastanduno, 92–114. Oxford: Oxford University Press, 2003.

*The Globalizers: The IMF, the World Bank, and Their Borrowers*. Ithaca; London: Cornell University Press, 2006.

'Whose Aid? Whose Influence? China, Emerging Donors and the Silent Revolution in Development Assistance'. *International Affairs* 84, No. 6 (2008): 1205–21.

World Bank. *IDA in Retrospect: The First Two Decades of the International Development Association*. New York; Oxford: Oxford University Press, 1982.

*Task Force on Portfolio Management (the Wapenhans Report)*, October 1992a.

*IDA10 Burden Sharing*. IDA10 Discussion Paper. World Bank, 1 June 1992b. http://documents.worldbank.org/curated/en/1992/06/1832060 3/ida10-burden-sharing.

*IDA10 Size and Burden Sharing*. IDA10 Discussion Note. World Bank, November 1992c. http://documents.worldbank.org/curated/en/1992/1 1/18320862/ida10-size-burden-sharing.

*Review of World Bank Conditionality*, 9 September 2005a. http://sitere sources.worldbank.org/PROJECTS/Resources/40940-1114615847489 /ConditionalityFinalDCpaperDC9-9-05.pdf.

*IDA-14* Press Release: Largest Funding Increase in Two Decades, *But More Resources Needed*, 2005b, www.worldbank.org/ida/ida-14-replenishment.html, accessed 16 March 2012.

*Good Practice Principles for the Application of Conditionality: A Progress Report*, 6 November 2006. http://siteresources.worldbank.org/PROJEC TS/Resources/40940-1114615847489/Conditionalitypaperfinal.pdf.

*China and the World Bank: A Partnership for Innovation*. Washington, DC: World Bank, 2007a.

'World Bank Group Pledges $3.5 Billion for Poorest Countries', 27 September 2007b. http://go.worldbank.org/FWCMXFT1U0.

*The World Bank's Safeguard Policies: Proposed Review and Update*, 10 October 2012a, http://siteresources.worldbank.org/EXTSAFEPOL/ Resources/584434-1306431390058/SafeguardsReviewApproachPaper .pdf, accessed 16 June 2013, accessed 16 March 2014.

'World Bank President Calls for 'Solutions Bank' to Meet Global Challenges'. *Press Release*, 11 October 2012b. www.worldbank.org/e n/news/press-release/2012/10/12/world-bank-president-calls-solutions-bank-meet-global-challenges.

'Financing for Development Post-2015', October 2013a, www.worldbank .org/content/dam/Worldbank/document/Poverty%20documents/WB-PREM%20financing-for-development-pub-10-11-13web.pdf, accessed 15 November 2013.

'Financing for Development Post-2015', 2013b.

*Contract Awards under Bank-Financed Investment Projects*. http://go .worldbank.org/GM7GBOVGS0, accessed 25 February 2014.

2014. IBRD/IDA management's discussion & analysis and financial statements. 30 June 2014.

Xinhua News Agency. 'World Bank Pledges More Co-Op with China, Welcomes the Country's Contribution to IDA', 18 December 2007. http://news.xinhuanet.com/english/2007-12/18/con tent_7276921.htm, accessed 28 May 2012.

'China proposes an Asian infrastructure investment bank', 3 October 2013, www.chinadaily.com.cn/china/2013-10/03/content_17007977 .htm, accessed 18 June 2014.

'China pledges 40 bln USD for Silk Road Fund', 8 November 2014, http:// news.xinhuanet.com/english/china/2014-11/08/c_133774993.htm, accessed 12 November 2014.

Xu, Jiajun, and Richard Carey. 2015a. 'China's Development Finance: Ambition, Impact and Transparency'. IDS Policy Briefing 92. Brighton: IDS. http://opendocs.ids.ac.uk/opendocs/handle/123456789/ 5996#.VhYaNPmqpBc.

2015b. 'Post-2015 Global Governance of Official Development Finance: Harnessing the Renaissance of Public Entrepreneurship: Post-2015 Global Governance of Official Development Finance'. *Journal of International Development* 27 (6): 856–80. doi:10.1002/jid.3120.

2015c. 'The Economic and Political Geography behind China's Emergence as an Architect of the International Development System'. Multilateral Development Banks in the 21st century: Three Perspectives on China and the Asian Infrastructure Investment Bank. London: Overseas Development Institute.

Yu, Qiao. 'Relocating China's Foreign Reserves', Brookings-Tsinghua Center Working Paper. 21 November 2013.

Zhou Xiaochuan (Governor of the People's Bank of China), 'Reform the international monetary system', 23 March 2009, http://www.bis.org/r eview/r090402c.pdf, accessed 25 April 2012.

Zoellick, Robert B. (Deputy Secretary of State) 'Whither China: From Membership to Responsibility?' *Remarks to National Committee on U.S.-China Relations*, 21 September 2005. http://2001-2009.state.gov/ s/d/former/zoellick/rem/53682.htm.

Zou, Jiayi, and Xiaolong Mo (International Department, Ministry of Finance, P.R. China). 'Analysing the Globalisation Paradoxes and the Role of Development Assistance from the Perspective of Policy Changes in the World Bank'. *World Economics and Politics*, No. 1 (2002): 36–41.

# Index

Lightning Source UK Ltd.
Milton Keynes UK
UKOW01n0626140617

303321UK00003B/18/P